Marine Policy and the Coastal Community

THE IMPACT OF THE LAW OF THE SEA

Edited by DOUGLAS M. JOHNSTON

ST. MARTIN'S PRESS NEW YORK

 For information, write:
St. Martin's Press, Inc., 175 Fifth Avenue, New York, N.Y. 10010
Library of Congress Catalog Card Number: 76-1337
Printed in Great Britain
First published in the United States of America in 1976

CONTENTS

EDITORIAL INTRODUCTION

Nothing has been more dramatic in the 1970s than the impact of natural resource issues on the international system. As we approach the next decade it is evident that many of the most serious conflicts will arise from intensified uses of the ocean. Even now, the arrival of impressive ocean technologies has produced radical changes of national attitude, interest and policy, and these in turn have generated wholly new demands on the processes of international law and organization.

Up to the mid-twentieth century the uses of the ocean were confined mostly to vessels and limited by the gradualness of developments in vessel technology. Through this kind of technology a relatively small number of nations acquired access to all parts of the ocean, albeit for restricted purposes, and their shared interest in reciprocity led naturally to the classical principle of the freedom of the high seas. Today, in a vastly expanded system of independent nation states, the classical assumption of equality is under attack as spectacular new opportunities unfold under the impetus of modern technology. In marine affairs the result is likely to be an unprecedented and somewhat uneasy combination of claims to a new equity in international relations and to a new level of technological efficiency in ocean management.

At the same time, it is now being learned with increasingly painful clarity, especially in federal states, that governmental structures inherited or copied from the nineteenth century are not well suited to the economic, social and environmental goals of 'coastal zone management'. Even as we begin to focus on the special problems of the coastal zone, the very concept of such a management system is on the point of spectacular expansion. Current trends in the law of the sea virtually ensure the enclosure of vast ocean areas under the jurisdiction of the coastal state and the subjection of the resources in these newly acquired areas to very unequal experiments in government planning, management and regulation. Yet there is little in the past to suggest that the citizens most directly affected, the coastal communities themselves, will be encouraged to participate effectively in the critical phases of decision-making.

This collection of articles consists of original contributions by fourteen well-known specialists in marine policy and coastal community studies from the United Kingdom, Canada, the United States and

Australia. The disciplines represented include public international law and organization, international and comparative politics, marine geography, resource and shipping economics, sociology and anthropology. These studies are written and edited with a view to assisting the teaching of marine and coastal affairs in a multidisciplinary setting at a post-graduate or senior undergraduate level. In providing a blend of policy-oriented studies of marine affairs with the humanistic literature of community welfare, this book attempts to cast new light on the relationship between man and technology.

PART I: INTRODUCTION

1 THE RISE OF THE COASTAL STATE IN THE LAW OF THE SEA

Edgar Gold

1. General Introduction

The subject of this introductory chapter is vast. Learned treatises have been written about almost every matter which will be discussed. Consequently much of what follows will be superficial and very selective. All that is attempted is a rapid overview of particular aspects of the law of the sea – a sort of framework around which the following, more specialized, chapters will be built.

The history of the coastal state's rights in the law of the sea cannot be reviewed, however briefly, without reflecting the author's own sympathies in some degree. In this chapter the rise of the coastal state is seen in a favourable light. Perhaps this is not surprising as it is written by a Canadian international lawyer and mariner. In any event, it is hoped that the obvious prejudices in favour of the coastal state do not derogate from the accuracy of the presentation.

2. The Jurisdictional Problem

The Nature of the Problem: Most of the surface of the world is water. The oceans cover over 70 per cent of the earth's surface – an area roughly equal to fifteen times the area of the North American continent. The very immensity of the seas is staggering. It is quite possible to be on a ship over 1,500 miles from the nearest land and, at one point in mid-ocean, over 3,500 miles from the nearest continent. And yet man has for over three millennia not only attempted to conquer this endless liquid continent by navigating it with his frail craft but has also tried to appropriate large areas of it for his own varied uses. Naturally, human nature being what it is, there were others who resisted these attempts at appropriation. What we know as the law of the sea today is essentially the response of international society to the need for regulating ocean navigation and the need for reducing conflicts arising out of the appropriation of ocean space.

The law of the sea, like virtually all other areas of international law, has been developed from two main sources: custom and treaty. In addition, there have been various other juridical sources, such as the decisions of national and international tribunals and the opinions of publicists, but the evolution of the law of the sea has also been affected by numerous non-legal influences, including the effects of wars. Generally speaking, however, it is not too distorting to say that the main 'elements' in the existing law of the sea are still custom and treaty.

Yet it must be remembered constantly that whatever the source of the rules, the self-interest of the maritime and coastal states ultimately controls. It has often been argued that the whole history of the law of the sea should be seen as a continual conflict between two diametrically opposed, yet coexisting and even complementary, concepts: the territorial sovereignty of the coastal state and the freedom of the seas for the use of the maritime states.[1] Freedom of the seas is an expression of the community interest in the free flow of commerce, without interference, constraint, danger or discrimination among nations. The concept of territorial sovereignty, opposed to that of unfettered freedom, is an outgrowth of the coastal state's concern to protect itself in terms of military and economic security.

Despite a general belief to the contrary today, these two concepts have always been understood as mutually dependent. The actual state of either one at a particular time has been largely determined in accordance with the self-centred interests of the most powerful maritime nations of the day. Throughout the history of the law of the sea, these nations have provided flux in using these concepts to achieve their own ends, whereas the weaker coastal states have had more to gain in contributing continuity and stability. However, it is really necessary to examine the history a little more carefully.

Historical Evolution: The origins of the first rules of the law of the sea are lost in pre-history, except for parts of those early rules which have been adopted by later civilizations as customary law. It is reasonably clear that in the 'cradle of civilization', the Mediterranean, nations considered the sea free and open to any legal and legitimate use.[2] However, even at this early stage there is some evidence that this 'freedom' was subject to limitations designed to satisfy the ambition of the leading states of that era of antiquity. Carthage, for example, restricted use of its port by foreign vessels, whereas Rhodes encouraged the use of what it considered 'its' waters.[3]

The earliest comprehensive code of the law of the sea that has survived is known as the Rhodian Maritime Code.[4] Rhodes conducted some of the most widespread and comprehensive maritime commerce in the ancient world, and thus developed a successful code of sea law. It is generally accepted that the great part of modern private international law of the sea – that is, commercial maritime/admiralty law – has descended from that code, for its principles were accepted by both Greek and Roman law, the latter forming the basis of the modern law of the sea. However, the important factor of the Rhodian Code is that it recognizes the right of all nations to freely use the sea for legitimate commerce. The right was made part of Roman law – according to Vulpian, the sea being open to everybody by nature and, according to Celsus, the sea, like the air, being common to all mankind.[5] However, the political reality of that time was that Rome was in virtual control of the Mediterranean and did not even need to consider dominion over the ocean in a jurisdictional sense.

With the collapse of the Roman Empire most law virtually ceased to exist. From this time until almost the mid-fifteenth century there was little law of the sea beyond survival of the fittest. Exceptions were to be found in certain areas where commercial transactions warranted the establishment of mutually acceptable maritime codes. Examples are the Basilika, which regulated seventh-century Levantine commerce; the Assizes of Jerusalem, a further development in the same area during the Crusades, principally as a replacement of trial by battle; the Rolls of Oleron, promulgated in 1160 by Queen Eleanor of Aquitaine in order to regulate expanding Atlantic seaboard commerce, and which passed from France to form the basis of Spanish sea law eventually; and the Black Book of the Admiralty, which probably dates from the reign of Edward III and provides a practically useful collection of the English rules of maritime law and practice.[6]

Nevertheless these early maritime codes were isolated rays of light in an otherwise dark era during which chaos reigned on the oceans known to man at that time. In a perverse sense it could be said that the Norman and Saracen pirates who ravaged commercial shipping during this long period enjoyed the greatest freedom of the sea in its history.

The Early Coastal State Claims: Thus for the best part of two thousand years a highly developed and established body of law relating to the seas was lost until necessity required its resurrection. There were two main contributory factors which brought about this necessity. First, in the Mediterranean, still the centre of a Europe recently awoken from the Dark Ages, commerce was slowly recovering from the ravages of the lawless period. The great trading centres and city states of the Mediterranean had begun to assert their dominance. The commercial ascendancy of Marseilles, Barcelona, Valencia, Genoa and Venice was soon followed by territorial claims to large parts of the ocean. This new development, intended to establish true dominance of the oceans, is one which has a surprisingly modern ring to it. Medieval Venice claimed the entire Adriatic Sea. The Republic of Genoa claimed not only the Ligurian Sea but also the Gulf of Lions.[7] Elsewhere other states followed suit: Denmark and Sweden claimed the Baltic Sea; Norway, followed by Denmark, decided that parts of the North Sea were under their sovereignty;[8] and England claimed extensive belts of water around the British Isles, including the Atlantic Ocean from North Cape to Cape Finisterre.[9] The culmination of this territorial expansionism was probably reached when in 1493 Pope Alexander VI Borgia divided the Atlantic Ocean from pole to pole between the two Iberian 'superpowers', Spain and Portugal, who had also steadily expanded their jurisdiction over the oceans.[10]

The type and degree of jurisdiction which states exercised in these ocean areas varied considerably. In general such states tried to exclude pirates from 'their' sea spaces; exercise criminal jurisdiction; prohibit navigation or levy tolls from foreign ships; forbid or regulate fishing by foreigners; prohibit naval battles of other states in the area; and demand that the flag of the coastal state be saluted as a symbol of dominance.

It should be understood that this coastal state ascendancy was dictated, to a large extent, by very different aims from those used by coastal states today. The claims in the period following the Dark Ages were all made by powerful maritime states and the coastal expansionism of these states was generally part and parcel of their overall maritime policy. Like its counterpart today, the maritime state of medieval times was a 'coastal state' (in the modern geopolitical sense) except that at that time its maritime ambitions and coastal state expansion meant 'having the cake and eating it too' – a choice which is not so readily available today.

The Early Counter-claims: Not surprisingly, the new expansionism of the large maritime states was to be challenged by other states. After all, this was a period of history when, unlike Roman times, there was no longer a single dominant power which could benevolently rule the oceans and speak of freedom at the same time. The very expansionism which had occurred was proof of this. Up to the mid-sixteenth century the nations who asserted 'ownership' had appeared to be well able to enforce their claims, but by then some of the counter-claimants were themselves becoming effective powers.

First the Polish king, allied with the Hanseatic League, effectively disputed the Danish-Norwegian claims to the North Atlantic.[11] However, it was the Elizabethan period of discovery which really resulted in the first politically significant articulation of the concept of the 'freedom of the seas'. The Elizabethans rejected the Iberian oceanic expansionism at a time when they themselves had not fully developed their own claims over the seas and they were supported in this rejection by the United Provinces of the Netherlands.[12] In 1604-5 the first major legal treatise on the law of the sea, *Mare Liberum,* was written by Hugo Grotius of the Netherlands to establish the rights and the freedom of Dutch trade in the East Indies against Portuguese interference. In this famous book, published in 1609,[13] Grotius fully supported the Elizabethan theory that the seas belonged to all nations and are not subject to unilateral appropriation by any nation.

Mare Liberum was, of course, a work of enormous importance based heavily on the Rhodian/Roman law and current Mediterranean practice. It remains to this day one of the most brilliant and convincing defences of the principle of freedom of the seas. Sight has, however, been lost of the fact that the principle was even at the time of Grotius gaining such acceptance that it probably needed relatively little defence. Suddenly the 'great ocean business' of the seventeenth and eighteenth centuries was thrust upon an expanding world and quite naturally the freedom of the seas became something which appeared to benefit everyone.

When in 1635 John Selden of England replied to Grotius in his work *Mare Clausum,* advocating that coastal states had the right to appropriate large sections of the sea, the Elizabethan period of discovery and its use of the concept of the freedom of the seas had given way to the preoccupation of James I with the British fisheries in opposition to the superior sea power of the Netherlands.[14] But the period of discovery had resulted in an accretion of new territories, and the vision of new opportunities swept away all that would interfere with this kind of expansionism – the sea power of the large maritime states.

It has been written recently that the principle of the freedom of the seas was not a policy favoured by the stronger states and imposed by them on the weaker ones, but that, on the contrary, it was a principle for which the latter had to fight bitterly by every means available against the strong maritime powers in order to achieve its recognition and implementation.[15] This is, of course, quite correct, but must again be seen in the general framework of the times which shows that the powerful states were only giving up something which they no longer wanted anyway. They could gain much more by supporting universal ocean freedom. From the beginning of the nineteenth century, Great Britain, the leading maritime state, pursued and consolidated its oceanic ambitions on a world-wide scale, fully exploiting the new freedom which she had found constricting less than three generations earlier. Most, if not all, maritime nations followed suit, and the precedence of sea power over coastal power was to last for the next century and a half.

3. The Re-emergence of the Coastal State

The Modern Era: Despite the passage of three-and-a-half centuries since the doctrinal clash between Selden and Grotius and despite the fact that technological and scientific advances since then have expanded our functional notion of the sea, the fundamental juridical-political problem – the extent of the limits of national jurisdiction – has remained. Indeed, despite the clear military superiority of the superpowers, the nations of the world are more divided than ever over the question of where to draw the lines of national jurisdiction at sea.

Since 1930, three international conferences on the law of the sea have tried and failed to agree on how to apply the opposed, but complementary, principles of freedom of the seas and territorial sovereignty. However, that they took place at all illustrated the changing balance of ocean power. The Hague Conference of 1930 consisted of delegations from 38 states,[16] and the First and Second United Nations Conferences on the Law of the Sea, which took place in Geneva in 1958 and 1960, attracted delegations from 86 states.[17] It can be seen that even in three decades the ranks of maritime-oriented states had swelled by almost 50 – most of which were coastal states in every sense of the word. Nevertheless the maritime powers were still able to muster a sufficient majority to defeat any inroads on their supremacy. However, the re-emergence of the coastal state was not to be halted, for a variety of reasons. In a full analysis it would be necessary to trace developments in five jurisdictional zones or 'regimes': (i) internal waters; (ii) territorial sea; (iii) functional zones; (iv) continental shelf; (v) high seas. In such a study it would be seen how certain functional problems, such as fishing and marine pollution control, overlap two or more of these zones. But to examine all of this in some detail is not possible in an introductory chapter. Instead the rise of the coastal state will be illustrated only against the background of developments in the territorial sea and the functional zones.

The Territorial Sea: The territorial sea of a state is the belt of ocean which extends seaward from the shoreline or the outward limits of internal waters. Getting universal uniformity in the extent of the territorial sea has always involved the most considerable difficulties.

More than ever today, state practice exhibits a variety of claims and a lack of stability, as the claims are changing almost daily.[18]

Generally, a coastal state possesses the same sovereign rights in territorial waters that it has in its internal waters, with the very important exception that territorial waters are subject to a right of free and innocent passage by merchant vessels of all nations which must, however, conform to the laws and regulations of the state claiming the waters. Ships thus have the right of passage although they are within the coastal state's jurisdiction.

The concept of the territorial sea is one which has been with us for centuries. By the beginning of the twentieth century a zone limited to 3 miles had been established by most then existing states, including Great Britain, the United States, Germany, France and many other maritime powers.[19] The original 3-mile limit probably grew out of the ancient 'cannon shot' rule which effectively gave the coastal state those areas of the sea that could actually lie under the protection of coastal gun batteries.[20] Although there is some doubt about this, as a matter of technical feasibility it was generally accepted as a legal proposition that, in order to preserve certain national rights and interests, nations could exercise a measure of control over certain areas of their coastal waters. An opposing view of earlier times was that the coastal belt was subject only to certain limited and well-defined rights in the coastal state. This view, based on the theory that territorial waters remain essentially a part of the high seas, saw the coastal state as a strictly limited guardian of its territorial waters, but it was eventually discarded in favour of the other concept which viewed the territorial sea more in terms of ownership.[21]

Despite agreement on the nature of the coastal state's authority in the territorial sea, the question of its scope has remained unsolved. In recent times there has been a consistent failure to reach any sort of lasting agreement on this issue and the differing views seem to grow further apart as new claims are made and new settlements attempted.

As stated above, at the beginning of the twentieth century most maritime nations had accepted a territorial sea limit of 3 miles. Within a very short time, however, the situation was changing as many coastal states began to extend their claims to distances up to 12 miles. Some claimed absolute, others limited, jurisdiction in these new areas. The new claimants were a mixture of coastal states which had altered their marine policies in favour of an extension of sovereignty and coastal states which, not being maritime states themselves, were challenging the unfettered rights of the maritime states. This finally led to such conflict and confusion that the League of Nations called the Hague Conference of 1930 in order to codify a general rule for the breadth of the territorial sea.

As indicated above, the delegations from 38 nations, despite considerable effort, failed to reach agreement. The main point of conflict was the wish of many coastal states to include in the new code national rights to exercise limited jurisdiction in a zone contiguous to the territorial sea. However, as expected, the maritime powers, in particular Great Britain, displayed the sort of inflexibility which discouraged any sort of compromise. Although the conference was deadlocked on this issue, as well as on that of the breadth of the territorial sea, it was at least able to achieve broad general agreement on the legal status of territorial waters.[22]

Between 1930 and 1945 the unsettled international situation obviously did not encourage further efforts to come to grips with the problem. In 1945 the maritime powers lost one of their strongest supporters to the 'other side'. The United States, long a supporter of the 3-mile limit, appeared to be opting for a wider recognition of the existence of contiguous zones. In that year it established a new fishery conservation zone outside the US 3-mile limit and announced that similar claims by other nations up to a limit of 12 miles from the coast would be recognized by the USA.[23] Almost at once a large number of jubilant coastal states followed suit although some went far beyond the 12 miles established by the USA.[24] This result was influenced by the fact that the US fishery conservation claim was accompanied by another unrelated claim to sovereign rights over the mineral resources offshore, the famous Truman Declaration on the Continental Shelf.

The general political situation prevailing in the post-World War Two period naturally increased the conflicts related to the territorial sea. The world had become divided into the ideological camps of the Cold War, making it even more difficult to reach any reasonable settlement on non-ideological global issues such as the breadth of the territorial sea. In addition, this period also saw the beginning of the end of the colonial era and the emergence of a large group of new states intent on asserting their new-found political rights as sovereign nations. These new states were to swell the ranks of the coastal states and provide the real catalyst for the renaissance of coastal state rights which was still some years away.

In the meantime, the task begun by the League of Nations in 1930, in attempting to codify the laws of territorial waters, was placed in the hands of the International Law Commission (ILC) of the United

Nations. By 1951, the ILC, declaring that the legal requirements of the territorial sea was one of the most urgent matters needing codification in international law, urged immediate action. The maritime states, sensing the writing on the wall, resisted. Finally in 1958 the first international conference on the law of the sea under the aegis of the United Nations (UNCLOS I) took place in Geneva. Overall, the conference was moderately successful as it was able to produce four international conventions.[25] As in 1930, however, no satisfactory settlement could be reached on the breadth of the territorial sea, even though some of the major underlying problems appeared to have been solved by the four conventions adopted. Nor was agreement reached on the extent of the coastal state's exclusive fishing rights.

Two years later at the Second United Nations Conference on the Law of the Sea (UNCLOS II), also held at Geneva, the territorial sea and exclusive fishing rights were virtually the sole subject of debate, but the conference was unable to break the deadlock.

At both conferences notable changes in position on the jurisdictional question were apparent. Great Britain, for example, proposed a new 6-mile limit which did not gain much support. On the other hand, the compromise by the United States and Canada – the well-known 'six-plus-six' proposal – failed by only one vote. This proposal involved a 6-mile territorial sea plus a 6-mile contiguous zone for fishery control. It failed basically due to the bloc voting practices of the East European socialist states, some of the Arab states, and some of the newly independent states.

The international situation at the end of these two conferences was one of even greater confusion than ever before. One definite result was the virtual end of general adherence to the traditional 3-mile limit. More important, the issue of coastal state jurisdiction was in the process of becoming much more complex. It was no longer simply an argument of wide versus narrow territorial seas – in terms of sovereignty versus freedom. It is really quite doubtful whether many of the delegations at Geneva in 1958 and 1960 had quite grasped the new complexities. Nor perhaps could the ILC have anticipated the new ocean expansionism which was to follow a few years later. At Geneva the two sides still debated in traditional legal terms. On one hand, the supporters of a narrow territorial sea expounded the need for the free flow of seaborne commerce and the efficient exploitation of marine resources (though these resources were being exploited by only a handful of nations), and emphasized the problems which coastal states would experience in properly exercising their policing in extensive coastal areas. Less often mentioned, but ever present, was the concern, particularly by the superpowers, for questions of security.

The coastal states advocating a wider territorial sea, on the other hand, did so for reasons of national security and fishery development, and the enforcement of customs and fiscal legislation.

The Geneva Conferences thus tried to discuss in strictly legal terms a problem which in one form or another had baffled the world for three millennia: the nature and extent of the state's authority over adjacent areas of the ocean. For the newly emergent coastal states this problem would have quite different socio-economic as well as political undertones. The luxury of hindsight has now proven that when the delegations returned home from Geneva in 1960 the new battle lines were only being drawn.

The Functional Zones: The whole history of the jurisdictional problem has been one of spatial concern. The more functional approach is comparatively recent, although the contiguous zone proposed in the Geneva conferences – considered by many to be the first rational approach to the issue of coastal state jurisdiction – is based on earlier proposals along similar lines.

Soon after the 1945 Truman Declaration on the Continental Shelf, which displayed the desire of the United States to have the best of both worlds – that is, to be an 'expansionist' coastal state as well as a maritime power – several Latin American states began to claim extensions in maritime jurisdiction, some of them in extreme form.[26] El Salvador, for example, claimed a full 200-mile territorial sea and enshrined this claim in its national constitution. Argentina and Mexico claimed an 'epicontinental' sea which encompassed not only their continental shelves but also superjacent waters. But the best known of these initiatives was the 1952 trilateral decision of Chile, Ecuador and Peru to establish a 'maritime zone' which was to extend not less than 200 miles from their shores.[27] These and other Latin American claims to extend maritime jurisdiction varied significantly from one another in form and content, but most, unlike the claim of El Salvador, appeared to encompass something less than complete territorial jurisdiction. In contemporary language they could be said to be early proposals for a multipurpose functional zone within which the coastal state could exercise exclusive jurisdiction for designated purposes, but allegedly without prejudice to existing rights of navigation and associated uses of the ocean.[28]

The reasoning behind these early Latin American claims is set out in voluminous literature and is confusing at best. The difficulty is that whilst these claims were based on cultural, as well as very realistic socio-economic grounds, they were generally expressed in a type of legal language that was regarded outside the region as subversive of the existing legal system. For example, the 1952 Santiago Declaration on the Maritime Zone, ratified by Chile, Ecuador and Peru and acceded to by Costa Rica, stated quite clearly and in remarkably contemporary language that the governments of coastal states had a duty to preserve and conserve natural ocean resources and the right to protect and control these resources as a means of developing their economies.[29] At a later Inter-American Conference on the same theme a resolution was adopted with one dissenting vote (USA) which recognized: 'that each state is competent to establish its territorial waters within reasonable limits, taking into account geographical, geological and biological factors, as well as the economic needs of its population, and its security and defence.'[30]

At the Geneva conferences, however, instead of following up this realistic economic argument and developing a new conference strategy based on it, the Latin American delegations presented their claims as legal propositions and as a result were treated almost with disdain.[31] The new claims were much too extreme for the majority of delegations at Geneva and the type of argument used by the proponents of these new claims was based on a vague mixture of natural law, geographical disadvantage and sovereign rights.[32] The Peruvian delegate in withdrawing his proposal charged both conferences with having 'failed to study adequately the technical, biological and economic aspects of the law of the sea'.[33] He was, of course, quite right – the conferences had been a legal gathering and not really concerned with such a broad spectrum of policy considerations. However, Peru and its fellow-claimants had also not been able to present these new aspects adequately to the conference. It was really like trying to transcribe space-age technology into ancient Greek – it just did not fit. However, even the Latin Americans were unaware that a new economic stage in the law of the sea was just around the corner.

4. The Emergence of the Third World

Shipping and the Third World: The years between the end of World War Two and the end of UNCLOS II in 1960 had brought about remarkable changes in the political atlas of the world. The most important change was in Africa and Asia with its many newly independent sovereign states. At the Geneva conferences there were only 14 of these new states represented, and the law of the sea was still, to these states, of minor concern compared with the many pressing problems of newly-won independence.

The newly independent nations were all, without exception, states with developing economies faced with considerable problems in a competitive, unequally developed world. Despite the efforts by the industrialized states to inject foreign aid into these ailing economies the gulf between rich and poor widened steadily. As a consequence the United Nations General Assembly decided to convene the United Nations Conference on Trade and Development (UNCTAD I) at Geneva in 1964. It was at this conference that the economic difficulties, trade inequalities and living disparities of the new nations were first compared to the economic superiority, trade monopolies and living affluence of the developed countries. It was found, for example, that the joint income of the developing states, with over two-thirds of the world's population, was not much more than one-tenth of that of the developed industrialized countries.[34] The world which had already politically divided itself into two opposing political worlds of East-West ideology had suddenly realized that there was a huge, demanding, hungry Third World. Almost overnight, it seemed, the really important gulf between states was that between North and South. Yet surprisingly, this rather sudden realization of the anachronistic nature of the world's economic structure was not to be felt in the area of marine affairs for some time.

At UNCTAD I the developed industrialized nations vowed, in an aura of optimism, that they would do everything to eradicate economic inequalities, and detailed machinery to put this plan into effect was set in motion by the conference, which became an integral and permanent part of the United Nations General Assembly.

At the request of Third World developing states and against strong opposition from the traditional maritime powers,[35] shipping was placed as a permanent item on the UNCTAD agenda and a separate UNCTAD Division for Invisibles (Shipping, Insurance and Transfer of Technology)[36] was subsequently formed. At the time of UNCTAD I the economic and commercial aspects of shipping were a forbidden territory to which neither international organizations nor developing countries had access. It has been correctly stated that on the international scene shipping was one of the several untouched strongholds of anachronistic private enterprise, invoking the credo of *laissez faire* and operating within shipping conference systems by virtue of oligopolistic privileges.[37] There was virtually no available information on the economics of ocean transport, primarily due to the secrecy which shrouded the practices of the shipping industry of the major maritime powers.

Since 1867 the major co-ordinating body of the shipping industry has been, and to a great extent still is, the Comité Maritime International (CMI). This non-governmental organization is composed of the various national Maritime Law Associations, which in turn are composed of the main shipping interests in the various maritime states. These interests are the shipowner, merchant, underwriter, average adjuster, broker, banker and lawyer directly involved in shipping. The main objective of the CMI was to contribute towards the unification of maritime and commercial law, maritime customs, usages and practices. For this purpose it has prepared draft conventions or sought to achieve a consensus of opinion in other ways on matters relating to maritime law.[38] The CMI has undoubtedly played a substantial role in the preparation of a good number of international conventions which deal with various aspects of maritime law, such as liability for collision between ships, assistance and salvage at sea, limitation of liability for shipowners, and rules relating to bills of lading, maritime liens and mortgages. Although the CMI has been quite effective in its role, it should not be forgotten that it constitutes a fairly well-organized interest group seeking to deal with problems from the point of view of a comparatively small circle of like-minded shipping-oriented members.[39]

The Division of Public and Private Law of the Sea: CMI discussions have been strictly limited to the private sector of international shipping and have refrained conscientiously from becoming involved in the broader political-economic issues of shipping policy. It was felt that such areas were best left to diplomats and politicians and that pressure from the CMI and its members would only be applied if international diplomacy and political realities jeopardized the carefully constructed *status quo* of international shipping in any way.

However, the CMI was not the only group involved with international shipping which divided marine law into public and private sectors. This is a matter which deserves much broader treatment than it can receive here, but the division is one of the most persistent and damaging myths operating to this day. The legal aspects of the ocean cannot, in this complex world, be divided so arbitrarily. Yet even the UNCTAD Shipping Division blithely separates itself from the realities of public international aspects of marine law and feels bound by restricted terms of reference, even although the decisions made in the public sector, such as the Law of the Sea Conferences of the United Nations, affect every single aspect of marine affairs. This is borne out by the fact that the grievances expressed by developing states both at UNCLOS III and in the more specialized setting of UNCTAD's Shipping Conferences have remarkable similarities and are often expressed by the same delegates speaking of their state's overall ocean policy. The significance of this seems to have been completely lost in both forums.

In any case the area of shipping has become one of vital interest to the new group of developing coastal states. In order to export their products the majority of these states rely almost completely on ocean transport. Yet, even in 1968, less than 8 per cent of the total world merchant fleet belonged to developing countries.[40] International shipping was thus a new field of conflict between the traditional maritime powers and the coastal states, and it is an area of conflict that has not been emphasized sufficiently in the recent debate on the law of the sea.

The Maltese Catalyst, 1967: However, even before UNCTAD II, which was to take place in New Delhi in 1968, a new 'decade of the sea' was ushered in. This was in 1967, when the then Maltese Ambassador to the United Nations, Arvid Pardo, first raised the question of the seabed in the UN General Assembly. In his speech and draft resolution Ambassador Pardo urged the exclusion of the seabed and the ocean floor 'beyond the limits of present national jurisdiction' from national appropriation and the establishment of an international agency to regulate, supervise and control all ocean bed activities beyond such limits.[41] Although there was no intention at that time to reopen considerations of the law of the sea in general, it quickly became evident that the ultimate resolution of the seabed issues required nothing less than a complete and radical reappraisal of the law of the sea – one that treats the sea conceptually as part of the whole marine environment. After some preliminary work which lasted until 1970, the 25th General Assembly of the United Nations moved from the relatively narrow focus of the seabed issue to the broader field of preparations for a new conference on the law of the sea, in an historic and decisive resolution which called for the convening of a Conference on the Law of the Sea in 1973 to deal with a staggering agenda of marine issues:

... The establishment of an equitable international régime –

> including an international machinery – for the area and the resources of the seabed and the ocean floor and the subsoil thereof beyond the limits of national jurisdiction, a precise definition of the area, and a broad range of related issues including those concerning the regime of the high seas, the Continental Shelf, the territorial sea (including the question of its breadth and the question of international straits) and contiguous zone, fishing and conservation of living resources of the high seas (including the question of the preferential rights of the coastal states), the preservation of the marine environment (including, *inter alia,* the prevention of pollution) and scientific research.[42]

In explaining the reasons for this far-reaching proposal by the General Assembly, a scant decade after the conclusion of the Geneva conferences, references were made not only to the necessity for considering problems of ocean space as a whole, but also to political and economic realities. Together with modern scientific and technological advances, these realities have established the urgent need for progressive development of the law of the sea in a world community of over 150 states, most of which are coastal states and many of which did not have the opportunity to take part in previous conferences on the law of the sea.

Unilateral Functional Claims: Many of these states, mostly in the developing world, were in any case dissatisfied with the results of the previous Law of the Sea Conferences, which they considered to be legalistically conceived and still oriented towards a smaller world of major maritime powers. Some of these states had taken their own unilateral action in spatially enlarging their coastal ocean areas. Amongst these were, of course, many of the Latin American states who had put into unilateral practice what they had preached in the 1950s.[43] Most of this new legislation dealt with fishing regulations and conservation, reflecting a growing coastal state sophistication in national fishery needs and problems. In Third World economic planning the growing importance of the living resources of the ocean and the potential wealth to be derived from the non-living resources of the seabed, which had become scientifically discernible and technically exploitable, gave an air of reality, and even urgency, to the new onslaught on traditional law-of-the-sea conservatism.

The Emergence of the Exclusive Economic Zone Concept: In 1971 the

Organization for African Unity (OAU) endorsed a recommendation for member nations which stated that '212 nautical miles would constitute the national economic limit in the oceans surrounding Africa.'[44] Emphasis was placed on the word 'economic' giving a completely functional connotation to the proposed zone – an 'exclusive economic zone' (EEZ) which was to serve the economic development of African coastal states through jurisdictional expansionism of a non-territorial kind. These proposals were further consolidated by the African states in Yaounde[45] and by a group of Caribbean countries in Santo Domingo[46] in 1972.

In the interim the UN Resolution calling for a new law of the sea conference had resulted in the expansion of the United Nations Seabed Committee. This body had been set up originally to study the Pardo proposal for establishing a 'common heritage' régime over the deep ocean floor but it now became a preparatory committee for the new conference. With an initial membership of 86 states this committee met twice annually in 1971, 1972 and 1973 in Geneva and New York. It was almost completely politically oriented and its method was strikingly different from that of the ILC which carried out the preparatory work for UNCLOS I in an atmosphere of legal scholarship under much narrower terms of reference. The 'Seabed Committee', now basically misnamed, established three subcommittees: Subcommittee I dealing with the proposals for an international seabed régime; Subcommittee II dealing with an enormous list of issues for the conference including the territorial sea, innocent passage, functional zones, high seas, fisheries and straits; and Subcommittee III dealing with marine pollution, scientific research and the transfer of technology.

During the July 1972 session of the UN Seabed Committee the functional approach to the law of the sea was given its greatest boost when the delegation of Kenya submitted the 'Draft Articles on Exclusive Economic Zone Concept'.[47] This initiative constituted a formal and coherent presentation of the EEZ concept, which had become the most catalytic of all the new law of the sea ideas. Although it is conceived by and for coastal states, the EEZ sought to avoid unnecessarily abrasive confrontations with the 'freedom of the sea' stand of the maritime powers. In his introduction of the Draft Articles the Kenyan delegate stated his purpose quite succinctly:

> The economic zone concept offers a good basis for resolving the impasse between those who believe in a narrow and those who believe in a broad belt of territorial sea. Basically, the purpose of

> the exclusive economic zone concept is to safeguard the economic interests of the coastal states in the waters and seabeds adjacent to their coasts without unduly interfering with other legitimate uses by other states.[48]

This new generation of coastal states was not confined to developing states in Africa and Asia. As already indicated, the Latin American states, who also are members of the Third World and pioneered much of the functional approach, were very much part of the new movement. Even more significantly, the ever-growing ranks of militant coastal states were also swelled by such states from the developed world who for a variety of reasons had become disenchanted with the dominance of the maritime powers. Important members of this new group were Australia, Canada, New Zealand and Norway, and to a lesser extent Iceland and Yugoslavia.

5. UNCLOS III

Final Preparations: During the summer meeting of the Seabed Committee in Geneva in 1972 it was decided that UNCLOS III should commence with a short preparatory session, mainly to discuss procedural matters, at New York in November–December 1973. The first substantive session was to be held in Santiago, Chile, in April–May 1974. Santiago was chosen because many states, particularly in the developing world, felt that this new, most important conference should be held in a developing coastal state. As a Latin American developing country, with a democratically elected Marxist government, with its long history of contributions to the law of the sea, Chile appeared to be ideally suited to be the venue of the Conference. However, the subsequent political events in Chile precluded holding the Conference there. After the preliminary session of UNCLOS III at New York in December 1973, the UN General Assembly accepted an offer from Venezuela to host the next session in Caracas from June to August 1974.[49]

The Caracas Session: The 1974 Caracas session of UNCLOS III was the largest intergovernmental conference in history. Almost 5,000 delegates, advisers, observers, officials, journalists and UN personnel from some 140 states had gathered for an historic meeting which had been in preparation since 1967.[50] The aim was, of course, to codify a new, more equitable law to regulate almost every aspect of the oceans. This aim was not to be realized.

The conference did not reach full agreement on a single one of over 100 items before it.[51] Even a very general basis for a new law of the sea could not be spelt out. The only progress which the Conference could show was in the adoption of a complex set of Rules of Procedure,[52] a compromise settlement to have a third session for eight weeks at Geneva in March 1975, and a unanimous agreement to have a final formal session in Caracas so that a 'Caracas Convention' could be concluded as a token of gratitude to the host country Venezuela.

The Caracas session has often been labelled a 'failure' but this would be a short-sighted assessment indeed. The work accomplished was an important stepping stone in the long history of the law of the sea and a necessary part of its evolution towards more equitable boundaries. At Caracas the traditional maritime states were, for the first time in ocean law history, at a voting disadvantage and, as a consequence, had to resort to delaying tactics or procedural manoeuvres. It appeared to be rather obvious that the maritime powers were unwilling, at times almost unable, to negotiate seriously. Many of them did not really want this conference and there was thus a very discernible shift in diplomatic (and intellectual) leadership from the traditional states to the coastal states – particularly those in the Third World. The Caracas session was thus not only a triumph for coastal state rights but it was also the conference of the Third World. The performance of the 'Group of 77', the banner under which the almost 100 states of the Third World operates, contributed directly to whatever success the conference could claim. However, this was not enough. The fact that a new law of the sea would be unworkable without at least the tacit co-operation of the major maritime states gave that small group of countries a virtual veto against the imposition of ocean rules unacceptable to them.

Nevertheless, it was hoped that the Caracas session, having disposed of procedural wrangles, listened to the general positions of over 100 states, and debated hundreds of items at great length, would clear the path for real negotiations at the third session in Geneva. Unfortunately this was not to be the case.

The Geneva Session: The third session of UNCLOS III, which took place in Geneva from March to May of 1975, began quietly yet full of promise, with delegates chastened by the difficulties encountered at Caracas. This time there were few speeches, fewer public sessions, but once again very few meaningful negotiations. In general, this session was a disappointing one and hardly reflected the efforts which had been put into the preparation for UNCLOS III since 1967. The session ended with a rather vague and very informal single negotiating text prepared by the Chairmen of the three Committees of the conference[53] which were roughly similar to the original subcommittees of the UN Seabed Committee. It was precious little to show for the total of 22 weeks that UNCLOS III had been in progress.

Of course, the jurisdictional problem plagued this session, as it had the previous session and as it had the whole history of the law of the sea. However, this fundamental difference was now only one of the many divergent views and self-interests of such a large gathering of nations representing every possible ideology, geographical position and economic area. The Geneva failure cast serious doubts on whether even a generally acceptable compromise can be achieved in this type of conference, no matter how well prepared. The sea area outside national jurisdiction which had been seen by Ambassador Pardo in 1967 as falling under 'common heritage of mankind' had now emerged as an area in which nationalistic ambitions, economic greed and territorial acquisitiveness vied with each other. Although less than pleasant, this is nevertheless the reality within which the New York session of UNCLOS III, slated for the spring of 1976, and further sessions beyond that, must operate. It is the result of a long chain of events, some of which have been traced back to the beginning of the nation-state system.

6. General Conclusion

The coastal state which has risen or re-emerged over this long period has itself undergone many fundamental changes in social, political and economic terms, and today some coastal state ambitions are as suspect as the ambitions of the dominant maritime states were in an earlier period of history. However if these new ambitions result finally in a more equitable division of the resources of the sea, in greater responsibilities for conserving resources now endangered by the action of man, and last but not least in a more tolerable world economic order, then the end will have justified the 3,000-year struggle for reason and equity.

Notes

1. For a recent account of these conflicting tendencies, see E.D. Brown, 'Maritime Zones: A Survey of Claims', in R. Churchill, K.R. Simmonds and J. Welch (eds.), *New Directions in the Law of the Sea, Vol. III*, 1973, p. 157.

2. C. Colombos, *International Law of the Sea,* 6th ed., Ch. 1, 1967.
3. Ibid.
4. Id.
5. R. Lapidoth, 'Freedom of Navigation – Its Legal History and its Normative Basis', 6 *J. Mar. L. & Comm.*, pp. 259, 261, 1975.
6. Colombos, note 2 above.
7. G. Gidel, *Le Droit International public de la Mer,* Vol. I, 1932, pp. 129–33.
8. Ibid.
9. Colombos, note 2 above.
10. Ibid.
11. Id.
12. Id.
13. H. Grotius, *On the Freedom of the Seas* (ed. and trans.), Hogoffin, 1916.
14. Colombos, note 2 above.
15. Lapidoth, note 5 above, at pp. 271–2.
16. *Conference for the Codification of International Law, The Hague,* 1930.
17. *Second United Nations Conference on the Law of the Sea,* Official Records, Annexes and Final Act, U.N. Doc. A/CONF. 19/8, 1960.
18. One of the most recent summaries shows Territorial Sea claims as follows: 3 miles – 25 states; 3–6 miles – 11 states; 6–12 miles – 55 states; 12–50 miles – 11 states; 50–150 miles – 3 states; 200 miles – 8 states. FAO Legal Office, 'Limits and Status of the Territorial Sea, Exclusive Fishing Zones, Fishery Conservation Zones and the Continental Shelf', FAO Doc. FID/C/127, Rev. 1, Rome, 1975.
19. Colombos, note 2 above, at p. 69.
20. Id., p. 92.
21. H. Smith, *The Law and Custom of the Sea*, 2nd ed., 1950, pp. 10–11.
22. Note 16 above, Minutes of the Second Committee, p. 123 ff.
23. US Federal Regulations, Vol. 10, No. 12,304, 1945.
24. See, for example: 41 *A.J.I.L.* (Suppt.) pp. 11–12, 1947; 2 *I.L.Q.*, 135, 1948.
25. See: *Final Act of the United Nations Conference on the Law of the Sea,* UN Doc. A/CONF. 13/L.58, 30 April 1958.
26. Note 24 above. See also: F.V. Garcia Amador, *The Exploitation and Conservation of the Living Resources of the Sea,* 2nd ed., 1963, and K. Hjertonsson, *The New Law of the Sea: Influence of the Latin American States on Recent Developments of the Law of the Sea,* 1973.
27. See: S.H. Lay, R. Churchill and M. Nordquist (eds.), *New Directions in the Law of the Sea,* Vol. I, 1973, p. 23.
28. See: D.M. Johnston and E. Gold, *The Economic Zone in the Law of the Sea: Survey, Analysis and Appraisal of Current Trends*, 1973, p.1.
29. Note 27 above.
30. M.S. McDougal and W.T. Burke, *The Public Order of the Oceans: A Contemporary International Law of the Sea,* 1972, p. 443.
31. Ibid., p. 496. See also, *United Nations Conference on the Law of the Sea,* Official Records, Vol. III, UN Doc. A/CONF. 13/39 (1958).
32. See: Garcia Amador & Hjertonsson, note 26 above.
33. *United Nations Conference on the Law of the Sea*, III, Official Records 176, and *Second United Nations Conference on the Law of the Sea*, 1960, Official Records, p. 61.
34. *UNCTAD I, Proceedings,* p. 6.
35. See: B. Gosovic, *UNCTAD: Conflict and Compromise*, 1971, ch. 2.
36. Shipping is now dealt with in a newly established separate Shipping Division of UNCTAD.
37. Gosovic, note 35 above, p. 138.

38. Comité Maritime International, *Documentation 1973*, Vol. IV, p. 274 ff.
39. In 1973 the CMI had 33 member states only seven of which were from the developing world.
40. Gosovic, note 37 above.
41. See: UN Doc. A/6695, UN General Assembly XXII Session, 18 August 1967.
42. UN Doc. A/Res/2750(XXV), UN General Assembly, 17 December 1971.
43. See: Garcia Amador and Hjertonsson, note 26 above.
44. *Asian-African Legal Consultative Committee, Report of the 13th Session,* Lagos, January 1972 ,App. VI, p. 452.
45. *Report of the African States Regional Seminar on the Law of the Sea,* Yaounde, 1971. UN Doc. A/AC138/79.
46. *Declaration of Santo Domingo*, 1972. UN Doc. A/AC 138/80.
47. UN Doc. A/AC138/S.C.II/L.10.
48. Ibid.
49. UN Doc. A/Res/306(XXVII), UN General Assembly, 16 November 1973.
50. See: E. Gold, 'The Third United Nations Conference on the Law of the Sea. The Caracas Session, 1974', *Marit. Stud. Mgmt.*, 2, 102, 1974.
51. See: UN Doc. A/CONF.62/69.
52. UN Doc. A/CONF.62/30.
53. UN Doc. A/CONF.62/WP.8/Parts I, II & III.

Further Readings

1. S. Oda, D.M. Johnston, J.J. Holst, A.L. Hollick and M. Hardy, *A New Regime for the Oceans,* The Triangle Papers, No. 9, 1976.
2. H.G. Knight, 'International Fisheries Management: A Background Paper', in Knight (ed.), *The Future of International Fisheries Management,* 1975, at pp. 1–50.
3. D.M. Johnston and E. Gold, 'The Economic Zone in the Law of the Sea', *Survey, Analysis and Appraisal of Current Trends,* Law of the Sea Institute Occasional Papers, No. 17, Kingston, Rhode Island, 1973.
4. R. Churchill *et al.* (eds.), *New Directions in the Law of the Sea,* 4 vols., 1973–5.
5. E.D. Brown, *The Legal Regime of Hydrospace,* 1971.

PART II: THE MARINE ECONOMY

2 THE ECONOMIC GEOGRAPHY OF THE SEA

Alistair D. Couper

1. Introduction

There is little doubt that the resources of the sea will become of vital importance over the next decade, and technological advance will allow exploitation of the marine environment to proceed at an unprecedented rate. Because of this increasing reliance on the sea we must continuously examine the relationships between man and the marine environment; for we know only too well from experience on land that man is the only species capable of systematically destroying an environment on which he depends, either by mismanaging and squandering the non-renewable elements, or by overexploiting the naturally renewable resources to the point of extinction.

It is one of the functions of economic geography to explain the relationships between man's economic activities and his environment. In particular the economic geographer is interested in the interaction between the natural environment and the processes of production, consumption and exchange which man enters into, and in the ways in which he perceives, evaluates and uses the resource potential of his environment.

It is obvious that the ways in which man has perceived economic opportunities in his environment have varied over space and time according to technology, culture, politics and other criteria. As a result so also have the stocks of resources available to man. Consequently the relationship between man and those stocks is complex. Different people recognize different stocks and uses of resources. Capitalist man, socialist man, Third World man, coastal man, and landlocked man – and the many sectoral interests within these divisions – may have quite different sets of priorities in terms of ocean resource exploitation.

Because resources are evaluated from various points of view, an inventory of the resources of the sea would reveal little about their values to different users. Marine resource evaluation is particularly complicated, for in contrast to the land most of the sea is still free and open for any nation to pursue economic and other activities without seeking the permission of other nations, and many of the resources of the sea are living and highly mobile. Furthermore, for any one area there is a multiplicity of possible uses: the sea is a transport resource which links places on the earth's surface; it may also be used as a buffer separating nations; it can be used for fishing, the disposal of waste, the extraction of minerals, chemicals, cooling water, and fresh water; it is a source of energy to be derived from tides and waves; it can be used for the testing of weapons, scientific research and recreation, and for the mining of minerals on and below the seabed. Many of these activities can take place simultaneously in the same area but several of them are incompatible with each other.

For most economic activities the sea is a difficult and alien environment. It is vast and the physical forces are great; most of the ocean resources are hidden below the surface; and boundary lines are not normally visible on the surface of the sea. In the past man's use of the sea has been strongly influenced by physical conditions, and these still exert an influence in political as well as economic terms. For these reasons an essay on the economic geography of the sea would be meaningless without close reference to the physical basis on which economic and other activities take place.

2. The Physical Basis – Geology, Currents and Primary Production

Apart from shipping and the testing of weapons man's activities on and below the surface of the sea are concentrated mainly in the area of the continental margins. This is the zone where continental and oceanic elements interact to the greatest extent. It should be noted that there is also a fundamental geological division between the continental margin (which comprises the continental shelf, slope and rise) and the deep sea floor. The rocks of the margin belong to the light sial part of the earth's crust, and are mainly granitic and rich in silica and aluminium. The continental margin represents a prolongation seawards of the adjacent land. In contrast, the rocks of the deep sea floor are of the denser simatic part of the crust, mainly comprised of basalt and related rocks; they are rich in magnesium. These contrasting characteristics of continental and oceanic rocks provide the justification for the claims by nations to the mineral deposits which lie on and below the continental margin adjacent to their coastlines.

Economically, the most important physical subdivision of the continental margin is, at the present time, the continental shelf. This has an aggregate area equal to 18 per cent of the land surface of the globe, and covers 7 per cent of the ocean floor. The continental shelves are, however, unequally distributed around the land masses. In some locations the shelf has a width of less than 1 kilometre, elsewhere it extends to 1,500 kilometres, and there are many coastal areas completely devoid of shelves. The average gradient of the continental shelf is less than 1 degree, but its surface varies in geomorphological characteristics. It can be relatively smooth, or it may be dissected by channels and overlain by moraines and mobile sand waves. But everywhere the continental shelf contains a coverage of sediments eroded from the adjacent land. The bed rock below the sedimentary deposits may comprise the seaward extension of continental sedimentary, igneous or metamorphic rocks.

The continental shelf terminates at the continental edge which is marked by an increase in gradient to about 4 degrees, on average. Conventionally, and for purposes of certain legal definitions, the edge of the continental shelf has been taken to be the 200-metre isobath (100 fathoms), but the increase in incline which marks the termination of the shelf, and the beginning of the continental slope, occurs in waters varying from 50 to 500 metres in depth.

In many parts of the earth the slope of the continental shelf exceeds 4 degrees. It can be particularly steep (over 45 degrees) where geological processes such as faulting accounts for part of its formation. In some areas the slope is smooth, whereas in others it is deeply dissected by submarine canyons. Usually the sediments of the continental shelf extend down the continental slope to terminate in a thick sedimentary apron at the continental rise. The continental slope covers some 11 per cent of the ocean floor.

The continental rise has a gentler gradient than the slope and it lies at an average depth of 2,500 metres. The rise may extend seawards to a distance of 600–6,000 kilometres from the bottom of the continental slope. Taken together the continental margin (shelves, slopes and rises) has an area equal to 50 per cent of the land surface of the globe, and covers about 21 per cent of the total ocean floor.

Beyond the continental rise is the abyssal floor of the deep ocean basin. The predominant feature is the uniform surface of the basaltic bedrock, covered by a thin veneer of sediments, broken only in places by small hills and volcanic cones. The abyssal floor has an area equal to 79 per cent of the submarine surface of the globe. In the mid-oceanic regions basaltic rocks rise from the abyssal floor to near the surface of the sea thus forming a chain of submarine mountains with a total length around the earth of over 70,000 miles. The abyssal floor is broken also by deep trenches, the deepest of which, the Mariana trench in the Pacific, has a depth of 11,304 metres.

The geomorphological characteristics of the continental margins and abyssal floor have an important bearing on the nature of marine life, and on the exploitation of mineral resources. The circulation of the sea, both horizontally and vertically, is affected also by this physiography. In general, surface currents correspond to the planetary wind systems but they are modified in direction and rate by the land masses and by the disposition, extent and shape of the coasts.

On the western sides of ocean basins the strong northward setting currents, such as the Gulf Stream in the Atlantic and the Kuroshio in the Pacific, bring warm waters from low latitudes. As these flow polewards there is an exchange of temperature, an increase in density, and a tendency to sink, thus contributing to vertical circulation and a supply of oxygen to lower depths. The compensating equatorial setting surface currents on the eastern sides of ocean basins flow less strongly but are, like the western region coastal currents, important for marine life.

Of particular importance for primary production in the sea are the areas of upwelling. These are most pronounced on the eastern sides of oceans (the west coasts of continents) in subtropical latitudes where there are prevailing winds parallel to the coast. In such conditions there is a horizontal displacement of water and a compensating upwards vertical current. This upwelling, which characterizes the coasts of Peru, California, North West and South West Africa, and Western India, brings subsurface nutrients to the sunlit euphotic layer, thus stimulating a high productivity of phytoplankton. Such zones of upwelling are the source of almost half of the world's fish supply.

Especially rich plankton pastures exist also in the waters above the continental shelves. This results from the supply of nutrients from the land, the shallowness of the waters which allows sunlight to penetrate to the seabed in places, the mixing of water due to tidal effects, the breaking of oxygenating waves in the shallow seas, and the varied sedimentary spawning areas available to a variety of fish. Most of the balance of the world's fish catches are obtained from these waters.

Life in the high seas beyond the continental shelves is much less prolific and varied. In the lower depths of the sea, and on the seabed, the species are highly specialized but they too depend ultimately on organic materials from the upper sunlit zones. These take the form of detritus brought to the deeper layers by slumping from the continental slopes, or by turbidity currents, and especially from the rain of decaying organic materials falling from higher levels.

It should be emphasised that although life exists at all depths, and in every part of the ocean, from the intertidal rock pools to the deep oceanic trenches, by far the most productive areas, in terms of population and species, lie in the continental shelf areas and in the zones of upwelling.[1]

In the past the physical geography of the sea was reflected in the design of vessels adapted to specific coastal conditions in types of fishing gear; in the discovery and use of oceanic wind and current systems for navigation; and in the location and layout of ports. Man in the age of advanced technology has been able to overcome many of the physical constraints on the use of the marine environment. Ports and harbours, for example, have been adapted and changed to meet the requirements of ships which have been designed almost specifically to commercial criteria; artificial protection by breakwaters and the construction of locks have ameliorated the effects of weather and tides, and dredging technology has allowed better access. In several other respects, however, the advances in marine technology have increased the influence of certain physical conditions. Very deep-draughted ships, for example, have been constrained to specific routes; and, in the face of advanced fish locational instrumentation and fishing gear, it has been brought home that the living resources of the sea are not necessarily renewable. But advanced technology has also enabled man to reassess the potential of the seabed by allowing him to descend into very deep water and to sample and quantify the resources.

Because of the complexity of the marine physical and biological conditions, and the diversity of interests and peoples using the oceans, the economic geography of the sea is difficult to encompass in a brief essay. It must, therefore, be highly selective. Each of the prime activities of man in the marine environment is considered separately and the essay is concluded with a consideration of the extent to which the various conflicting uses of the sea may be reconciled.

3. Sea Transport

Since prehistoric times the sea has been used primarily as a means of transport, and in the modern period the high density and low viscosity of sea water has made it possible for enormous tonnages to be moved with ease over vast distances. This has allowed the uneven distribution of resources in the world to be more evenly spread, and specializations to emerge in many parts of the world based on comparative advantages in terms of climate, land, labour or capital. One result of the development of world-wide sea transport has been, therefore, to knit the economies of individual countries into a world economy. The well-being of many nations thus depends on the efficiency and cost of sea transport.[2]

There are about 35,000 merchant ships in the world at the present time. Perhaps about 12,000 of these are at sea on any one day. Between them they transport annually some 2,700 million tons of cargoes (1972), of which over half is oil. This represents a little over three-quarters of all international trade by volume. Table 1 gives some measure of international seaborne trade by geographic area.

Table 1: Seaborne Trade by Geographic Area, 1972 in '000 tons

	Loaded		Unloaded	
	dry cargo	oil	dry cargo	oil
W. Europe	245.5	98.4	455.9	743.5
USSR/E. Europe	79.4	71.3	41.3	22.4
Africa	117.0	268.6	53.1	47.5
Middle East	6.6	775.6	22.7	18.0
Far East	151.1	66.0	321.9	307.8
Australasia	123.9	3.0	18.6	137.7
North America	276.5	5.8	170.4	192.6
Latin America	152.5	240.6	49.8	146.9
	1,152.5	1,529.3	1,133.7	1,616.4

Source: British Shipping Statistics 1974, Chamber of Shipping of the United Kingdom.

The freight bill for carrying out these sea transport activities is in the order of $50 billion per annum, which is the highest value placed on any single maritime economic activity. This figure is ultimately passed on to importers and exporters in various proportions, so that any increase in the operating costs of shipping means lower returns to producers, or additions to the price of raw materials, foodstuffs and manufactured goods traded internationally.

The merchant fleets engaged in conducting international seaborne trade are discussed by Dr. Ronald Hope in Chapter Five of this volume. All that requires to be emphasized here is that the operating costs of modern vessels are high. A 200,000 ton oil tanker, for example, costs about $17,000 per day to operate and a 2,000 unit container ship has total costs of around $20,000 per day. Fast turn-round in port and minimum route distance at sea are therefore important, for loss of time means higher freight bills for the countries dependent on sea transport.

The main determinants of time on voyage, in addition to ship and port technology and operations, are weather conditions, the physical characteristics of the routes, and the political and legal divisions of the sea. A vessel trading on the high seas has freedom of movement, but the actual route followed will be dictated by distance and by wave or ice conditions. Sometimes the master will choose to follow a least-distance route by great circle sailing which takes him into high and possibly stormy latitudes; or he may follow a rhumb-line route in lower latitudes which involves increased distance but may avoid stormy conditions. Increasingly it is the practice of ships to be 'weather routed'; that is, to follow a least-time track by plotting a course each day through wave fields of lowest gradient. These are depicted on radio-linked wave contour maps, or the information is relayed from a shore-based meteorologist. By weather routing it is possible that a vessel in the North Atlantic can, in winter, save 24 hours or more on a single passage.

Ice continues to be an obstacle on some routes. Ice closes the northern sea route across the Siberian Sea for almost 200 days in the year, but during the open period this north-east passage reduces the distance between Europe and the Far East by some 2,000 miles compared with voyages via the Suez Canal. The route is not, however, always open to the flags of all nations. The north-west passage across North America is even more ice-bound, but the route has been shown as feasible following the successful transit of the s.s. Manhattan in September 1969. This confirmed the possibility of oil and mineral shipments from Alaska and the Arctic islands being made most of the year round, and it opened an alternative high-latitude route for shipping between the Atlantic and Pacific. It should be noted that a more economic solution for the trade of ice-bound polar regions may lie in submarine tankers and freighters. A nuclear-powered submarine of 100,000 tons and upwards could follow trans-polar routes beneath the ice, the navigational problem being overcome by the placing of acoustic transponders along the sea bottom over the route.[3] This, however, could involve questions of legality and problems of jurisdiction over the seabed in high polar latitudes.

Closer inshore, the principal physical constraints on shortest route distance lie in depth of water. This is particularly so in relation to straits and canals, the use of which avoids long deviations around headlands, or even continents. The increased draught of many ships to 21 metres and over limits their choice of certain important waterways. The Malacca Strait, for example, through which about one-sixth of the world's oil is transported, has a depth of only 20 metres in places so that ships of over about 200,000 DWT are prevented from making fully loaded transits. The alternative route for bigger ships is through the

Lombok Strait, adding another 1,000 miles to a voyage from the Arabian Gulf to Japan. The Dover Strait has a limit of about 21 metres, the entrances to the Baltic Sea have draught limits of 11 and 8 metres and the Kiel Canal can take ships up to 9.45 metres draught. In the case of the major canals, Suez has currently a depth of about 11 metres and Panama to between 10 and 12 metres, depending on water levels in the lakes.

Because of the importance of some straits for reducing time it is natural that a great number of ships converge on them. The Strait of Dover, for example, has a traffic volume of 350 vessels per day plus 200 ferry crossings, in addition to the usual movements of fishing and pleasure craft. To minimize the hazards which such a traffic density presents, internationally agreed traffic lane separations are in force; and some coastal states adjacent to high-density routes wish to introduce stricter traffic control over shipping. This applies also to the Cape of Good Hope route where, because of the dangers of collision, grounding, and consequent pollution, vessels have been required to maintain a distance of 12 miles from headlands. This periodically brings ships close to the edge of the continental shelf where a combination of complex currents and bad weather can lead to freak waves. Severe damage to ships and several total losses have occurred in this region as a result of these factors.[4]

Shipowners are concerned by the possibility of increased coastal state jurisdiction which may involve diversions from least-distance routes, needless exposure to bad weather, or the hazarding of their ships through being stopped in busy sea lanes for purposes of inspection. But coastal states are concerned with their exposure to pollution, and other dangers, from the proximity of high-density shipping. So far, international rules to protect the environment have been framed in such a way that they do not delay vessels. Since 1967, for example, there has been a complete ban on the discharge of persistent oils within 50 miles of any coast (and within 150 miles of coasts in the North Atlantic) and ships above 20,000 GRT built after May 1967 are prohibited from discharging oil, or mixtures of more than 100 p.p.m., anywhere at sea. Under a 1973 IMCO convention no oil may be discharged anywhere in the Mediterranean, Black Sea, Red Sea, or Middle East Gulf; and ships ordered after December 1975 must be fitted with segregated ballast tanks.

If fully adopted and complied with, these measures could eliminate the release each year of some 1.25 million tons of oil into the sea from tank washings, and another 0.5 million tons from ships other than tankers. Traffic control in narrows, compulsory pilotage, mandatory lanes, segregation of dangerous vessels, and the enforcement of high-quality manning on ships could, in turn, greatly reduce the number of marine accidents which lead to catastrophic spills and explosions. These latter measures necessarily curtail the customary freedom of the master to determine his course and speed in certain limited areas, but they preserve freedom of navigation over most of the seas.

The need to avoid costly delays to modern shipping, while ensuring the protection of coastal state interests, has led to support for port state rights of enforcement, whereby infringements would be dealt with at ports of call, thus also overcoming any reluctance on the part of flag states in enforcing regulations.

Some measures of the costs to the world economy through interfering with the free flow of shipping may be appreciated from the effects of the closure of the Suez Canal. The additional ocean transport costs of closure amounted to $4,400 million between 1967 and 1971. The costs sustained by the developing countries of East Africa and South-East Asia in their export trade with Europe came to $560 million.[5]

4. Fishing

In many ways fishing is the most important extractive use of the sea. As a biological resource it is renewable and can always be available to man. The stock of fish may even be increased in quantity and quality in the course of time by proper management; but it can also be exhausted or destroyed through overexploitation, or as a result of conflict with other users of the sea. The landed value of the world fish catch in recent years has been between $8 and $12 billion per annum.

As may be appreciated from the outline of the physical basis, the richness of sea fisheries is ultimately determined by the phytoplankton crop. On this the zooplankton graze, and in turn are fed on by small fish and other carnivorous creatures. Only a small proportion of the phytoplankton is directly consumed by fish such as the sardine. Most other near-surface feeding pelagic fish (herring, pilchard, anchovy) feed on zooplankton, while the demersal round fish (cod, haddock, hake), and the bottom feeding flat fish (plaice, sole, halibut), are even further removed from the primary source. There is a complex web of life in the sea extending from the nutrient components in sea water through many interrelated levels to the higher fish stocks directly consumed by man.

As well as being distributed vertically in the sea, fish migrate over various distances. Generally there are four species recognised in terms of their horizontal mobility. (i) Sedentary species, including oysters, clams and crabs, which are immobile at the harvestable stage, other than by constant physical contact with the seabed or subsoil. (ii) Coastal species which are free swimming and are generally associated with the waters of the continental shelves, and the nutrients carried to the sea by rivers, or with the zones of coastal upwelling. Several of such species, including the cod and herring, are highly migratory. (iii) Anadromous species which spawn in fresh water but spend much of their life in the oceans. The salmon is the best known of this species. (iv) Wide-ranging species, such as whales, tuna and swordfish, are the most highly mobile fish in the sea. They are found at great distances from land as they migrate over vast areas of the ocean.

The mobility of fish is associated with their life cycles and with seasonal and other environmental factors. They move freely through areas of national jurisdiction and may cover several thousand miles in their annual migrations. Fishermen have tended to pursue fish shoals on the high seas over the continental shelves and in the coastal zones of upwelling as a common property resource. Their freedom to fish in these waters has been regarded traditionally as a principal freedom of the sea.

To have commercial significance, a fishery must consist of a large aggregation of one or more marketable species abundant enough to withstand regular exploitation. Modern vessels, detection systems and fishing gear have allowed shoals to be pursued over the whole area of the sea and catches to be continually increased. In 1948 the world catch amounted to 19.6 million tons, in 1971 it reached 69.7 million tons, and estimates of optimum yields from the sea vary from 80 to 200 million tons per annum. Not every species can undergo increased exploitation. Many are already overexploited. The maintenance of the balance of life in the sea depends on an extraction rate of various species which permits their continuing reproduction, as well as the maintenance of a marine environment free from toxic pollutants.

The reasons why certain species are in danger from overfishing are discussed in the next chapter. Most fish are caught within 200 miles of land, and of the total catch a little over 50 per cent is obtained from the Pacific region and 40 per cent from the Atlantic. Most of this is taken by some 17 countries as shown in Table 2.

Table 2: Fish Catches by Country (1971)

	'000 metric tons
Peru	10,611
Japan	9,894
USSR	7,337
China	6,880
Norway	3,075
USA	2,767
India	1,845
Thailand	1,572
Denmark	1,400
Canada	1,289
Indonesia	1,250
United Kingdom	1,073
South Africa	1,084
Korea Rep.	1,074
Phillipines	1,050
France	742
Iceland	685

Source: FAO statistics.

Most highly productive areas of the sea are very heavily fished, and in most cases a reduction in fishing effort would, in the course of time, be rewarded by increased levels of catches. By contrast the application of more labour and capital in the fishing effort is likely to reduce catch levels and the profitability of fishing.

On a world scale man depends to only a limited extent on fishery resources, but degrees of dependence vary greatly between countries and coastal regions. Division can be made between domestic and distant water dependencies. In the high latitudes of the northern hemisphere, for example, there are communities which depend on domestic fishing for most of their cash incomes, as in Iceland, West Greenland, Newfoundland, Faroes, Western Norway, Western Scotland and Western Ireland.[6] In the Pacific and parts of South-East Asia and the West Indies the inhabitants of the low coral islands in particular (which like the northern communities have a difficult agricultural base), also depend on near-sea fish stocks;[7] as do many coastal communities in Africa, India and Asia. Normally such groups combine fishing with farming and other activities.

The second broad geographical division of fishing activities is the distant water group, comprising mainly fleets from industrial countries. The two are not of course mutually exclusive (fishermen from Iceland and Western Norway visit distant waters, and the industrial coastal regions of the United Kingdom have inshore fishermen) but it is nevertheless possible to designate distant-water fishing as belonging to the advanced industrial nations operating out of major ports, while domestic fishing is carried out by the less industrialized countries from many small coastal settlements.[8]

It is the activities of the distant-water fleets which have increased to the greatest extent in recent years. In several cases the distant-water fleets include freezer trawlers, and factory ships served by numerous catchers. The Soviet Union, Japan, United States and most of the industrial nations of Europe are engaged in distant-water activities as well as in domestic fishing. Such fleets are most active in the north-west Atlantic, east central Atlantic, south-east Atlantic, north-east Pacific and south-west Pacific. In these areas the distant-water fleets caught more than 40 per cent of the total catch in 1971.

There seems little doubt that, properly managed, the fish stock could increase in quantity and continue to provide support for coastal communities, possibly to supply as much as a quarter of the world's protein requirements in a relatively short time. In managing fisheries it is also technically feasible to cultivate species in coastal fish farms and restock areas of the sea. But the problem of retaining ownership over the fish released is one factor which currently prevents this. Even fish farming in confined inlets and bays for domestic harvesting has not proceeded to the extent it could, due to legal complications and conflicts with other sea users – in particular with those using the sea for the disposal of waste products.

5. Hydrocarbons

Oil and gas deposits are found in very large sedimentary basins. Such basins underlie 57 per cent of the world's continental margins, and 32 per cent of the world's land area. Consequently it is expected that in the course of time most of the world's hydrocarbons will be extracted from beneath the sea. Already some 20 per cent of oil production and over 10 per cent of natural gas is won from below the continental shelves, and has a value of over $10 billion. About one quarter of the world's proven reserves lie in the shelf and slope areas within 200 miles of land. Other possible source locations include the continental rises with their great depths of sediments, and possibly the mid-oceanic ridges. By the early 1980s about half of the world's oil production may be obtained from offshore wells in the continental shelves.

The extraction of oil and gas from beneath the sea started in Lake

Maracaibo during the 1920s. By the mid-1940s the use of fixed platforms was widespread in the Gulf of Mexico, and in 1949 mobile rigs were active off the coast of Louisiana. Since then semi-submersible craft have been developed for work in the North Sea at water depths exceeding 300 metres, while dynamic positioned drill ships are able to operate in depths of 1000 metres.

In the early 1970s there were 200 mobile drill units and 40 drill ships active, and drilling was taking place on the continental shelves of 70 countries. By 1975 about 30 of these offshore operations had reached the production stage. Areas of highest potential for hydrocarbons are the continental shelf of the North Sea, the Siberian Arctic, Spitzbergen, Alaska, the Mackenzie Delta, Bering Sea and Beaufort Sea, the east coast of North America (especially the Gulf of Mexico, Louisiana and Florida), Trinidad and Tobago, Brazil, Argentina, Southern California, Ecuador and Peru. In the Mediterranean the areas of high potential occur off Algeria, Libya, the Nile Delta, Southern Italy, and the Aegean. The whole of the West African continental shelf has considerable potential, as has the Arabian Gulf and the Black Sea, the Caspian and the Sea of Azov. In Asia the continental shelf off China is considered very rich in hydrocarbons and likewise the area between Taiwan and Japan. The Indonesian region has proven reserves, and gas has been found off North West Australia and in the Bass Straits. Prospecting is proceeding off New Zealand and in parts of the Pacific. In most areas of younger sedimentary rocks in the world there is interest in hydrocarbon prospecting (see Table 3).

The most active area currently is the North Sea. Interest in this zone was stimulated in 1959 when gas was discovered onshore in Holland. In 1964 offshore jurisdictional problems were largely solved and exploration of the North Sea started. Gas was discovered in the southern area in September 1965 and soon afterwards a productive oil-well was drilled further north. It is now the most productive offshore area in the world and in the mid-1970s estimates of the recoverable oil stood at around 44,000 million barrels. Estimates of unproven reserves have been put at two or three times this level.

Estimates of recoverable oil reserves in the world are also continually being updated, but Table 3 gives some indication of the orders of magnitude of proven reserves of oil and Table 4 of gas in the continental shelves of various countries. The estimates of recoverable oil reserves in the world range from 1,600 to 4,000 thousand million barrels, the upper figure assuming vast offshore reserves yet to be proven.[9]

The extraction of hydrocarbons from offshore is expensive. A semi-submersible rig costs about $50 million to build and equip, and about $50,000 per day to operate. The Forties Field cost over £650 million to bring into production. Extraction is also hazardous. In the 1960s three oil rigs were lost in the North Sea due to stress of weather. Since then rigs have been built to withstand winds of 150 knots and the likelihood of 100-foot waves.

The methods of bringing oil from offshore depends mainly on the life and yield of the field. In long-life wells pipelines are laid to the nearest low-lying area of coast, or in some circumstances tanker loading is carried out from buoy moorings at well-head terminals. The bigger terminals comprise massive structures resting on the bed of the continental shelf with a storage capacity for 1 million barrels of oil.

6. Minerals and Chemicals

The mineral deposits on and below the seabed and dissolved in sea water have not been extensively exploited on a world scale. The total value of marine minerals probably amounts to less than $600 million per annum, which represents about 3 per cent of the world's annual mineral output.

The continental shelves account for most of the offshore solid mineral production. In order of importance the minerals currently obtained from the seabed and sub-soil are: sand and gravel, shells, tin, diamonds, iron sands, and other mineral sands (ilmenite, rutile, zircon, garnite, gold). Most of these placer deposits are formed by gravitational segregation during transportation seawards from erosion, or mining, on land. They are found mainly at depths of less than 130 metres.

In the deeper areas beyond the continental shelves placer deposits are likely to be limited, and seawards of the margins there are only thin sediments of wind-borne or chemical origin which have settled on the seabed from the surface. Below the bed of the continental shelves minerals may also be found, as in the deposits of sulphur of the cap rocks of salt domes off Louisiana and in the Gulf of Mexico. The rocks below the continental slopes and rises may likewise contain minerals but at great depths.

An important mineral which is yet to be comprehensively surveyed is the phosphorite nodules which have been found at various water depths off the coast of California and other parts of the ocean. But the main interest currently focuses on the manganese nodules lying on the surface of the deep sea floor. These are found in water depths of between 3,000 and 6,000 metres and are particularly widespread in the Pacific. Mero states that there is probably no extensive area, other than

Table 3: Offshore Oil Reserves

	(millions of barrels) Estimated ultimate recoverable offshore oil reserves 1972
North America	15,640
Canada	na[a]
US	15,640
Europe	12,011
Denmark	na
Italy	152
Netherlands	na
Norway	3,013
Spain	150
UK	6,400[b]
USSR	2,296[c]
Middle East	95,933
Abu Dhabi	5,494
Dubai	1,581
Iran	6,072
Iran Saudi Arabia	10,000
Saudi Arabia	57,878
Qatar	12,374
Saudi Arabia – Kuwait neutral zone	2,534
Rest of Asia	3,054
Malaysia–Brunei	3,030
Malaysia–Sarawak	200
Indonesia	400
Japan	24
Latin America	26,073
Argentina	na
Brazil	na
Mexico	2,124
Peru	142
Trinidad and Tobago	420
Venezuela	23,287[d]
Australasia	2,876
Australia	2,864
New Zealand	12
Africa	9,401
Angola–Cobuda	1,232
Congo (Brazzarrue)	500
Egypt	4,681
Gabon	478
Nigeria	2,510
World Total offshore	165,588[e] (i.e. 25%)
World Total all reserves	672,700[f]

Notes

a Potential for Canada has been estimated to be 7 billion barrels but has not been confirmed as ultimate recoverable.
b Estimate of ultimate recoverable reserves in North Sea, south of 62°N parallel are 42 billion barrels.
c Conservative estimate.
d May be high because it includes some offshore reserves of onshore/offshore fields.
e Extensive exploration now under way plus recent discoveries in five countries not noted, will doubtless add substantially to this figure.
f World total proved oil reserves at end of 1972 according to BP.
na Not available.

Source: US Geological Survey, *Chemical and Engineering News,* 4 March 1974.

Table 4: Offshore Gas Reserves

	Ultimate recoverable offshore gas reserves Billion cubic feet
North America (US)	39,463
Western Europe	40,000
Denmark	500
Italy	na[a]
Netherlands	na
Norway	10,000
UK	29,500[b]
Middle East	6,640
Kuwait	875
Saudi Arabia	3,600[c]
United Arab Emirates	2,165
Latin America	3,500[d]
Trinidad and Tobago	3,500[d]
Australasia	16,300
Australia	10,300[d]
New Zealand	6,000
Africa	1,000[e]
Egypt	1,000
Gabon	na
World Total	106,903[f]

a Estimated to be 3.2 million cu.ft. but not confirmed as ultimate recoverable.
b Seven new fields were found in 1972 and 1973, but recoverable reserves are not available yet.
c An additional 11 million cu.ft. are estimated, but are not confirmed as ultimate recoverable.
d A minimum figure.
e The estimate for Nigeria is 10 million cu.ft. but not confirmed as ultimate recoverable.
f A minimum figure, as statistics are not available for small countries.
na Not available.

Source: US Geological Survey, *Chemical and Engineering News,* 4 March 1974.

the trenches of the Pacific, more than 200 miles from land where manganese nodules of one form or another cannot be found.

The manganese nodules of the seabed vary in size from 1 to 20 centimetres and may contain quantities of manganese copper, nickel, aluminium, cobalt, calcium, strontium, cadmium, nickel and molybdenum. The estimates for the Pacific Ocean vary from 1,000 thousand million to 2,000 thousand million tons. This represents a vast reserve of minerals far in excess of the proven reserves on land. Indeed the mineral content of the nodules could supply world industry, at present rates of consumption, with manganese, aluminium, nickel and several other elements for hundreds of years.[10] Drechsler records the average concentration in the Pacific Ocean as 1.12 grams per square centimetre so that if the United Nations proposal of licensed areas of 40,000 km^2 was adopted for mining then each area would contain 400 million metric tons. Allowing for only 100 million being recoverable each mine could extract one million tons per annum for 100 years providing each year 260,000 tons of manganese, 12,000 tons nickel, 10,000 tons copper and 2,400 tons cobalt.[11] There could be several hundred such mines working in the Pacific, Indian and Atlantic Oceans in an area of 300 million km^2.

It is the awareness of these vast resources of the abyssal plains which will stimulate technological advance, and also engender debates as to how exploitation should proceed so that the resources are used for the common heritage of mankind.

Sea water also contains an enormous reserve of minerals, though these will be difficult to extract. The 350 million mls^3 of sea water contains dissolved solids amounting to 35 thousand parts per million, thus each cubic mile contains some 165 million tons of minerals.[12]

The main chemicals gained from sea water are, in order of value: salt, magnesium, bromine, heavy water (D_2O) and minor quantities of potassium, calcium and sulphate. In certain areas of the sea the concentrations of minerals are particularly high, as in the hot, high-density brines discovered in the middle Red Sea. In addition to minerals, sea water is significant as a direct source of fresh water, and this will increase in importance with the industrialization of the oil-producing countries. Table 5 provides some indication of the resource potential of sea water. Mero identifies 47 minerals in addition to those shown in the table. Of particular note is the vast deuterium oxide (D_2O) content of sea water, which, if only a relatively small percentage could be extracted, would meet much of the world's nuclear energy input requirements for several thousands of years.

Table 5: Concentration and Amounts of Elements in Sea Water

Element	Concentration (mg/h)	Amount of element in sea-water (tons/mile^3)	Total amount in oceans (tons)
Chlorine	19,000.0	89.5×10^6	29.3×10^{15}
Sodium	10,500.0	49.5×10^6	16.3×10^{15}
Magnesium	1,350.0	6.4×10^6	2.1×10^{15}
Sulphur	885.0	4.2×10^6	1.4×10^{15}
Calcium	400.0	1.9×10^6	0.6×10^{15}
Potassium	380.0	1.8×10^6	0.6×10^{15}
Bromine	65.0	306,000	0.1×10^{15}
Carbon	28.0	132,000	0.04×10^{15}
Strontium	8.0	38,000	$12{,}000 \times 10^9$
Boron	4.6	23,000	$7{,}100 \times 10^9$
Silicon	3.0	14,000	$4{,}700 \times 10^9$
Fluorine	1.3	6,100	$2{,}000 \times 10^9$
Argon	0.6	2,800	930×10^9
Nitrogen	0.5	2,400	780×10^9

Source: J.L. Mero, *The Mineral Resources of the Sea,* New York, 1967.

7. Energy

The enormous forces of waves, ocean currents and tides have always presented opportunities and challenges. In the search for renewable sources of energy these forces are being reappraised. It is theoretically possible to utilize the temperature differences between warm and cold currents. Off the coast of Florida, for example, the difference is 19–25°C; and Sebo estimates that, at present levels of technology, about 4,000 relatively small power plants, each with a capacity of 400 mw, clustered in a 15-mile by 550-mile swath off the coast of south-east USA, could supply the electricity energy requirements of the whole country.[13]

The mass transport of water in the oceans is also theoretically possible to harness, as is wave energy; and experimental work is proceeding in relation to the latter. But the most immediate use of ocean energy potential lies in tidal energy conversion. This is established in the Rance Estuary of north-west France where an energy output of 500 gwh/yr is generated; and in the Soviet Kislaya Guba project on the White Sea. Areas of very high tidal power potential exist in the Bay of Fundy between New Brunswick and Nova Scotia where there is a tidal range of 16 metres, and in the Severn Estuary between South Wales and Somerset. It has been estimated that the Severn power generator could supply 10 per cent of the United Kingdom electricity requirements. Other areas of high potential include Alaska, Southern California, the south-east of South America, India, China and Australia.

Tidal power is a renewable resource and the technology for harnessing it is already available. Sebo calculates that the continuous tidal power potential of the world is about 1,100 gw. At the present time only 240 mw is harnessed.[14]

8. Military Use

The great powers have used the sea as a means of defence and of aggression. In spite of long-range weapons, conventional surface naval forces are still deployed internationally, and the deep sea offers concealment for missile-carrying submarines. The seabed may also be used for installing listening devices for the monitoring of ship passages. The main naval forces reported as deployed at sea during 1974 are shown in Table 6.

In addition to the forces shown in Table 6 the navies of Australia, China, and some of the developing countries are deployed in many oceans.[15]

Table 6: Military Use of the Sea

	NATO Bloc	Soviet Bloc
Missile submarines	45	136
Other submarines	209	267
Aircraft carriers	24	0
Cruisers	29	34
Destroyers	505	440

Source: 'Why Navy', HMSO, 1974.

The sea has also been used as a military range, a missile testing zone, and for nuclear tests. For these purposes nations have banned vessels from entering certain areas of the high seas, as for example during the nuclear tests at Mururoa where a prohibited zone of 60 miles was declared beyond the 12-mile limit. But naval authorities are also in general proponents of the principle of freedom of the high seas. In particular they wish the right of unimpeded transit through international straits.

9. Dumping of Waste

The sea has an enormous capacity for diluting and degrading waste materials, but because it appears to be a free resource it has tended to be overused for these purposes. The use of the sea for waste disposal is not of course free. It merely appears so, since users for dumping purposes are not obliged to take account of the costs they impose on others, such as those in the fishing and recreational sectors.

The shipping industries have tended to use the sea as a sink for tank washing to the order of about 2 million tons of crude oil per annum, but this is being largely curtailed by technological advance and legislation. The deep sea has also been used for the dumping of radioactive waste by the countries of Europe, Japan and North America. Between 1946 and 1970 it is recorded that 86,758 containers of radioactive waste, with estimated activity of 94,673 curies, were dumped in the North Atlantic.[16] Although these have been dumped in very deep water at least one container has been brought to the surface in a fishing zone by upwelling. In December 1971 the USA effectively ceased to license sea disposal of radioactive waste. Some countries, including the United Kingdom, continue, however, to release nuclear waste from pipelines extending within their territorial waters; and an unknown quantity of explosives, gases, and other surplus military weapons and substances continue to be dumped in the deep ocean.

The most serious areas of marine pollution lie in coastal waters, into which vast quantities of domestic and industrial wastes are poured from land-based sources, and there is a continuous run-off of fertilizers from agricultural land. These include non-degradable materials, persistent heavy metals, and toxic substances. This is particularly serious in the enclosed and semi-enclosed seas such as the Baltic, Black Sea and Mediterranean. Marine life may be killed off in coastal waters by toxicity, or be rendered inedible to man as a result of absorbing sublethal doses of radioactivity, mercury, lead or cadmium. The effects of coastal marine pollution are seen at various levels: the destruction of around 40 million fish in the Rhine in July 1969 due to the spillage of some toxic chemicals, the loss of 30,000 sea birds on the coast of Denmark in 1972 due to oil spillages,[17] and the poisoning of the coastal population on the Japanese island of Minemata by methol-mercury absorbed by shell-fish.

Most of the estuaries in the advanced industrial nations are suffering from overuse as a sink for waste. The polluting loads discharged into an estuary are measured in terms of biochemical oxygen demand (BOD). When organic effluence is discharged into the water the decomposition lowers the oxygen content of the water, and if the load of organic matter is very heavy oxygen levels may be so reduced that the purifying activity of the bacteria in the water ceases. In the Tees Estuary of the United Kingdom, for example, the polluting load discharged in lb/BOD per day has increased by 716 per cent from 1930 to 1966.[18] This has, of course, been due to the enormous increase in industrial activities which tend to concentrate at estuary locations. It has meant the destruction of amenity, and also the loss of nursery grounds for young fish, again demonstrating that what appears to be a free resource to the disposers of waste has considerable negative spillover effects on other users of the sea.

International legislation relating to the dumping of pollutants at sea is becoming more stringent, but enforcement remains very difficult. In the future pollution offences by ships, while remaining the responsibility of the flag state, may also be open to prosecution by the coastal state and port state. In the case of land-based pollution, however, the establishing of standards and the enforcement of regulations are the sole responsibility of the coastal state. It is likely that each state, while noting the desirability of international harmonization of standards, will decide on the amount of deterioration of the marine environment which appears socially acceptable and ecologically permissible in relation to its own area of sea. It will also compare the costs of abating pollution with the costs to its own economy of the effects of pollution. The view of various states will be coloured by their industrial priorities and by the dependence they have on the sea for fishing and the use they make of it for recreational purposes. As with fishery management it is clear that the sea as a resource for dumping waste has to be managed on an international, or at least regional, basis.

10. Impact of the Land–Sea Interface

All sea activities make demands on the coast, and many land-based activities have their effects on the sea. Sea activities are moving landwards with the extension of marine transport on to inland waterways by LASH barges, and with the development of inland container depots. Land activities have in turn moved seawards, in the form of ports and terminals to outer areas of estuaries in order to accommodate deeper draughted ships, the reclamation of tidal zones for oil service bases and industry, and the creation of artificial islands offshore for the location of marine installations and power plants.

There is considerable competition for coastal land in many countries, and this will increase with sea-related activities. In the older industrial nations industries have tended to move to the coast as imported raw materials have taken over from indigenous resources. Such industries as steel, oil refining, petrochemicals, grain milling and paper manufacturing reduce the weight and bulk of raw materials after they are unloaded from bulk carriers. These industries are consumers of vast areas of flat land, they use estuarine water for cooling purposes, and discharge thermal emissions and waste products to the sea. Other activities attracted to the coastal zone include sewage and water treatment plants, fish processing, gas terminals, power stations and airports. Port installations in themselves involve the use of considerable acreages of land, particularly where container facilities are built.

The coast has also been the scene of urban sprawl, and has attracted hotels, holiday homes, amusement parks, marinas and other recreational facilities; as well as activities as diverse as underwater marine parks and military firing ranges. There is clearly a special attraction to coastal land and considerable competition for it as well as conflict of use.

This has been made more intense with the expansion of offshore industries. The impact of offshore developments is frequently felt first at ports where storage facilities have to be established and service vessels berthed. As ports are often circumscribed by urban areas they cannot easily be expanded, and competition for space becomes a matter of conflict between the needs of commercial shipping, the fishing fleet, and the offshore industry – and often with the inhabitants of the adjacent urban area which may be under threat of demolition to provide additional storage and servicing infrastructure. This has been the experience of some Scottish ports under the impact of the rapid development of North Sea oil.

An oil rig engaged in exploring activities, for example, requires about 12,000 tons of materials delivered over a year, and when involved in development drilling a total of 30,000 tons has to be taken to the rig. This has to be delivered from bases within a maximum of 200 miles from the oil field. The 30 or so rigs in the North Sea represent, therefore, a high service requirement. Aberdeen handles over 200 supply vessel turn-rounds per month and Peterhead 300, thereby greatly overtaxing and changing these ports.

The service bases for offshore oil also stimulate manufacturing and supply activities. Aberdeen has now nearly 300 oil-related firms and unemployment has dropped from 3.5 per cent in 1970 to 1.4 per cent in 1974.[19] But there appears now to be some stress on local labour and an influx from other areas. The effect is to render local non-oil-related industries (e.g. fishing) less attractive, raise the price of land and housing, and overtax social services and transport.

The main problems of the coastal impact of offshore oil, however, relate to 'blue coast' sites and smaller rural communities. In the building of steel and concrete platforms, for example, specific coastal land and water requirements have to be met. In the case of steel jacket structures about 40 hectares of land is required with access to 10 to 20 metres of water, and a work-force of 1200 to 2200 men. Concrete structures require about 20 hectares of land, access to 60 metres of water, and a work-force of 600 to 800 men.

These conditions can only seldom be met in existing industrial areas of the coast. Steel structures have therefore been built in rural north-east Scotland, occupying enormous coastal areas and requiring an influx of labour, materials and infrastructure of such a magnitude as to change completely the character of the region. Concrete structures have tended to be built in even more remote areas since they require very deep water. This is found in the highland regions of glacial erosion, as in the lochs of western Scotland, and the fjords of Norway. Because these areas have been heavily glaciated and eroded they tend not to have retained an agricultural population; and lacking the younger coal deposits they did not experience the industrial revolution – other than by a loss of population. Consequently they tend to be occupied by the traditional crofter/fisherman, living in communities with distinct cultural heritages. They are also regions of great natural beauty and amenity. The construction of enormous concrete platforms necessitating excavation of land for building, and for materials, as well as the influx of labour, changes drastically these remote areas of the coast.

In landing the oil it is necessary to run pipelines ashore. The best route is over a gently shelving bed to a low sandy coast, as close as possible to the oil fields. Where the landfall is remote from refineries or markets, tanker terminals may have to be established at deep-water locations. Thus remote Shetland, as well as providing service bases, has been chosen for the development of the biggest tanker port in Europe, at Sulom Voe. Shetland, from a stable population of only 18,000 previously relying on fishing, handicrafts and tourism, is now on the threshold of a way of life which will change in many unforeseeable ways.

Where gas is brought ashore, it is necessary to install a processing plant on the coast, and this may occupy over 500 acres of land. As with oil pipelines the routes of gas lines are chosen to cross a gently shelving, and preferably sandy seabed – which is, however, also good trawling ground and thereby conflicts occur with the fishing industry.

The impact of offshore hydrocarbon developments on the coast and coastal communities has been a source of debate in many regions. Frequently the struggle is between users of the marine environment for fishing and recreation and the industrial developers; and between local people who wish more employment opportunities in an area of declining population and the distant urban dwellers who wish to preserve the area for its amenity value and holiday homes.

The alternative to the use of scarce coastal land for industry which requires maritime locations, and for urban expansion, lies in artificial islands.

Already there are several, 10-acre, man-made islands constructed by oil companies off the coast of Long Beach, California, which are associated with drilling in the East Willmington Field; and a 40-acre man-made island is proposed for the location of nuclear power plants off south-west California.[20] Similar schemes are being suggested by Japan, France, Belgium, The Netherlands, West Germany and the United Kingdom. In relation to the latter country the reclamation of the Goodwin Sands in the North Sea has been advocated for airport development; as well as for oil and gas terminals, refineries and other noxious industries.[21] In the North Sea, a sea-city of glass and concrete has been proposed to be built 15 miles off the coast of Norfolk for a population of about 30,000.

There have also been various schemes for the erection of artificial islands in more remote areas of the high seas, in some cases through the conversion of uninhabitable reefs (awash at high water), such as Minerva Reef in the south-west Pacific. The legal questions of entitlement to a territorial sea, an economic zone, and a continental shelf for all such islands are still unsettled. Presumably detailed rules concerning deployment, accommodation of conflicting uses of the sea, establishment of safety zones and jurisdiction, protection of marine environment, and scientific research, will have to be laid down for artificial islands.[22]

11. Conclusions

From a brief outline of selected aspects of the economic geography of the sea it is apparent that the rate of exploitation, and change, of oceanic and coastal environments will accelerate over the next few years.

The conflicts which will emerge are many, ranging from local ecological problems such as the destruction of fish breeding grounds as a result of dredging, to major global disputes as to who may appropriate what in the sea.

The basic difficulty lies in the fact that the sea is a unified system, within which the various subsystems, including the socio-economic, interact. Political decisions relating to the use of marine resources, including marine space, at local or regional levels, are likely therefore to have effects on a much wider scale.

Many disciplines will clearly have to contribute to an understanding of the oceans as a resource, as distinct from a physical system with the human factor removed. One of the essentials for this is a conceptual approach which translates the physical environment into resource terms, but with an appreciation on the one hand of the unity and limits of the physical environment, and on the other of the economic and cultural characteristics of the various human communities which depend on, or are threatened by, the exploitation of these resources. What is being, hopefully, sought is a multidisciplinary approach to ocean resource management which adopts this more global view against which local decisions can be made.

Notes

1. C.A.M. King, *Introduction to Physical and Biological Oceanography*, Edward Arnold, 1975 (contains detailed discussion and Bibliography).
2. A.D. Couper, *The Geography of Sea Transport*, Hutchinson, 1970.
3. J.A. Cestone and E. St. George, 'Underwater Arctic Navigation', Vol. 27, *Journal of Navigation*, 1974, pp. 342–61.
4. I.C. Little, 'The Problems of Operating Mammoth Tankers on the Cape Route', *Navigation*, Vol. 22, No. 1, 1975, p. 83.
5. UN, *The Economic Consequence of the Closure of the Suez Canal*, TD/B/C4/104/Rev. 1, 1973.
6. J.R. Coull, *The Fisheries of Europe*, Bells-Advanced Geographies, 1973.
7. A.D. Couper, 'Change and Maritime Economics of the Pacific', in H.C. Brookfield, *The Pacific in Transition*, Edward Arnold; Lewis Anderson, *Offshore Geography of North West Europe*, 1966.
8. Christy T. Francis, *An Alternative Arrangement for Marine Fisheries. An Overview*, Resources for the Future, Washington DC, 1973.
9. A. Hutchenson MacGregor and A. Hogg, *Scotland and Oil*, Oliver and Boyd, 1975, p. 4.
10. Evan Luard, *The Control of the Sea Bed*, Heinemann, 1974, pp. 15–16; UN, Secretary-General Report E/CM 20 DD2, 1971; J.L. Mero, *The Mineral Resources of the Sea*, New York, 1967.
11. H.D. Drechsler, 'Exploitation of the Sea: A Preliminary Cost Benefit Analysis of Nodule Mining and Processing', *Maritime Studies and Management*, Vol. 1, 1973, pp. 53–65.
12. Edward Wenk, 'The Physical Resources of the Oceans', *The Ocean*, Scientific America, 1969, pp. 83–91.
13. A. Sebo Stephen, 'Ocean Power', *Maritime Studies and Management*, Vol. 2, No. 4, April 1975, pp. 202–15.
14. Sebo, op. cit.
15. HMSO, 'Why Navy?', Information Service, 1974.
16. R.A. Shinn, *The International Politics of Marine Pollution Control*, Praeger, 1974.
17. A.H. Joensen, 'Danish Seabird Disasters in 1972', *Marine Pollution Bulletin*, August 1973, Vol. 4, No. 8, p. 117.
18. Elizabeth Porter, *Pollution in Four Industrial Estuaries*, HMSO, 1973.
19. MacGregor and Hogg, op. cit.
20. J.F. Hoffman, 'Man Made Islands Can Solve Many of Our Problems', *Ocean Industry*, February 1970, p. 48.
21. *Land Reclamation from the Sea*, UWIST DRU/MAST/019D, 1975.
22. N. Papadakis, 'Artificial Islands in International Law', *Maritime Studies and Management*, Vol. 3, No. 1, July 1975.

3 THE ECONOMICS OF MARINE RESOURCE MANAGEMENT

Lee G. Anderson

1. Introduction

Economics is often defined as the study of the proper allocation of scarce resources (i.e. land and other natural resources, labour and capital) among unlimited competing ends. Marine resources are only a part of the total resources of any society, and therefore this discussion of their management must take place with a view for the whole picture. Nevertheless, because marine resources are subject to peculiar problems and uses, a detailed look at them is clearly justified. These peculiarities, which also apply to certain other resources, generally guarantee that a free market, or, more formally, a purely competitive economy will improperly allocate most marine resources, thus necessitating some form of outside regulation (assuming, of course, that the process of regulation will not divert an inordinate amount of resources from other productive uses).

The proper management of marine resources is a difficult task that has not been successfully accomplished in theory or practice to this date, although a good deal of important and useful work has been done in both areas. Therefore it should not be expected that this short discussion will be able to solve the problem finally. It is possible however to define it clearly in such a way that appreciation of its many parts is possible. We will attempt to describe the reasons for the necessity of management which will, at the same time, offer a glimpse of the myriad potential problems involved. We will also describe the various types of regulations and discuss their relative strengths and weaknesses, both from an efficiency and a distributional point of view. The main discussion will be in terms of efficiency only; the very important distributional aspects of management will be discussed separately.

2. The Peculiarities of Marine Resources

Marine resources, like most environmental resources, are different than other ordinary economic resources such as factories, skilled labour forces, etc., in four somewhat interrelated ways. They are common property or open-access resources in that there is often little or no control as to who can use them nor to what extent. Also, there are often external effects among and between users. For example, a fisherman who trolls may foul the equipment of one who uses traps, and leaks or spills from tankers may affect the total catch of both. A third point, related but still somewhat different, is that the marine environment may be used for several different purposes simultaneously. These uses may be complementary (as in the case of factories that release thermal wastes and aquaculture), conflicting (as in fishing for two species, one of which is a source of food for the other), or merely compatible (such as shore line residences and quiet recreational activities). Finally, there are some uses for marine resources for which economic markets do not exist. Marine recreation is a good example. These four problem areas, open-access, externalities, multiple use and lack of markets, each deserve further comment.

Common property or open-access is one important difference between a cattle rancher and a commercial fishery and between the mining of copper on land and deep-sea mining, and it is a difference that is responsible for many of the resource allocation problems in commercial fishing and deep-sea mining. Although the first pair both deal with the biological reproductive capacity of a stock, there is very little concern about the extinction of cattle. Likewise, although the second pair deal with the extraction of a non-renewable resource, there is comparatively little concern about wasteful techniques or proper temporal utilization of land-based facilities. Since the cattle rancher owns the herd it is in his best interest to weigh the differences in long-run costs and revenues of different slaughter rates. He not only makes sure that slaughter takes place at the proper age and weight, he is also careful to ensure that proper types and amount of animals are kept as a breeding stock. On the other hand, since no one owns the fish stock, as long as there is free access, each fisherman will be concerned only with his own immediate catch. Using gear selectivity devices to ensure that the fish are taken at the proper size is irrational from an individual point of view because there is nothing to keep others from taking the fish at a smaller size and thus obtaining all or most of the catch. Similarly individual attempts to reduce catch in any one year in order to increase catches in following years will be of little value to a particular fisherman because there is no guarantee that others will not harvest the fish this year or that others will not obtain the increased catches, if any, in the future. To look at it from the other way around, each fisherman will find it in his best interest to harvest as many fish as he can. It is no wonder then that there is great concern over the stocks of many of the heavily exploited ocean fisheries.

The same general conclusions follow from an analysis of open-access mining. On land, the rights to a mine are usually vested in one person. This person will find it to his advantage to operate the mine so that the ore is utilized at that point in time when the discounted difference between total revenues and total costs will be maximized. That is, if the owner expects the price of the ore to go up and the cost of extracting it to go down due to improvements in technology, it will be to his advantage to postpone utilization if the increase in profit from waiting is greater than could be earned by loaning current profits out at existing interest rates. Under such conditions, even if the owner needed money immediately, it would be to his advantage to sell the mine to someone else who is willing to wait for the increased profits. Because of the expected increase in profits relative to the existing rate of interest, the owner could sell the mine for a price greater than current profits. In any case the ore will not be utilized by society until such time as the discounted net worth is a maximum. At the same time since the owner can only be concerned with ore in his mine, he will make sure that every ton that is worth more than the cost of mining it is utilized.

In the case of deep-sea mining neither of these results will occur. Open-access will force potential miners to utilize ore as soon as the cost of extracting them is less than revenue without any regard to how the difference between revenues and costs will change over time. Similarly there will be a tendency to abandon an area once high-grade deposits have been extracted and then move on to other areas with high-grade ores. In fact the race to get the wealth may encourage techniques that are extremely wasteful but do enable a rapid extraction of higher-grade ores.

Open-access not only leads to waste of the marine-based resources through improper rates of use, but it does so at the expense of land-based resources. The race for the fish or for the minerals that open-access encourages, means that too many resources will be allocated to fishing or to mining – resources that could be used more advantageously in other parts of the economy.

Externalities, the second peculiarity of marine resources under discussion, occur when the production or use of one good affects the production or use of another. They can be positive, as when the production of honey increases the harvest of nearby apple trees because of the pollination, or negative, as when the waste water from a steel plant lowers the productivity of a fishery downstream. Whenever there is a positive externality, the good that causes it is generally underproduced. For example, since the beekeeper only receives revenue from his honey, he will expand his bee production as long as the increases in cost of maintaining them is less than the extra revenue earned by the increased honey production. From society's point of view, however, it makes sense to expand bee production as long as the increase in the cost of maintenance is less than the revenue from increases in honey production *plus* increases in apple production. Unfortunately the beekeeper will pay attention to his own costs and revenues only, and so the number of commercial hives will be less than it should be.

Whenever there is a negative externality, the good that causes it is generally overproduced. A steel producer will increase production as long as increases in revenue are greater than increases in his private costs of production. But from society's point of view, the cost of producing the steel includes the loss in net revenues to the fishery, and so it makes sense to expand steel production only as long as the extra revenue earned is greater than the sum of the increased cost of producing steel *and* the decrease in revenue to the fishery. But since the steel producer decides how much steel is to be produced and he only uses his private costs in his calculus, he will produce too much steel.

Because the marine environment is capable of providing many different services and because they are all related in one way or another via the seabed, the water column, the surface, or the atmosphere above it, one would correctly deduce that externalities would be commonplace. Unfortunately most of them are negative externalities. Spills and leaks from vessels affect fisheries, recreation, and other forms of marine-related production; vessel movements can affect fixed fishing gear and cause wakes in harbours or coastal waterways which can, over time, weaken structures on shore; and so on.

Closely related to the concept of externalities, but still conceptually distinct, is multiple use. Because of the many dimensions and features of the marine environment it is capable of providing many uses at the same time. In terms of pure economic efficiency, the proper goal for management would be to select that combination of uses that maximizes the sum of the discounted net values obtained from all uses. To see this, imagine a situation where a specific area of the marine environment is suitable for only two uses, fishing and transportation. Assume further that only two combinations of uses are possible. In the first, shipping is allowed only in certain types of boats and along specified routes. If the fishermen adjust as best they can to the disturbances caused by the coming and going of the transport vessels, their net revenue will be $300 while the net revenue of the transport sector is $100. In the second, there are no constraints on the transport sector and they are able to rearrange their operations so that their net revenues increase to $500, but even after adjusting as best they can, the net revenue of the fishing sector falls to $200. According to the general rule, then, the second combination of uses is the one that should be chosen because it has the larger of the net values in use. Of course there is a distribution problem here: although the second case will maximize net revenue, the fishing sector will be earning less than they could in the first case. This problem will be discussed in detail in the final section of the chapter. Of course the problem of multiple use is much more complicated than this example. For one thing there are many different uses and many different ways and rates at which they can be operated. This means that there is a very large number of possible combinations of use that must be studied in order to see which one has the highest value in use.

The final point under discussion is the lack of markets for some of the services provided by the marine environment. A fundamental justification of a free market economy is that owners of resources will be motivated to put them to their highest valued uses in order to earn the highest profits. This conclusion only follows, however, if the owner can sell or rent the services provided by the resources under his control. For example, consider an individual who owns a large tract of shorefront property, which is capable of producing many types of services. Undeveloped it will provide a habitat for marine animals, a site for limited recreational opportunities, and perhaps a pleasing view to people on a nearby highway or in an adjoining community. At the other extreme, it could be developed into high-rise apartments thereby providing housing services and a different type of recreational experience. Obviously there are other uses between these two extremes, but for our purposes let us only consider these. If the property is developed, those who desire to live in the apartments will have to reach a mutually agreeable arrangement with the owner. There are readily accessible real estate markets where buyer and seller can get together and a system of easily enforceable laws that prohibits the use of apartment buildings without the owner's consent and also protects a tenant or a new owner after a transaction has occurred. If the land is not developed, however, the owner has very little chance for collecting revenues for the services his property provides. Who will pay for the services provided by the natural habitat? Fishermen appear to be the most likely candidates, but how much should they pay and what is there to force them to pay? The same problem applies to the scenic and recreational and aesthetic uses of the land. The people who enjoy the view may be easy to identify but what institutions are available to enable the owner to collect a fee or to prohibit those who do not pay from 'peeking'? The problem is made more difficult by the fact that this is a public good; that is, if one person enjoys the scenery, this will not significantly detract from the enjoyment of others. Therefore the value in use must be the sum of the values to all 'consumers' of the view. The case for recreation is somewhat different, but if it is a large piece of land with many access points, the expense of enforcing a paid admission policy may be quite high relative to potential revenues.

It appears likely then that the private owner will prefer to have his property used for development. If in fact people value all of the services provided from the undeveloped site more highly than those of the developed site, then the lack of markets will have forced the private owner to use his property such that the highest value in use is not achieved.

The difficulties posed by these four peculiarities of marine resources are compounded by the fact that they are often multinational in character. The problem of open-access is difficult enough without having to contend with the additional problem of fishermen of different national origins, with their different customs, productivities and valuations of the resources in question. Similarly, the problems caused by externalities become more confusing when the production of a good in one country affects the production of a good in another. It is possible that each country will place a different value on the same good, thus making the determination of the optimum output of the externality causing good quite difficult. The possibility of different valuation of the same use in different countries will also make the solution of the multiple use problem much more difficult.

Open-access, externalities, multiple use and lack of markets, with the possible confounding influence of multinational use: these are attributes of marine resources which make a special study of their use both interesting and worthwhile. It is to this subject that we now turn our attention.

3. Management of Marine Resources

To keep the discussion of management straightforward, let us concentrate first on the management of a single resource, a fishery. The principles gleaned from this discussion will apply with only modest expansion to marine resource management in general. The basics apply directly; modifications are only required to consider different underlying physical or biological phenomena or interrelatedness of use.

The key to the management of a fishery is the reproductive capacity of its fish stock. The fundamentals of this can be expressed in the sustainable yield curve which shows the relationship between different levels of fishing effort and sustained yield or harvest. A sustained yield is one that can be harvested year after year without affecting the fish stock, which means that sustainable yield for any given stock size is equal to its rate of growth at that size. Initially increases in effort, where effort can be conceptualized as days of fishing weighted by a factor to correct for differences in size and efficiency of different vessels, will lead to increases in sustainable yield but eventually because of adverse effects on the stock size, further increases in effort will actually lead to a decrease in sustained yield. While there is more fishing effort, it is applied to a smaller-sized stock and so sustainable yield falls.

As a result of the shape of the sustained yield curve, the total revenue curve of a fishery when the price of fish is constant is as pictured in insert on following page. Increases in effort per period of time for the fishery as a whole will eventually lead to a decrease in total revenue because there will be a decrease in total catch. If we can assume that total cost for the fishery as a whole increases in proportion to effort (in other words, each additional boat, when operated in the most efficient manner, can be added to the fishery at the same cost as was the previous one), then the total cost curve of fishery will be a straight line as in Figure 1. In accordance with normal economic analysis, assume that cost includes a normal return, one that is sufficient to keep vessel owners operating. Using these two simple curves it is possible to predict where an open-access fishery will operate and also to show where an optimally regulated fishery should operate.

With no regulation, the equilibrium level of effort in the fishery will be E_3, where total revenue equals its total costs. It is also the point where the average revenue per unit of effort equals average cost per unit of effort. To see why this is an equilibrium, consider any level of effort to the left of E_3. Total revenue for the fishery as a whole is greater than total cost, therefore each boat will earn profits. To put it another way: to the left of E_3 average revenue per unit of effort is greater than average cost per unit of effort. This agreeable state of affairs will not only encourage existing boats to expand their effort; it will also motivate new boats to enter the fishery. Now consider a level of effort greater than E_3, where total costs are greater than total revenues. Now the boats will be suffering losses (average cost per unit of effort will be greater than average revenue per unit); therefore each boat will decrease its effort, and some may even leave the fishery. Since effort will tend to increase below E_3 and to decrease above it, the equilibrium level of effort in an open-access fishery will settle at this point, which can be called the open-access equilibrium yield.

It must be admitted that this static analysis which assumes that the fishery is always operating on the sustained yield curve is somewhat of a simplification. It may take a fish stock several years to adjust to a once and for all change in effort, such that the specified level of effort acting on the existing stock size will produce a catch equal to the growth rate. In the meantime of course the level of effort can change again. This leads to the possibility of drastic reduction in the size of the fish stock if changes in effort due to differences in revenues and costs are slow relative to changes in stock size due to differences in catch and growth values.

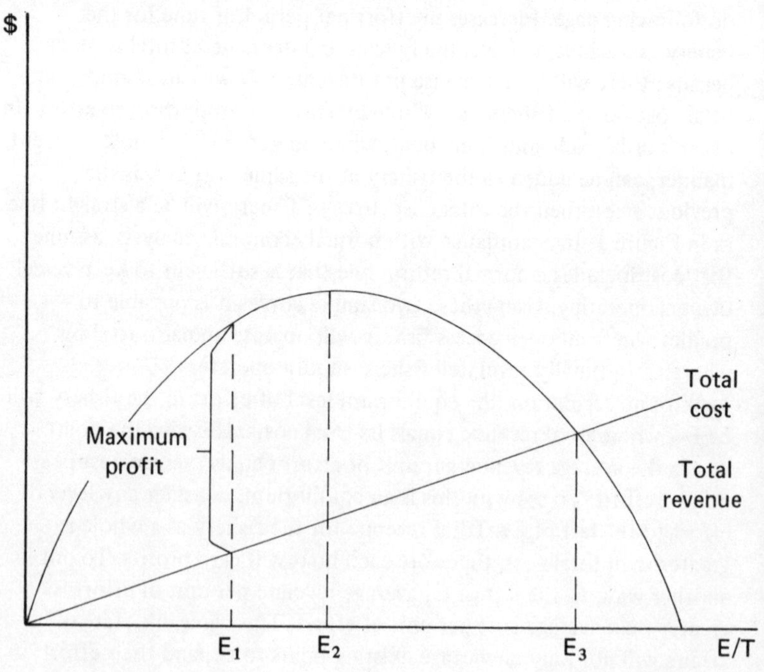

Fig. 1

Now turn to the question of how much effort should be applied to the fishery. If costs and revenues have been correctly measured, the proper amount of effort in this static analysis is E_1 where profit or rent to the fishery (i.e. the difference between revenue and cost) is a maximum. Such maximization of profit is not an end in itself; rather its achievement means that all of society's resources have been properly allocated.

Consider a fishery operating at E_1. Any increase in effort will decrease profits, because costs will increase more than revenue. Revenues measure what people are willing to pay for the fish, and costs represent the value of the next-best use of the resources necessary to produce the effort used to catch the fish. Therefore, when the addition to cost of producing one more unit of effort is greater than the resultant increase in revenue, society is losing, since fish are being taken at a cost greater than their value to consumers. In other words, when effort is increased, then inputs are being diverted from producing other goods of higher value to society. On the other hand, if effort were to be reduced from E_1 profit would fall, implying that revenues must fall faster than costs. Therefore, although resources were being released for other production, the resultant goods would have a lower value than the fish that could have been caught.

Thus we find that E_1 is the optimal allocation of effort to the fishery, since the value to society of the last unit of fish caught (marginal revenue) just balances the cost of providing it (marginal cost). This point is usually called the maximum economic yield, MEY, of the fishery. It is worth emphasizing that what is desirable about MEY is not that the profit to the fishery as a whole is maximized, but rather that society's inputs are not being used to exploit the fishery unless they cannot be used more advantageously elsewhere.

Again to get a true picture of MEY, it is necessary to consider the time it takes a fish stock to react to a change in effort. A reduction in effort from E_3 to E_1 will initially decrease the catch. The yield will increase only as the stock is able to grow. Decreases in effort are only worthwhile if the increase in future net revenues discounted by the interest rate more than compensates for the initial revenue decrease. From the proper viewpoint of maximizing the present value of the net revenues of the fishery, MEY will occur at E_1 only when the discount rate is zero.

The reason the open-access equilibrium yield is different from maximum economic yield is directly traceable to the common property nature of the fishery. Individual vessel-owners are not concerned with the marginal costs and revenues of the fishery as a whole but rather only with their own costs and revenues. Therefore as long as average revenue is greater than average cost (regardless of the relationship between marginal revenue and marginal cost of the fishery), individual boat-owners will find it profitable to enter the fishery. And with open-access there is nothing to prevent them from doing so. Therefore open-access will result in an improper use of the fish stock stemming from an incorrect amount of resources being allocated to fishing.

Since it has been demonstrated that an open-access fishery will not operate at the optimal level of effort, the problem becomes one of finding the optimal way of causing a readjustment in the level of effort. It should be remembered, however, that the problem is one of too much effort and too many resources being used to produce that effort. Reducing effort without releasing resources for productive utilization in other parts of the economy is only a partial solution. It will indeed reduce pressure on the fish stock and may even lead to an increased sustained yield, but it will still result in a waste of resources. Therefore the goal of fishery management from an economic point of view is to ensure that the proper amount of effort is produced and that it is produced in the most efficient manner. There is, of course, a time dimension to shifting to the optimal level of effort. In addition to the fact that it takes time for net revenues to increase, it is also the case that resources released from fishing need time to be absorbed by other sections of the economy. There are also distribution problems involved but they will be discussed separately. There are many ways of regulating fishing effort, each with their corresponding strengths and weaknesses. The most commonly discussed ways are closed seasons, quotas, gear restrictions and other limitations on efficient production, various types of taxes, and creation of ownership rights to the fish stock. Unfortunately all except the latter and some forms of taxes result in inefficiently produced effort.

Closed seasons and quotas have very similar final results. The former forbids fishing except in a given period of time, but since the open-access problem has not been removed, fishermen will be encouraged to increase the amount of effort that they can produce in that period as long as revenues are still greater than costs. This increased rate of production will increase average cost and this, combined with the fact that the vessels must remain idle for part of the year, obviously means that the unit cost of producing effort is greater than it need be. A quota means that fishing effort must cease after a specified harvest has been obtained. Again in an open-access situation existing fishermen will be motivated to increase their harvesting ability so that they can obtain a larger share of the quota. This will also have the tendency to increase costs. With both closed seasons and quotas a new equilibrium will be reached where total revenues are equal to total costs. It will occur at a lower level of effort than the open-access equilibrium yield because costs will be higher as a direct result of open-access operation constrained by the regulations.

A second type of regulation, limitations on efficient production, directly results in increased costs that come as a consequence of closed seasons and quotas. For example, by preventing fishing vessels from using anything but sail power (a restriction that has been implemented on more than one occasion) the cost of producing effort goes up because individual fishermen are forced to use a suboptimal combination of inputs. This increase in cost will result in a decrease in the amount of effort produced at the open-access equilibrium yield. Limitations on efficient production can be graphically represented by an increase in the cost curve in Figure 1. The new equilibrium will occur at the intersection of the revenue curve and the new cost curve. While in the short run this will result in a decrease in effort it will do so at the expense of efficiency. In the long run, the policy is subject to even more serious drawbacks. Again because the basic problem of open-access has not been confronted, the individual fisherman will still try to maximize his profits, except that they will be constrained in the type of power they can use. They will, therefore, try to increase the actual amount of effort they can produce subject to the constraint and to the fact that the revenues must be greater than costs. For example, they may use different vessels, or stay out longer on each trip to try to compensate for the restriction on sail power. In this way they may partially make up for the initial restriction. Therefore in the long run it is possible that the reduction in effort caused by forced inefficiencies will be less than originally expected.

A third type of regulation is taxation. A tax levied on fishing effort or on fish can obtain a maximum economic yield, but one applied to vessels or to individual fishermen will not. As far as the fisherman is concerned, a tax on fish is, for all practical purposes, the same as a reduction in the price of fish and a tax on effort is equivalent to an increase in the cost of providing effort. In terms of the graph this means that a tax on fish will lower the effective total revenue curve and a tax on effort will increase the cost curve. Therefore that tax on fish, which has the result of lowering the new revenue curve in Figure 1 such that it intersects the original total cost curve at E_1, the point of static maximum economic yield, will force the open-access fishery to operate there because effective total revenue will equal total cost. Not only will the proper amount of effort be produced, but since nothing has been done to affect the actual costs of products, effort will be produced in an efficient manner. Likewise that tax on effort which has the effect of shifting the adjusted cost curve up till it intersects the original total revenue curve at E_1 will also result in the proper amount of effort produced in an efficient manner.

However other types of taxes will not have these favourable results. For example, a tax on each vessel will encourage a fisherman to increase the amount of effort per unit of time that he gets from each vessel rather than obtaining any needed expanded effort by utilizing extra vessels. This readjustment in the combination of inputs used to produce effort will increase its average cost, and thus while it will tend to reduce effort it will not do so in an efficient manner.

Because the crux of the fisheries' overexploitation problem is the lack of property rights, one solution is to create properly defined rights to the fishery. To see this, consider the result if rights to our hypothetical fishery described in Figure 1 were granted to one individual. This person would be motivated to operate it in the same manner that we would expect any private entrepreneur would operate an income-producing asset; he would try to maximize profits. Specifically he will add extra units of effort only if the increase in revenue for *the fishery as a whole* was greater than the cost of the effort. (Recall that, above, each fisherman tried to maximize profits for his individual vessel.) Of course he will always strive to produce the effort as efficiently as possible. This means that he would operate the fishery at the point of maximum economic yield. The fact that average revenue per vessel is greater than average cost per vessel at this point will not influence his decision about total effort; he will be concerned only about maximizing the difference between total revenues and total costs.

The same general results follow if the rights to produce the proper amount of effort are distributed among many fishermen. Each will then know how much effort he can produce. He will be self-motivated to produce as inexpensively as possible, and as long as the amount he can produce is not relatively large or small compared to the capacity of his vessel, he will be able to produce it in the most efficient manner. Distributing the rights to many people will eliminate any possible monopoly problems.

Actually the taxation method and the property right creation method can be combined by auctioning the proper number of rights to the fishery to the highest bidders. This will guarantee that the correct amount of effort is used while at the same time it will result in government revenues. It will also encourage efficient production of effort because those that are most efficient will be able to submit the highest bids for the rights.

These four types of control or management techniques fit into categories that are applicable to the management of marine resources in general. Quotas and closed seasons are *restrictions in use*, forced inefficiencies are *restrictions in method*, property right creations are *internalizations*, and of course, the fourth category is *taxation*. (Taxation could be considered a form of internalization, but for our purposes we will consider them separately.) The first two can usually accomplish certain specified management goals but only at the expense of general efficiency. Internalizations and proper taxes are not subject to inefficiency weakness, but they do have some practical application problems. Internalizations generate specific distribution problems, because unlike other restrictions which apply to all with equal force, these have an all or nothing characteristic. You either have the right to fish or you do not. Taxation programmes will not be very popular with fishermen which may increase the cost of enforcement. They also suffer from time lags. It takes time for operators to adjust their level of output to new taxes and since the highly variable price, cost and yield conditions in many fisheries may require new output levels each year, taxes will not obtain these rapid changes. Before drawing any conclusions on proper management policies let us see how these four categories of management techniques apply to other marine uses.

Consider first seabed mining. It generally requires regulation for two reasons: open-access and externalities. Open-access is a problem, not because the stock will be destroyed (it is a non-living and essentially non-renewable resource that must be 'used up' to provide services) but because it will be exploited too rapidly. As pointed out earlier, the proper rate of use of a non-renewable resource depends upon the cost of extracting it and its value in use at different points in time, and upon the existing interest rate. If expected improvements in technology suggest lowering of extraction costs in the future or if demand conditions suggest that prices will go up, then depending on their relative expected changes and the rate of interest, it may pay a private owner to put off exploitation until a later date. Specifically, if the net profits from mining in the present when loaned out at the prevailing interest rate will yield a total amount that is smaller than the expected net profit from mining at a specified date in the future, then it pays to postpone exploitation. This makes sense for society as well because the minerals will be utilized when their net value in use, weighted over time, is a maximum.

In an open-access situation, however, pressures exist to speed the rate of exploitation. Specifically, as soon as the cost of exploitation is less than the selling price, then the motivation is there for exploitation to take place. It makes no difference that a greater profit could be made by exploiting at a later time, even considering the cost of waiting, because there is no guarantee that if an individual postpones exploitation that someone else will not utilize the resource in the meantime.

The problem is compounded by the fact that during the process of extraction waste products will be produced, which if not properly handled may cause externalities by increasing costs or decreasing revenues or values in use of other marine resources. Therefore not only is there a need for regulation as to the temporal aspects of extraction but perhaps also for method and extent of extraction.

It is possible to account for both of these problems by utilizing one or, more likely, some combination of regulations from the four categories discussed above. By forbidding extraction or by forcing operators to use unnecessarily expensive extraction techniques until such time as utilization is deemed desirable, it is possible to prevent the minerals from being utilized too early. This of course assumes that the proper information is available so that the restrictions can be removed at the proper time. Even so, this procedure will not handle the problem of efficiency during the year extraction is allowed. There is still the potential of a 'race' to get the minerals, favouring rapid rather than efficient extraction methods. These problems could be handled by regulations that specify certain techniques or which allocate, by one means or another, the available areas to specific individuals.

Similarly, restrictions on location or type of extraction method used can prevent or reduce some of the externality causing by-products of extraction. These will accomplish the goal but may do so at the cost of overall efficiency. Prohibitions and restrictions are inflexible and thus do not allow for proper adjustments to minimize the costs of handling the externality. Placing a unit tax on the by-products or placing a limit on the number that may be produced will also reduce their output but will encourage the operators to do so as efficiently as possible. This of course leaves open the questions of how high the tax of what the absolute limit on the by-product should be in order to guarantee that the extra revenue of mining the last unit is at least equal to the total costs to society, including extraction costs and other social costs imposed on other users of the marine environment.

Another way that is theoretically possible to obtain the proper rate and type of extraction in a given year is to allow a merger of the mining interest and the other uses that are damaged. This is another form of internalization. This will force the miner to fully consider the ramifications of the waste products because they will directly affect the total revenue of the newly merged firms. This has obvious practical restrictions however. For one thing, because of the many uses that mining could affect, the merged firm would have to be very large, not to mention the fact that it would have to be made up of firms from many different nations. Also, uses such as recreation are not produced by firms and so a merger would not be possible. In some special cases, however, a formal or informal merger of relatively small and simple production activities may be a viable option.

In summary, it is fairly easy to identify the type of problems that will result from utilization of seabed minerals. It is also possible to categorize the types of regulations that are available to control these problems and to visualize their strengths and weaknesses. The problem then becomes one of selecting a combination that will most nearly accomplish the conflicting goals of obtaining utilization at the right point in time and doing so at the proper rate and in the most efficient manner. And of course, all of this must be done in the context of the given mores and other institutional factors of the society and the cost and availability of the proper information.

If this seems difficult when just considering seabed mining, it must appear impossible when considering the more general task of coastal zone management of a densely populated marine environment capable of accommodating multiple uses. The problem may not be impossible, but it certainly is a very, very difficult one. The overall goal should be to obtain the proper allocation of all resources, including the marine resources with their special problems, to obtain the maximum satisfaction, i.e. maximum value in use, for the community. Determining the proper combination of regulations to accomplish this in the face of open-access, the many interdependencies caused by multiple use and externalities, and the fact that many of the uses are not provided in any formal market is a very formidable problem. However, careful consideration of the strengths and weaknesses of the various categories of regulations when viewed in the context of the exact nature of the problem, the types, amounts, and cost of management information, important social constraints on actions, and other such variables should go a long way in helping to select a management strategy that would vastly improve the allocation over that which would occur in the absence of regulation.

To summarize this section, recall that there are four basic categories of resource management regulations, each with their own strengths and weaknesses. *Restrictions in use* and *restrictions in method* can often physically obtain such short-run goals as saving a fish stock or halting the flow of a particular waste product. They normally do so, however, at the cost of economic efficiency, and in the long run they sometimes encourage further inefficient behaviour that diminishes their short-run effectiveness. They should therefore be avoided if these weaknesses are too great. But they still can be a valuable short-run regulation when immediate results are called for, or in other cases where information is not complete enough to utilize advantageously more complex regulatory methods. An example of this last case may be uniform pollution control devices on all automobiles regardless of location, care, or extent of use. This may not be the most inexpensive way to reduce waste emissions into the air. (Perhaps cars in crowded metropolitan areas, where the environment is saturated with wastes, should have very powerful control devices, and those in isolated wide-open spaces should have weaker or no controls at all.) But efforts to find and institute a less expensive way would more than likely be more expensive than any expected savings.

Internalizations such as creating property rights or mergers, if utilized correctly, will accomplish proper use of resources but they are subject to practical and institutional constraints. For example, there are limits to the extent that mergers can take place both on internal management criteria and on the grounds that too much market power may be placed in the hands of one firm. Also there are serious problems in determining who should receive the property rights and in how they are to be enforced if granted. *Taxation* is a very good regulation device if the proper thing is taxed, but it can be a slow and difficult to manage policy. In addition they can be very unpopular with the people who are directly affected.

One other point should be brought up at this time. Regulation costs money. More formally it utilizes resources that could be used to produce other goods and services for society. This means that in selecting the proper combination of regulations, the cost of implementing them (for example information, management, and enforcement costs) is a variable that should be considered in relation to how well that combination works. Specifically, care should be taken to ensure that the costs of regulation are less than the benefits (measured in terms of the value of the increased flow of services) that result. If not, society is better off with no regulation.

4. Distribution Aspects of Management

Thus far the discussion of management has been restricted to aspects of economic efficiency: resources should be allocated such that the total value in use is maximized. While there may be reasons why this goal should be modified, it is not as narrow and materialistic as may be thought. Notice that throughout earlier discussions care has been taken to include all types of values provided by the environment. For instance if the environment provides solitude, or nursery grounds for marine species valued for their aesthetic beauty or their commercial potential, or sites for recreation, then the value of these uses should be directly considered when making decisions about resource allocation. Granted these things are not considered in most free market situations, and they are often ignored in governmental policy, sometimes intentionally and sometimes because of a lack of information, but nonetheless they should be a part of any consideration of values in use.

One potential weakness with strict economic efficiency however is that although it strives for a maximum value of output, it makes no stipulation about how the income derived from it should be distributed. It is obvious of course that distribution of income is an important consideration, both for the people concerned and as an element in governmental policy. Each individual likes to feel that he is getting his 'fair share,' and usually has some notion about what is an equitable share for everyone. This latter notion is translated into such policy actions as graduated income taxes, unemployment compensation and welfare for the poor.

By logical extension it is often proposed that resource management take distributional considerations into account. That is, the distributional aspects of the various regulation procedures should be an important factor in determining the proper management scheme as are efficacy, practicality, cost and efficiency aspects. Indeed it is sometimes suggested that the management goal itself be reformulated to include some distributional objectives. Let us discuss each of these points in turn.

Consider first the distributional effects of the various categories of control techniques. In fishery management restrictions in method such as closed seasons, quotas and gear restrictions are fairly neutral in effect as long as all fishermen are equally well equipped, since each will then be equally hindered in the race for fish. In other cases, those that are better equipped to fish under the constraints placed by the regulations will enjoy a larger catch (if the regulations are physically effective) and hence will earn a larger income from the fish stock. Those that are less well equipped and who because of age, lack of skills or credit are not able to become better equipped, will suffer a loss of income and perhaps may be forced from the fishery altogether.

Internalization through the granting of property rights has straightforward distributional effects. Assuming that the proper number of rights were distributed, those that receive them will receive a part of the economic profit earned at maximum economic yield, the size of which depends upon the relative size of their share. Those that are forced out of the fishery or are prevented from entering lose the net income they could have earned in the controlled fishery and they have no chance to obtain part of the profit that is earned by a properly managed fishery. The amount of their loss will depend upon the size of the real income in their next best employment alternative.

Taxes or auctions for fishing rights, which have the same potential for achieving maximum economic yield as the granting of property rights, do however result in a different distribution of the wealth. The more productive fishermen will be the ones who can pay the taxes or the auction price and so will be the ones who will continue to earn income. They will not enjoy all of the benefits of the properly regulated fishery, however, because of the payments they will have to make. The net result is that the general public will benefit from increased tax revenues (they receive nothing if property rights are granted to individuals), the productive fishermen will benefit to the extent that their net incomes increase, and the less productive fishermen, who are unable to pay the taxes, will suffer a loss in income.

Although there is no golden rule to determine what a proper income distribution should be, the effects management schemes can have on distribution can be very important, especially if they are counterproductive to other income distribution policies in the economy. Therefore the management authority may have good reason to take them directly into account.

Now to consider the reformulation of management goals in light of distributional objectives. Distributional uses can be introduced directly or indirectly. Regulation can directly increase the income earning potential of certain individuals or it can give special consideration to the provision of certain types of services. Let us consider the indirect way first. Examples are management goals such as maximization of hunting and fishing opportunities, maximization of the beauty of the coastal environment, or minimization of the changes in the coastal environments. If, for example, the first one does in fact provide more opportunities for fishing than would the situation where regulation was geared to maximization of total value in use, it would be a transfer of income in kind to those individuals who enjoyed fishing and had the wherewithal to participate in it. It should be remembered, however, that achievement of the goal is at the expense of some other productive uses that would provide more value than the fishing. Therefore, the management authority should compare the benefit of the redistributional objectives achieved with decrease in the value of total services.

An example of a regulatory goal that directly affects income distribution would be a fishery management policy that aimed for the maximization of employment opportunities for geographically isolated individuals who are not trained for other types of work. To accomplish this goal the fishery may have to be operated beyond maximum economic yield and little consideration could be given to the costs of producing effort. In deciding if this is a proper goal it should be remembered that the extra employment is achieved only at the expense of greater efficiency in the total economy. This means that policy-makers should be sure that the gain in employment and the increased self-esteem that it generates are worth the loss of efficiency and also that there is no other less expensive way of achieving the income transfer.

When faced with arguments that regulation or management policies take distributional aspects into account, defenders of the strict efficiency goal argue that these things should be handled independently. That is, the economy should be operated to produce the highest valued combination of goods and services, and if it is felt that the income distribution that results is not proper, then redistribution policies should be adopted. This makes perfect sense from a theoretical point of view, but its application is sometimes very difficult. For one thing, it will not work for transfers of income in kind such as the number and quality of fishing opportunities or environmental beauty. With regard to straight income transfers, people are often very much opposed to transfer of wealth between segments of the population, that is, taxing one segment to subsidize another, while they may favour indirect transfers through increased opportunities for employment or direct provision of goods made possible by regulation even if it does come at the expense of overall efficiency. Closely related to this is the distaste for straight doles regardless of who pays for them. People would often rather see disadvantaged groups be given the opportunity to work even if the work could be done more efficiently in another manner than see them get a straight handout. For these reasons direct and indirect distributional policies are often a part of management.

5. Summary

Proper utilization of marine resources implies the correct use of all resources. Nonetheless, the special problems of open-access, externalities and multiple use associated with them, and the resultant improper use of resources, necessitates special management of marine resources. The proper goal for this management is to maximize their value in use over time and proper management requires that both market and non-market services to be considered. The types of possible management policies can be placed into four categories: restrictions in use, restrictions in method, internalizations and taxation. Each of them have their strengths and weaknesses as far as efficacy, practicality, distribution, cost of operation and efficiency of resource use. The problem of management is to select that combination of regulatory techniques that most nearly satisfies the efficiency goal and does so at a cost that is both as small as possible and lower than the dollar value of the benefits to be achieved. In cases where distributional goals are also utilized it is essential that benefits from redistribution be compared with the costs of lowered efficiency.

Further Readings

1. L.G. Anderson, 'Criteria for Maximum Economic Yield of an Internationally Exploited Fishery', in Knight (ed.), *The Future of International Fisheries Management,* 1975, pp. 159–82.
2. F.T. Christy Jr., 'Disparate Fisheries: Problems for the Law of the Sea Conference and Beyond', *Ocean Development and International Law,* 1973, pp. 337–53.
3. Charles S. Pearson, 'Extracting Rent from Ocean Resources: Discussion of a Neglected Source', *Ocean Development and International Law,* 1973, pp. 221–38.

4 ECONOMIC ORGANIZATION AND THE EXPLOITATION OF MARINE RESOURCES

Giulio Pontecorvo and Roger Mesznik

1. The GNP of the Ocean

Despite the unusually hostile environment and international status of the world's oceans, the basic determinants of the technology and the production functions utilized in exploiting their resources are not materially different from what they are on land. There are, however, compelling reasons for a separate discussion of what may broadly be described as the 'economics of the oceans'.

Historically, the oceans have been used for trade and transport, military purposes and as a source of food. Today, we must add to this list deep-sea mining, the recovery of hydrocarbons, scientific enquiry and environmental and pollution problems. Furthermore, as a result of technological change, the traditional uses are undergoing significant modifications.

In the most general sense we may say that the abundance of ocean resources has given way to scarcity. For example, at one time the supply of fish was considered infinitely elastic relative to the demands placed on the stocks.[1] Today, however, increases in demand, which result from rising real income throughout the world and population growth, combined with the new technology, embodied in the long-distance, capital-intensive fishing fleet, have pushed fish populations to the point where the supply functions for almost all species has moved from being infinitely elastic to highly inelastic. More simply put, there is strong evidence of overfishing throughout much of the world and only a small likelihood of a significant expansion in the catch from ocean fisheries in the future.[2]

The once vast open spaces of the oceans are becoming crowded. Today, the number of vessels using the English channel has given that waterway the look of a major truck route, and for the first time, important harbours are being forced to install traffic control systems analogous to those found at major airports. At the same time ships are increasing in size and complexity. The supertanker and the LNG (liquefied natural gas) carrier pose entirely new problems in terms of port requirements, storage and transfer facilities, threats to the environment and the creation of potential liabilities that extend beyond the current risk-bearing capacity of the marine insurance industry. These are the dramatic changes in technology and scale of the uses of the oceans that suggest the need for a separate examination of the economics of ocean resource exploitation.

Furthermore, changes in technology often result in economies of scale which create economic pressures that affect the pace and organizational form of ocean resources exploitation. These forces are in turn affected by supply and demand conditions. The location and richness of the resource base utilized by various industries, the pattern of world and national demand and the institutional arrangements that are particular to the various nations all influence the form of the economic organization that is utilized to exploit ocean resources.

Finally, there are certain conditions that are unique to the exploitation of ocean resources. The most significant of these is the common property condition of ocean fisheries.[3] The common property conditions of fish stocks is an important determinant of the organization of fisheries. This is true even though certain stocks are found entirely within territorial waters. Good illustrations of the effect of the common property status of the resources on the industrial organization of the oceans may be seen in the over-capitalized, small-boat inshore lobster fisheries in the state of Maine and the maritime provinces of Canada, the Norwegian winter herring fishery, or the world's largest industrial fishery, the anchovetas in coastal waters claimed by Peru. Solutions such as the imposition of quotas do not solve the economic problems imposed on the fisheries by the common property condition of the resources.

In this chapter we will analyse six uses of the oceans: transportation, fishing, offshore petroleum, deep-sea mining, scientific research and recreation. In this evaluation we will stress the particular economic, technological, legal and other institutional constraints that may be imposed on the pattern of use. We will also note any substantive national or international conditions that influence the pattern of activity.

From this examination of the structure of the industrial organization in the six sectors we will deduce tentative hypotheses about the workability of the structure. Workability is defined as the social desirability or, more specifically, the adequacy of the results of resource use from the point of view of society.

One complicating feature of the industrial structure that is used to exploit ocean resources is the fact that we are dealing simultaneously with two levels of analysis. In some aspects of the analysis, national boundaries are unimportant and we are able to consider an effective, unified world market. In other aspects, national policy and unilateral arrangements are crucial and we must consider separate national markets. For example, some fish stocks in the north-west Atlantic are divided among nations in a purely political process. Market forces only take over when allocating a country's share to its respective fishermen. Under these circumstances, the efficiency of the international market is always suboptimal since it is subject to the predetermined share of each country.[4] In other areas, the separation of the impact of national acts on submarkets as compared to a truly international market is not easily discernible. It is almost impossible to disentangle the impacts of different national shipbuilding subsidies, export subsidies, and the availability of flags of convenience on the inter- and intranational markets for shipping services.

However, before we can evaluate each sector of ocean activity it is useful to provide an overview of them all. The appropriate analytic tool for this overview is the national income accounting concept of the gross national product, roughly defined as current output at market prices. The utilization of an ocean 'GNP' statement will give us a crude measure of the relative importance of the various sectors. Examination of GNP data as a time series would have provided insight into the rates of growth in the several sectors. Unfortunately, data are not available for this latter analysis so we are limited to examination of our own set of benchmark 'GNP' estimates. From these estimates, we will draw some tentative hypotheses about the direction of movement in the several sectors, but we must be cautious about the utilization of such a limited data base.

The gross national product of a nation's economy is defined more precisely as the sum, in monetary units, of all goods and services produced by the economy during the period of one year. A similar measure may be established for the oceans. However, since the oceans are not a nation the data for an ocean 'GNP' must be estimated from world-wide sources, and the data that follows should be regarded as a set of preliminary estimates of index numbers rather than as accurate measurements.

We estimate the GNP of the oceans at some $75 billion per year.[5] The main components of the GNP and their relative shares are as follows:

Table 1: Preliminary Estimates of Ocean GNP

Component	Billion	% of Total
Shipping	app. 40–60	app. 60–73
Fishing	app. 15	app. 18–23
Offshore Oil	app. 6–8	app. 10–11
Mining	app. 1	app. 1
Recreation	app. 4–5	app. 7
TOTAL	app. 66–82	

Source: Pontecorvo and Mesznik, 'The Wealth of the Oceans and the Law of the Sea: Some Preliminary Observations', *San Diego Law Review* (1974). *Note:* The value for oil does *not* reflect the price increases since 1974.

One sector of ocean activity, scientific research, is not included in the total. This omission points both to a strength and a weakness of the 'GNP' approach. Since 'GNP' measures output, we cannot include the total scientific research in it. This is because scientific research does not produce an immediately visible output that has a market price. Yet scientific research is an important facet of ocean activity which has long-range implications for resource use, technology, and ultimately the level of output.[6]

Despite its nominal omission from the table, the value of scientific research is reflected indirectly to the extent that it is embodied in the knowledge and technology utilized in other categories.

A second problem of the table is in the 20 per cent approximation represented by the fishing industry. In all probability this estimate is understated for two reasons. An unknown but significant part of fishing activity is subsistence fishing. As with 'income in kind' on the farm, the output of the subsistence fishery does not enter the market and is, therefore, not included. The second aspect of fishing for which there is no adequate measure of output is sports fishing or recreational fishing.

The details of the estimates for each sector will be discussed as part of the sectional analysis, but it is important to note that, to date, transportation has been, by a wide margin, the most important economic activity associated with the oceans. Also, it is reasonable to hypothesize that in the future, resource utilization and recreational uses will increase relative to transportation.[7]

Finally, it is important to note the relative size of ocean activity. At the level of 70 plus billions, it is roughly 5 per cent of the GNP of the

United States, which exceeds $1300 billion per year.

But the 'GNP' of the oceans is comparable with that of many national states and in all possibility ocean 'GNP' will grow in the foreseeable future at least as rapidly as the world average. It may grow faster as ocean resources become more valuable and world trade increases more rapidly than world income.

2. The Shipping Industry

Introduction: As indicated in Table 1, shipping accounts for the largest share of the oceans' 'GNP'. But shipping, a measurement of the output of shipping services, is in turn just an activity measure of the world's fleet of ships. In 1970 the total world fleet tonnage had the following structure:

Table 2: The World Shipping Fleet by Type of Vessel

	Percentage of Total Tonnage
Oil Tankers	38
General Cargo	30
Ore & Bulk Carriers	16
All Others	16

This breakdown of present tonnage underestimates the future proportion of tankers and bulk carriers in the fleet since they represent a large portion of the ongoing building programmes. In 1971, tankers accounted for 63 per cent of the dead weight tonnage (DWT) of all new production, and ore and bulk carriers for 19.6 per cent. In the same year, general cargo ships accounted for 13.8 per cent of all production, or less than half their current position in the fleet.[8]

Responsiveness of the Shipping Industry to Market Forces: These numbers suggest that the world's fleet is undergoing a rapid structural transformation, and indicate the dynamic characteristic of the shipping industry, its response to the pull of market forces, and its ability to keep step with the growing volume of world trade.

Apparently the industry faced no unusual problems in securing the capital and other resources necessary for expansion of the fleet. By inference, one may then assume that the inputs required for expansion (especially capital) are paid competitive prices. Otherwise the expansion would have been slower and it would have been accompanied by a disproportionate increase in prices. The same figures also suggest that the industry is operating within a reasonably efficient set of markets for both the inputs required and the output that is produced. Of the total DWT commissioned for 1973 some 50 per cent were for export into the world market for ships. The proportion is even higher for some notable ship-building countries like Japan and West Germany. The high proportion of production for sale abroad suggests that the proportion of DWT produced for domestic ownership and, therefore, potentially subject to direct government controls which may offset market considerations is not large. On the other hand, the lack of disproportionate increases in construction costs in shipping may be partly attributable to substantial, growing and proliferating governmental subsidies to ship-building. If this is so, it will tend to keep the initial costs and the corresponding depreciation artificially low.

Technological Change and Economies of Scale: The industry has responded rather well to technological change, such as the introduction of the container ship. At the same time, the rapid tenfold increase in tanker size from the 30,000 ton range to the 300,000 ton range within a few years reflects the presence of economies of scale. These changes are the basis for regarding the industry as reasonably competitive and sufficiently flexible to accommodate the new technology. However, one cannot accept the conclusion of workability of the industry without reservation. The quick acceptance by the industry of supertankers may mean that the oil companies are reasonably efficient in terms of reducing their costs, but it does not follow that they are compelled by the forces of competition to pass the cost savings, realized as a result of the technological change, to the consumer of the delivered product.

We observe bilateral oligopoly in the market for shipping where the small number of buyers, in significant part oil companies, are actively engaged in the ordering of new ships. They are buying from an equally concentrated group of sellers. Japan has provided approximately half the output of ships for the world market and Sweden, Germany, Japan and the UK together account for over 70 per cent of the world market output.[9]

These conditions of bilateral oligopoly will tend to yield a reasonably efficient market. In this case, cost-saving technologies will be quickly adopted, but since what is true for the market for ships does not necessarily apply to markets for the finished product, it is not certain that the cost savings are passed on to the ultimate consumer. In general, though, quick acceptance of technological innovation is in itself a good incentive for further development of innovations.

Secondary Markets for Ships and Shipping Capacity: Good secondary markets are, also, an indication of an efficient market in shipping. Efficient secondary markets mitigate the impact of concentrated ownership by extensive leasing agreements which tend to increase the flexibility in use of the ships. The extensive secondary markets and leasing agreements are also a function of the very high operating leverage. Operating leverage is defined as the ratio of per cent changes in profit to per cent changes in output. It is a measure of the sensitivity of the profit to changes in output. The leverage is determined by the proportion of fixed costs in total costs. The higher the fixed cost, the higher the leverage and the more sensitive is the profit to changes in output. Accordingly, if a high fixed cost facility like a ship is utilized below capacity, the profit will improve substantially if incremental uses can be obtained. But, at the same time, the marginal cost of providing this incremental service is very low. Under such conditions there is likely to be an active search for a substantial amount of secondary markets.

Adjustment to Changes in Demand: A reasonable ability to adjust quickly to changes in volume and composition of demand for shipping is important. Two examples that come immediately to mind are the closure of the Suez Canal and the highly erratic changes in the shipping volume of grains. The rapid adjustment of the shipping industry to these two situations permits the inference that ships are reasonably substitutable and reasonably elastic in supply and that the response lag of the industry to changes in demand is reasonably short.

All of the above attributes are characteristic of a competitive and efficient industry. This would suggest that the present industry structure is, on balance, economically reasonably efficient and policy, both national and international, should act to hold this position.

Future Conditions: A gaze into the future, though, does suggest that some qualitative changes may be expected. Pollution, congestion and accidents which represented a minor annoyance until recently are rapidly becoming major concerns. A satisfactory solution will require some standardization of requirements for vessel construction and equipment. This will in turn increase the need for negotiations, agreements and regulations with all the attendant delays, trade-offs and inefficiencies. Such an increase in regulation and control will also increase the per unit costs of shipping.

Pollution and congestion are two textbook examples of externalities. Externalities are said to occur whenever the production or consumption process of one economic agent influences the consumption or production processes of another agent in a way which is not captured by the price system. Thus, polluting effluents discharged by a ship accrue as a cost to society but they are not reflected in the price of the good unless the pollutor is regulated, licensed, penalized or financially held accountable for in some other way. Externalities are a classic example for the kind of problems which are not dealt with effectively in a private, profit-maximizing environment. Accordingly, one ought to expect an increase in governmental interference with the shipping industry. This is also true since the potential destruction caused by accidents is no longer local, nor limited, nor easily insured against.

A second source of concern and consideration is the possibility that the OPEC countries will buy or otherwise control a disproportionately large share of the shipping capacity. This possibility has been hinted at as a way to increase their bargaining power in future price changes, output changes and embargoes.

Another major concern is the possibility that countries that straddle important sea-traffic lanes or straits will attempt to extract a monopoly 'toll', limited only by the availability of substitute lanes and passages. The country that controls a minimum-cost lane between two points of trade can charge and collect a toll as long as the toll is less than the additional cost that would be incurred by the shipper if he were to shift to the next more expensive shipping alternative. The corporate role will be limited to collecting this toll in the form of higher prices and delivering it to the claiming country.

The pending expansion of national rights to the 200-mile limit will increase the opportunities for such tolls. The explicit recognition of the national exploitation of economic resources within that limit might provide a good justification since owning a strait might be considered equivalent to owning a unique natural monopoly. The increased regulation of ocean traffic might provide a convenient vehicle for such a toll.

3. Oil and Gas

The search for and the exploitation of deposits of oil and gas poses a completely different picture. Presently, offshore output represents some 15 per cent of the global output; but it is growing proportionally much faster than land-based production. Two factors with strong influence on the structure of the industry justify an expectation of rapid change. One factor is the search for hydrocarbons presently being undertaken off the shores of some 68 countries.[10] The second factor is the rapid nationalization of presently known, land-based and shore-based sources.

As a result, the corporations and nations which are presently engaged in the search for and exploitation of oil and gas resources are facing two contradictory trends. On the one hand, the increased importance of offshore resources is widening the focus of activity by drawing an increasing number of countries into the process. On the other hand, the former role of the corporations as unchallenged arbiters of prices, outputs and location of exploitation is being eroded and reduced through nationalization and government intervention.

In the long run, one might expect that the increasing number of supply sources and the widely divergent needs, priorities and political affiliations of the supplying countries will increase supplies, reduce prices and make cartel-type actions more difficult to realize. But this development is predicated upon the assumption that the aggregate growth in supplies will more than offset the aggregate growth in demand, and that at least some of the new source countries will generate supplies which exceed their own requirements.

Whereas at present four countries control the sources of some 55 per cent of the world's output and eight countries produce 75 per cent of the world's export, it is to be expected that these concentrations will drop over time as new fields are opened up. As more countries nationalize the exploitation of their hydrocarbon resources, different oil wells which were formerly under the single management of one company and thus subject to the company's unique objectives in terms of rate of output, price and expansion will now have to respond to a wide array of national objectives which vary in terms of priorities, social discount rate, need for development funds, and so on. As these widely divergent national objectives are translated into objectives of oil-well management, one should expect substantial frictions within the existing cartel and substantial pressure against the erection of a new one. This process will be enforced by the rapid increase in the number of countries with proven and exploitable reserves and the low marginal costs for the extraction of output once the initial outlay has been undertaken.

Under these changing circumstances, one ought to expect an increase in the number of legal entities acting in the market and a change in the role of the corporations.

4. Mining

A different picture is presented by the mining industry. At present, the mining of minerals in the oceans is negligible, amounting only to $1 billion per year. But the potential expansion of mining activities into the deep sea for the extraction of manganese nodules represents a quantitative and qualitative jump. Since the industry has not formally started operations, it is possible to write alternative scenarios depending upon the underlying assumptions one makes about costs and markets. If one assumes that investments in the order of $200 to $500 million are sufficient to cover initial costs, and if one accepts the argument that the technology of deep-sea mining is comparatively simple and obtainable, one may foresee a large number of firms and countries entering the industry and creating a reasonably efficient market for the extraction and processing of manganese nodules. This scenario presupposes that the supply of nodules is very large relative to future demand and that the supply is distributed widely throughout the oceans. In this possible scenario the corporations presently scurrying to enter the industry are lured mainly by the short-term excess profit expected in the early stages of development.

Under such circumstances, the role of the corporation will be in accordance with the classical model of a profit-maximizing entity operating in a reasonably competitive market, contributing to the long-run minimization of costs and to technological developments.

On the other hand, the denial of the validity of the aforementioned assumptions leads one to foresee monopoly prices and non-optimal behaviour from the point of view of society and to ask for some control and overview.

A slightly different argument might be made if one looks at the impact of the development of new sources of raw material on the distribution of wealth and income among nations. Under conditions of perfect markets, the minimum cost for the output of sea mines will benefit all users of the raw material in proportion to their volume needs. Thus, the developed countries will benefit most, whereas some less developed countries (LDCs) will benefit only eventually, as the prices of metal-consuming investment and consumption goods are scaled down to reflect lower raw material prices. Conceivably, the LDCs might prefer an international monopoly extracting monopoly profit from the resource and redistributing the profit to LDCs in accordance with some formula which reflects the need. Under such circumstances, the corporations will at best be the concessionaires which operate with permission from the international body. They will also act as suppliers of technology and equipment.

5. The Organization of the World's Fisheries

Two conditions complicate the analysis of the organization of the world's fisheries.[11] One which we have already noted is the common property condition of the resource. The second is that some of the fishing activity throughout the world is not undertaken as a simple profit-maximizing business activity but rather as a 'way of life'. The phrase 'way of life' is suggestive but not analytically useful. In this context it includes a wide mix of factors; the psychological needs of individuals, the sociology of rural life, the effect of severe poverty on labour skills and labour mobility, national economic and military policy, to mention only the most important. These factors influence in varying degree the pattern of fishing activity in both the most developed as well as in the developing states.

For example, in Norway the historical vision of the fisherman-farmer has been sustained by extensive government subsidy of coastal fishermen in Western and Northern Norway. This subsidization policy has been both direct and indirect, covering medical, educational and transportation services to the coastal villages as well as vessel and catch subsidization.

In varying degrees similar policies are followed in the UK, Canada, the United States, etc. The conditions of life differ but the organization of labour-intensive subsistence or near subsistence fisheries is analogous to those in developing countries in Africa, Asia and Latin America.[12]

The remaining part of the world's fishing activity tends to be a capital-intensive business whose behaviour is similar to that of other industries. This is true even for the socialist states where one measure of profitability is the opportunity cost of alternative sources of protein.

Chapter Three in this book analyses in detail the economics of fisheries and stresses the effect of the common property condition of the stocks on economic result. Here, therefore, we only note those effects and suggest how they influence the structure of the organization of some fisheries. The simplest model is to assume a fishery or set of fisheries with the following conditions. A given supply of fish, that is, a stock or set of stocks that may be fished to a sustainable yield for maximum physical supply. (The maximum sustainable yield is usually not identical to the optimum economic output which will maximize the net yield from the resource.) If fished beyond the sustainable, yield output will decline as the stock is depleted. At the point in its development at which we are considering this fishery, its output is at or beyond the sustainable yield. The demand for the fish is increasing over time as population and incomes rise. In addition, there is easy entry of capital and labour into the fishery.

In this model the fishery will move toward greater and greater inefficiency. The demand curve will shift outward, reflecting the increasing pressure on the fish stock. At the same time, rising prices and short-run increases in profit will attract more and more capital and labour into the fishery to catch the declining supply of fish. The preceding analysis, though, is oversimplified. It does not distinguish between the international level of analysis and the national one. For fisheries which are subject to open access only by one country the problem of the open access nature and the resulting inefficiencies are purely internal. The world community at large is only involved to the extent that the overcapitalization threatens the perpetuation of the stock or the extent that the world market tolerates the inefficiencies either because the stock is unique (e.g. Alaskan crab) or because all other producer countries are equally inefficient. If the resource is accessible to a selected few countries, bilateral or multilateral agreements will usually divide the harvest into national quotas, leaving it up to the individual countries to allocate and utilize their respective shares. Under such circumstances the survival of the fisheries is reasonably guaranteed, the national entry is controlled, but the overcapitalization and inefficiency still exists at the national level to the extent that the nations do not control entry. For widely migrating pelagic fishes, the open entry problem is raised to the international level since very few barriers are imposed upon countries intending to enter the fishery. An example might be an agreement between a country with an extensive distant fishery fleet and a country that straddles the migration path of tuna, allowing the former to catch the tuna within proximity to the latter.

The only obvious exceptions to the above problems would be in new fisheries which have not yet developed to the point of overcapitalization or in those cases where the demand for the fish in question does not grow or actually declines. A classic case in disvestment is the California sardine fishery. Heavily fished, the sardine population was essentially eliminated and the fishery collapsed. Interestingly enough, some of the processing equipment was dismantled and used to help start the Peruvian anchovy fishery.

Table 3: World Fisheries

Country	1972 Thousand Metric Tons	Millions lb.	Millions $
Japan	10,248	22,593	3,366
USSR	7,757	17,101	1,573
China (Mainland & Taiwan)	7,574	16,698	2,171
Peru	4,768	10,512	91
Norway	3,163	6,973	235
US	2,650	5,842	704
Thailand	1,679	3,702	342
India	1,637	3,609	357
Spain	1,617	3,565	602
Chile	1,487	3,278	39
Others	23,020	50,749	5,620
TOTAL	65,600	144,622	15,100

The total catch and the order of the countries in accordance with their catch has been changing rapidly, particularly because of the rapid and disproportionate increase and subsequent fluctuations in the Peruvian anchoveta fisheries.

Table 4: World's Five Leading Fishing Nations

1965		1970	
Country	Thousand Tons	Country	Thousand Tons
Peru	7,632	Peru	12,613
Japan	6,908	Japan	9,315
China	5,333	USSR	7,252
USSR	5,100	China	6,255
US	2,724	Norway	2,980

Source: Yearbook of Fisheries Statistics, Vol. 34, Food and Agricultural Organization – United Nations, 1972. As quoted in *Fisheries of the United States 1973*, Nat. Oceanic and Atmospheric Administration–National Marine Fisheries Service, March 1974.

A reinforcement of the argument that world fisheries have been reaching their peak output is provided by a comparison of the total output since 1966.

Table 5: Total World Catch 1966–72 (thousand tons)

1966	1967	1968	1969	1970	1971	1972
57.3	60.4	63.9	62.7	69.5	69.7	65.6

Source: Yearbook of Fisheries Statistics, Vol. 34, FAO, 1972

If one excludes from this series the only two growth fisheries – tuna and anchoveta – the series shows a downward trend.

6. Recreation

The use of the ocean for recreational purposes is heavily intertwined with the use of the shore line. It is also exclusively under the direct control of the shore states, and as in the US, even subject to the direct jurisdiction of political entities within national states. As a result, very few generalizations are permissible. One can say for sure, though, that the demand for recreational uses will grow disproportionately fast as a result of increases in income. It is also safe to suggest that the increasing interdependence of ocean uses will rapidly limit the growth in supply and will force a better evaluation of the relative merits of contradictory and incompatible uses. At a low level of utilization of the oceans, the mutual infringement of different uses, e.g. sports and commercial fishing, was barely perceptible. But as the level of utilization increases, these contradictions become predominant and constraining, particularly with respect to recreational uses. This is caused by the fact that recreational uses are more likely to be incompatible with many other uses.

7. Scientific Research

As was pointed out in the introduction, scientific research does not appear explicitly in the ledgers of the 'GNP' in spite of its underlying importance. Research and the resulting technological progress might be hidden or embedded in either of the following:

(a) Increases in supply through the discovery of new sources: for example, new submarine oil fields and nodule deposits.

(b) Improvement in the rate of recovery and utilization. This corresponds to a shift in the production function towards a level of higher efficiency. This shift is the main motor of technological progress and increased productivity. This is the process by which erstwhile 'uneconomical' resources become useful and are made to yield. For example, nodules have been known to exist since the early part of the twentieth century, and the Canadian tar sands have disturbed hunters since the nineteenth century. But only the steady progress in the production process, fuelled by scientific discoveries, is making them useful at this point.

Under these circumstances, the costs of scientific research are embedded in military and civilian budgets, and the revenues are hidden in the long-term decline of costs and increases in supplies.

8. Summary

Progressing industry by industry, we have attempted to explain how technological constraints, supply and demand conditions, barriers to entry and institutional arrangements tend to prescribe and shape the development. We have also tried to identify the main problems and policy issues that the ocean community will be facing when attempting to utilize the ocean's resources to the benefit of man in the most 'appropriate' way. The following table is meant to represent a brief summary of the main findings.

Table 6: Utilization of the Oceans*

	Category 1 Mineral Resources Including Oil	Category 2 Stocks of Fish	Category 3 Shipping
Entry Conditions	Licence—grant of monopoly in oil & possibly in nodules.	Common property—open access. National & international fisheries pose different problems.	No barriers. Increasing specialization might increase non-optimal structure of industry. Increasing density and standardization might make the extraction of tolls possible.
Industrial Structure	Large-scale efficient producers with extended time horizons due to monopoly position. Importance of the monopoly positions partially dependent on the nature of the market for the end product.	Excessive number of small producers, unstable structure, employment considerations historically very important, low level of research and financial weakness in firms.	Parts are reasonably competitive others are bilateral oligopolies. Increased government interference because of and through subsidies and restrictive legislation.
Economic Policy Objectives	(a) To keep a balance dependent on the relative profitability in the several sectors. (b) To capture the rent from the resource for societal benefit.	Same as a-c of category 1. Items (d) and (e) are not likely to be relevant. Also: (f) Limit entry and turn potential rent into realized net yield.	(a) Forecast and plan for the necessary increase in government interference due to externalities like congestion, pollution and accidents.

(Table 6 cont.)

Economy Policy Objectives (Continued)	(c) Mitigate fluctuations in supply and demand which have strong negative influence on world economic conditions.	(g) To avoid excessive losses from dislocation of labour and capital by policies directed toward creating greater factor mobility.	(b) Try to increase propensity of shippers to pass on cost savings to the ultimate consumer.
	(d) Forestall and cushion the impact of new sources of raw material on old supply countries, particularly for minerals.	(h) To capture portion of rent created by barriers to entry.	(c) If possible, co-ordinate and decrease expensive but mutually cancelling government subsidies.
	(e) Use newly discovered resources to redress injustice in wealth distribution. (Objective accepted by some countries but not by all.)		

*Parts of this table are extracted from: Charles S. Stewart and Giulio Pontecorvo: 'Problems of Resource Exploitation: The Oil and Fishing Industries , published in *Pacem in Maribus,* Vol. II, No. 4A, Center Occasional Paper, Center for the Study of Democratic Institutions.

Notes

1. In a supply and demand graph an infinitely elastic supply function is a horizontal line parallel to the quantity (X) axis. It indicates that there is no limit to the amount of the commodity that may be supplied at the given price.
2. The forecast of only modest increases in the supply of fish protein from the oceans assumes that fishing effort will be directed at fish populations currently known. If it becomes possible to shift fishing efforts to lower trophic levels (simpler organisms) output could expand. This does not appear to be likely in the foreseeable future.
3. Historically the concept of a 'commons' as opposed to property held in fee simple is not unique. But while today there are still instances of resources held in common, or not owned at all, the fish stocks of the oceans are the most important instance among the ones which are currently utilized.
4. Suboptimal economic efficiency means less than the best possible use of ocean resources.
5. See Giulio Pontecorvo and Roger Mesznik, 'The Wealth of the Oceans and the Law of the Sea: Some Preliminary Observations', *San Diego Law Review* (1974). Adjustments to the source are taken from *Fisheries of the United States 1973* (National Oceanic and Atmospheric Administration, National Marine Fisheries Service, March 1974).
6. One aspect of the problem of measuring the value of scientific contributions is illustrated by the present value formula $PV = \frac{A}{(1+i)} + \frac{B}{(1+i)^2} + \ldots$ Earnings that are in the distant future, that is, greater than five years hence, tend to have small present values. Since science, unlike industrial activity, tends to have long-term rather than short-term payouts, the present value of scientific activities is on the average lower than for other investment opportunities. This is particularly troublesome when benefit/cost analysis is used to establish priorities among alternative investment opportunities. It would, of course, be possible to include scientific research at cost. This should be done in the future but the data for this estimate as well as for 'military' expenditures in the oceans are extremely difficult to collect and beyond our current capability to make reasonable estimates.
7. As noted, another important omission from the Table is the value of military activity that takes place in the oceans. Clearly, many of these are transportation services. There are also important linkages between the volume of scientific research and military uses just as there are between scientific and commercial uses.
8. Commission on American Shipbuilding, 1973, quoted in C. Chryssostomidis, *International Transfer of Shipbuilding Technology.*
9. Ibid.
10. John F. Gamble, *Global Marine Attributes* (Cambridge, Mass., 1974), pp. 106–7.
11. If we wished to examine the organization of fisheries from a historical point of view we could add a third factor, the role of fisheries in foreign policy. The charters given to English fishing companies indicate the position of fisheries in international conflict over the seas during the early modern period. See, for example, H. Innis, *The Cod Fisheries* (rev. ed., 1954).
12. Subsistence is, of course, a relative term. Life is quite different for a marginal lobster fisherman in Eastern Maine than it is for a villager in a coastal village on the east coast of India.

Further Reading

1. L.M. Alexander, 'Indices of National Interests in the Oceans', *Ocean Development and International Law,* 1, 1973, pp. 21–50.

5 THE POLITICAL ECONOMY OF MARINE TRANSPORTATION

Ronald Hope

1. The Purposes of Marine Transport

It is customary to define economics as a social science concerned with the uses to which scarce resources can be put. It is probably equally enlightening to describe it as the art of bargaining. In the field of marine transport it is impossible to exclude politics, and it is therefore warrantable to revert to the eighteenth-century term 'political economy'. But if economics is the art of bargaining, then political economy may be defined as the art of bargaining from strength: in other words, in political economy the dice can often be loaded, and in the field of marine transport they frequently are.

The purpose of marine transport is to carry goods, people and ideas. Thus Henry the Navigator's aim was to carry the word of God to heathen peoples, though he was not averse to receiving gold in exchange: gold for God or goods for an immortal soul might prove a satisfactory bargain on both sides, though there can be little doubt who had the strength when the bargaining began. But beads and baubles had to be added to ideas at an early stage in the bargaining process, and since the invention of wireless telegraphy the transport of ideas by ship has become of slight significance.

The transport of people lasted longer. It started on a modest scale in the sixteenth century. In the seventeenth and eighteenth centuries the slave trade was its pre-eminent feature, though where the slaves went European masters had settled already. On the grand scale, the European exodus took place in the nineteenth century and great shipping companies were largely supported by it. Emigration by sea continued in the first half of the twentieth century and this movement of people was augmented by a growing tourist traffic. In the 1960s the number of passengers carried across the Atlantic by air overtook the number carried by sea and now there is no regular transatlantic passenger service by sea. In 1950 the number of passengers entering and leaving the United Kingdom from and to non-European countries was 602,000 by sea and 255,000 by air. Twenty years later these figures were 285,000 by sea and 5,715,000 by air. In 1956 the last British troopship, *Nevasa*, was launched; a few years later the British Government went over

Table 1: Passengers Entering and Leaving the United Kingdom from and to non-European Countries (thousands)

	1950	1959	1970	1972
Arrivals				
by sea	269	312	135	96
by air	125	428	2,334	3,057
Departures				
by sea	333	334	150	105
by air	130	414	2,381	3,093

Sources: Annual Abstract of Statistics, No. 97, 1960, p. 39.
Chamber of Shipping of the UK: *British Shipping Statistics*, 1973, p. 96.

entirely to air transport for troops and *Nevasa* was converted to a school cruise ship. In 1975 the ship was withdrawn from service. Few emigrants now travel by sea; tourists are to be found on the sea on short-sea passages only, probably with their cars; practically all that is left of the marine transport of people is the cruising business, a growth area in absolute terms but hardly a growth area in relative terms when holiday traffic as a whole is considered. The cruise ship is labour-intensive and as a holiday the cruise can never be cheap. The demand for cruising must be subject to high income elasticity and cruise business trends are likely to be closely correlated to the fluctuations in the economies of the industrialised countries.

This leaves the carriage of goods and, despite the growing amount of valuable cargo moved by air, and somewhat fanciful talk of dirigibles which might move even heavy cargoes cheaply, it is in the carriage of goods that sea transport still has a considerable edge, economically speaking, on other means of transport. Freight, inclusive of mail, carried on international air routes in 1972 amounted to 27,600 million ton-kilometres. If the average length of journey were only 100 kilometres – and it will certainly be longer – this would give to air freight less than one-tenth of the tonnage – 2,861 million tons – loaded in ships on international routes. Peter Masefield wrote twenty years ago of the British shipping industry: 'The mean operating cost for the shipping industry as a whole works out at only one-seventh of a penny for each capacity-ton-mile worked, and is substantially the lowest of any means of transport. It is, in fact, half the mean rate for all forms of transport. In other words, bulk transport by sea in large vessels is the cheapest way of carrying goods over long distances at

Table 2: World Seaborne Trade: Cargo Loaded (million metric tons)

Year	1937	1950	1960	1970	1972
Tanker cargo	105	225	540	1,440	1,637
Dry cargo	389	325	540	1,165	1,224
Total	494	550	1,080	2,605	2,861

Sources: UN Statistical Yearbook, 1973, Table 17. *British Shipping Statistics,* 1973, p. 73.

relatively slow speeds.'[1] Road and rail have eroded coastwise traffic because of handling costs across the quayside and the increased risk of pilferage in any operation where door-to-door transfer is subject to pause and interruption. Nevertheless, deep-sea, the ship remains unrivalled and tonnage grows with trade.

Table 3: World Merchant Fleet (million gross registered tons)

Year	1939	1950	1963	1970	1972	1973
Tanker	12	19	50	88	108	119
Dry Cargo	50	67	95	127	146	156
Total	62	86	145	215	254	275

Source: British Shipping Statistics, 1973, pp. 22-4.

2. A Model System of Marine Transport

If the purpose of marine transport is to carry goods, then those goods should be carried as cheaply as possible if the system is to be economic. What are the most cost-effective forms of marine transport?

There is no simple answer to this question because world trade is not a simple business. From the figures given above it would appear that much more cargo is being shifted nowadays by a given tonnage of shipping than was the case twenty or forty years ago. To do this the ships must be fuller, faster, or both, speed being taken to include the whole operation, that is, fewer delays or quicker turn-round in port and a higher operating speed at sea.

To operate ships full of cargo, other things being equal, is clearly economical, but in many bulk trades other things have proved by no means equal since the Second World War. Handling costs have been reduced by building larger and specialised carriers operating one way in ballast, and much of the old trampship trade, in which an owner so tried to place his ship that she was reasonably full of cargo most of the time, has disappeared. Only in the cargo-liner trades is it probable that tonnage has operated more fully laden in most of the post-war period when compared with the inter-war period, because of a relatively long period of prospering world trade and the effect of such political influences as the Korean and Vietnam wars and the closure of the Suez Canal.

Ships have certainly become faster in the past forty years and, in many cases, in doing so, have passed the point of most economical operation. Time, of course, is money, and if a machine ordered from Europe can reach Singapore a week earlier an economic value can be put on that week's operation and the price of time worked out. If, however, there is a steady flow of, say, grain from one area to feed a stable population in another area, speed in transit is not essential once the flow has been established. The problem in an internationally competitive business is that if one operator offers speed all may feel impelled to offer speed even though the unit cost goes up. This appears to have happened in the Europe–Far East liner trade in the 1960s. When oil prices quadrupled in 1974 the reaction of the tanker companies in response to some decline in demand was to reduce the speed of their ships so that the ton-mile cost of transporting oil fell and more oil was 'warehoused' at sea.

The speed of turn-round has also increased in the past forty years, and port delays and labour troubles in the docks were the driving force which induced the great container revolution in the years immediately following 1965. A container ship can be loaded and unloaded in a few hours. However, containers themselves still have to be 'stuffed', or filled, and 'unstuffed', and empty containers often have to be returned. It is too early to say whether the container revolution has cheapened transport in real terms.

The wooden ship could not be built beyond a certain size. The limit on the size of the modern ship is largely determined by the depth of the waters through which it must pass, and actual size is largely determined by terminal facilities and the size of the market. The only other significant factor in post-war years has been the closure of the Suez Canal which has strengthened the forces that have impelled tanker operators to build vessels of rapidly increasing capacity – the 'very large' and 'ultra large' ships of 200,000–350,000 deadweight tons. If trade of any description grows there is an incentive to build bigger and, in the circumstances, more economical ships. The size of the average ship (a purely statistical concept) has more than doubled since 1939.

Table 4: World Tonnage and the Number of Ships

Year	1939	1950	1960	1970	1974
Tons gross	68,509,432	84,583,155	129,769,500	227,489,864	311,322,626
Number of ships	29,763	30,852	36,311	52,444	61,194
'Average' size (tons gross)	2,302	2,742	3,574	4,338	5,087

Source: Calculated from *Lloyd's Register of Shipping:* Statistical Tables, 1974.

In a model world it would be relatively simple to devise a model marine transport system. Technology, markets and such physical factors as depth of water would determine the sizes and types of the vessels operated. From the main statistics of world trade, classified according to oil movements, other bulk cargoes, containerized cargo and residual parcel movements, it would not be difficult to discover what shape the ideal world merchant fleet should take. The operational movements of the fleet would be dictated by a computer as fluctuations in demand were programmed to the machine. Replacements could be planned for in a less haphazard way than now, and a constant review of relative costs would indicate if the time had come to build underwater tankers, atomic-powered merchant ships or even to revert to sail in some updated and sophisticated way if fuel costs continued to escalate. Enough slack in the system would be needed to allow for 'normal' fluctuations, but it is easy to imagine that the whole system – a world network of container liner services with feeder lines operating in the 'hinterseas' of ports of call plus the bulk trades on computerised tramping schedules – would be cheaper than it is now. The object would be to provide the cheapest transport service and liner conferences would become redundant.

The problem of ownership need not be insuperable. Ownership could be apportioned to countries on the basis of the volume of their trade, for it is volume rather than value that counts in shipping except in so far as packaging is expensive; a packaging element might be allowed for in the container and parcel trades and 'weighting' introduced to give such traffic its due. The shares of shipping apportioned to particular countries could be government-owned or privately owned according to the ideology prevalent in the country concerned. The capital costs of modern shipping are, in fact, so huge that already a number of multinational consortia have come into being.

The problem of where ships should be built can be left on one side because ships could be put out to tender as now, though in the model world governments would not rival one another in offering special inducements for ships to be built in their country.

Manning might, however, be given some consideration here. In practice it would no doubt be apportioned to countries according to the number of tons owned because no country would ignore the political question of defence and would see a need for national seafarers in times of emergency. In the model world, the cheapest seafarers adequately trained would be employed. The theory of this is a simple extension of the comparative cost advantage princip

3. Flags of Convenient Necessity

The purposes of describing a simple model are to see how it compares with the real world, to point to differences, to ask ourselves why these differences arise, and to examine trends in the real world to see if the model and the world grow more alike.

Table 5: National Merchant Fleets and National Trade*

	Size of merchant fleet (million gross tons)	Percentage of world tonnage	Goods loaded and unloaded as percentage of world total	Value of imports and exports as percentage of world total
World	331	100	100	100
Liberia	55	17	0	0
Japan	39	12	10	6
UK	32	10	5	6
Norway	25	8	1	1
Greece	22	7	0	0
USSR	18	6	2	4
US	14	4	9	12
Panama	11	3	0	0
Italy	9	3	5	5
France	9	3	4	6
German Fed Rep	8	2	2	10
Sweden	6	2	1	2
Netherlands	6	2	5	4
Spain	5	2	1	1
Denmark	5	1	1	1
India	4	1	1	1
Cyprus	3	1	0	0
Total of countries listed	271	84	47	59

Sources: Lloyd's Register of Shipping, 1974; *UN Statistical Yearbook*, 1973.

*Although the tonnage figures relate to 1974 the other figures relate to 1971 and

1972 respectively because these were the latest available, but this is not considered significant within the terms of the discussion. The figures have been rounded up or down to the nearest whole number.

It has been suggested above that in the model world ownership could be apportioned to countries on the basis of the volume and/or value of their trade. In the real world this is clearly not so. There are countries, like Japan, Sweden, Denmark and the German Federal Republic where it might be said to be broadly true. There are countries like India where it has been government policy to make it so; and there are other developing countries like Nigeria where the government has tried to obtain some share of the carrying trade. It may be thought that political effort will be directed, on the part of many countries, to establishing a fleet which will carry up to 50 per cent of their total trade, and there are some pressures in this direction.

On the other hand, some economists might argue that it is in the interests of all parties that maritime transport should be cheap, and hence that such transport should be provided by 'maritime nations', nations which have a comparative cost advantage over others in the provision of shipping, just as some nations might have a comparative cost advantage over others in, say, the provision of bauxite. If the table above is examined with this in mind, the 'maritime nations' – that is, those which register merchant fleets considerably in excess of the size required for their national trade – would appear to be Liberia, Norway, Greece, Panama, and, in some lesser degree, the United Kingdom and the USSR. The picture thus obtained is not, perhaps, quite the picture which the nations of Western Europe have presented to the world in the past.

What then constitutes a 'maritime nation'? The Norwegians, Greeks and British can, perhaps, lay claim to having been maritime nations since time immemorial. The Greeks were in the field as early – or almost as early – as the Phoenicians, and the Celts in British waters were not far behind. The Vikings appeared later in history – having learned their oceanic navigation from the Celts, no doubt – but that history is now a thousand years old. However, the maritime nation myth can soon be dispelled. Why have the Greeks survived and the Phoenicians disappeared? Why do the Danes and Dutch not appear among the maritime nations when they have as much claim to a seafaring history as the Norwegians and the British? The fact is that the maritime nations are those with flags of convenient necessity: the countries in which the ships are registered have to be 'convenient' or 'suitable' or 'not troublesome' (to use the synonyms offered by the Oxford Dictionary), and the necessity arises from constraints or compulsions of different kinds. Politics and economics are difficult to separate in this field – hence the political economy of marine transport.

Table 6: The Growth of the Liberian Merchant Fleet (million tons gross)

1949	1954	1959	1964	1969	1974
.05	2.4	11.9	14.5	29.2	55.3

Source: Lloyd's Register of Shipping.

'Flags of convenience' are largely a post-World War Two phenomenon. Ships registered in Panama totalled less than one million tons gross in 1939 but had increased to nearly 3 million tons gross by 1948 and have since increased further to over 11 million tons gross in 1974. Most frequently the term is used to describe this fleet and that registered in Liberia, the phenomenal post-war growth of which is indicated above. It is for these fleets that United States nationals – the Norwegian-born Mr. Erling Naess being the most prominent of their spokesmen – have coined the phrase 'flags of necessity'. Other flags are used. 'So far as the United Kingdom owned and registered fleet is concerned the tonnage owned by overseas parents is approximately 10,000,000 tons gross, out of a total fleet of 28,000,000 tons gross.'[2] It may be that non-nationals own parts of Norwegian, Greek, Japanese and other fleets. Recently the Cypriot flag has been favoured by some, and this flag was flown over 3.4 million tons gross of shipping in 1974. Chinese capital has gone into ships registered in the republic of Somali, a flag flown over close on two million tons of shipping in 1974.

Why have such flags become convenient and necessary?

The necessity claimed by those in the United States is that that country requires a large merchant marine subject to American control in time of national emergency and cannot obtain it under the US flag because of national manning requirements and the American inability to compete in the international market if US rates of pay are paid to seafarers and if US shipbuilding costs have to be met. The outsider may suggest that there is nothing sacrosanct about US manning requirements; nor is it decreed from heaven above that US subsidies should be confined to scheduled line and certain tanker operators and limited to something in excess of half the bills. Necessity arises only in that, if a problem cannot be solved in one way, people with reason to solve it will try to solve it in another. The flags of Panama and Liberia were chosen, among other reasons, because it did not seem likely that they would be alienated from the United States.

However, these flags are also convenient – as are some others – because the demands made upon the shipping companies that fly them are not as rigorous in one way or another as are those made upon shipping companies flying the flags of other maritime nations. Generally speaking, the profits made by ships flying the main flags of convenience are lightly taxed or not taxed at all; the employers – subject to modest international controls and the demands made by insuring institutions – can employ any labour they like, and – subject to the availability of seafarers and to the limitedly powerful International Transport Workers Federation – they can pay these seafarers any wage that will be accepted; and, finally, these ships are subjected to a minimum of 'red tape'. A minimum of 'red tape' means that the standards of operation and crew accommodation need not be, even if they often are, as high as the standards in more rigorously controlled countries. Even where the standards of operation are generally high, important economic advantages will accrue to those who can 'bend the rules' when it suits them to do so. It is because most of what has been said in this paragraph cannot be applied to countries like the United Kingdom, however much of their tonnage is owned by foreigners, that such countries are normally excluded from the term 'flags of convenience'. 'The OECD Maritime Transport Report for 1971 listed a number of features common to such flags, in particular that the country of registry has neither the power nor the administrative machinery effectively to impose any Government or international regulations; nor has the country the wish or the power to control the companies themselves.'[3]

That 'convenient necessity' pays some people is clear from the statistics. In negligible use a generation ago, convenient flags now fly over 30 per cent of the world's shipping and the proportion grows year by year.

The situation also grows increasingly complicated, and to establish a genuine link between convenience countries and convenience ships, as the 1958 United Nations Law of the Sea Conference decreed, becomes more and more difficult. In the *Torrey Canyon* case – where large areas of coast and sea were polluted by shipwreck due to bad navigation – a ship owned by the Barracuda Tanker Corporation of Bermuda and registered in Liberia was under lease to the Union Oil Company of California, which had sub-leased the ship for a single voyage to British

Petroleum Trading, Ltd., a subsidiary of the British Petroleum Company. This ship had been built in the United States, had undergone extensive structural changes in Japan, was insured in London, and manned by an Italian crew. After repeated failures to obtain compensation for the damage done, or even consideration, through the courts, the British and French governments eventually collected $7,500,000 when British Treasury agents seized the sister ship, *Lake Palourde*, in Singapore and issued an arrest writ against her which was paid by her insurers.

That the use of convenient flags can mask unsafe operation may be illustrated by the loss of the Liberia-registered cargo ship *Seagull* (6,507 tons gross) with all 29 or 30 crew (the thirtieth possible crew member was a lady who was believed to have been on board) somewhere between Pantellaria and Sicily in February 1974. The master was the only qualified bridge watchkeeper; the mate had been promoted from the position of radio officer; there was no second mate; and no qualified engineer officers. A Liberian investigation concluded that it was doubtful whether either of the senior desk officers had the professional ability and experience to deal with any emergency arising from bad weather, and it was doubtful whether the unqualified radio officer had the ability to secure and pass on to the master any weather information. In 1973, when flags of convenience flew over some 23 per cent of the world's tonnage, over half the tonnage lost at sea was attributable to these ships, and the true position was even worse than these figures suggest by reason of the potentially safer nature of the trades in which many of these ships engage[4] and the relatively young age of convenience-flag ships.[5] The point need not be laboured further, but it may also be illustrated from the side of the closely controlled flags: the average tonnage lost at sea by the United Kingdom in relation to tonnage at risk from 1964 to 1973 was the lowest of the seven largest merchant fleets for which comparable figures were available, and over three times better than the world average.[6]

Flag of convenience shipping is a classic case of operation in which social costs are likely to be borne by others, and the operator himself escapes them. Curiously, highly reputable shipping companies operating ships under flags which demand high standards have been slow to call for more rigorous control of convenient-flag operators and the running has been left to the International Transport Workers Federation which is now demanding port-state rather than flag-state jurisdiction. In other words, port authorities, under the port-state control, should be able to detain foreign flag ships which do not measure up to internationally agreed standards of operation until these standards are realised. This approach seems to have obtained British Government support judging from proposals being made to the Inter-Governmental Maritime Consultative Organisation (IMCO) in 1975. There appears, however, to be no reason why any state should wait upon international agreement before implementing rules of its own in its own territorial waters, and if territorial waters are to be extended – as seems likely – the area under national control will greatly increase.

Who provides the capital? It may be suggested that this discussion of flags of convenience has been disproportionately long in an essay which purports to deal with the political economy of marine transport. However, it is not merely central to any discussion of marine policy in relation to coastal communities, and the general desire to nurture what is in the sea and to save the oceans from destruction, but it is also central to any discussion of what may more narrowly be thought of as 'economic'.

Who provides the capital for convenient-flag ships? Overwhelmingly, of course, this capital is American – that is, from the United States – and it is provided by the major American oil companies and a number of large independent owners, some of them financed by banks. There are, however, serious gaps in our information. If convenience-flag shipping totals something like 100 million tons gross, and S.A. Lawrence is right in suggesting that 32.3 million tons gross was American controlled in 1970, at a time when only 9.8 million tons was under the American flag,[7] who owns the other 75 million tons? According to Charles H. Blyth, as much as 75 per cent of convenience tonnage is owned by American and Greek interests lumped together, but where do the Greeks obtain their capital from? Others involved are the Italians, the Hong Kong Chinese (using capital provided in part by the Communist Chinese), the Japanese, the Germans, and perhaps other European banking and commercial interests.

If Table 5 above which details national merchant fleets and national trade could be redrafted in terms of the ownership of the merchant fleets concerned, would it look more like this?

Table 7: Hypothetical National Merchant Fleets (by Ownership) and National Trade

	Size of merchant fleet (million gross tons)	Percentage of world tonnage	Goods loaded and unloaded as percentage of world trade	Value of imports and exports as percentage of world trade
US	70	21	9	12
Japan	42	13	10	6
Norway	25	8	1	1
UK	22	7	5	6
Greece	22	7	0	0
USSR	18	6	2	4
German Fed. Rep.	12	4	2	10
Italy	12	4	5	5
France	10	3	4	6
Netherlands	8	2	5	4

In the section above devoted to a 'model' system it was suggested that the ownership of the world fleet could be apportioned to countries on the basis of the volume of their trade, and subsequently it was suggested that the registered tonnage figures indicated that ownership and trade were roughly proportional in the cases of Japan, Sweden, Denmark, the German Federal Republic and India. The figures above seem to indicate that genuine ownership makes this truer than it appeared formerly in the cases of the United Kingdom, Italy, France and The Netherlands, as well as in those countries already listed.

Up to the present the countries of Western Europe have tended to oppose flag discrimination, and the insistence of certain nations – notably South American republics and, in the case of 'aid' cargoes, the United States – that 50 per cent of their trade should be carried in their own ships. It may be doubted, in the light of the evidence, whether they know their own business best. The major countries that might lose out on a 50–50 basis, or on the 40–40–20 basis (that is, where 40 per cent of the trade is carried in national hulls, 40 per cent in the vessels of the trading partner, and 20 per cent in third-party tonnage), would appear to be the United States, Norway, Greece and the USSR. The most striking difference, of course, between Table 7 above and Table 5 is the change in the position of the United States, which in the table above clearly appears as a provider of shipping services to the rest of the world.

4. The Bargaining Situation

There are many unsatisfactory features in the marine transport scene. The conference system, which seems to have served world trade reasonably well for a century, has an inherent weakness in that the established suppliers of shipping services can only lose in any bargaining situation: outsiders can always force their way into the conference and secure a share of the trade (as many Communist countries and many developing countries have done already); and shippers are often in a more powerful position than shipowners, especially where they have government backing. In the realm of new investment in shipping, a leap-frogging situation often arises, a situation in which to a new set of investors it may seem economic to build new and probably bigger ships, but it seems economic only because the losses suffered by the owners of the obsolescent capital thus created fall on another set of investors. Developing countries are also tempted to create a merchant marine for prestige reasons or for the purpose of earning foreign currencies or for both reasons, even though it is not difficult to show that standards of living might be raised more effectively by using such capital in other ways.[8] Enough has been said already to indicate that the standards of ship operation, particularly under flags of convenience, leave much to be desired, but the return on capital invested in this way obviously makes it attractive to certain companies and institutions which do not have to cover the full social costs.

In the model world which has been described it was suggested that the cheapest seafarers adequately trained would be employed. If the dangers inherent in inadequate training are to be avoided, however, the training required will have to be spelt out in detail and internationally agreed upon and, where not internationally agreed upon, insisted upon by individual coastal states anxious to protect their environment. In these circumstances there are not likely to be a few 'maritime' nations in the sense in which that term has sometimes been used. If proper training facilities are provided, most nations can become 'maritime', though some will have the advantage of an existing well-established training system. Moreover, it is unlikely that some seafarers will continue to be much cheaper than others. The maritime unions will push for parity; and wage costs or salaries as a proportion of operating costs are likely to diminish, thus making higher wages more acceptable. The comparative cost advantage of employing Sicilians or Asians or Somalilanders will be whittled away if proper qualification is insisted on and if success attends the efforts of the International Transport

Workers Federation. In these circumstances nations are likely to insist eventually on the employment of their own nationals in their own trade on a negotiated basis.

Where labour is dearest, capital is cheapest. This explains the most dramatic change in world shipping in the past sixty years – the decreasing proportion of world shipping owned by the United Kingdom and the increasing proportion owned by the United States. The truly maritime nations are those that find it profitable to invest in shipping. Greece and Norway are countries where the rate of return on internal investment is not likely to exceed the rate which can be earned in shipping, because both countries are poorly endowed with natural resources. The United States in the twentieth century, like the United Kingdom in the nineteenth century, has had a surplus of capital for investment overseas. Because of their native shares in world trade, and their relative wealth, the industrialized countries find some investment in shipping – roughly proportionate to their trade – profitable. Now the oil-producing countries have capital for possible investment in shipping.

If all this is so, why is it suggested in the model system that ownership be apportioned to countries on the basis of the volume of their trade?

The answer is to be found in the way the world is going. Further regulation of convenience-flag shipping is inevitable, and regulation will make such investment less profitable. At the same time, developing nations will demand their share of trade and some developed nations may be forced to re-examine their own policies. The United States has always reserved its 'coastal' trade, extending its coast as far as Hawaii. The time may yet come when the United Kingdom will feel impelled to do the same. Furthermore, the Western nations may well be compelled to act politically to prevent encroachment upon their trade by subsidized Communist fleets. Shipping is already a multinational business. What is in process of being worked out – and the task is urgent – are the ways in which it should be licensed, taxed and properly regulated in the interests of the world at large.

There is nothing new in much of this. A very much younger industry than shipping may have set the pattern already. The political economy of marine transport may grow more and more to resemble the political economy of air transport.

Notes

1. Presidential Address to Institute of Transport, 1955.
2. N.W. Douglas, Press Secretary, General Council of British Shipping, *Fairplay*, 30 May 1974, p. 7. Possibly an underestimate, according to a paper, 'Under which Flag', read to members of the Honourable Company of Master Mariners on 12 March 1975 by Charles H. Blyth, General Secretary of the International Transport Workers Federation.
3. Douglas, op. cit., p. 6.
4. Blyth, op. cit.
5. *Maritime Transport 1971* (OECD).
6. Mr. John Archer, head of the Department of Trade's Marine Division, at a lecture at University College, London, 1975.
7. See S.A. Lawrence, *International Sea Transport: The Years Ahead*, Lexington Books, 1973.
8. Cf. R.O. Goss, *Studies in Maritime Economics*, 3, 'Investment in Shipping and the Balance of Payments'.

6 THE FUTURE OF THE WORLD'S FISHERIES

Donald A. Pepper

The Present Situation

1. The Role of Fisheries in World Food Supply

The future of the world's fisheries is inextricably linked with a number of recent phenomena that have contributed to the present crisis situation in the world's food supply. Tremendous population growth in the underdeveloped nations, rising income levels in the developed nations and perhaps some fundamental changes in the world's weather are all part of the same equation that has resulted in a scramble for protein that is changing the fishing industries throughout the globe. Traditionally, fisheries have been conducted by coastal peoples, usually for a single or few species, in nearby local areas for local markets. This has been dramatically changed with the advent of 'industrial fishing' by high-seas fishing fleets that range all over the oceans in search of fish, any fish, as a source of protein. Slowly but surely the world's fisheries are being bound into the total problem of the world food shortage and a small traditional fishery off West Africa conducted by fishermen in canoes must compete with modern factory trawlers employing all the techniques of advanced technology. It is by now a trite observation that a change in the weather in Western Canada, a slight shift of the 'El Nino' current off Peru, or a change in the price of Arab oil will produce changes in prices that fishermen in Newfoundland will receive for capelin and ultimately the price the consumer will pay for poultry products. What has brought this about?

A few clues to answer the question of changes in the world's fisheries can be supplied by examining the trends in the world's food supply. One observer, Lester R. Brown (1974) notes that grain reserves of about 100 million metric tons are necessary as a carry-over from one harvest to the next and when reserves drop below these levels shortages exist and prices then rise at a fast rate and to a high level. Another form of reserve has been idle crop land (most of it in the US where farmers have been paid not to farm), because it represents potential production and Brown has constructed an 'index of food insecurity' from these two statistics that shows these reserves in days of annual grain consumption by the world. Since 1961 the number of days of consumption in reserves, that is, amount of food available, has declined from 95 days to 26 days in 1974. This is shown in Table 1 which also shows that the total amount of reserves has fallen from 222 million metric tons to 90 million in the same period. According to Brown, this constitutes a measure of food insecurity and one response to overall world food insecurity has been the expansion of fishing effort through the construction of high-seas fishing fleets.

Table 1: Index of World Food Security, 1961–74

Year	Reserve Stocks of Grain	Grain Equivalent of Idled US Cropland	Total Reserves	Reserves as Days of Annual Grain Consumption
	(millions metric tons)			
1961	154	68	222	95
1962	131	81	212	88
1963	125	70	195	77
1964	128	70	198	77
1965	113	71	184	69
1966	99	79	178	66
1967	100	51	151	55
1968	116	61	177	62
1969	136	73	209	69
1970	146	71	217	69
1971	120	41	161	51
1972	131	78	209	66
1973	106	24	130	40
1974	90	0	90	26

Source: Lester R. Brown, *By Bread Alone*, Praeger, New York (1974).

While some of the shortfall in grain production which is part of the world food shortage has been offset by an expansion in fish landings, it is doubtful whether this increase in landings has contributed much to those who really need it – the world's poor. A close examination of the increase shows that the major expansion has been the Peruvian anchoveta fishery which produces fish meal which is used on animal food for poultry, hogs and beef which is consumed by the more developed nations. The pattern of the world's fish landings is shown in Figure 1 which illustrates the increase of landings from over 20 million metric tons in 1950 to over 70 million metric tons in 1973. If one subtracts the Peruvian fishery it is evident that there has been pressure placed upon the more conventional species that one used for food. Indeed, many stocks have been seriously overfished and many more are in a precarious position.

The amount of food available varies considerably throughout the world and the consumption of fish is equally varied. The reasons for this are the result of many factors, traditions, government policy, changing tastes, and so on, but it is necessary to outline the role fish play in national diets to gain an appreciation of past and future development. Table 2 shows the daily intake of calories in different parts of the world, *per capita* consumption and fish as a percentage of the animal proteins. The world average is for a daily intake of 2,367 calories with a *per capita* consumption of 11.8 kilograms (25.9 pounds) per year and fish accounts for about 14 per cent of the total animal protein. However, this percentage varies from a high in Japan of 47.5 per cent to less than 4 per cent in North America, so the range is considerable. In addition, the total amount of calories consumed is different throughout the world, so that fish may have a different relative importance. For instance, the developed countries and the USSR and Eastern Europe countries have an intake of calories about 30 per cent above the world average (about 3,100 calories per day compared with about 2,300 calories per day for the world). The daily *per capita* caloric intake in Japan is only 2,429, but its *per capita* consumption of fish is one of the highest in the world at 49.9 Kg. per year, while that of the USSR is half that, 23.9 Kg. per year, but the percentages of fish in animal protein are markedly different, 48 per cent for Japan and 8.4 per cent for the USSR. The next section traces the development of the high-seas fleets and one can make the assumption that it is directly related to the role of fish in national diets.

2. Development of the High-Seas Fleets

The post-World War Two expansion of the high-seas fishing fleets is one of the significant trends in world fisheries. The impact of this expansion has been felt upon various stocks of fish previously exploited by coastal fishermen and has led to many conflicts. Many of these gear conflicts are not resolved and the 200-mile 'exclusive economic zone' concept has received some of its adherents from nations whose coastal fisheries have been affected by the high-seas fleets, although these fleets have discovered many stocks not previously exploited.

The total number of fishing vessels and tonnages of vessels greater than 100 gross registered tonnage is shown in Table 3, which ranks the nations by tonnage. Russia has the greatest number, 3,917 vessels for

Table 2: World Fish Consumption,[a] Nutritional Standards, and the Role of Fish, 1970[b]

	Daily Intake of Calories	Consumption Total '000 tons live wt.	Consumption Food '000 tons live wt.	Population '000	P.C. Consumption kg/year	Fish as % of animal proteins
World	2367	65,266	43,933	3,718,979	11.8	14.0
Developed countries	2962	32,736	17,064	726,976	23.5	11.2
North America	3166	6,081	3,492	226,612	15.4	4.8
Western Europe	2991	17,251	7,235	355,645	20.3	10.2
Oceania	3199	328	191	15,344	12.4	5.0
Japan and Others	2191	9,076	6,147	129,875	47.5	47.5
Developing countries	2106	15,787	12,950	1,760,143	7.4	19.3
Africa	2161	2,103	2,015	282,221	7.1	22.8
Latin America	2447	3,097	1,842	283,467	6.5	8.1
Near East	2284	521	409	167,436	2.4	7.0
Asia	1977	10,036	8,651	1,022,883	8.5	31.6
Centrally planned countries	2858	16,743	13,949	1,201,860	11.3	14.9
Asian centrally planned	2035	7,190	7,190	883,548	8.1	27.0
USSR	3165	6,740	5,808	242,554	23.9	8.4
Eastern Europe	3058	2,813	922	105,758	8.7	6.4

a. Excluding fish meal and fish used for pet food and other miscellaneous purposes.
b. Source: W.A. Robinson and A. Crispoldi, 'The demand for fish to 1980', FAO Fish Circ. No. FIEF/C131 – FAO, Rome, September 1971.

Table 3: Fishing Vessels, Factories and Carriers, Number and Tonnage, 1974 by Rank

	Country	Number of Vessels	Number as % of Total	Tonnage 1000 Gross Tons	Tonnage as % of Total
				(Vessels over 100 gross tons)	
1.	USSR	4,043	22.5	5,610	52.6
2.	Japan	3,198	17.8	1,255	11.6
3.	Spain	1,616	9.0	496	4.7
4.	USA	1,577	9.0	358	3.4
5.	Poland	265	1.4	271	2.5
6.	UK	614	3.4	242	2.3
7.	Norway	616	3.4	203	1.9
8.	France	616	3.4	196	1.9
9.	West Germany	156	0.8	158	1.5
10.	East Germany	166	0.9	146	1.4
11.	Canada	466	2.6	133	1.3
12.	Peru	604	3.4	125	1.1
13.	Portugal	187	1.0	123	1.1
14.	Italy	233	1.3	90	0.7
15.	South Africa	143	0.8	75	0.7
		14,500	80.8	9,481	88.7
	All Other	3,688	20.5	1,202	11.3
	World Total	18,188	100.0%[a]	10,683	100.0%

Source: *Lloyd's Register of Shipping,* 1974.

a. Figures do not add up to 100 per cent exactly because of rounding.

5,383, 000 GRT for 51 per cent of the world total and Japan is second with 2,959 vessels for 1,207,000 GRT for 13 per cent of the world total. Total world tonnage has increased from 5 million GRT in 1969 to 7.3 million GRT in 1974. The contribution of these high-seas fleets engaged in the distant-water fisheries has been estimated by Gulland (1973). While these fleets take only about 12 per cent by weight of the world's catch this is misleading as the species usually caught are the high-value ones for human consumption such as tuna (which is almost entirely taken by the high-seas fleets). This information is contained in Tables 4 and 5. These fleets contribute substantially to domestic consumption of fish as very few of the fleets land their catch for sale in other countries. For instance, in 1970 the USSR caught 48 per cent of her domestic consumption with her distant-water fleet and Japan caught about 22 per cent with her ocean-going fleets.

Similarly, the third largest fleet, Spain, had 48 per cent of her consumption from her distant-water fleet. The surprising entry of Poland into world fisheries has resulted in over 55 per cent of her domestic consumption coming from her expanding distant-water fleet.

The development of the Japanese fleet is not unusual given the traditional role of fish in the national diet but the expansion of the Russian and Polish fleets was a response to the desire to increase the amount of protein in national diets. Also, these socialist-bloc nations maintain that the cost of catching fish is substantially lower than beef production. In addition, Russia and Poland have policies of cheap food and it appears that fish in various forms is a convenient way of solving food distribution problems and providing variety to their protein requirements.

Other countries have also pursued, through fisheries, national objectives related either to development or to domestic food policies. Spain and Portugal consume salt cod, 'bacalhau', in their traditional diets and their governments have subsidized the construction of fishing vessels to take cod off the Grand Banks of Newfoundland. The Republic of South Korea has expanded its distant-water fleet to satisfy its own needs and also as a means of earning foreign exchange. The dependence of the Canadian maritime provinces upon the fisheries has led to a number of direct and indirect subsidies to bolster an industry that is suffering from foreign fleets depleting stocks on the Grand Banks. Peru exists as the classic case of development that has been brought about through exploitation of a fish stock, in this case a single species, anchoveta. The collapse of this fishery has had a profound effect upon the prices for fish meal and has raised feed costs in the developed world.

Table 4: Catches in Thousand Tons and, in parentheses, Percentage of National Total Taken by Local and Distant-Water (DW) Fleets in Different Regions of the World

Fishing Areas		1964	1965	1966	1967	1968	1969	1970
Atlantic	Local	1,665 (49)	1,785 (47)	2,047 (52)	2,080 (52)	2,275 (50)	2,110 (48)	2,170 (51)
North West	DW	1,725 (51)	1,975 (53)	1,973 (49)	1,950 (48)	2,315 (50)	2,250 (52)	2,050 (49)
Atlantic	Local	7,536 (87)	8,224 (85)	8,736 (86)	9,063 (87)	9,411 (92)	9,251 (92)	9,734 (91)
North East	DW	1,114 (13)	1,396 (15)	1,464 (14)	1,287 (13)	839 (8)	769 (8)	926 (9)
Atlantic	Local	1,500 (97)	1,561 (97)	1,210 (95)	1,245 (97)	1,844 (99)	1,435 (99)	1,460 (99)
Western Central	DW	50 (3)	49 (3)	60 (5)	35 (3)	16 (1)	15 (1)	10 (1)
Atlantic	Local	569 (50)	603 (50)	729 (53)	748 (49)	716 (42)	782 (38)	866 (34)
Eastern Central	DW	571 (50)	597 (50)	686 (47)	782 (51)	974 (58)	1,288 (62)	1,714 (66)
Mediterranean	Local	960 (100)	990 (100)	1,030 (100)	1,140 (100)	1,030 (100)	970 (100)	1,170 (100)
and Black Sea	DW	— (—)	— (—)	— (—)	— (—)	— (—)	— (—)	— (—)
Atlantic	Local	443 (94)	502 (96)	559 (87)	566 (45)	612 (76)	594 (84)	611 (58)
South West	DW	31 (6)	22 (4)	85 (13)	686 (55)	198 (24)	146 (16)	444 (42)
Atlantic	Local	1,583 (84)	1,580 (72)	1,615 (70)	1,978 (75)	2,412 (73)	2,289 (74)	1,620 (66)
South East	DW	307 (16)	600 (28)	695 (30)	662 (25)	888 (27)	801 (26)	840 (34)
Indian Ocean	Local	1,170 (96)	1,158 (93)	1,241 (90)	1,232 (91)	1,308 (91)	1,350 (90)	1,545 (91)
Western	DW	50 (4)	82 (7)	139 (10)	128 (9)	132 (9)	150 (10)	145 (9)
Indian Ocean	Local	692 (90)	704 (93)	778 (96)	868 (93)	959 (94)	1,076 (96)	1,051 (96)
Eastern	DW	48 (10)	56 (7)	32 (4)	62 (7)	61 (6)	44 (4)	39 (4)
Pacific,	Local	659 (44)	640 (44)	661 (40)	476 (25)	473 (25)	391 (18)	492 (19)
North East	DW	826 (56)	821 (56)	1,007 (60)	1,431 (75)	1,452 (75)	1,797 (82)	2,145 (81)
Pacific,	Local	9,920 (100)	10,700 (100)	10,800 (100)	11,160 (100)	12,170 (100)	12,110 (100)	13,030 (100)
North West		— (—)	— (—)	— (—)	— (—)	— (—)	— (—)	— (—)

Table 4 (Continued)

Pacific, Western Central	Local	2,360 (100)	2,500 (100)	2,700 (100)	2,890 (100)	3,280 (100)	3,440 (100)	3,900 (100)
	DW	— (–)	— (–)	— (–)	— (–)	— (–)	— (–)	— (–)
Pacific, Eastern Central	Local	498 (80)	497 (83)	560 (87)	680 (88)	663 (83)	645 (85)	738 (86)
	DW	122 (20)	103 (17)	80 (13)	90 (12)	137 (17)	115 (15)	122 (14)
Pacific, South West	Local	84 (56)	100 (62)	110 (58)	105 (62)	114 (60)	102 (51)	106 (56)
	DW	66 (44)	60 (38)	80 (42)	65 (38)	76 (40)	98 (49)	84 (44)
Pacific, South East	Local	10,399 (100)	8,260 (100)	10,148 (100)	11,171 (100)	11,852 (100)	10,240 (100)	13,694 (100)
	DW	12 (0)	15 (0)	17 (0)	11 (0)	20 (0)	26 (0)	18 (0)
World Total	Local	41,590 (90)	41,300 (88)	44,640 (88)	47,580 (88)	50,880 (89)	49,170 (89)	54,590 (88)
	DW	4,620 (10)	5,430 (12)	5,810 (12)	6,330 (12)	6,090 (11)	6,320 (11)	7,140 (12)

Source: J.A. Gullard, op. cit.

Finally, the dependence of some national economies upon fish is well known. Iceland is prepared to wage a 'mini-war' with the British and German fleets to protect her economy. While the reasons for the development of high-sea fleets are varied the end result is the same: greater competition for fish in the world's oceans.

The Future Supply and Demand for Fish

1. Demand for Fish

In any discussion about fish, and particularly one about future supplies and consumption, a *caveat* is necessary. The amount and kind of fish consumed varies over the globe because of historical factors related to cultural or religious tastes, which makes it difficult to supplant one type of fish in a national diet with another, perhaps slightly inferior, species. Recent advances in product development have minimized this problem considerably. For instance, the American consumer appears not to have minded the substitution of Alaska pollock for Atlantic cod in breaded fish sticks and fish portions. Previously unexploited species appear to be finding consumer acceptance but a certain amount of consumer education and promotion appears necessary before some species are marketable. At present, 'table-grade' species are near maximum sustainable yields so any substantial increase in consumption must come from species that are not being exploited. The acid test is consumer acceptance of these new species and this depends upon a myriad of factors that are almost impossible to quantify. The reasonable expectation is that within a few years consumers will be eating what were previously considered 'trash' fish.

One of the major trends in the factors affecting fish consumption has been the increase in world population; another the rising standard of living in the developed countries. The continued increase in population will affect fish consumption which will in turn be influenced by when and where the population growth takes place and the relative increases in income levels. The present world consumption of about 44 million metric tons of fish for food will have to be substantially increased to accommodate it and prevent a lowering of *per capita* levels of consumption.

A recent FAO study (Robinson, 1971) has estimated the future demand for fish under a number of assumptions about population growth and rises in income levels. It is, in effect, a 'best guess' of what one can expect. The most optimistic view is that the world's population will increase from its present 3.8 billion to about 4.5 billion in 1980

Table 5: The Contribution in Thousand Tons and, in parentheses, Percentage of Total Catch of Local and Long-range Fisheries to the Catches of Certain Selected Countries

	Year						
	1964	1965	1966	1967	1968	1969	1970
Cuba							
Total	37	41	44	65	66	79	105
Local	37 (100)	41 (100)	42 (98)	62 (95)	62 (94)	69 (87)	62 (59)
Long-range	— (0)	— (0)	1 (2)	3 (5)	4 (6)	10 (13)	43 (41)
Japan							
Total	6232	6760	6961	7713	8515	8449	9147
Local	5390 (87)	5844 (86)	5870 (84)	6169 (80)	6814 (80)	6615 (78)	7135 (78)
Long-range	842 (13)	916 (14)	1091 (16)	1544 (20)	1701 (20)	1834 (22)	2012 (22)
Korea (Rep. of)							
Total	599	640	701	749	841	879	934
Local	596 (100)	638 (99)	692 (99)	733 (98)	815 (97)	831 (95)	881 (94)
Long-range	1 (+)	2 (+)	9 (1)	16 (2)	26 (3)	48 (5)	53 (7)
Poland							
Total	244	280	316	321	386	387	451
Local	193 (79)	199 (71)	201 (64)	154 (48)	153 (40)	165 (43)	204 (45)
Long-range	51 (21)	81 (29)	115 (36)	167 (52)	233 (60)	222 (57)	247 (55)

Table 5 (Continued)

Spain														
Total	1200		1328		1351		1429		1503		1483		1483	
Local	763	(64)	795	(60)	733	(54)	729	(51)	738	(49)	755	(51)	781	(53)
Long-range	437	(36)	533	(40)	619	(46)	700	(49)	765	(51)	728	(49)	702	(47)
USSR														
Total	3749		4273		4560		4959		5301		5752		6399	
Local	2238	(60)	2414	(56)	2547	(56)	2624	(53)	3003	(57)	2992	(52)	3316	(52)
Long-range	1511	(40)	1859	(44)	2013	(44)	2335	(47)	2298	(43)	2760	(48)	3083	(48)

Source: J.A. Gullard, 'Distant Water Fisheries and Their Relation to Development and Management', in *Journal of the Fisheries Research Board of Canada,* Vol. 30, No. 12, Part 2, Dec. 1973.

and in the range of 6.1 – 8.0 billion by the year 2000. The impact of this increase upon the demand for fish has been calculated on a country-by-country basis and is aggregated in Table 6. It shows that under the assumption of constant *per capita* consumption of fish that the demand for fish products (meal and food) would increase by 8 million tons to a total of 73 million tons in 1980 and by the year 2000 this demand would increase by 27 million tons for a total demand of 93 million tons, more than double 1970 consumption.

While it is accepted that fertility rates are tricky things, subject to change due to individual perceptions, preferences about family size (and trends are only discerned over the long term), it is apparent that they are presently declining in the developed world and might possibly be in other parts of the world. The UN 'medium variant' shown in Table 6a assumes that the world population will increase at a rate of 2 per cent per year up to 1985 and thereafter at about 1.7 per cent to the year 2000. Where the population increase occurs will naturally affect the kind and amount of fish required to satisfy the demand. The UN experts expect that much (over one-third) of the population increase will take place in the market economies of Asia. This has implications for aquaculture as this is a traditional source of fish and although *per capita* consumption is relatively low, about 8.5 kilograms per year, fish is an important part of the diet and the population increase will require an additional 2.6 million tons of fish by 1980 for this area alone and over 9 million tons by 2000. It should be stressed that these calculations assume 1970 levels of *per capita* consumption.

Historical trends have indicated that as income levels rise the *per capita* consumption of protein (which includes fish) rises. Given that fish is a traditional part of many national diets, it can be expected that rising income levels will also increase the demand for fish. Table 6b contains the conservative estimates of population growth ('medium variant') used in Table 6a and adds some estimates of rises in income levels and estimates the ultimate demand for fish as a result of population and income growth. The result of better standard of living will be to increase the *per capita* consumption of fish a further 1.5 Kg. by 1980 and a further 3.1 Kg. by 2000. The effects, of course, will vary from country to country. For instance, in Japan it is expected that in spite of a levelling off of growth and present high fish consumption rates that the demand for fish will still be higher than in other countries. It is also possible that in the USSR a 'saturation' level may be reached and fish consumption will not continue to rise. The net effect of these population and income variables is expected to increase

Table 6a: Additional Supplies of Fish[a] Required to Maintain 1970 *per capita* Consumption in 1980 and 2000, in Thousands of Tons Live Weight

	Actual Consumption 1970	Increase Required if Population Growth is					
		1980			2000		
		Low	Medium	Constant Fertility	Low	Medium	Constant Fertility
World	43,933	7,316	8,228	9,412	23,069	27,252	38,210
Developed countries	17,064	1,938	1,952	1,952	5,916	6,073	6,208
North America	3,492	416	416	416	1,507	1,507	1,507
Western Europe	7,235	551	551	551	1,692	1,692	1,692
Oceania	191	41	41	41	133	133	133
Others	6,147	930	943	943	2,583	2,740	2,875
Developing countries	12,950	3,554	4,015	4,354	12,004	14,670	20,714
Africa	2,015	570	623	621	2,199	2,711	2,958
Latin America	1,842	560	604	666	2,071	2,386	3,027
Near East	409	113	125	133	438	516	701
Asia	8,654	2,302	2,654	2,923	7,264	9,022	13,983
Centrally planned countries	13,919	1,824	2,261	3,106	5,149	6,509	11,288
Asian centrally planned	7,190	1,116	1,553	2,398	2,908	4,268	9,047
USSR	5,808	627	627	627	2,027	2,027	2,027
Eastern Europe	922	80	80	80	213	213	213

a. For direct human consumption excluding fish meal.

Table 6b: Estimated Demand for Fish in 1980 and 2000 due to Income and Population Increase

	P.C. consumption Kg/year			Est. population millions		Total demand '000 tons live weight		
	Actual	Projected		Medium variant		1980		2000[a]
	1970	1980	2000	1980	2000	Human consumption	Fish meal	Human consumption
World	11.8	13.3	16.2	4,575.2	6,640.3	60,969	33,295	107,548
Developed countries	23.5	26.5	28.7	805.3	977.6	21,372	25,140	28,075
North America	15.4	16.7	17.7	253.8	324.6	4,230	4,180	5,745
Western Europe	20.3	24.0	26.6	383.5	439.8	9,208	15,710	11,699
Oceania	12.4	13.6	15.2	18.7	26.1	254	375	397
Others	47.5	51.4	54.7	149.3	187.1	7,680	4,875	10,234
Developing countries	7.4	8.7	11.7	2,306.0	3,789.9	20,131	3,165	44,405
Africa	7.1	8.7	9.3	371.5	665.7	3,249	260	6,191
Latin America	6.5	7.6	9.2	376.2	650.5	2,854	1,965	5,985
Near East	2.4	3.0	3.5	222.6	385.3	658	110	1,349
Asia	8.5	10.0	14.8	1,330.3	2,079.5	13,324	810	30,777
Centrally planned countries	11.3	13.3	18.7	1,463.9	1,872.8	19,466	4,990	35,068
Asian centrally planned	8.1	9.5	14.8	1,079.4	1,414.6	10,253	–	20,936
USSR	23.9	29.7	37.9	269.3	327.8	7,996	2,600	12,424
Eastern Europe	8.7	10.6	13.1	115.2	130.4	1,217	2,390	1,708

a. Estimates of fish meal demand in 2000 are not reliable enough to be useful.

Source: M.A. Robinson, *Journal of the Fisheries Research Board of Canada,* Vol. 30, No. 12, Part 2 1973

total demand by over 63 million tons by the end of the century. In other words, fish production will have to more than double 1970 levels. It is appreciated that since these estimates were made in 1970, the possibility of increases in the standard of living are perhaps a little more remote but the estimates of population increase still appear to be valid.

2. Future Supply of Fish

One of the dominant trends in fishing has been the consistent increase in landings during the last century (except for interruptions due to wars). From a modest beginning of 2 m. metric tons in 1850 landings increased to ten times that amount in 1950, about 20 m. metric tons. Landings appear to have levelled off in the last few years at about 70 m. metric tons and in 1971 actually declined to about 65.6 m. metric tons. A large portion of the increase, and the decline, has been due to the Peruvian anchoveta fishery which contributed as much as 13 m. metric tons to the total. The collapse of this fishery has seriously affected the total landings but its impact upon direct fish consumption is not much as it was made into fish meal.

Leaving aside the anchoveta fishery there is still concern for the fisheries as a number of conventional species are in danger of being overfished, if not wiped out. The pressures upon these stocks and conflicts between states has led not only to a wide variety of international agreements but also to some realistic quotas and restrictions upon fishing effort. The question that needs to be answered is whether or not the future supply exists and is there an upward limit? As has been noted, there is a potential demand increase and it is necessary to examine the supply potential of the oceans to see if supply and demand can be equated.

Estimates have been made many times of the potential supply using a variety of methods and assumptions. These are contained in Table 7, and range from the low of 21.6 m. metric tons made by Thompson in 1949 to the high of 2,000 m. metric tons by Chapman in 1965. These estimates vary principally because of differing assumptions about the trophic level at which fish are harvested (i.e. at what stage of the food chain fish are caught). It is also interesting to note that the estimates are continually being revised upwards (underlining the hazards of making predictions). The most recent estimates by Moiseev (1973) and Suda (1973) envisage an increase from the present 70 m. metric tons to about 82 m. metric tons for the former and 93–110 m. metric tons for the latter. Moiseev's estimate was made in 1970 when the catch was 61.7 m. metric tons and his estimate appears to have been conservative (in spite of declining catches in some species). Suda's estimate is higher because he feels there will be much more concentration upon the unconventional species.

While the potential supply exists there remains the unanswered question of the cost of catching and processing the fish necessary to satisfy the demand created by population increases and general shortage of protein. The recent increase in world prices has escalated the cost of catching fish by the world's high-seas fishing fleets. It is difficult to estimate the impact of inflation and the real rise in costs of fishing but one can expect the socialist-bloc countries to continue their distant-water fisheries as long as their costs are substantially below other protein costs and as long as they are self-sufficient in oil. The impact of oil price increases upon the Japanese fleets is more difficult to assess but the trend appears to be towards the use of other nationals as crew (paying lower wages) and the use of joint-ventures. The nations that possess surplus oil are in an excellent position to develop high-seas fleets to supply the future demand for fish. The big unknown is the cost of catching, which must be below prices received in the market place to make it economic.

Table 7: Estimates of Total Yields of Marine Animals

Author	Forecast (million metric tons)	Year	Method
Thompson	21.6	1949	ext
FAO	55.4	1955	ext
Finn	50–60	1960	ext
Graham and Edwards	55 (bony fishes)	1962	ext
Meseck	55 (by 1970)	1962	ext
Graham and Edwards	60 (bony fishes)	1962	ext
Schaefer	66 (by 1970)	1965	ext
Meseck	70 (by 1980)	1962	ext
Alverson	80	1965	ext
Bogdanov	70–80	1965	ext, f
Graham and Edwards	115 (bony fishes)	1962	f
Schaefer	160	1965	ext
Schaefer	200	1965	f
Pike and Spilhaus	200	1965	f
Chapman	1000	1966	f
Pike and Spilhaus	180–1400	1962	f
Chapman	2000	1965	f

From Schaefer and Alverson (1968).
ext = extrapolation from catches.
f = flow of organic material through the food chain.

Source: A. Suda, *Journal of the Fisheries Research Board of Canada*, Vol. 30, No. 12, Part 2, Dec. 1973.

Fishing Fleet Expansion and Future Catch Rates

It may be fruitful to examine the development and fishing patterns of a number of the national fleets in greater detail to outline some of the fundamental reasons for expansion and to possibly predict some future activities. For obvious reasons we shall consider (i) Russia, (ii) Japan, the two largest fishing nations and (iii) the US tuna fleet and (iv) the Portuguese cod fishery. The latter two are included to show the difference between an innovative expanding fleet in a fishery with high values and a traditional, slowly contracting fishery.

(i) The Soviet Fleet

The growth and development of the Soviet fleet since the end of World War Two has been phenomenal. Almost completely destroyed during that war, it was rebuilt and by 1967 it had the largest high-seas fishing fleet in the world and was third in fish landed, after Peru and Japan. The investment to achieve this has been variously estimated and is believed to be of the order of $4 billion in the 1964 to 1966 period. In addition, a large infrastructure of ports and shipyards as well as research and development facilities had to be created. That the development has been successful is demonstrated by the fact that fish is now an integral part of the diet of Soviet people, fish being about one-third of the animal protein consumed. Catches have steadily increased up to about 1970 where they appear to have reached some sort of peak at around 6,400 thousand metric tons. This catch comes from practically every ocean in the world, and due in part to particularly dramatic increases in the western part of the Indian Ocean in recent years. The ability to fish the oceans of the world attests to the fishing ability of the fleet which, it should be remembered, delivers almost all its catches for domestic consumption in Russia. During the period 1966 to 1971 the consumption of fish in various forms increased by 30 per cent, from 3,419 thousand metric tons to 4,433.5 metric tons. As shown in Table 5, a steadily increasing percentage of it came from the high-seas fleet (local catches and inland waters production also increased over the same period).

The increase in the number and tonnage of Russian vessels in the high-seas fisheries makes Russia one of the dominant forces in the world fisheries. An extensive modernization and replacement programme appears to be under way and while there may be no significant increase in the number of vessels, the newer ones tend to be larger and more sophisticated and hence more efficient.

It is only natural that such a fleet would have pioneered the development of a number of on-board processing techniques which are not duplicated by other nations and that the Soviets have also discovered new fishing grounds and are able to exploit species such as the previously unexploited grenadier *(Marcrurus rupestris)* which has developed into a major fishery for them. They are also conducting exploratory fishing operations upon Antarctic krill *(Euphasia Superba)* which they fully expect to be a valuable new source of protein. While world catches appear to have peaked, the response of the Soviet fishing industry will probably be to increase the efficiency of its present fleet by improved fish finding and fish-catching techniques to exploit conventional species. Further, under-utilized species may be exploited by making fish protein concentrate and reconstituting it into new food products.

While there is little or no data on the economic performance of the Soviet fleet as a whole (indeed there is little for most nations) some information does exist on the catch rates for USSR vessels in the International Commission for the Northwest Atlantic (ICNAF) area. This data shows a declining trend in the catch-per-unit-effort (CPUE) for the Soviet fleet. In 1965 the large factory-trawlers were able to catch about 44 tons of fish per fishing day. This has gradually declined and in 1971, which was a bad year, this type of vessel was only able to catch 29 tons per day fished. The smaller USSR fishing vessels in the ICNAF area have experienced a similar decline. A good year for them in the ICNAF area was 1966 when they were able to average over 8 tons per day of fishing, but this has also declined to about 5 tons per day in 1972, the most recent data reported. Indications are that in 1973 and 1974, these catch rates will be lower because of the quotas imposed upon the fleets by ICNAF.

It is difficult to predict the response of the USSR fishing fleet to their declining catch-rates. They must obviously search for new fishing grounds and new species but the overall impact is to increase the cost of fishing. According to the Soviets' method of calculating economic performance (Sysoev, 1972) the factory-trawlers are very profitable, paying for themselves in about five years. This implies that the USSR will continue to build more factory-trawlers. Thus, in spite of declining catch-rates and increased costs, we can expect the Soviet fleet to continue its expansion. The implications of this are many, but it does not augur well for coastal states who wish to exploit their shelf area to its fullest.

(ii) The Japanese High Seas Fleet

Preceding but paralleling the development of the Soviet fleet has been the expansion of the Japanese high-seas fishery. Like the Russians their fleet was negligible after World War Two, but they had traditionally participated in distant-water fisheries, and faced less problems in building it up. The domestic demand for fish products and the declining landings of nearby traditional grounds forced the fishing companies to expand their fisheries further and further from Japan. The first expansion was into the East China Sea, Korea and the Gulf of Tonkin. However, international disputes led to a limit of expansion in these areas. The expansion of the mainland Chinese fleet, the build-up of the Korean fleets and the Vietnam conflict finally forced the Japanese to expand into what is called the 'Northern Seas' fishery in the Bering Sea, around Kamchatka, and the Aleutians. The expansion of the fleet in these areas has led to the major commercial stocks being seriously endangered, although it should be noted that the Japanese fleet is not the only one in these waters. The Russian fleet is quite extensive and the recent build-up of the Korean fleet fishing in the North Pacific has intensified the pressure upon these stocks. The notable expansion of the pollock *(Theragra chalcogrumma)* fishery has been made to sustain the production of the Japanese fleet and the introduction of on-board processing facilities to make minced pollock meat ('surimi') has helped the phenomenal increase in landings of this species. In addition to this trawl fishery is also a net and long-line fishery for salmon and a large trap fishery for crab. These latter two fisheries have led to conflicts with US and Canadian fishermen.

The Japanese have also expanded into the area off West Africa for species such as hake (in the south), squid, octopus, mackerel and others. There is also an extensive shrimp fishery off the north-west coast of South America as well as the highly-developed tuna fishery using either long-line or pole-and-line techniques. This latter fleet ranges the world's oceans, tuna being one of the most prized species for Japanese markets. The one notable lack of success in Japanese efforts has been in the ICNAF area, one of the world's most productive areas. The reasons for this are rather complex but given the high demand for fish products it is probable that there may be an expansion of the fleet into this area, especially for squid.

Closely allied with the development of the high-seas fleets has been the policy of joint-venture between Japanese companies and other foreign companies to exploit species that lie close to the shores of coastal states. This appears to be an increasing trend and is expected to increase as more and more states increase their jurisdiction over the continental shelf waters.

The rise of the Japanese high-seas fisheries has been documented by Kasahara (1972) and he notes that the important Japanese fisheries are 'strictly controlled by the Central government under the licensing system'. All of these fisheries, including domestic aquaculture, have had severe limitations placed upon expansion either through the licensing system, increased costs or international agreements that have established quotas or limits to Japanese fishing effort. One can expect the increase of joint ventures by the Japanese as they continue their attempts to overcome the domestic shortage of fish. The previously mentioned world oil prices and domestic inflation can only pressure the Japanese high-seas fleets into substantial changes.

(iii) US High-Seas Tuna Fleet

As pointed out by Broadhead (1971) the two countries that consume the major share of the world's tuna landings are also the two that catch the most. For example, in 1969 Japan and the US caught about two-thirds of the world's catch and consumed slightly more, about three-quarters of the total. Individually, the US catches about 20 per cent and consumes about 45 per cent while Japan catches 30 per cent and uses 30 per cent (Joseph, 1972).

The US fleet is noteworthy from a number of viewpoints. It is highly mobile, fishing effectively anywhere in the world. It is sophisticated in its techniques, using electronic navigational aids operated by satellites, helicopters, specialized freezing techniques and uses one of the most significant modern methods of net-handling, the Puretic power-block. Also of significance is the high degree of vessel ownership by the captains and fishermen (although the amount of vessel ownership by the processing companies is increasing). The rapid expansion of this fleet is the result of a number of factors: an increasing domestic demand for tuna as a result of rising income levels, high profits accruing to the vessel-owners, and the existence of a relatively under-exploited resource with the necessary technological innovations to catch this wide-ranging species.

While the status of the stocks has been the cause of concern for the few regulatory bodies that exist, the increase in the number of tuna vessels continues at a very high rate. The ratio of the catch to the vessel capacity has been steadily decreasing in the last few years from about 2.5 tons of catch per ton of vessel capacity to about 1.3 tons per ton of capacity in 1971 and is still declining (Joseph, 1972). This trend is indicative of a serious problem, an increase in fleet capacity and very little increase in catches, the traditional recipe for disaster. Secondly, this scramble for tuna intensifies conflicts with coastal states which may wish to exploit this species.

The tuna fishery merely highlights the traditional expansion path of a new fishery but also reveals some of the complexities that may arise in attempts to control high-seas fisheries. The US, as one of the most powerful nations, will be brought into conflict with many nations because of its need for tuna if 200 miles (and higher) limits are imposed by nations either from the result of law of the sea negotiations or through unilateral declarations. Already well known are the conflicts this US fleet is having with South American countries which do not exploit the species themselves but continually find US vessels pursuing tuna within their 200-mile limits. As this fleet expands, it will be ranging further and further and this can only lead to more conflicts with nations that seek to develop this fishery themselves. The trend seems irreversible: high domestic demand, large profits, expansion of the fleet to ensure supplies, and ominously declining catch rates.

This has been the experience of a number of fisheries that had to have an almost total collapse before some sort of effort limitation was placed upon them. Because tuna and the fishing fleet occupy all the oceans of the world and are far-ranging, it appears that this fishery may exist relatively free from any controls other than those imposed by economic conditions in Japan and the US. There are two international commissions that regulate the quotas for a number of species but they cannot control the construction of new vessels which appears to be the key to management of fishing stocks. If 200-mile limits are to be the new order, then this fleet will have conflicts with many nations.

(iv) The Portuguese Cod Fleet

The Portuguese have been going to the Grand Banks of Newfoundland and to Greenland for several hundred years. There they fish for cod, salt them down on the vessel and return to Portugal where the fish are a traditional part of the Portuguese diet. As many as 50 vessels and 3,000 men went on sailing vessels which were about 1,200 gross registered tons (and were known as the 'White Fleet' from the colour of the hulls). Change has been slow in this industry, the use of sail existing until the late 1950s. Sail was gradually replaced by diesel for travelling, but sail was used on the fishing grounds.

It was one of the most hazardous of all fisheries, the individual fishermen going out each morning from the mother ship in a little dory equipped, until recently, only with a sail, oars and a compass. Miraculously, they returned each night laden with fish. This was done in an area notorious for sudden gales, fogs and icy temperatures. The persistence of this particular fishery in an age where technological change is rapid highlights some of the peculiarities of fishing.

The reason the Portuguese fleet was able to exploit these fishing grounds and remain in a relatively primitive state technologically was due to a unique continuation of factors that give it a comparative advantage. It was able to exploit grounds that modern trawlers cannot (it is a hook-and-line fishery), and it had a traditional market for fish in a form that required no technological improvements to the fishing fleet. Also, the earnings of the fishermen were substantially above any alternative employment in their own country, but below that of other fishermen in the same area. Being relatively isolated from influences that have forced changes upon other nations' fisheries it appeared an anachronism, but changes did come. One, the use of nylon gillnets, is the most notable technique adopted by the Portuguese and now these gillnet dories have small diesel engines replacing the sail and oars of the dories. The cod is still salted, but unfortunately they are getting smaller, making them less desirable to the Portuguese.

Ultimately, the long-term impact of increased effort in the ICNAF areas has been the depletion of the cod stocks and the disappearance of large cod which the Portuguese favoured. The process was a gradual one, but as the catch-per-unit effort of the dory vessels slowly declined, fewer and fewer vessels went to the Grand Banks and the icy shores of Greenland until the traditional method has now disappeared after a long and colourful history. The Portuguese have been forced to modernize their fleet and have built trawlers to compete with the other nations. In the world struggle for protein, the Portuguese dory-vessel fleet finally succumbed to a superior technology.

Conclusions

The conclusions from the preceding discussion are obvious: the demand for fish will place pressures on all fish resources in the world and the world's fishing fleets will have to adapt to some new realities, such as the cost of oil and increased competition from protein-hungry nations. Some that already have a comparative advantage in species or area may be insulated from these changes, but the long-term trend will be for coastal states to increase their jurisdiction over shelf areas. There will be a form of 'exclusive economic zones' that follow either from unilateral declarations or from a new Law of the Sea Convention.

These changes in fisheries will be mirrored in the rise of more and increasingly complex institutional and economic arrangements for the regulation of fishing and processing of resources from these shelf areas. The potential for conflict remains very high as nations either seek to maintain a fishery or to enter it.

The resolution of this conflict will surely test whatever institutional organizations exist. The economic arrangements will see a 'transfer of technology' as those nations with the expertise (or markets) engage in joint ventures for the exploitation of fish in the 'fishing zones' of coastal states. Part of this technological transfer must be in the area of aquaculture which will be amongst the alternatives for a number of nations with increasing populations.

Finally, there are two dominant trends that will ultimately shape each nation's fishery policy: increasing population and the increase in energy costs. The trade-off here may force some difficult choices to be made. For example, high-seas fishing consumes 8–10 times the energy per caloric output of coastal fishing. The cost of distant-water fishing may be just too high to continue and already there are changes in these fleets. Whatever the ranking of priorities by each nation, for the coastal states and those in high-seas fisheries one thing is clear: the world's hungry must have food and the world's areas must supply more. The danger is international conflict and overfishing: the opportunity is to feed people starved for protein.

Fig. 1: World Landings and Landings of Selected Countries 1956–72

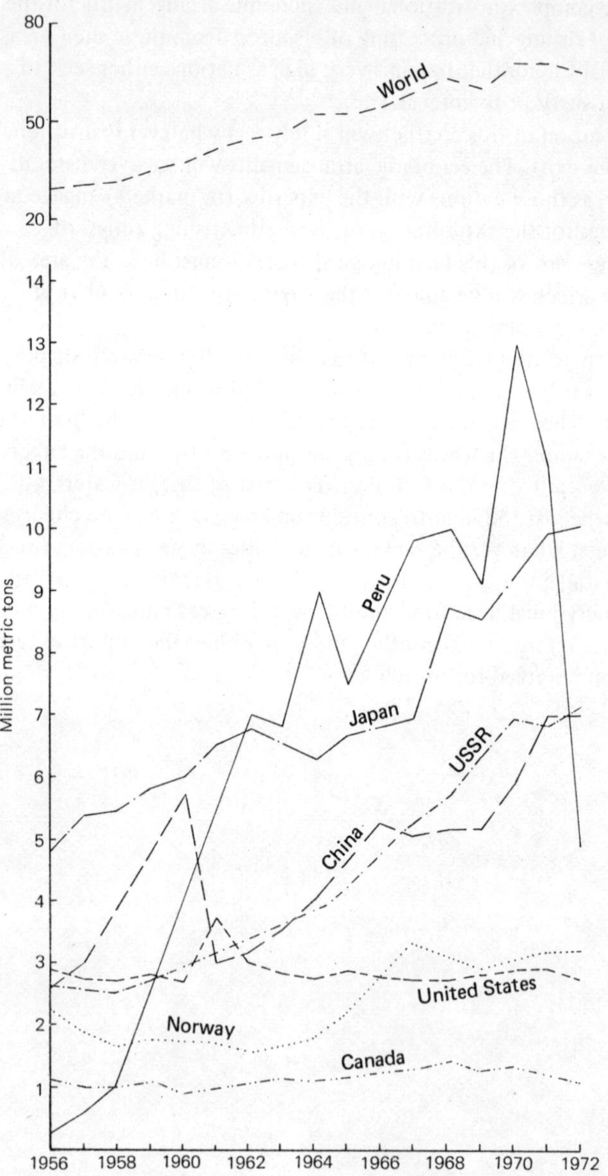

Source: FAO, United Nations

References

Braun, Lester R., (with Erik Eckholm): *By Bread Alone*, New York, Praeger Publishers, 1974.

Broadhead, G.C., 'International Trade-Tuna', IOFC/Dev/71/74 FAO, 1971.

Gullard, J.A., 'Distant Water Fisheries and Their Relation to Development and Management', in *Journal of the Fish. Res. Board of Can.*, Vol. 30, No. 12, Part 2, Dec. 1973.

International Commission for the Northwest Atlantic Fisheries (ICNAF), *Statistical Bulletins*, 1 – 23.

Joseph, J., 'Scientific Management of the World Stocks of Tunas, Fillfishes and Related Species', *Journal of Fish. Res. Board of Can.*, Vol. 30, No. 2, Part 2, Dec. 1973.

Kasahara, Hiroshi, 'Japanese Distant-Water Fisheries: a Review', *Fishery Bulletin*, US Dept. of Commerce, Vol. 70, No. 2, April 1972.

Lloyd's Registry of Shipping, 1974.

Moiseev, P.A., 'Development of Fisheries for Traditional Exploited Species', in *Journal of Fish. Res. Board of Can.*, Vol. 30, No. 12, Part 2, Dec. 1973.

Robinson, M.A. and A. Crispoldi, 'The Demand for Fish to 1980', FAO Fish. Circ. No. FIEF/C131, Rome 1971.

Sealey, T.S., 'Soviet Fisheries: A Review', *Underwater Journal*, August 1973.

Suda, A., 'Development of Fisheries for Nonconventional Species', in *Journal of Fish. Res. Board of Canada*, Vol. 30, No. 12, Part 2, Dec. 1973.

PART III: OCEAN POLITICS

7 THE DYNAMICS OF GLOBAL OCEAN POLITICS*

Edward Miles

The purposes of this chapter are four-fold: first, briefly to describe the existing global political system for the oceans, emphasizing the interrelationships of states with different capabilities facing different biogeophysical conditions; secondly, to identify the dynamics of global ocean politics; thirdly, to analyze the impacts of these dynamics on the negotiations at the Third United Nations Conference on the Law of the Sea (UNCLOS III); and fourthly, to make some projections about the future of global ocean politics.

1. The Global Political System for the Oceans

The range of participants covers the usual three categories of states, intergovernmental organizations (IGOs), and international non-governmental organizations (INGOs). The relative importance of each type of participant on ocean-related issues has already been analyzed.[1] The focus in this case will be on states since these are the most significant players in developing the law of the sea.

States differ both in the variety of ocean-related capabilities they command and in the biogeophysical conditions which they face.[2] These differences have always been economically and politically significant[3] and have assumed special importance in strategies pursued at UNCLOS III. In fact, the concentration of capabilities within very few advanced industrial countries is a major cause of one of the two basic confrontations at UNCLOS III; that between the 'haves' and the 'have-nots'.

For instance, with respect to fisheries, six countries (according to 1972 FAO statistics) account for about 58 per cent of the total world catch. Two of these, Peru and China, derive their large shares either

*The research upon which this chapter is based was done between 1973 and 1975 and was supported by a number of sponsors, none of whom should be held responsible for the views expressed herein. The author wishes to record his gratitude to the Carnegie Endowment for International Peace, the University Consortium for World Order Studies, Woods Hole Oceanographic Institution, The Institute for Marine Studies, University of Washington, and to the National Sea Grant Program (Grant No. 61-8246 UW). In addition, the author is grateful to Professor William T. Burke for detailed comments on an earlier draft.

primarily from a single coastal species (anchoveta in the case of Peru) or from combined inland and near-shore fisheries. Two countries, Japan and the USSR, fish on a global basis. The last two countries, Norway and the United States, derive most of their catch from coastal species but also engage in a certain amount of long-distance fishing.

By itself, the USSR accounts for 49 per cent of world fishing tonnage in vessels of 100 gross tons or larger and Japan accounts for an additional 13 per cent.[4] Spain, the United Kingdom, France, Norway, Poland and the Federal Republic of Germany are also significant long-distance fishing countries and it should be pointed out that several developing countries are making observable strides in this activity, e.g. the Republic of Korea, Taiwan, Ghana and Nigeria. In the category of merchant shipping, looking either at gross registered tonnage or dead weight tonnage, Liberia, Japan, the UK, Norway, the US, USSR, Greece and the Federal Republic of Germany are the major players but the position of Liberia is clearly an artefact of flags of convenience registration.[5] The major players with respect to marine scientific research are again very few; viz. the US, USSR, Japan, the UK, Canada, France and the Federal Republic of Germany.[6] The US and the USSR, however, are the only countries with global research programmes in the ocean. Finally, with respect to the exploitation of offshore oil and gas and hard minerals, the capabilities are again concentrated within very few countries, in particular the US, Norway, Canada, France, the UK, The Netherlands, USSR and Japan. In the relatively near future, however, these capabilities are likely to be diffused among members of the Organization of Petroleum Exporting Countries (OPEC), Indonesia and China.

The evidence shows that only in the field of fisheries are capabilities being increasingly diffused. In all other categories of marine activity, most of the costs are borne and most of the benefits derived within a very small group of countries comprising the US, USSR, Japan, the UK, France, Canada and the Federal Republic of Germany. The concentration of capabilities became politically significant globally because the Maltese initiative of 1967 was coincident with one structural change taking place within the United Nations and the link between the two was activated by four sets of participants seeking to derive certain benefits.

The structural change was the decline in the intensity of the East/West confrontation and the emergence of a superpower coalition, first on issues of outer space regulation and then on the issue of arms control for the deep seabed. The specific objectives which were put into the crucible at this time (1966–70) were: (i) the interest of the superpower coalition to convene a limited conference on the law of the sea to resolve issues of the territorial sea and passage through straits used for international navigation left unresolved by the 1958 and 1960 Geneva Conferences on the Law of the Sea; (ii) the interest of Ambassador Arvid Pardo and others in using the issue of the seabed beyond national jurisdiction to bring about major innovations in the structure, authority and performance of international organizations and therefore in official approaches to world order; (iii) the aims of certain Latin American states to legitimize their claims to a 200-mile territorial sea; and (iv) the awakening of several imaginative individuals within the African Group who saw in this issue the potential of making drastic changes in the distribution of some of the world's wealth.

The North/South confrontation is, however, not the only major dimension of conflict at UNCLOS III. The other global issue is a fight between coastal states, especially those which are considered 'geographically advantaged' in the length of their coastline, size of continental margin, and distribution of living resources off their coasts, and landlocked and other states which are considered 'geographically disadvantaged'. It is to this aspect of the political system that we now turn.

2. Biogeophysical Marine Attributes of States

Recently, several attempts have been made to calculate the extent to which states would gain or lose if some of the major proposals being negotiated at UNCLOS III were to be included in a final treaty. These biogeophysical marine attributes of states have become politically significant primarily because those major proposals are based largely, and even solely, on spatial criteria. For instance, Njenga calculates, on the basis of criteria emphasizing length of coastline provided by the delegation of The Netherlands, that using the measure of a 200-mile economic zone, 68 coastal states are 'disadvantaged' in the sense that they would get less than the global average; 29 landlocked states are also 'disadvantaged'; 34 states are 'advantaged' in the sense that they get more than the global average and in some cases very much more; and 15 states are neither 'advantaged' nor 'disadvantaged'.[7]

In another approach based on the relationship of a 200-mile economic zone to the width of the continental margin (i.e. the continental shelf, slope and rise), Kanenas estimates that 20 states would possess margins wider than 200 miles, 52 states would have margins approximately the same as 200 miles while 33 would have margins less than 200 miles.[8] In yet another approach based on the relationship of a 200-mile economic zone to the depth criterion of the 200-metre isobath used in the 1958 convention on the Continental Shelf, Alexander calculates that 50 landlocked and shelf-locked[9] states would gain between 20,000 and 200,000 square nautical miles; and 24 states would gain more than 200,000 square nautical miles.[10]

However, if the outer edge of the continental margin were used as a criterion instead of the 200-mile economic zone this would have no impact on the 50 landlocked and shelf-locked states which would gain nothing. But now 49 states would gain up to 20,000 square nautical miles in seabed area; 36 would gain up to 200,000 square nautical miles; and 13 would gain more than 200,000.[11] If the continental margin criterion were used, the big winners would be: Australia, New Zealand, Norway, Indonesia, Canada, USSR, USA, Japan, Argentina and Mexico in that order. But if the 200-mile criterion were used the rank order would change to: USA, Australia, New Zealand, Japan, USSR, Indonesia, Mexico, Brazil, Chile and Norway.[12] Obviously, the biggest difference would be felt by Brazil and Chile, states which do not have wide continental margins.

A logical next question is: What is the relationship between either limit and the actual distribution of living and non-living resources? For non-living resources, more than 90 per cent of the world's proved offshore hydrocarbon reserves are situated within 40 nautical miles of states.[13] While it is likely that some petroleum deposits exist at great depths at the edge of continental margins, there is considerable uncertainty surrounding the potential significance of such deposits. In any event, with present technology the costs of exploitation increase dramatically as a function of increasing depth and there is no possibility of exploiting such deposits in the near future, even if they exist. On the other hand, while there are certainly deposits of manganese nodules within 200 miles of coastal states, the most promising known deposits discovered to date exist well beyond any state's potential economic zone.[14]

Perhaps the greatest impact of a 200-mile economic zone will be on the living resources of the world ocean, since all the world's demersal species and most of the commercially significant pelagic species will either be totally or occasionally encompassed within such zones. But for most countries, it is never a simple matter to determine what their position should be relative to any major proposal before the conference. The rest of this chapter will therefore focus on the determinants of state positions and negotiating behaviour at the global level.

3. The Dynamics of Global Ocean Politics

Political behaviour in different systems, and at different levels within systems, is usually very complex, but if the system can be demarcated from its links with others it is often possible to observe a clearly defined substructure or pattern of behaviour which effectively cuts through much of the complexity without sacrificing too much of the richness of detail. In the case of global ocean politics, the evidence suggests that the substructure consists of five types of conditions:

(i) Differences in capabilities of ocean use and therefore in the distribution of income and other values generated by such use.
(ii) Differences in biogeophysical conditions of states.
(iii) Differences in national objectives *vis-à-vis* ocean use.
(iv) The extent to which the substantive issues are 'pure', i.e. pertain only to the activities of ocean use, or 'contaminated', i.e. penetrated by external, non-ocean-related issues.[15]
(v) The organizational demands of conducting negotiations in institutionalized settings at the global level.

By themselves these elements do not usually result in spontaneous combustion. A catalyst is required. This has most often been provided by changes in people's expectations about ocean exploitation and the ways in which these changes affect the first three elements. The catalyst starts the process but does not control it, since the interaction of the five conditions itself generates outcomes and longer-term effects that may be quite different from what was originally intended. In that sense, the system is a Pandora's Box. Let us proceed to illustrate the theoretical point with examples from UNCLOS III and the preparatory phase which led up to it.

4. The Dynamics of Global Ocean Politics in Operation UNCLOS III

The immediate catalyst for UNCLOS III lies in Pardo's perceptions of major developments in the exploitation of the ocean floor beyond limits of national jurisdiction. Perhaps in part because he overestimated both the rate at which such exploitation would be possible and the extent of income to be generated by it, the issue was penetrated by the North–South confrontation which was increasing in the General Assembly at that time. The reason for such linkage is obvious. Only a few countries dominate the exploitation of the oceans and benefit from it. Those same countries are the ones seen to be on the verge of making major gains with resources which, some claim, should be regarded as *res communis* (belonging to all) rather than *res nullius* (belonging to none).

Phrased in this way the oceans issue becomes linked not only generally with the North–South dimension but specifically with a growing fight over the concentration of capabilities for marine scientific research taking place within the Intergovernmental Oceanographic Commission (IOC) of UNESCO. The specific agents making this link were several Latin American countries, among them Brazil and Argentina, seeking in the General Assembly legitimation of the 200-mile territorial sea for the one and coastal state ownership of the entire continental margin for the other.

Several developing countries underscored the necessity of the claim for coastal state control of scientific research in waters adjacent to the territorial sea. Resenting what they saw as an incipient trend by the superpowers to break away from the General Assembly, where the majority was becoming increasingly independent, to smaller, more easily handled bodies like the 18-nation Disarmament Committee, denunciations of the IOC as a rich man's club of restricted membership and concern began to grow.[16]

This movement later received unexpected support from some advanced industrial countries like Australia and Canada which sought to impose tighter controls over exploration. In doing so they foreshadowed the very different approach they would take at UNCLOS III compared with their positions at the conferences of 1958 and 1960. The foci of Australian concern were Soviet and Japanese investigations in the Indian Ocean, while the Canadian Government was more concerned about US and Soviet activity in the Arctic. These attempts to control scientific research seemed to strike a responsive chord in the minds of many delegations, most of whom wanted more information on who was exploring where, for what, with what results. As the debate developed, the concentration of capabilities fed the distrust of those who did not possess them and emphasized the desirability of controlling information gained from scientific research and, as a further safeguard, of vesting property rights over marine living and non-living resources in the coastal state.

However, the push to extend coastal state jurisdiction inevitably activated the element of biogeophysical attributes since these, to a considerable extent, would determine winners and losers. The only hope of those who already were losers by an accident of nature would be in the skill with which they could use the rules of the game governing large intergovernmental conferences. This essentially meant the size of the coalition they could create, given the two-thirds majority rule for decision.

It took about three-and-a-half to four years (1968–72) for this coalition, called the Landlocked and Geographically Disadvantaged Group, to be built, since there were considerable difficulties to be overcome. In particular, since the membership had to be drawn from all regions of the world, this implied an assault on the membership of some strong regional groups (Africa) as well as some less cohesive ones (Asia and Western Europe). Later also, the Disadvantaged Group had to compete with the supercoalition of the Conference, the Group of 77, which aggregated the interests and demands of all the 'have nots'.

The state which mobilized the Disadvantaged Group coalition was Austria, the representatives of which perceived that in the world at large there were more than 50 potential members of such a coalition, though no more than 25 were members of the UN at the time. This meant that the coalition would be at its greatest strength in a Plenipotentiary Conference and not in the UN Seabed Committee where it amounted to no more than 15 or 16 countries. The universe of potential allies was defined to include: (i) landlocked states; (ii) states with only short coastlines; (iii) states bordering marginal seas; and (iv) states with very narrow shelves or no continental shelf at all.[17]

As a group this coalition had only two basic strategies to play: (a) to seek at all times to control a blocking third of votes; and (b) to press at all times for the establishment of strong international control over the exploitation of marine resources and the distribution of income. This is expressed in phrases like the 'common heritage of mankind' and 'benefits for all regardless of geographical location'. On some issues the coalition could actually increase its size, since the interest of the Group relative to increasing the scope of international organizations occasionally coincides with the interests of the superpowers, Japan and the EEC, seeking to restrict the extension of coastal state authority.

But let us return to the penetration of the oceans issue by the global North–South confrontation then developing in 1967–8. At that time the Group of 77 was not yet a cohesive coalition in the Seabed Committee. In particular, the Afro-Asian Groups looked at the issues differently from the Latin American Group. The focus in the Afro-Asian Groups appeared to be on the geomorphological configurations of the various countries and this emphasized a diversity of interests. Very few of the African countries, for instance, have significant continental shelves and this accounted for the early emphasis on a strong international régime. The response of the Latin American Group was to push for the legitimacy of regional and subregional solutions on the assumption that it would be easier to sell their 200-mile position if they catered to the different sets of special interests around the world.

The Latin American Group also urged a number of Afro-Asian countries to extend exclusive jurisdiction unilaterally. Table 1 shows that there was a definite trend toward such unilateral extensions by 1972 but it is difficult to attribute all of this to the Latin Americans.

In the judgement of some delegates, some extensions were more a reaction to the uncertainties surrounding negotiations on the List of Subjects and Issues in 1971. From this point of view these extensions were attempts to pre-empt a conference solution. Whatever the cause, the fact is that the change in state attitudes towards unilateral extensions of jurisdiction over the ocean and its resources received a major boost between 1968 and 1972 in the context of bargaining within the Seabed Committee. This development was facilitated by a crucial compromise fostered by Kenya within the African Group and Venezuela within the Latin American Group. The result of that compromise was the emergence of the Group of 77 as a cohesive unit declaring allegiance to the concept of the economic zone or patrimonial sea. The effect of this was to displace the problem of the disposition of the seabed beyond national jurisdiction as the major issue of UNCLOS III.

Table 1: The Trend toward Unilateral Extensions of Jurisdiction over the Ocean, 1968–72

	Miles							
	Territorial sea limits					Exclusive fishing zones/ fishery conservation zones		
Year	3	6	12	200	Other 3	12	200	Other 12
1968	30	16	31	5	8	30	5	4
1972	29	12	52	10	11	39	6	12

Sources: FAO, *Limits and Status of the Territorial Sea, Exclusive Fishing Zones, Fishery Conservation Zones, and the Continental Shelf,* FAO Fisheries Technical Paper No. 79, FID/T79, (Rome), FAO, 1968; Dept. of State, Bureau of Intelligence and Research, the Geographer, International Boundary Study, Series A, Limits in the Seas, *National Claims to Maritime Jurisdictions,* No. 36, 3 January 1972.

Before proceeding with a detailed analysis of the negotiations on the economic zone, let us pause to summarize the argument about the dynamics of global ocean politics and how they have worked within the context of UNCLOS III. It is instructive to do so in stages since the process feeds on itself and changes thereby over time as depicted by Figure 1.

There are twelve major variables in this process though several of them are made up of many components. In the beginning there are three major players, if the US and USSR, given their shared respective claims, are counted as one. However, Pardo's initiative activates a fourth, the African Group. The locus of activity is the UN General Assembly, a global forum itself experiencing a sharp increase in conflict along the North/South dimension. This activates and intensifies concern over differences in marine capabilities and attributes. The crucial question is who gets what from the ocean and how can the skewed distribution of benefits be changed.

Stages I and II can therefore be regarded as the incubation period of this process. The salience of the issues increases rapidly, more countries become aware and join the Seabed Committee (from 35 in 1968 to 91 in 1971). Information is diffused but unevenly distributed among the delegations. Expertise is built up among a number of delegations from Africa and Asia who had never before been involved with these questions. The primary substantive focus is on the disposition of the seabed beyond the limits of national jurisdiction. During 1970 the process begins to change. Groups are mobilized, strategies are more explicitly followed, and the substantive focus begins to expand to include a reappraisal of the entire Law of the Sea.

Stage III is activated when the General Assembly decides to convene a Third United Nations Conference on the Law of the Sea and to make the Seabed Committee into a Preparatory Committee for UNCLOS III. The Seabed Committee in turn decides to reopen the entire law of the sea to negotiation against the wishes of the major maritime countries. The scope of the conference, as defined by the List of Subjects and Issues, is shown in Table 2. The shape of the process is determined by the interaction of national objectives with the dynamics of conference diplomacy: that is, with the special concerns of building and maintaining coalitions, seeking majorities as defined by the Rules of Procedure. This variable of 'national' objectives warrants further explanation.

Fig. 1: An Illustration of the Dynamics of Global Ocean Politics in Operation at UNCLOS III

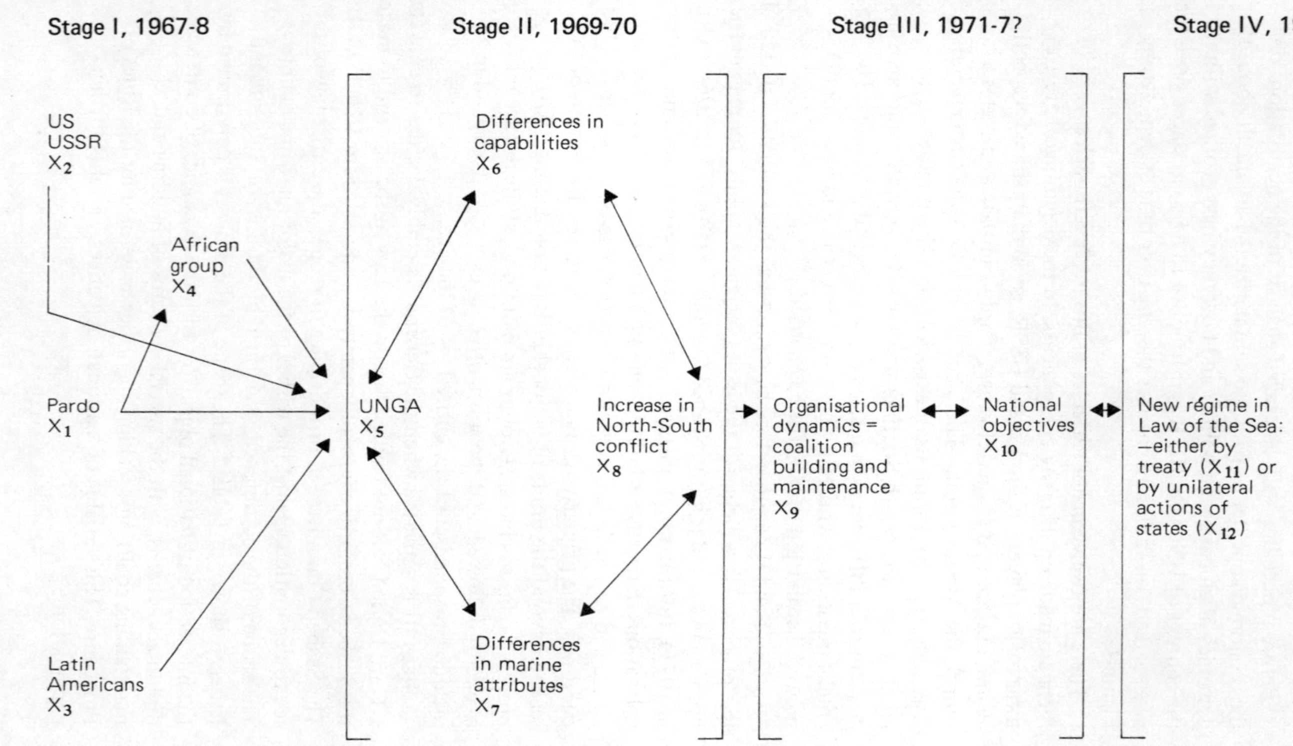

Table 2: Condensed List of Subjects and Issues at UNCLOS III

I. The international seabed area

- A. Definition, nature and characteristics of.
- B. Machinery: structures, functions, powers.
- C. Economic implications of seabed exploitation.
- D. Equitable sharing of benefits.

II. Jurisdictional issues

- A. Definition and limits of the territorial sea.
- B. Innocent passage.
- C. Straits used for international navigation.
- D. Continental shelf limits.
- E. Exclusive economic zone: definition, limits; nature of coastal state jurisdiction over living and non-living resources; control over marine pollution and scientific research; freedom of navigation and overflight; management and conservation of anadromous and highly migratory species; preferential rights; full utilization; settlement of disputes.
- F. Rights and interests of landlocked states.
- G. Rights and interests of shelf-locked states and states with narrow continental shelves and/or short coastlines.
- H. Régime of archipelagoes.
- I. Régime of islands.

III. Preservation of the marine environment, control of marine pollution, scientific research and transfer of technology

- A. Preservation of the marine environment, general obligations.
- B. Control over marine pollution.
- C. Scientific research.
- D. Transfer of technology.

Source: United Nations, *Report of the Committee on the Peaceful Uses of the Seabed and the Ocean Floor Beyond the Limits of National Jurisdiction*, New York, United Nations, 1973, 2:24–38.

It is important to remember that states, and the delegations which represent them, are rarely if ever monolithic.[18] Politically they are coalitions and the degree of internal cohesion is usually a variable rather than a constant. Country positions (the so-called 'national interest') are generally the result of compromise among government agencies, each with its own set of interests and constituents varying in their domain of influence. In some cases, country positions have also been determined by single individuals or very small groups. The point is that within the context of UNCLOS III, each delegation must try to reconcile the interests of different and often conflicting national uses and users of the ocean. (This problem is, of course, not unique to the oceans.) For some delegations this is not necessarily a difficult undertaking while for others it can be very difficult indeed. Consequently, where the substance of negotiations is a very complex package, the political process consists of almost simultaneous sets of negotiations between countries, groups of countries, and within country delegations. This adds to the complexity, to the time it takes to find solutions, and to the difficulty of arriving at acceptable compromises.

Stage IV overlaps with Stage III since it is an outcome of the growing frustration many coastal states feel with the entire process of UNCLOS III and the length of time it takes to get results. A growing number of delegations now speak privately about the unsatisfactory nature of agreement on available terms relative to the benefits to be had from acting unilaterally. The uncertainty has increased in 1975 given moves by several countries, the US in particular, to act unilaterally in extending a 200-mile economic zone around their coasts. It is therefore very much in question whether the new régime of the oceans will arrive by way of a treaty or not.

Let us now look in some detail at the dynamics of global ocean politics as they can be observed in operation in the negotiations on the issue of the economic zone.

5. The Economic Zone

In their detailed analysis of the concept of the economic zone, Douglas Johnston and Edgar Gold correctly trace its origins to the claims and practices of several Latin American countries reacting to the US Declaration on the Continental Shelf made by President Truman in 1945.[19] Originally (1971–2), the concept was intended as a mechanism which allowed the coastal state to exercise exclusive jurisdiction over living and non-living resources without enlarging the scope of such jurisdiction to the extent that the area claimed became a territorial sea. The outer limit of 200 miles was simply taken from the Latin American claims pushed by Peru and Ecuador at first and later by others. This limit is entirely arbitrary and has no functional relationship to the medium in which the asserted jurisdiction is to be exercised.

The crucial questions posed in the ensuing debate on the economic zone are: what is the extent of coastal state control over the conservation and allocation of living resources in the area claimed, especially as it relates to the interests of states historically fishing in that area? What is the outer limit of the continental shelf over which the coastal state exercises exclusive jurisdiction? What is the nature and extent of coastal state control over scientific research and activity generative of marine pollution in the area claimed? What is the relationship between coastal state control and the traditional 'freedoms' of the law of the sea, such as navigation, overflight and the laying of submarine pipelines and cables? And how are the residual rights in the area to be characterized?

The reason for the emergence of this concept lies in the fact that an unqualified territorial sea of 200 miles did not effectively aggregate the interests of more than a few states within the diverse grouping of 'have-not' countries, members of the Group of 77. Moreover, as indicated previously, the major issue at the beginning of this round of negotiations on the law of the sea was the disposition of the seabed beyond national jurisdiction. Dominated by Arvid Pardo, the debate centred on a proposal for a very strong international organization to be created in which such rights would be vested. At first, the Afro-Asian Groups went along with this formulation both because they lacked the capabilities to exploit the medium and because their delegations generally had little expertise in ocean management and the law of the sea.

As the debate developed over time, however, the focus shifted under active prodding from the 'territorialist'-inclined Latin Americans, from the need for a strong international organization to control all seabed resources beyond relatively narrow belts of coastal state control to one of extending coastal state control over extensive portions of the oceans. This was seen to be an alternative approach which gave developing countries much better opportunities for deriving revenue from ocean use. But, given variations in biogeophysical marine attributes, a growing number of countries feared that only some developing countries would benefit.

This history of the negotiations on this issue is therefore characterized by: (i) a concerted, well-organized strategy utilized by the Territorialist Group led by Peru and Brazil to legitimize their claims for a 200-mile territorial sea or, failing that, to extend the scope of coastal state control in the economic zone to the point where the zone becomes the functional equivalent of a territorial sea; (ii) a search among the Africans, some Asians, and the more 'moderate' Latin Americans led by Venezuela and Mexico to accommodate the conflicting interests of regional groups and thereby produce a 'package' solution which the Group of 77 could accept as a whole. In this they are strongly supported by a coalition of developed countries, particularly by Canada, Australia, Iceland, New Zealand and Norway;

(iii) the insistence by some developing countries like Jamaica and Trinidad-Tobago that since the natural marine endowments of countries in a region varied, they could not accept such a zone unless it were accompanied by clear guarantees of access to the living resources within neighbouring zones for geographically disadvantaged developing countries within that region; (iv) opposition to the concept of coastal state sovereignty over resources, control of scientific research and ship-generated pollution by the major maritime countries; and (v) attempts by the landlocked and geographically disadvantaged group to go beyond guarantees of access to the sea and include access to the living and non-living resources of neighbouring coastal states. In the development of this debate since 1971 one can observe in striking fashion the interaction of all the dynamics of global ocean politics.

6. The Claims and Strategy of the Territorialist Group

The Territorialist Group presently consists of seven Latin American countries: Brazil, Ecuador, El Salvador, Nicaragua, Panama, Peru and Uruguay; and three African countries: Dahomey, Guinea and Somalia. One Latin American country, Argentina, has declared a 200-mile territorial sea but has not been an active member of this group, while one African country, Sierra Leone, has declared a 200-mile territorial sea but has chosen to support the position of the African Group on the economic zone. The claims of this group are the most extensive and, among the challengers of traditional law of the sea, have the longest history. Four specific proposals were tabled in the Seabed Committee in 1973, and one was tabled at the Caracas session of UNCLOS III in 1974.[20]

By adopting such a position, these countries have all chosen to resolve the five questions enunciated above completely in favour of the coastal state. Since the zone is given the status of a territorial sea, coastal state sovereignty is exercised over all resources and over all activities. The approach to the problem of residual rights in the extended zone as they affect navigation has been explicitly treated by both Brazil and Peru. In fact, two régimes affecting navigation within the 200-mile zone have been proposed. The first would apply the rule of innocent passage within a relatively narrow belt (perhaps corresponding to the traditional territorial sea) adjacent to the coast while the second would create a rule of 'free transit' between the outer edge of this belt and 200 miles. The traditional concept of freedom of navigation would apply only beyond 200 miles.[21] The concept of 'free transit' is not intended to proscribe all activities unconnected with navigation and not already specifically reserved to the coastal state.

Why have these particular countries chosen this particular approach? Biogeophysical marine attributes provide only a partial answer. For instance, with respect to areal gains in the water columns, and therefore with living resources, El Salvador and Panama would make small gains on the west coast of South America. Peru would be the biggest winner but Ecuador would also gain considerably. On the east coast of South America, Brazil and Uruguay would also gain.

On the west coast of Africa, Guinea and Sierra Leone would make gains relative to foreigners fishing in that area but there will be problems with neighbouring states given the migratory pattern of the resources. Dahomey would gain very little since they have a very short coastline. On the east coast, Somalia would make no significant gains in fisheries but could conceivably attempt to regulate some of the Suez Canal tanker traffic.[22]

With respect to the continental shelf, only Ecuador and Costa Rica would make significant gains on the west coast of Central and South America, otherwise the shelf is uniformly narrow. On the east coast, Brazil, Uruguay and Argentina would make significant gains but Argentina's would be the biggest of all. Nicaragua would be shelf-locked by Colombia. In Africa Guinea is shelf-locked by Portuguese Guinea and Sierra Leone, Dahomey is shelf-locked by Togo and Nigeria. Sierra Leone would gain somewhat and Somalia would make significant areal gains with a narrow shelf but a wide continental rise.[23]

To sum up, within the Territorialist Group, substantive gains would be made either in living resources or seabed area by Peru, Ecuador, Brazil, Uruguay, Argentina, Sierra Leone and Somalia. But this is not enough to explain their choice of this position since the same gains could be made under several of the proposals on the Economic Zone currently before the Conference. For Dahomey this position makes no sense whatever, while for Guinea it seems that the point being made is an ideological one against the major maritime, and primarily Western, countries. In the case of Somalia, its position may also be determined in part by its conflicts with Ethiopia and Kenya. For Peru, Brazil, Ecuador and Uruguay the point may be in the tactics of negotiation.

When the concept of the economic zone/patrimonial sea was first broached in 1971 by Venezuela and in 1972 by the African Group led by Kenya, the emphasis was on the control of resources. The Territorialists, however, consistently sought to stall the preparatory proceedings, to increase frustration and thereby to feed the fires of unilateral action. In doing so, their hold on the Latin American Group was firm. Even those Latin American countries which did not want a 200-mile territorial sea were unwilling to break ranks between 1973 and 1975 and consistently sought formulae that Brazil and Peru could accept.

This had two effects. First, it delayed movement in the conference as a whole leading in 1973 and 1974 to public accusations addressed to Peru by the Soviets and others of stalling. In fact, privately in the corridors, non-Latin members of the Group of 77 expressed a great deal of annoyance with Peru and Brazil for stalling but never did so publicly. Secondly, the major role played by Peru and Brazil in the Group of 77 helped to facilitate the transformation of the economic zone concept into the functional equivalent of a territorial sea via extensions of coastal state control on scientific research and pollution. This development is itself coincidentally related to a general radicalization of certain African members of the Group of 77, in particular Algeria, Tanzania and Mauritania. The focus of their ideological attack was Committee I on the seabed régime but it spilled over to Committee II, on the economic zone, and III on scientific research and pollution. It should be mentioned here that the original catalyst for the Group of 77 on the pollution issue was Canada, pursuing some of its own national objectives and the link with the Group appeared to have been made primarily via the Kenyan delegation who took the lead on this issue as on so many others, within the Group. We will deal with the problem of pollution in more detail in the next section.

7. The Structure, Development and Internal Strains of the Coalition Supporting the Concept of the Economic Zone/Patrimonial Sea

This coalition is an extremely heterogeneous grouping since its membership is drawn from five different subgroups within UNCLOS III. These are: (i) primarily the coastal state segment of the African Group, even though the entire Group professes allegiance to the concept via the OAU declaration of 1972;[24] (ii) the 'moderate' Latin Americans led by Venezuela, Mexico and Colombia rallying around the patrimonial sea concept as defined by the Declaration of Santo Domingo of 1972;[25] (iii) several coastal states from the Asian Group but in particular India and Sri Lanka; (iv) a coalition of industrially advanced coastal states seeking sovereignty over resources in a zone adjacent to the territorial sea, consisting of Canada, Iceland, Norway, Australia and New Zealand; and (v) the Archipelagic Group, consisting of Indonesia, the Philippines, Fiji and Mauritius.

This coalition has sought on three occasions in 1973, 1974 and 1975 to pre-empt the conference by resolving internal difficulties and co-opting the membership of the Group of 77 coalition, thereby automatically controlling a two-thirds majority. Each time it has failed primarily as a result of differences in perceived interests determined by differences in capabilities and biogeophysical marine attributes. For instance, among developing countries there are at least three distinct groupings based on level of marine-related capabilities. There are those countries, like Argentina, Brazil and Mexico which possess significant potential in all areas of marine activities. There are others, like Peru, Nigeria, Ghana, Indonesia, Thailand, Republic of Korea *et al.*, which possess significant potential in one or more areas but not in all. And, finally, there are all the others which possess no significant potential. These include all the landlocked countries, some of the shelf-locked countries, and some coastal states like Somalia and Mauritania.

The strongest supporters of this coalition are (i) coastal states possessing either significant potential or existing capabilities and significant marine resources off their coasts; (ii) coastal states with significant resources but as yet no significant capabilities; and (iii) a few countries possessing neither significant resources nor capabilities but wishing to expand and maintain the integrity and influence of the Group of 77 coalition, to score some ideological points in the North/South confrontation and to bring about radical changes in the distribution of income from ocean-related activities. The predominant members of this group are Kenya, Tanzania and Algeria, the representatives of which are effective leaders of the African Group and the Group of 77.

The outlines of the 'package solution' sought by this group were very clear even before the end of the preparatory sessions in August 1973.[26] The approach called for a territorial sea of 12 miles and an economic zone/patrimonial sea of up to 200 miles in which the coastal state would exercise sovereignty over *all* living and non-living resources and would control scientific research and ship-generated pollution. There are about 20 countries adhering unreservedly to this position. An additional 34–40 countries support some variant of this position but seek protection for a variety of special interests.

For instance, at the Caracas Session in 1974 most members of the coalition supported the idea of coastal state sovereignty over living resources. However, most countries with advanced capabilities and considerable experience in fisheries management favoured writing in to the Treaty obligations for full utilization of the living resources within the economic zone. This would require the coastal state to negotiate with foreign fishermen for that portion of the resource which the coastal state would be unable to catch and use. This was strongly opposed by developing countries, the representatives of which wanted no derogation on the authority of the coastal state to decide. Yet some developing countries like Ghana, Nigeria, Ivory Coast, Jamaica, Barbados and Trinidad-Tobago are developing distant-water fishing capabilities as a result of their inability to satisfy domestic demand solely from the resources available off their coasts. These countries sought protection by another route. They asked for guarantees of equal access to living resources within a region by developing countries belonging to that region.[27]

This latter demand has always been more potent within the African Group than within either the Latin American or Asian Groups. There are two reasons for this. There are 13 landlocked countries among the 42 members of the African Group and some concessions have to be made to them in order to prevent open revolt. In addition, only in the West African region between Mauritania and Angola encompassing the Gulf of Guinea are fisheries a significant component in domestic protein consumption. The cost of this concession is therefore less for the Africans than for either the Asians or Latin Americans where there are fewer landlocked countries and where fisheries represent a significant proportion of domestic protein intake. Consequently, the proposal on the patrimonial sea (A/AC.138/SC.II/L.21) contains no such guarantees of access while these guarantees have always been a part of African proposals on the economic zone. The African impact was also felt on the only compromise 'package solution' to be presented to the conference at the Caracas Session (A/CONF.62/L.4).

Another serious strain within the coalition concerns the definition of the outer limit of the continental shelf. Most of the core supporters of the economic zone claim coastal state sovereignty over the entire continental margin. The African Group, however, strongly opposes this and recommends instead that the outer limit of the shelf be the outer limit of the economic zone (i.e. 200 miles). There seem to be again two reasons for this. First, the problem of the landlocked described above leads to an insistence on the Group's part that some resources be left for disposition on a 'common heritage' basis. But, secondly, this is once more a relatively cheap solution for the Group since very few African countries possess wide shelves. In fact, in Africa only the Republic of South Africa would be a big winner if the margin were defined as the outer limit.

The question of residual rights in the economic zone is a major contentious issue in the conference as a whole but the Africans (except for Kenya and Tanzania) have generally been less adamant on this than some of the Latin Americans. In addition, though all groups appear to be united on the demands for coastal state control of scientific research and ship-generated pollution within the economic zone, there are variations in the scope of control perceived as desirable.

For example, the Group of 77, led by Kenya, India and Yugoslavia on this issue, has consistently proposed all-encompassing coastal state control of scientific research, on occasion even to the point of holding publication rights.[28] But the Group experiences erosion on two fronts. On the one hand 'geographically disadvantaged' European countries, like the Federal Republic of Germany and The Netherlands, have succeeded in garnering the support of some African landlocked countries plus that of some developing shelf-locked countries like Singapore and have jointly co-sponsored some lenient draft articles on scientific research.[29] In explaining this breakaway at the Caracas Session Singapore and the African landlocked claimed that the Group of 77 had consistently neglected their interests on this issue.[30]

On the other hand, a group of developing countries, some of which have considerable potential in scientific research, wished to avoid too restrictive a régime being created. There emerged in Caracas, therefore, an informal coalition between countries like Mexico, Venezuela and Colombia, plus Spain and Ireland. These delegations sought to find some middle way between the obligations approach of the US and others and the very restrictive approach of the Group of 77.[31] This coalition bore fruit at the Geneva Session in 1975 when Colombia, El Salvador, Mexico and Nigeria introduced an alternative approach to the Group of 77 position.[32] For tactical reasons neither Spain nor Ireland was asked to co-sponsor these draft articles and this is the approach which found its way into the Informal Single Negotiating Text presented by the Chairman of Committee III.[33] As such it will be the basis of all future negotiation.

With respect to ship-generated pollution, the issue began as a confrontation between Canada, arguing for coastal state standard-setting authority, and the US and the UK arguing against. Early in the summer session of the Seabed Committee in 1973, the US informed Sub-Committee III about US proposals to make the Intergovernmental Maritime Consultative Committee (IMCO) the lead international agency on this problem with sole authority to set standards and thereby to affect ship construction. These proposals were to be made at the IMCO Conference planned for October 1973. The Canadian delegation in reply made this into a major issue of the meeting not only on the merits of the case but also on the symbolic issue of US attempts to pre-empt a solution of this problem at UNCLOS III.

The political behaviour generated by this conflict was most instructive. Over the course of summer 1973, the Canadian delegation activated a coalition between Canada, Kenya and UNEP. For Kenya, this appeared to be both a symbolic issue affecting the degree of coastal state authority to be exercised in the economic zone and one in which Africa had substantive interests. These interests were graphically demonstrated in maps showing major routes of tanker traffic from the Persian/Arabian Gulf around the Cape of Good Hope to Western Europe during the period in which the Suez Canal was closed (i.e. after 1967). The third member of that coalition, UNEP, was at the time engaged in a major jurisdictional fight with FAO and appeared to see this proposal by the US as creating the potential for future erosion of programme support for UNEP. The tactics adopted were threefold: (i) press for coastal control over standard-setting, at least on an equal basis in special circumstances with an international organization; (ii) propose that such authority be shared with UNEP and not with IMCO; and (iii) strongly urge the Group of 77 to attend the IMCO conference in October to vote against the US proposals.

As events unfolded in the Seabed Committee, at the IMCO Conference, and at the Caracas Session of UNCLOS III, it appeared that there were disagreements within the Canadian Government on desirable policy as well as within the Group of 77. At the Seabed Committee debate the US delegation expressed surprise at the Canadian position saying none of these reservations had been expressed by the Canadian IMCO delegation who had supported the proposed changes in IMCO structure and programme. The Canadian delegate angrily denied this but the statement was accurate. It remained accurate at the IMCO meeting in October also.

The fact is that the Canadian UNCLOS delegation was caught between the special circumstances of the Arctic Ocean, the symbolic politics flowing from the Canadian Arctic Waters Pollution Act of 1970 and the competing interests of the Canadian shipping industry which opposed giving coastal states the authority to set standards regulating ship construction. Moreover, the coalition between Canada, Kenya and UNEP had no impact beyond the UNCLOS arena and specifically did not affect acceptance of US proposals at the IMCO Conference in

October 1973. Finally, at the Caracas Session it also became clear that Norway and Liberia, among others, were less than enthusiastic about the original Canadian position and Norway proposed a compromise which Canada later accepted. This provided for concurrent jurisdiction in special circumstances between coastal states and appropriate international organizations but the exercise of coastal state authority would not extend to ship construction.[34]

Given the internal conflicts described above, this coalition was unable to resolve its differences either at Caracas or at Geneva.[35] This has had a fateful impact on the conference as a whole since no group has yet been able to construct a two-thirds majority on the economic zone, perhaps the most crucial issue of the conference.

8. The Coalition of the Landlocked and Geographically Disadvantaged States and the Economic Zone/Patrimonial Sea

The position of the landlocked and GDS coalition, as it is called, was developed in a series of working papers and draft articles presented in 1973 and 1974.[36] The first demands made in 1973 (A/AC.138/SC.II/L.39) relative to the economic zone sought only guarantees for equal access to the living resources of neighbouring coastal states. In addition, developed coastal states establishing a zone were to contribute a certain portion of the revenues derived to the international authority for equitable distribution among 'disadvantaged' countries. A similar procedure was to be applicable to all coastal states exploiting non-living resources within the zone.

During the summer session in 1972, the delegation of Zambia made its first appearance. The Austrian delegation, still busily engaged in mobilizing the Disadvantaged coalition, assiduously courted the Zambian delegate, explained the thinking of the Group on the major issues and convinced him of the rights of landlocked states in the oceans. This strategy bore fruit late in the summer when Zambia and Uganda jointly submitted a paper on the economic zone (L.41). The approach adopted called for the establishment of regional economic zones, the exploitation of fisheries by all states within the region, and the exploitation of non-living resources by 'relevant regional or subregional authorities'.

This paper was proposed at the same time that the African Group was preparing draft articles implementing the OAU Declaration. It represented, therefore, the first effective penetration of the African coalition by the Austrians on behalf of the Disadvantaged Group. Privately the Africans were furious, especially since the Zambian delegate refused to withdraw the proposal. The tactic then employed by the African Group was to utilize the Council of Ministers of the OAU, the source of the Declaration, to put pressure on Zambia and Uganda to withdraw the proposal. This tactic was successful, perhaps because it came at a time when Zambia faced increased conflict with Rhodesia which had cut off the traditional Zambian outlet to the sea. President Kaunda was then receiving the full support of his colleagues in the OAU and could not therefore ignore the request.

The position of the Disadvantaged Group was fully worked out during the Caracas Session in UNCLOS III and it was then that Singapore emerged as a major leader of the Group along with Austria. Tactically, of course, this improved the Group's ability to resist countervailing pressures from the Group of 77. The most significant change in position occurred with the inclusion of a demand that landlocked and other geographically disadvantaged states should have the right to explore and exploit *both* living and non-living resources in the economic zone on an equal and nondiscriminatory basis (A/CONF.62/C.II/L.39). In addition, all coastal states deriving revenues from exploitation of non-living resources in the zone would be required to contribute a portion of those revenues to the international authority for later distribution.

The last variation on the Disadvantaged position came also at Caracas when Bolivia and Paraguay jointly introduced a much more extreme version of the regional economic zone approach (L.65) than had been suggested by Zambia and Uganda. This approach called for the establishment of regional economic zones jointly by coastal states and neighbouring landlocked states. Within these zones regional sovereignty over living and non-living resources would apply. The exploitation of all natural resources would be managed in the same way as resources beyond national jurisdiction.

Between the Caracas and Geneva sessions the Disadvantaged coalition appears to have become impatient and more radical in their tactics. Privately, members of the group argued that there was little difference for them between unilateral action by states and coastal-state-oriented versions of the economic zone. Consequently, they assumed that their only hope of having a major impact on the outcome, if a treaty were to be signed, was by 'flexing their muscles' in terms of voting power. This, of course, infuriated the Group of 77 and especially the African Group who denounced the 'unholy alliance' between developing and developed disadvantaged states. The discussions in the Group of 77 grew increasingly acrimonious on this issue, especially when delegations tried to make specific distinctions as to which disadvantaged states were developed or developing.

In addition to this tactic, coastal states from the Group of 77 had recourse to a much more potent threat. This was that if developing landlocked states actually flexed their voting strength, they would lose their most important interest in the ocean, which was access to the sea. On several occasions in the corridor these countries were threatened with the loss of transit rights and this is a threat which cannot be ignored. As the strain increased in the Group of 77, the Disadvantaged Group attempted to produce their own paper for submission to the chairman of Committee II in preparation of the Informal Single Negotiating text, but they failed. In fact, two papers emerged from these meetings. One, for landlocked countries, was based on the old Zambian/Ugandan paper of 1973. Another, for geographically disadvantaged states, attempted a compromise between the original approach (A/AC.138/SC.II/L.39 and A/CONF.62/C.II/L.39) and the regional approach. At the same time, it sought to allay some coastal state fears by acknowledging the need for negotiations on a number of items. As such, it was less radical but no more acceptable since the Asians and Latin Americans continued to refuse guarantees of equal access to fisheries and everyone refused access to non-living resources. The most the Disadvantaged coalition was offered were: (i) transit rights, (ii) equal access to fisheries by the Africans, and (iii) access to whatever portion of the allowable catch the coastal state did not use. Of course, the coastal state would determine what was the allowable catch. If they refused this, the Disadvantaged Group were bluntly warned they would get nothing.

9. The Interests and Strategies of the Major Maritime Countries Relative to the Economic Zone/Patrimonial Sea

The major maritime countries do not constitute a homogeneous grouping since, like all countries, they have conflicting interests arising out of differences in capabilities, biogeophysical marine attributes, and national objectives. For instance, the US and USSR are the only governments in the world which have a global security interest in the ocean. This affects the EEC countries as well as Japan since the major trade-off of the conference is between unimpeded passage through straits used for international navigation and the economic zone. While the superpowers and, to a lesser extent, the UK and France have direct military interests involved via the submarine-based deterrent, they all share an interest in protecting tanker traffic from coastal state interference. The major issues on which differences have arisen among the major maritimes concern the management of fisheries, the outer limit of the continental margin and, occasionally, scientific research.

The significance of fish in the national diets of the major maritime countries varies as shown in Table 3. For Japan and Iceland the significance is major but the dependence of Norway and Denmark is also considerable. It is interesting that Iceland joins the Coastal States Group alliance with the Group of 77 purely for living resource reasons. Norway (like Canada) joins for reasons of resource acquisition mixed with ideology and a tendency to side with the South in the North/South confrontation. Denmark, as a result of acceding to membership in the EEC, is forced into a stand against the economic zone even though this puts it in a difficult position *vis-à-vis* Norway.

Table 3: Fish as per cent of Protein Supply in the Major Maritime Countries

Country	Fish as per cent of total protein supply	Fish as per cent of animal protein supply
Japan	20.5	57.8
Iceland	22.8	30.5
Norway	11.9	19.4
Denmark	11.0	16.5
Democratic Republic of Germany	7.1	13.3
France	5.8	10.0
Italy	4.0	9.8
USSR	3.3	8.4
UK	4.7	7.9
Poland	3.2	7.0
Federal Republic of Germany	4.4	6.8
Canada	3.8	5.7
Bulgaria	1.3	4.8
USA	3.4	4.8
The Netherlands	2.8	4.4

Source: FAO, Dept. of Fisheries, *The Economic and Social Effects of the Fishing Industry – A Comparative Study*, Rome, FAO, 1973, Doc. No. FIE/C/314, Table I, pp. 3–5.

When one compares, however, protein dependency with how the balance of consumption over local production is acquired the nature of the problem changes somewhat. Italy, The Netherlands, and the US acquire that balance primarily from import while Bulgaria, France, both Germanies, Japan, Poland, the UK and the USSR all acquire their balance from non-local fishing.[37] These are the countries with the heaviest investments in long-distance fishing fleets and therefore among those potentially hardest hit by the extension of 200-mile economic zones. Japan and the USSR will be the most affected since their fleets are by far the largest.

The positions pursued by delegations from these countries are only partially explained by these considerations. It is necessary to add two other ingredients to explain their responses to the challenge. These are the domestic political significance of the fishing industry, and how calculations about trade-offs are arrived at.

For example, from the very beginning it was clear that the US conceptualized the major problems of UNCLOS III as involving a trade-off between resources and navigation.[38] The US proposed as a package a solution including a 12-mile territorial sea, a guarantee of unimpeded passage through straits used for international jurisdiction and preferential rights for the coastal state over demersal species beyond 12 miles based on a formula involving the harvesting capacity of the coastal state. Later, separate treatment was claimed for anadromous and highly migratory oceanic species (mainly tuna).[39]

This policy is a striking example of the way in which states attempt to reconcile their own conflicting internal interests while negotiating with the outside world.[40] The initial perception of the trade-off between resources and navigation clearly signalled US preoccupation with security interests as its highest priority. However, the willingness to trade on the governmental position regarding fisheries was constrained by nervousness within the Department of Defense (DOD) about 'creeping jurisdiction' and by the need to reconcile the conflicting interests of the US fishing industry divided among coastal fishermen (mainly demersal species), salmon fisheries and long-distance fisheries for tuna and shrimp.[41] The DOD concern was met by restricting extended coastal state jurisdiction to fisheries and by vesting control over allowable catch in international organizations which all signatory coastal states would be obliged to join. Conflicting fisheries' interests were initially reconciled by separating out coastal species, over which the US would exercise extended jurisdiction, from anadromous and highly migratory species.

There was an appealing elegance to this formulation but it was only an initial submission in a very long series of negotiations. The implication, therefore, was always that as the US moved towards the opposing coalition, as it would have to in order to get a treaty, it was more likely to compromise on the living resources than on either the military interests or the non-living resources. In fact, at the beginning the US package included a significant concession on mineral resources in the continental shelf but this was vigorously and continuously opposed by US oil companies. It was therefore not likely that further concessions would easily be forthcoming. In any event, most coastal states seemed to be moving towards control of the entire continental margin. The compromises would, as a result, have to be at the expense of the fishing industry, the shipping industry, including oil companies as owners of tanker fleets, and the oceanographers. The latter two were embroiled as the proponents of the economic zone began to do just what DOD feared, i.e. facilitate the creeping of coastal state jurisdiction.

It is possible from this perspective, to look at US policy in the negotiations at UNCLOS III as fighting a rearguard battle on fisheries, scientific research within the economic zone and ship-generated pollution, giving away as little as possible each round but consistently giving nonetheless; at the same time, indicating that absolutely no deal could be made unless there was a guarantee of unimpeded passage through straits. But at every turn of the wheel each concession generated furious fights within the delegation, sometimes involving allies outside, in Congress and elsewhere, as the various parties tried to minimize or recoup their losses. Meanwhile the delegation increased in size to the point where it was almost as large as the Group of 77, experiencing equal difficulty in arriving at common positions on the economic zone as well as on other issues.

Compared with the US experience, the Japanese and Soviet choices appeared relatively simple, though conceivably no less painful. For Japan, the economic zone was regarded as a disaster, given its domestic needs, its investment in fleet, its pattern of fishing, and the domestic political significance of the Japanese fishing industry. Japan appeared to follow a policy of denying legitimacy to any claim which did not take the Grotian postulate as its basic premise.

In 1972 Japan tabled a proposal which conceded to *developing* coastal states only the right to a portion of the allowable catch based on their harvesting capacity. However, a developed coastal state could acquire jurisdiction only over that portion of the allowable catch '. . .which is necessary to maintain its locally conducted small-scale coastal fisheries.'[42] Since both Japan and the USSR derive over 50 per cent of their catches off the north-east and north-west coasts of North America, it was not difficult to discern what was at stake here. Japan was also hostile to preferential rights for anadromous or highly migratory oceanic species. The USSR also tabled a similar proposal in 1972.[43] The same concession is made to developing states but no provision for separate treatment of anadromous and highly migratory species is allowed. Soviet interests with regard to demersal and anadromous species especially off North America would thereby be protected.

The positions of these countries have changed appreciably since 1972 in reaction to developments within the Group of 77 and the Coastal States Group. Both the USSR and the US in Caracas accepted a 200-mile economic zone which gave sovereignty to the coastal state over living and non-living resources.[44] But each still sought to circumscribe that 'sovereignty' by including obligations on full utilization of the catch and allowing foreign fishermen to take the excess. The US also retained its exception for highly migratory species. Not surprisingly, the supporters of the economic zone concept accused the superpowers of taking away with one hand what they were giving with the other and the stalemate continued.

During the Caracas Session, the EEC countries were finally able to agree on a common fisheries policy after two years of negotiations, but the UK refused to go along.[45] There is in fact an increasing conflict between the UK and the other EEC countries on the issue of the economic zone since, on the one hand, most of the EEC members are 'geographically disadvantaged' and the UK is not. Since 1973 the position of the UK has changed considerably from being initially opposed to the extension of coastal state jurisdiction beyond the territorial sea to one very closely akin to Canada, Norway, Australia and New Zealand in 1975.

The EEC approach is considerably more restrictive than either the US or the USSR and more closely akin to the original Japanese position. It denies, by implication, the establishment of an economic zone as defined by supporters of that concept and very narrowly restricts the jurisdiction of the coastal state to fisheries. But even relative to fisheries this jurisdiction is heavily circumscribed by international obligations and the authority of 'regional or sectoral fishery organizations'. This paper elicited a barrage from the Group of 77, the representatives of which described regional fishery commissions as being 'clubs for plunder'.

As indicated previously, there are differences between the major maritime countries on the question of the outer limit of the continental shelf. Only the US and the UK support the concept of the margin. The USSR, given the morphology of its own shelf, suggests either the 500-metre isobath or 100 miles. This would allow the USSR to control its continental margin while denying the same opportunity to countries claiming margins which extend beyond 100 miles. Japan supports a 200-mile limit while the EEC countries, given the configurations of the Western European coastline, have taken no position as a group. France, however, insists that the median line is not the only way of resolving these delimitation issues between adjacent states.

On the issues of control over scientific research and pollution, these countries may be closer together but even here there are nuances. For instance, both the UK and USSR are more restrictive about scientific research on the continental shelf than is the US. There is a much closer affinity between the US, Japan and Federal Republic of Germany on the issue. France appears to be ambivalent. There is not the same kind of variation on the control of pollution issue since interests seem to be symmetrical. Finally, on the issue of residual rights in the economic zone, this group would generally prefer to characterize the zone as high seas in which the coastal state exercises specific jurisdictions and this is another major source of contention with the supporters of the economic zone concept.

Conclusions

In the negotiations on the economic zone issue all five ingredients of the dynamics of global ocean politics are in operation. The penetration of the law of the sea by the North/South confrontation acts as the major backdrop against which most moves are made and heavily shapes the way the game is played within the global conference. States belonging to the Group of 77 coalition must calculate their moves not only in terms of perceptions of 'objective' interest but also in terms of the effects of these moves on the normative/ideological, almost religious, dimension along which the Group of 77 is mobilized. Defections are serious matters since they leave the country open to charges of traitorous behaviour and being 'tools of Western imperialism'.

It is also interesting to note that even though there is not always a simple, direct relationship between marine attributes and national objectives, the former figure heavily in country calculations of interests. In fact, comparing the types of claims made at UNCLOS III with those made in 1930, 1958 and 1960, it seems that marine attributes play a greater role than they have in the past when capabilities appear to have been the dominant ingredient. This difference may well be a function of how the negotiations are structured.

Up to 1960 the process was clearly controlled by the major maritime countries. There was an uneasy mix between a focus on activities and a focus on spatial criteria. Even then, however, countries showed a penchant for choosing spatial criteria when the going got rough. This was strikingly the case in connection with the contiguous zone issue on which the conference, even though it recognized that different activities were involved, opted for a single limit of 12 miles within which exclusive coastal state jurisdiction could be exercised. For this reason the conference was criticized for adopting an entirely arbitrary single limit when what was important was the 'concentration and dispersal of interests'.[46]

In the context of UNCLOS III, capabilities affect calculations of interest to be sure but spatial criteria based in part upon marine attributes are the dominant theme. This, we suggest, is because the major maritime countries no longer control the process. The process is now controlled by the coalition which largely lacks major ocean-related capabilities yet seeks to redress inequalities in the distribution of world income via the medium of the ocean. Moreover, this coalition was mobilized, some opponents would even say 'captured', by two groups: (i) those states pushing the 200-mile territorial sea claims; and (ii) those states ideologically seeking a redistribution of resources and therefore income.

As we have argued in previous sections, however, this coalition is not monolithic. The landlocked and GDS are a persistent splinter group precisely because spatial criteria are dominant in determining who gets what at UNCLOS III. But, given the constraints facing them, this splinter group cannot play the role of arbiter at the conference even though it aspires to. Outside the conference halls the law of the sea is almost solely a coastal states' game. The fact that the conference is dominated by the supporters of the 200-mile economic zone/patrimonial sea concept and that the major maritime countries are doing business on that basis means that it has become the focal point of the entire negotiations. It is now legitimate. Whether or not there is a treaty, it will be the focal point of future claims and counterclaims and therefore of the future law of the sea.

If there is no treaty it is quite likely that the probability of conflict over living and non-living resources and navigation will increase globally. In some parts of the world this conflict is likely to be violent. This may be the case in the Mediterranean and the Persian/Arabian Gulf over navigation, the west coast of Africa (the Gulf of Guinea) over resources, and the west coast of Central and South American over resources. There will also be serious difficulties in the Caribbean Sea.

It is likely that these conflicts will increase in salience and therefore infect non-ocean-related issues. Ironically, the danger of failure at UNCLOS III comes from a growing number of coastal states, the representatives and governments of which think that no agreement is better than agreement on available terms. Some ask why should these frustrating and unproductive negotiations be allowed to continue when the same or better fruits could be had by unilateral action? But the fact is that unilateral action will not solve the difficulties of the *long run*. Many claims will simply not be accepted by others and in their contention points of future conflict will be multiplied. In particular for the superpowers which have global interests in the ocean, unilateral action and no treaty will create more problems than it solves and will increase the probability of using force more often than they and others are likely to think acceptable. For these reasons we suggest that in the long run there is no alternative to a treaty and it is likely to be based almost entirely on the output of the 77 Group. This group has been the forum within which significant compromises on the jurisdictional issues have been worked out. It was organized by the Norwegian delegation and is led by the chairman of that delegation, the Honourable Jens Evensen, Minister without Portfolio of Norway. It is, however, oriented almost completely to coastal state interests.

Assuming, therefore, that a treaty will ultimately be written based upon terms currently available, who will win and who will lose? The potential winners are: (i) countries with long coastlines and significant living resources off their coasts; and (ii) countries with wide continental margins. The potential losers are: (i) the landlocked; (ii) countries with short coastlines and narrow continental margins; and (iii) shelf-locked countries without major petroleum deposits relatively near-shore.

The major losers in fisheries are likely to be countries like Spain, Portugal, Bulgaria and Poland with a high level of investment in fishing fleet, facing prohibitive opportunity costs of seeking alternative protein sources. These countries are also unable to employ a wide range of inducements for getting access to the productive economic zones of others. Partial losers, in the sense that they will face major increases in their costs of operations,are Japan, USSR, UK, both Germanies and the US tuna and shrimp fleets. The latter may also find substantial resources closed to them in the future. For the tuna fleet, which is heavily overcapitalized, this will be a disaster of major proportions.

With respect to scientific research, the major potential loser is the USSR which will have to seek to build a much wider range of global contacts than they currently have at their disposal. US oceanographers will also very likely be severely hampered and will find it necessary to expend considerable resources, both time and money, getting access to other countries' economic zones. This changed situation coincides with the effects of inflation (cost of food and fuel) and declining levels of ship support by the US government. Since similar difficulties will face all countries with the capability for significant marine science research, in the short run the total volume of global oceanographic research is likely to decline. The long-run picture will be substantially influenced by the relative effectiveness of whatever co-operative programmes are established for the emergence of viable marine science programmes in developing countries.

But, one could ask, would such a régime be stable? There are two dimensions to the answer. It will be stable globally if the most important coastal states support it. These are the coastal states with existing or significant potential capabilities as well as those with resources. These are therefore ones which are likely to benefit either directly or because the available alternatives create more problems than they solve. But there will actually be a great deal of variation in the implementation of the treaty at the regional level because specific situations differ. It is at this level that the implementation of the treaty may differ substantially from the global régime established since deals will have to be made, joint ventures established, technical assistance provided. These negotiations may erode exclusive jurisdiction of the coastal state in an operational sense.

On the other hand, there are four sub-regions in which this kind of régime will either create serious conflicts or add fuel to ones already existing. We have in mind the Eastern Caribbean, the north-west Pacific, the South China Sea, and the Eastern Mediterranean. In the Caribbean and Mediterranean particularly the multiplicity of shelf-locked islands and the paucity of living resources will leave those involved very dissatisfied. There will also be problems for the EEC and Scandinavian countries but in both areas pre-existing frameworks are available within which solutions can be sought. These do not exist for the other areas.

The long-run forecast for such a régime is therefore for 'stability' at the global level with a high degree of regional variation including increasing conflict in four subregions. But this 'stability' will not be everlasting. The law of the sea will continue to change as long as people's expectations about ocean exploitation change and thereby cut across differences in capabilities, marine attributes and national objectives.

Notes (Doc. No. in these notes refers to UN Documents)

1. Edward Miles, 'Transnationalism in Space: Inner and Outer', in Robert O. Keohane and Joseph S. Nye, Jr. (eds.), 'Transnational Relations and World Politics', *International Organization*, Vol. XXV, No. 3, Summer 1971, pp. 602–25.
2. States also differ in objectives sought in the ocean, assets available, methods employed and outcomes achieved. The analysis is restricted to capabilities and biogeophysical conditions in order to highlight a political connection which has emerged in UNCLOS III. The term 'capabilities' denotes capacity to utilize the oceans and the efficiencies of such use. This implies a range in both the scope of use (number of activities engaged in) as well as degrees of efficiency for each activity.
3. Edward Miles, 'Technology, Ocean Management and the Law of the Sea: Some Current History', *Denver Law Journal*, Spring 1969, pp. 240–60; Robert Friedheim, 'The Satisfied and Dissatisfied States Negotiate International Law', *World Politics*, October 1965, pp. 20–44; and Lewis Alexander (ed.), *The Law of the Sea*, Columbus, The Ohio State University Press, 1967.
4. Francis T. Christy, Jr., 'Fisheries and the New Convention of the Law of the Sea', *San Diego Law Review*, Vol. 7, No. 3, July 1970, Table 2, p. 466.
5. UNCTAD. *Review of Maritime Transport, 1969*, New York, The United Nations, 1969. Doc. No. TD/B/C4/66.
6. Panel Reports of the Commission on Marine Science, Engineering and Resources. *Science and Environment*, Washington, DC, GPO, 1969 Vol. 1, Table 4, p. 1–14 and Table 5, pp. 1–14–15. See also: Syed Zahoor Qasim, 'Development of Marine Science Capabilities in Different Regions of the World', *Report of the Marine Science Workshop*, The Johns Hopkins University, Bologna, Italy, October 15–19, 1973, Annex D, pp. 9–22.
7. Francis Njenga, 'Regional Approaches to the Law of the Sea', in *Perspectives on Ocean Policy*, Conference on Conflict and Order in Ocean Relations, sponsored by the Ocean Policy Project, The Johns Hopkins University, Washington, DC, GPO, 1975, pp. 91–3. The notion of a 'global average' in length of coastline is, of course, fictional.
8. Kanenas, 'Wide Limits and "Equitable" Distribution of Seabed Resources', *Ocean Development and International Law Journal*, Vol. 1, No. 2, Summer 1973, p. 149.
9. A shelf-locked state is one whose continental margin abuts that of another state in such a way that it is unable to extend its jurisdiction beyond the shelf down to the slope and rise.
10. Lewis Alexander, 'Indices of National Interest in the Ocean', *Ocean Development and International Law Journal*, Vol. 1, No. 1, Spring 1973, Table III, p. 40.
11. Ibid., Table II, p. 39.
12. Ibid., Table IV, p. 41.
13. United Nations, General Assembly, Committee on the Peaceful Uses of the Sea-Bed and the Ocean Floor Beyond Limits of National Jurisdiction,

Economic Significance, In Terms of Sea-Bed Mineral Resources, of the Various Limits Proposed for National Jurisdiction: Report of the Secretary-General. Doc. No. A/AC.138/87, 4 June 1973, p. 33.

14. Ibid., pp. 34–8. See also: D.R. Horn, B.M. Horn and M.N. Delach, *Ocean Manganese Nodules Metal Values and Mining Sites*, Technical Report No. 4, NSF–GX33616, 1973; and D.R. Horn *et al.*, *Factors which Control the Distribution of Ferromanganese Nodules and Proposed Research Vessel's Track North Pacific*, Phase II, Ferromanganese Program NSF/IDOE, Technical Report No. 8, NSF–GX33616, 1973.
15. This distinction is taken from Olav Knudsen, *The Politics of International Shipping*, Lexington, Mass., Lexington Books, D.C. Heath & Co., 1973, pp. 76–83 and 96–100.
16. See: William Burke, 'Law, Science and the Ocean', *The Natural Resources Lawyer*, May 1970, pp. 195–225; Robert Friedheim and Joseph Kadane, 'Ocean Science in the UN Political Arena', *Journal of Maritime Law and Commerce*, Vol. 3, No. 3, April 1972, pp. 473–502; and John Knauss, 'Developing the Freedom of Scientific Research Issue of the Law of the Sea Conference', *Ocean Development and International Law Journal*, Vol. 1, No. 1, Spring 1973, pp. 93–120.
17. Anton Prohashka, 'The Consequences of Nonagreement', in Lewis Alexander (ed.), *The Law of the Sea; A New Geneva Conference*, Proceedings of the Sixth Annual Conference of the Law of the Sea Institute, University of Rhode Island, 21–24 June 1971, Kingston, University of Rhode Island, 1972, pp. 61–2. For a detailed analysis of the concerns of this group see: Thomas M. Franck, Mohamed El Barader, and George Aron, 'The New Poor: Land-Locked, Shelf-Locked and Other Geographical Disadvantaged States', *International Law and Politics*, Vol. 7, pp. 33–57.
18. For very useful analyses of this point, see: Graham T. Allison, 'Conceptual Models and the Cuban Missile Crisis', *American Political Science Review*, Vol. 63, No. 3, September 1969, pp. 689–718; Graham T. Allison, *The Essence of Decision*, Boston, Atlantic, Little-Brown, 1972; Robert O. Keohane and Joseph Nye, Jr. (eds.), 'Transnational Relations and World Politics', op. cit., pp. 329–50 and 721–48; Graham T. Allison and Morton H. Halperin, 'Bureaucratic Politics: A Paradigm and some Policy Implications', in Raymond Tanter and Richard H. Ullman (eds.), *Theory and Policy in International Relations*, Princeton, N.J., Princeton University Press, 1972, pp. 40–79; and Robert O. Keohane and Joseph S. Nye, 'Transgovernmental Relations and International Organization', *World Politics*, Vol. XXVII, No. 1, October 1974, pp. 1–38.
19. Douglas M. Johnston and Edgar Gold, *The Economic Zone in the Law of the Sea: Survey, Analysis and Appraisal of Current Trends*, Law of the Sea Institute, Occasional Paper No. 17, Kingston, University of Rhode Island, 1973, pp. 1–8.
20. Uruguay, A/AC.138/SC.II/L.24; Brazil, A/AC.138/SC.II/L.25; Ecuador, Panama, and Peru on the territorial sea, A/AC.138/SC.II/L.27, and Corr. 1 and 2; Ecuador, Panama, and Peru, A/AC.138/SC.II/L.54; and Nicaragua A/CONF.62/C.2/L.17.
21. Statement by the representative of Brazil, Plenary, 28 June 1974, Third United Nations Conference on the Law of the Sea – Official Records, Vol. I, New York, United Nations, 1975, pp. 60–61; and statement by the representatives of Peru, Committee II, 1 August 1974, ibid., vol. II, p. 193.
22. These assessments are made from the following sources: Map prepared by the Geographer, US Dep. of State, 'Global Effect of 200 Nautical Mile Territorial Sea Claims; FAO, *Atlas of the Living Resources of the Seas*, Rome, FAO,

1972; and FAO Dep. of Fisheries, 'Yellowfin Tuna and Skipjack in the Eastern Pacific Ocean', Doc. No. FID/C148(Rev. 1), Suppl. 1, 1973.

23. From map prepared by the Geographer, US Dept. of State. 'Composite Theoretical Divisions of the Seabed' and 'Major Topographic Divisions of the Continental Margins.'
24. See: 'Organization of African Unity Declaration on the Issues of the Law of the Sea – CM Res. 289 (XIX)', Doc. No. A/AC.138/89, of 2 July 1973. The origin of this group position is to be found in *Report of the African States Regional Seminar on the Law of the Sea*, Yaounde 1972, Doc. No. A/AC.138/79. The original proposal on the economic zone introduced by Kenya in 1972 is an early reflection of this position (Doc. No. A/AC.138/SC.II/L.10). It was replaced by a revised version tabled by 14 co-sponsors from The African Group in 1973 (Doc. No. A/AC.138/SC.II/L.40 and corr. 1–3) and again by 17 co-sponsors from the African Group in 1974 at the Caracas session of UNCLOS III (Doc. No. A/CONF.62/C.II/L.82).
25. See: 'The Declaration of Santo Domingo', Doc. No. A/AC.138/80. See also: H.E., Ambassador Andres Aguilar, 'The Patrimonial Sea', in Lewis M. Alexander (ed.), *The Law of the Sea: Needs and Interests of the Developing Countries*, pp. 161–5; and Lewis M. Alexander (ed.), *Gulf and Caribbean Maritime Problems*, Kingston, Law of the Sea Institute, University of Rhode Island, 1973. The major proposal embodying this concept was tabled in 1973 by Colombia, Mexico, and Venezuela in the Seabed Committee: Doc. No. A/AC.138/SC.II/L.21.
26. The relevant documentation is provided by the following proposals: in 1972, A/AC.183/SC.II/L.8 (Canada); L.10 (Kenya); L.11 (Australia and New Zealand); in 1973, A/AC.138/SC.II/L.21 (Colombia, Mexico and Venezuela); L.23 (Iceland); L.36 (Australia and Norway); L.38 and Corr. 1 (Canada, India, Kenya, Madagascar, Senegal and Sri Lanka); L.40 (African Group); L.52 (Pakistan); in 1974, A/CONF.62/L.4 (Canada, Chile, Iceland, India, Indonesia, Mauritius, Mexico, New Zealand and Norway); A/CONF.62/C.II/L.21 (Nigeria); L.57 Rev. 1 (Australia and New Zealand); and L.82 (African Group).
27. See the proposals advanced by Jamaica: Docs. No. A/AC.138/SC.II/L.55 and A/CONF.62/C.II/L.35. For an excellent assessment of the conflicting interests of Caribbean countries, see: Harry Mayers, 'Guyana Wants 200 Mile Zone', *The Trinidad Guardian*, Tuesday, 26 March 1974, p.8.
28. Doc. No. A/CONF.62/C.III/L.13 and L.13, rev. 1.
29. Doc. No. A/CONF.62/C.III/L.19.
30. See Edward Miles. 'An Interpretation of the Caracas Proceedings.'
31. This is described in ibid.
32. Doc. No. A/CONF.62/C.III/L.29.
33. Doc. No. A/CONF.62/WP.8/Part III.
34. Miles. op. cit.
35. Ibid., pp. 82 and Edward Miles, 'An interpretation of the Geneva proceedings', *Ocean Development and International Law Journal*, forthcoming.
36. Afghanistan, Austria, Belgium, Bolivia, Nepal, and Singapore, 'Draft Articles on Resource Jurisdiction of Coastal States beyond the Territorial Sea, Doc. No. A/AC.138/SC.II/L.39; Uganda and Zambia, 'Draft Articles on the Proposed Economic Zone', Doc. No. A/AC.138/SC.II/L.41.
    Afghanistan *et al.* (15 co-sponsors), 'Explanatory Paper on Draft Articles Relating to Land-locked States', Doc. No. A/CONF.62/C.II/L.29.
    Afghanistan *et al.* (19 co-sponsors), 'Draft Articles on Participation of Land-Locked and Other Geographically Disadvantaged States in the Exploration and Exploitation of the Living and Non-Living Resources in the Area Beyond the Territorial Sea', Doc. No. A/CONF.62/C.II/L.39.

Afghanistan, Bolivia, Czechoslovakia, Hungary, Mali, Nepal and Zambia, 'Draft Articles Relating to Land-Locked States', Doc. No. A/AC.138/93.
Botswana, Lesotho, Uganda and Upper Volta, 'Amendments to A/CONF.62/L.5', Doc. No. A/CONF.62/C.II/L.45/Rev. 1.
Bolivia and Paraguay, 'Draft Articles on the "Regional Economic Zone"', Doc. No. A/CONF.62/C.II/L.65.
See also: Thomas M. Franck *et al.*, 'The New Poor: Land-Locked, Shelf-Locked and Other Geographically Disadvantaged States', op. cit.

37. Ibid., Table IV, p. 17.
38. See the President's Statement on United States Ocean Policy of 23 May 1970, *Dep. of State Bulletin*, 15 June 1970, p. 737. See also the statement by the US Representative, John R. Stevenson, before Subcommittee II of the Seabed Committee introducing Draft Articles on the Breadth of the Territorial Sea, Straits and Fisheries, 3 August 1971, Doc. No. A/AC.138/SC.II/L.4.
39. Doc. No. A/AC.138/SC.II/L.20.
40. For a full account of the background behind this policy see Ann L. Hollick, 'Seabeds Make Strange Politics', *Foreign Policy*, Vol. 9, Winter 1972–3, pp. 148–70.
41. It is important to realize that the US actually gains significantly in extending control over coastal fisheries to 200 miles. Only two fisheries are traded off thereby, i.e. tuna and shrimp. In the context of UNCLOS III, however, the real trade-off on fisheries was a trade-off on the *position* advocated by the Departments of State and Commerce and a retreat from the species approach.
42. Doc. No. A/AC.138/SC.II/L.12.
43. Doc. No. A/AC.138/SC.II/L.6.
44. 'Draft Articles on the Economic Zone', submitted by Byelorussian SSR, Bulgaria, German Democratic Republic, Poland, Ukranian SSR and USSR. Doc. No. A/CONF.62/C.II/L.38; 'Draft Articles for a Chapter on the Economiz Zone and the Continental Shelf', submitted by the United States, Doc. No. A/CONF.62/C.II/L.47.
45. 'Draft Articles on Fisheries', submitted by Belgium, Denmark, Federal Republic of Germany, France, Ireland, Italy, Luxembourg and The Netherlands, Doc. No. A/CONF.62/C.II/L.40.
46. Myres McDougal and William T. Burke, *The Public Order of the Oceans*, New Haven and London, Yale University Press, 1962.

Further Readings

1. J.S. Nye, 'Ocean Rule Making from a World Politics Perspective', *Ocean Development and International Law*, 3, 1975, pp. 29–52.
2. D.B. Bobrow, 'International Politics and High-Level Decision-Making: Context for Ocean Policy', *Ocean Development and International Law*, 3, 1975, pp. 171–80.
3. E. Miles, 'An Interpretation of the Caracas Proceedings', in Christy *et al.* (eds.), *Law of the Sea: Caracas and Beyond* (Proceedings of the Ninth Annual Conference of the Law of the Sea Institute, 1975), pp. 39–94.
4. D.M. Johnston, 'The Options for LOS III: Appraisal and Proposal', ibid., pp. 357–72.
5. T.M. Franck, M. El Baradei and G. Aron, 'The New Poor: Landlocked, Shelf-Locked and other Geographically Disadvantaged States', *International Law and Politics*, 7, 1975, pp. 33–57.

8 OCEAN POLITICS IN WESTERN EUROPE

Robert Boardman*

1. Introduction

Oceanic political culture has a long history in Western Europe. This background, from the trading routes and fishing grounds of ancient times to the beginnings of colonial expansion by the European powers from the late fifteenth century, predates the emergence of the modern state system. The attitudes and practices thus formed have served both to heighten tensions within the region, and yet also to contribute to the evolution of norms governing the behaviour of states and other actors in European waters. Both tendencies, of conflict and harmony, can be discerned in the ocean politics of the last two decades. Even the terms in which the oceans have been discussed have sometimes appeared to vary little through the centuries. One writer argued in 1975 that, 'Our seas are not merely an oil mine, a hunting ground for the world's fishermen, a drain, a wide road to carry our trade along. They are the condition of our wealth and of our food in the future, and we must plan their use just as carefully as we plan the use of our equally limited supply of land.'[1] The point echoes many such discussions in the past; more than two centuries earlier, a London publisher issued *The Fisheries Revived: or, Britain's hidden treasures discovered; proving that not only our future wealth, but security, will depend upon that inestimable trade, etc.*[2] Ocean disputes as well as practices span the medieval and modern eras. Discussing the British–Icelandic fishery dispute of 1972–3, one Icelandic observer cited the murder of the Governor of Iceland by English fishermen in 1468 as one of his country's grievances against the English.[3]

These kinds of questions have a dual fascination for the political scientist. On the one hand, we seem to be delving into a subject that

* I am grateful to the Research Development Fund of Dalhousie University for grants in support of research in the United Kingdom in the summer of 1973 and spring of 1975. I should also like to thank Dr. Albert W. Koers, of the University of Utrecht, Dr. E.D. Brown of University College London, and Dr. William Wallace of the University of Manchester, for the valuable help they gave at various stages of the research. Greig Macleod, a doctoral candidate in the Department of Political Science, Dalhousie University, collaborated on the section of the chapter on Scottish politics. All blemishes of the final version remain, of course, my own responsibility.

fits snugly, almost too perfectly, into classic definitions of the nature of politics, such as Harold Lasswell's particularly apt 'who gets what, when, and how'[4] : the 'what' in the present chapter being the fish and oil resources of the seas and seabed of Western Europe. Yet, on the other hand, the character of the political system that we are dealing with here is not clear. Some form of West European political system can be identified;[5] but it is one that is continually changing, and one whose processes may vary considerably between different issue-areas. Nor can it be assumed that contemporary intergovernmental bodies form the nucleus of an embryonic West European government of the future, equipped with legislative, executive and judicial branches. Although the European Community has developed some momentum in the fields of fisheries and energy, for example, it is constrained by the limited range of topics within its purview, the limited nature of its authority in relation to member states, and its limited membership.

The politics of each of these two functional areas, fisheries and oil, are complex. Ideally, attention would have to be directed as much at domestic and transnational politics in Western Europe as at interstate relations and the activities of intergovernmental organisations, if we were to grapple adequately with the questions of how decisions are reached about the allocation of the region's ocean resources, or of how resource conflicts are generated and dampened. The undertaking here is more modest. It is to sketch in the main features of the emergent regimes in each functional area, and to discuss some of the ways in which ocean activities have affected political behaviour within the states of Western Europe. More particularly, the chapter will look at the evolution of European Community policies, and at domestic politics in the United Kingdom.

2. The Politics of Fish

Other states, such as the Soviet Union, Canada and the United States, make use of the fishing grounds of the North Sea and the North-East Atlantic and have entered into bilateral or multilateral agreements with West European nations on the regulation of fisheries in the region. Of the regional powers themselves, three – Norway, Denmark and the United Kingdom – stand out as those with major fishing interests. And of these, Norway has consistently retained a leading position, with catches totalling 2,786.6 thousand metric tons in the North-East Atlantic area in 1973 (see Table 1). In each of these countries, fisheries form an important part of the national economies.[6] Notwithstanding the traditional freedoms, and the impression given by the confrontations

Table 1: North-East Atlantic Fisheries: Catches by Country 1965-73 (in thousand metric tons)

	1965	1966	1967	1968	1969	1970	1971	1972	1973
Belgium	59.7	62.7	63.8	68.2	58.7	53.4	60.2	59.0	52.7
Denmark	828.4	835.6	1,053.2	1,447.3	1,263.1	1,216.7	1,387.4	1,427.3	1,450.0
Faroes	62.9	85.1	93.1	162.4	135.9	181.5	171.7	176.0	220.0
France	582.6	592.0	577.3	534.9	564.5	598.5	592.1	608.5	659.1
GFR	443.2	458.1	419.5	387.4	388.1	391.6	357.2	314.4	364.0
Greenland	0.9	0.9	0.8	0.6	0.6	0.5	0.6	0.3	0.3
Iceland	35.7	39.6	50.2	53.1	66.5	78.9	74.0	92.0	90.7
Netherlands	363.3	337.2	299.0	313.2	314.6	298.7	318.2	345.8	340.8
Norway	2,258.8	2,825.6	3,205.2	2,779.0	2,435.0	2,843.7	2,837.7	2,944.7	2,786.6
UK	990.4	1,009.2	945.4	993.1	1,077.5	1,092.3	1,099.7	1,065.4	1,136.0
TOTALS	5,625.9	6,246.0	6,707.5	6,739.2	6,304.5	6,755.8	6,898.8	7,033.4	7,100.2

Source: United Nations, Food and Agriculture Organisation: *Yearbook of Fishery Statistics* (annually).

between Britain and both Norway and Iceland, the ground rules for a regional fisheries régime began to be constructed in the early nineteenth century. This background is important for assessing the ocean policies of the European Community.

Historical Background: For much of the present century, North Sea fisheries were regulated by the Hague Convention of 1882. Bilateral agreements between East European governments had been reached earlier. Following a convention signed in 1826, Britain and France in 1839 recognized the exclusive right of the nationals of the coastal state to fish inside the 3-mile territorial limit, and arrived at other understandings with respect to the high seas in the English Channel and the North Sea.[7] The Hague Convention itself was more ambitious both in geographical scope and subject matter. It was signed by the leading North Sea coastal states of the day: Britain, Germany, Denmark, France, The Netherlands and Belgium. The Convention recognized the exclusive rights of nationals within the 3-mile limit; other provisions related to fishing seasons, the use of nets, registration and the nationality of boats, surveillance of military vessels, and other questions.[8] A further major step was taken in 1959 on a broader intergovernmental front with the establishment of the North-East Atlantic Fisheries Commission (NEAFC), which has dealt with a variety of subjects including the conservation of fish, protection of breeding grounds, regulation of fishing methods and seasons, and so on.[9]

The 1960s and 1970s have been decades of change. Concern over the depletion of stocks resulting from growing industrial and consumer demand and technical innovations, and dissatisfaction with the outcomes of the 1958 and 1960 Law of the Sea Conferences, prompted unilateral extensions of their national fisheries limits by the Scandinavian states, and led Britain in 1963 to seek a major overhaul of the 1882 régime. The British action stemmed directly from fishermen's grievances at their progressive exclusion from traditional grounds. Resolution of the conflict with Norway over Norwegian limits had been reached in 1951,[10] but the declaration of 12-mile exclusive fisheries zones by Iceland and Denmark (for the Faroes) later in the decade brought strong pressures from British fisheries interests on the Government. Bilateral attempts at settlement broke down, one upshot being the series of incidents between Britain and Iceland that became known as the 'cod war'.[11] In 1961, Norway tightened her earlier position and declared a 12-mile zone; the following year, Denmark similarly toughened her attitude to British fishing rights within the

6–12-mile zone off the Faroes; and only temporary accommodation had been possible in Britain's dispute with Iceland. In 1963, London terminated British adherence to the 1882 Convention. The Government drew attention to the 'progressive restriction of the area of the High Seas on which the nations of the world can exercise their right of fishing'. The extensions of limits by other countries had imposed 'heavy sacrifices on the British fishing industry', and the Government had 'therefore been obliged to consider whether their duty to the United Kingdom fishing industry can be reconciled with the continuation of the traditional three-mile limit. . .While giving full weight to the legitimate interests of their friends and allies, their conclusion is that in the present state of international law they are no longer justified in denying to British fishermen some extension of their exclusive rights in their own coastal waters.'[12]

The resulting European Fisheries Conference of 1963–4 is significant in the light of later developments in that the participants included both the six EEC member states and the seven EFTA (European Free Trade Area) countries, together with Iceland, Spain and Ireland (also a later European Community member). The conference can be seen as a wider public setting for ironing out the central conflict that had emerged between Britain and the Scandinavian powers. Thus Iceland, Norway and Denmark (for fishing off Greenland and the Faroes) took the position that nothing less than international acknowledgement of their exclusive rights within a 12-mile zone would be acceptable, though each was prepared to recognize historic rights of the nationals of other countries for a short period. Agreement was eventually reached which recognized 'the exclusive right of the coastal state to fish and exclusive jurisdiction in matters of fisheries within the belt of six miles measured from the baseline of its territorial sea.' In the 6–12-mile belt, the right to fish could be exercised 'only by the coastal state and by such other Contracting Parties, the fishing vessels of which have habitually fished in that belt between 1 January 1953 and 31 December 1962.'[13] The conference also prepared the ground for a more comprehensive examination of outstanding fisheries questions which took place at a second London conference of 1966–7. The range of participants was expanded to include also the United States, Canada, the USSR and Poland, and the Convention which resulted was broad in scope. Again, much of the bargaining at the conference revolved around the conflicting positions adopted by Britain and the Scandinavian states. The latter took the view that the convention should apply only outside national limits; and that the jurisdiction of the coastal state pertained to all aspects of fisheries, including decisions on the right to fish, fishing methods and gear, measures of conservation, and the conduct of fishing operations generally. The outcome was an acknowledgement that 'within the area where a coastal state has jurisdiction over fisheries, the implementation and enforcement of the provisions of this Convention shall be the responsibility of the coastal state'; but the coastal state was also given the right 'to make special rules and exemptions. . .for vessels or gear which by reason of their size or type operate or are set only in coastal waters.'[14]

The conferences of the 1960s could not settle all issues. There has been an almost continuous process of consultation and bargaining between North-East Atlantic fishing states, both directly and under the auspices of intergovernmental bodies. Agreement was reached between Britain, Norway, Denmark and four other countries in 1973 on the regulation of fisheries around the Faroes, which included limits being placed on allowed catches of certain species.[15] Exchanges between Britain, Norway and the Soviet Union have been established on a regular basis for setting limits to the fishing of North-East Arctic cod.[16] Negotiations between the British and Norwegian governments on British fishing rights in Norwegian waters have continued. In 1975, the two governments agreed on the creation of a number of trawler-free zones.[17] Finally, intergovernmental consultation through the NEAFC machinery has contributed steadily to the evolution of accepted norms. Also in 1975, agreement was finally reached on a ban on industrial fishing for herring, a step that was hailed by conservation interests as a significant one towards the more rational management of fisheries.[18]

The EEC's Common Fisheries Policy. Brief though it is, the above historical account provides a useful perspective with which to view the European Community's attempts to formulate a fisheries policy common to all member states. The Common Fisheries Policy from 1970 has represented an important broadening of the developments just noted, since it has eaten much more deeply into areas of traditionally domestic jurisdiction. Interest in fisheries on the part of the EEC was more implied than explicit at the time of the signing of the Treaty of Rome in 1957. Indeed, the Common Fisheries Policy can be viewed almost as a spin-off of the Community's more general interest in the harmonization of the policies of member governments, its particular involvement with agriculture, and its goal of breaking down trade barriers and other forms of discrimination between member states.

The starting-point for Brussels' interest in the sea is Article 38(1) of the Treaty of Rome: 'The common market shall extend to agriculture and trade in agricultural products. The term "agricultural products" shall mean the products of the soil, of stock-farming and of fisheries and production of first-stage processing directly related to the foregoing.'[19] It was a relatively long time, however, before this concern became an active one. Partly this was due to the Commission's setting of other priorities in the early years of the EEC. A second factor was the existence of sometimes sharp differences of opinion on the extent to which the Community was legally empowered to involve itself with maritime issues. It could be argued that the EEC's jurisdiction under the Treaty of Rome is restricted to the territories of member states, and does not extend outwards into the sea. This was not, however, the interpretation that tended to be adopted in practice either by the Commission or by the Council of Ministers. Nevertheless, one writer has emphasized: 'Toute la difficulté résulte. . .de ce que le Traité ne contient pas de règle claire fixant l'étendue de la competence spatiale de la Communauté.'[20] And third, delay was perhaps an inevitable result of the initiative in fishery questions being taken during the 1960s in bilateral or multilateral settings outside the EEC framework, even where these forums included Community members as participants. Finally, North Sea fisheries raised questions that could not be effectively resolved by consultation between member states of the EEC; this problem was only partially eased by the enlargement of the Community in 1973, since in the event Norway declined to accept membership alongside Britain, Denmark and Ireland.

The EEC was granted observer status at the 1963–4 London conference. This, and the presence of its member states, led to the inserting of a provision in the London Fisheries Convention that 'Nothing in the present Convention shall prevent the maintenance or establishment of a special régime in matters of fisheries. . .as between Member States. . .of the European Economic Community.' The conference itself provided an impetus to the development of a Community fisheries policy. The Commission's interest was indicated as early as 1964, when it was decided to institute a special method of administrative co-operation for applying intra-Community treatment to the fish catches of vessels of member states.[21] In June 1966, the Commission sent its outline of the basic principles of a common fisheries policy to the EEC's Economic and Social Committee. The proposed market sought to create a competitive framework, but one that would remain relatively immune from trade fluctuations. It would cover such matters as common fishing standards, intervention and withdrawal prices, guide prices, approximations for some base products, and a Community levy system in place of the existing national customs arrangements. Other aspects which the Commission then had under consideration included the prevention of social hardship which might be caused by such intervention in the fishing industry; improvement of the living and working conditions on board fishing vessels; and the setting up of training and welfare schemes.[22] In 1968, for example, the Commission set up a Joint Advisory Committee on Social Questions arising in the Sea Fishing Industry, consisting of representatives of fisheries employers' and workers' organizations.[23]

This activity culminated eventually, after Commission proposals of 1968, in the two Council regulations of June and October 1970 (2140/70 and 2141/70) which established the basis for the EEC's Common Fisheries Policy.[24] The basic principle underlying the policy was defined as being that 'Community fishermen must have equality of access to fishing grounds and to their exploitation in maritime waters coming under the sovereignty or within the jurisdiction of Member States.'[25] However, 'as a transitional measure, an exception to this rule may be permitted for certain types of fishing carried on by local population whose employment is strictly dependent on inshore fishing.' This goal was elaborated in Article 1 of 2141/70: 'With a view to promoting harmonious and balanced development of the fishing industry within the general economy and to encouraging rational exploitation of the biological resources of the sea and of inland waters, a common system shall be adopted for fishing in maritime waters, together with specific measures with a view to appropriate action and the co-ordination of Member States' structural policies in this sector.' Systems applied by each Member State 'must not lead to differences in treatment with regard to other Member States.' In particular, states 'shall ensure equal conditions of access to and exploitation of the fishing grounds situated in [these waters], for all fishing vessels flying the flag of a Member State and registered in Community territory' (Article 2.) However, access to certain fishing areas within the 3-mile limit 'may be limited, for certain types of fishing and for a period not exceeding five years from the time of entry into force of this Regulation, to the local population of the coastal regions concerned if that population depends primarily on inshore fishing' (Article 4).[26]

It was later an additional source of irritation for British fishing interests that the Community established the Common Fisheries Policy on the very day that negotiations also began with Britain and the three other applicant states for membership of an enlarged grouping. Regulation 2140/70 had, it was felt, been rushed through without due regard being given to the issues posed by the enlargement of the Community to include the three major fishing states of Western Europe. Thus under the terms of the agreement on fisheries reached during the enlargement negotiations, the original policy was somewhat modified. In particular, member states of the EEC were authorised, notwithstanding the principle laid down in Article 2 of 2141/70, 'to restrict fishing in waters under their sovereignty or jurisdiction, situated within a limit of six nautical miles calculated from the base lines of the coastal Member State, to vessels traditionally fishing in those waters from ports in that geographical coastal area,' until 31 December 1982.[27] States availing themselves of this derogation, however, 'must not adopt provisions dealing with conditions for fishing in these waters which are less restrictive than those applied in practice at the time of accession.' In addition, a crucial point for British fishing interests, the 6-mile limit was extended to 12 miles in certain specified areas on the coastlines of the four applicant states, together with part of the French coast.[28] Given this checking of the trend begun in 1970, it is not surprising to find the original EEC members placing emphasis on the transitional nature of these arrangements. From the sixth year after accession at the latest, the Council, on proposals from the Commission, is to 'determine conditions for fishing with a view to ensuring protection of the fishing grounds and conservation of the biological resources of the sea'; and before 31 December 1982, the Commission is also to present a report to the Council on 'the economic and social development of the coastal areas of the Member States and the state of stocks.'[29]

Fisheries Politics in Britain: It has already been suggested that British fishermen's indignation over Scandinavian extensions of national fisheries limits was the major factor precipitating the Government's decision in 1963 to press for changes in the existing North Sea and North-East Atlantic fisheries régime. This pattern, of government policy being shaped in the context of a complex interplay between domestic pressures and international constraints, can be seen in operation on a number of recent occasions.

The industry itself is not a large one, providing employment for about 21,000 fishermen, of whom approximately two-thirds fish inshore. Larger numbers are, however, employed in other aspects of processing and production on land. Distant-water interests are concentrated in the three major ports of Hull, Grimsby and Fleetwood. Yet the political clout of the industry has been impressive and, moreover, would appear to be growing. This can perhaps be attributed in part to the nature of the issues involved; they can easily be portrayed in Parliament or the news media as conflicts in which British underdogs are doing battle with foreign opportunists from Iceland or the Common Market. More important has been the effective organization of fishing interests in Britain. Apart from specialized or *ad hoc* groups, those active in the disputes with Iceland have included the British Trawlers' Federation, representing the owners; the Trawler Officers' Guild, for the skippers and mates; and the mass-membership Transport and General Workers' Union, representing deckhands and dockers. Moreover, MPs representing fishing constituencies have been an active group in the House of Commons. It was estimated that between twenty and thirty Conservative votes might be dependent on a promise of revision of the EEC's Common Fisheries Policy at the time Parliament was deciding on British accession to the Community. In the subsequent renegotiations of the terms of entry by the Labour Government in 1974–5, a number of MPs, including Enoch Powell, seized on fishermen's grievances as one element in the general case against continued British membership of the European Community.[30]

However, the British Government's responsiveness to fishing interests' demands has not been uniform. Fisheries policy has been framed with an eye to the broader issues of British foreign policy and, in the case of the Iceland dispute at least, defence policy. This much is apparent from studying the conflict with Iceland in the early 1970s. Iceland's new coalition government of 1971 terminated the 1961 agreement, and gave notice of its intention to bring in a 50-mile limit with effect from 1 September 1972. In a study of British policy-making on this question, William Wallace points out that several government departments were involved in addition to the fishery experts, and moreover that the three most directly concerned came to sharply differing interpretations of the best course of action for Britain. It is arguable, he suggests, that the British and Icelandic foreign ministries could fairly quickly have reached some kind of compromise on the dispute, had not their actions been constrained by a need to accommodate domestic political pressures. In particular, on the British side, the campaign of the inshore fishermen against British acceptance of the EEC's Common Fisheries Policy made speedy settlement impossible in the context of the delicate negotiations then going on in Brussels. All sides of the fishing industry in Britain combined to form a

Fisheries Joint Action Committee to put pressure on Whitehall, and the demand for naval protection for trawlers was followed up by MPs in the House of Commons. A compromise between the two sides did eventually surface late in 1973; but this was arrived at only after incidents in which live rounds were fired by Icelandic coastguard vessels at British trawlers, after London had stepped up the protection offered to British fishermen, and after extensive diplomatic exchanges, both bilaterally and through NATO, and talks at the prime ministerial level. Throughout the course of the dispute, the closest contact was maintained between the Fisheries Department and the British Trawlers' Federation. Federation members were, for example, included in several delegations to Reykjavik, and official contact was kept up also with the group of MPs representing fishing constituencies.[31]

A comparable process is evident during the negotiations on British accession to the European Community in 1971–2 and on revision of the terms of entry in 1974–5. The objection of the fishery organizations to the basic principle of free Community access to all fishing grounds of EEC member states was heightened by other complaints during the first of these. It was claimed, for example, that Community fishermen were not following proper conservation measures, and were using finer-meshed nets than those commonly used by British vessels, or were using methods like chasing fish into trawls by trailing chains along the sea floor. In general, however, with some reservations, the provision for a Community market protected against third-country supplies was acceptable.[32] British fishermen's organizations pressed their case with novel tactics: in October 1971, inshore fishermen descended on the Conservative Party Conference in Brighton from two dozen boats with anti-EEC slogans and Very pistols. Yet this pressure, exerted also through Parliament, proved ineffectual in bringing fishery questions to a position of high priority on the agenda of the negotiating conference. The conference took up fishery questions only in June 1971, after other issues relating to British accession had been largely resolved, and by which time neither British nor EEC negotiators were prepared to see the talks flounder on questions of fisheries.[33] Britain did, however, demand either a full 12-mile limit for the bulk of her coastline, or else a more effective period of transition that would better guarantee British long-term interests. Agreement was not finally reached until December 1971.

The issue arose again with the return of a Labour Government in February 1974, having a commitment to renegotiate the terms of British entry agreed to by the outgoing Conservative administration.

During the campaign leading to the referendum on the renegotiated terms held in June 1975, fishery questions achieved greater prominence than they had during the earlier negotiations. More long-standing complaints in the fishing industry were now joined by others: a large expansion of imports of cheap frozen fish from Norway, Iceland, Poland and other non-EEC countries; a fall in fish prices because of increases in landings and the greater competitiveness in the consumer market of beef and chicken; the lack of adequate coastal protection afforded fishermen by the Government, which, it was claimed, had resulted in overfishing even inside British territorial limits by vessels flying foreign flags; the adoption of what was viewed as a soft line by the Government in Community quota negotiations; increasing anxieties about the post-1982 situation; increased costs in the industry which, with lower returns, had led to the laying up or scrapping of a significant proportion of Britain's trawler fleet; general questions of conservation and fishery limits; and the economic state of the industry as a whole, in particular in relation to the question of government and EEC subsidies and grants. There was also increasingly a Scottish dimension to protests.[34] Direct tactics were taken much further than on previous occasions. In March–April 1975, following similar action taken earlier by French fishing interests, British fishing vessels blockaded 200 miles of Britain's coastline. In the context of continuing law of the sea negotiations, representatives of fisheries organizations began more insistently to demand an extension of limits to 200 miles as a matter of urgency.[35]

The issue was taken up at Westminster by MPs other than those more closely concerned with the fishing constituencies. Enoch Powell, for example, pointed out that after 1982 Britain would have no territorial waters and fishing grounds of her own. These would be 'the common territorial waters and fishing grounds of the whole EEC, where we shall have no more rights than the nationals of any other province of the new super state.'[36] Fishermen's grievances were also aired sympathetically by the Liberal, Conservative and Scottish National parties, both before and after the referendum. The Conservative Party demanded changes in government fisheries policy, and called for the establishment of a 200-mile exclusive economic zone which would include an area restricted only to United Kingdom vessels.[37] Yet the Government's response remained a cautious one, which may have reflected anxiety by pro-Community forces lest the sensitivity of this issue – which had already played a large part in the Norwegian referendum vote against European Community membership –

jeopardize the chances of an affirmative vote in the 1975 referendum. Thus at one point the Prime Minister argued publicly that renegotiation had been successfully completed, even though no statement had been issued officially about the status of the Common Fisheries Policy; and the Minister responsible for fisheries on another occasion listed the main achievement of renegotiation as being in the area of Community concessions to British demands concerning the marketing of beef.[38] The spring harbour blockade was ended by fishermen after assurances had been given by the Scottish Office that the Government would seek changes in the Common Fisheries Policy and raise the question of limits. Their chief grievance at that time, the question of fish imports from non-EEC countries, was already being studied in Brussels.[39]

3. The Politics of Oil

Oil politics are different from fisheries politics. One key difference follows from the redefinition by Western nations in the 1970s of the 'high' policy issues involved in questions of energy resources. Consequently, as *The Times* commented at the beginning of the period of finds of commercially exploitable quantities of oil in the British sector of the North Sea: 'There is no industry in the world that is more mixed up with politics than oil.'[40] The discovery of large, indigenous supplies of oil in the North Sea had had far-reaching implications by the mid-1970s on the internal politics and external policies of states like Norway and the United Kingdom, and also on the fabric of intergovernmental exchanges through the European Community, the OECD, and other bodies. Small-scale oil fields have been tapped inside Britain for several decades.[41] It was the Shell–Esso discovery of the Groningen gas field in Nothern Holland in 1958 that first raised the possibility that the North Sea might become a rich source of hydrocarbons in the future. During the early and middle 1960s, the search was essentially for further natural gas fields. In 1968, Philips discovered the large Cod and Ekofisk oil fields in the Norwegian sector of the North Sea shelf close to the boundary with the United Kingdom sector, and the Tenneco field in the Dutch sector. There has followed an almost yearly count of major oil finds. In September 1970, Philips made a find in the British sector four miles from the Norwegian border, near Ekofisk; in the following month, British Petroleum announced the discovery of a major field east of Aberdeen.[42]

It was not long before talk of self-sufficiency in oil became a commonplace of British political debate on the North Sea finds. The rhetoric of this debate deserves mention if only for the role it has played in orienting publics towards the issues involved. As early as mid-1970, the specialist *Petroleum Press Service* of London declared that, 'The oil discoveries are to Europe what Prudhoe Bay was to the USA, an indigenous and secure source of oil.' The character of the industry itself was at stake, based as it was on 'the hitherto inviolable assumption that the world's second largest consuming area, which is Western Europe, must necessarily be supplied from areas remote from it.'[43] *The Times'* special correspondent on these questions wrote in 1972 that the finds had 'completely changed Britain's energy outlook for the rest of this century',[44] while one enthusiastic participant in a conference on North Sea oil held that year expressed the view that 'North Sea oil is God's last chance for the British.'[45] Yet estimates of the size of the oil reserves and projections of the proportion of British or West European energy needs that could be met by regional supplies have varied tremendously. More than that, the business of estimating the extent of exploitable reserves became itself one element in British political debates on offshore oil development policy. It produced, for example, the complaint by Lord Balogh that the oil industry was playing down the size of the finds in order to secure better conditions for oil exploration and in addition to obtain higher prices from the Gas Council, the sole customer for British North Sea gas supplies.[46] Official British Government estimates showed a steady increase during the early 1970s with some tapering off later. In March 1972, the Minister for Industry said that discoveries north-east of Shetland could lead to production figures of 25 m. tons per annum by 1975, and perhaps of 75 m. tons by 1980.[47] Forecasts by the National Institute of Economic and Social Research in November 1972 were that the share of oil and natural gas in the primary energy input was likely to rise to over two-thirds by 1980; and that by then, North Sea oil and gas could be meeting 45 per cent of Britain's energy requirements.[48] By April 1975, production in 1980 was being officially forecast at between 100 and 130 m. tons per annum. It was stated that Britain was still on schedule for becoming self-sufficient in oil by that date, and moreover that sufficient reserves existed to sustain production throughout the 1980s at 100–150 m. tons a year, and perhaps more than that for some years.[49]

Evolution of British Policy: The emphasis in the present discussion is on the broader picture of politics in Britain rather than the details of the formulation of British offshore oil policy. However, the origins and character of that policy require mention at the outset. While political debate on seabed resources did not begin in any major fashion until 1970–2, the main outlines of government policy in relation to the North Sea shelf had been laid down several years earlier. In 1964 Britain ratified the 1958 Continental Shelf Convention, and thus accepted the principle that the continental shelf fell under the jurisdiction of the coastal state, together with the provision for median lines to be drawn between countries facing each other across the shelf. Agreements and disputes on demarcation of the shelf between North Sea states, including Britain, continued into the 1970s.[50] Unlike fisheries, then, the initial ground rules for a regional offshore oil régime were set in the absence of even sketchy knowledge of the nature of the resource at stake; North Sea shelf demarcation was not an issue associated with public political activity in Britain. Only later did questioning of the fundamental principles involved arise in West European politics, for example in the context of French grievances at her 'exclusion' from the indigenous oil resources of the region. Britain, indeed, turned out to be specially favoured by the division of the continental shelf of the North Sea by the median-line principle. An estimated 46.7 per cent of the area fell under British jurisdiction (see Table 2). Moreover, when oil fields were discovered, they were located primarily in a north-south strip straddling the British–Norwegian sector boundaries, and then later increasingly in the northern provinces of the British sector. Demarcation of the shelf also provides a useful slant on the impact of offshore oil development on Scottish politics, which will be discussed shortly. The British area was further subdivided by an Order of 1968 for the purpose of specifying the parts of the North Sea falling respectively under Scottish or English civil and criminal law. As a result, the Scottish area became 62,500 square miles, almost double the English one of 32,800 square miles.[51]

The first allocations of licences by the Ministry of Power in Britain for seabed exploration were made in November 1964, when 364 blocks were allocated to 22 companies or groups. For the next four years, exploratory activity was geared primarily to the discovery of natural gas fields. Official policy on oil was shaped by the need to respond quickly to the discoveries of the late 1960s. The principles behind the thinking of the Conservative Government from 1970 were articulated in a number of official policy statements. In 1972 the Secretary for Scotland said that the Government's position was quite clear: it considered that any restrictive conditions on exploration and development could lead only to delay in exploiting a valuable resource.[52] The context of the remark was growing criticism from the

Table 2: Estimated Area of Coastal State Jurisdiction over North Sea Continental Shelf

	Area (in '000 sq. miles)	% of Total
UK	95.3	46.7
Norway	51.2	25.1
Netherlands	21.8	10.7
Denmark	18.8	9.2
West Germany	13.9	6.8
Belgium	1.6	0.8
France	1.6	0.8
	204.2	

Source: MacKay and Mackay, *The Political Economy of North Sea Oil*, London, Martin Robertson, 1975, p. 21.

Labour Party that corporations engaged in North Sea exploration had been given too free a hand by the Government. Later in 1972 the Prime Minister reaffirmed that the Government had adopted a licensing policy aimed at the fastest possible development of oil resources.[53] The course of government offshore policy in succeeding years, and its evolution in relation to energy policy more generally following the framework established by the Government's 1967 White Paper, is not traced in the present chapter.[54] However, it is worth while noting that the perceived necessity for speedy development tended in practice to determine a number of aspects of licensing and taxation policy. Thus competitive auctions for licences were not held. Rather, the Government used its discretion in assessing the proposed work programmes of the applicants, and in so doing looked favourably on applicants with intensive work programmes. Incentives to work at speed were introduced. Each licensee, for example, was required to surrender one-half of his area after a six-year period, which entailed some haste on the part of the company or consortium in coming to decisions about which part of any block would produce the best returns. Similarly, the annual rental of each block was relatively low. These and other points can best be discussed here by examining the issues raised in political debate in Britain on offshore oil policy, and touching on the kinds of changes in government policy that ensued.

The British Political Debate on Offshore Oil Policy: This debate reached something of a peak in the years 1971–3, for two main reasons: first, it was during this period that the political issues involved in the exploitation of the recently discovered oil were largely shaped; and second, the momentum of the Labour Government's own offshore development policy became channelled after 1970 into sustained criticism of the new Conservative administration.

The first issue related to the revenue accruing to the state as a result of offshore development. Critics maintained that the existing royalty rate of 12½% of the price at the well-head was too low; and that this was combined with a comparatively low corporation tax of 40 per cent, a proportion of which could be offset by companies under Double Taxation Agreements or against costs incurred in exploration and development. Companies and consortia engaged in the search for oil enjoyed, it was argued, more freedom than was politically acceptable. Thus they were benefiting positively from government investment grants; and the Government's hands were held to be tied since it had not acquired the right of direct access to the cost accounts or exploration data of companies with a view to preventing the emergence of excessive profits, and was in addition unable to exercise effective control over changes in the parenthood of individual companies. Opposition and other critics complained that a far-reaching debate on offshore policy was being unduly hindered by a serious lack of information about the relationship between the Government and the corporations, and in particular on the question of how officials of the Department of Trade and Industry were recommending the use of the discretionary powers in allocating licences to individual companies or groups – what work programmes had been imposed, how it proposed to assess taxes and royalties when the oil came ashore, and so on. It was suggested that the ways in which the price of oil was calculated for tax purposes was vague. Suggestions for changes included introducing sliding royalties or bonus systems to ensure that higher rates could be introduced on major finds, which in turn implied increased monitoring by the state of company activity; or the possibility of distinct oil production taxes, at rates higher than existing company tax levels.[55]

The question thus merged with the second issue: that of the role of the state in offshore development. One commentator criticized state participation in the search for oil in the British sector as 'an amazingly haphazard affair' when compared with the policies being developed in Norway and The Netherlands.[56] This had been a growing feature of Labour policies in the late 1960s.[57] In the natural gas domain, for example, priority had been given to consortia in which the Coal Board and Gas Council were members. By 1970, when it lost office, Labour had come round to the view that all applicants for new licences in the west coast should have at least 50 per cent state participation. An expanded role for the state became increasingly a factor in Labour thinking in opposition in the early 1970s, a trend that was accentuated by the general leftward shift of the Party during this period. Following a consultative document prepared by the Party in 1972, a commitment to nationalize North Sea oil was reached early the next year.[58] The Government's response rested partly on the general principle of the need for rapid development; partly on the conviction that the needs of oil exploration and exploitation called for corporation rather than for governmental expertise; and, finally, partly on some concern lest the OPEC states should seize on too demanding a British policy in relation to North Sea reserves as justification for demanding equity participation in the oil companies' concession areas in member countries.[59]

Third, MPs from constituencies particularly affected by offshore development raised the question of the potential benefits for local and regional industry and employment. In mid-1972, for example, the chairman of the Conservative Party in Scotland proposed that licences for exploration should have been made subject to the developing companies using local industrial facilities.[60] This view quickly gained ground, though not without company protests that the compulsory inclusion of local interests slowed down the search for oil, and public criticisms that British companies had themselves been slow to tackle the North Sea market. In September 1972, the Prime Minister declared that 'Now we are entering a new phase and this will be reflected in the allocation of future licences. We are watching carefully to ensure that British firms are given a full and fair opportunity to compete.'[61] Official steps taken during this period included the commissioning of a special report from the International Management and Engineering Group on the scope for British industry to benefit from the oil industry's North Sea oil expenditures; the public list of oil company requirements for exploration, platforms, transport, servicing, and so on, produced by the North-East Development Council and the Department of Trade and Industry; and the establishment of an Offshore Supplies Office to advise on problems connected with bringing more investment to Scotland and the north-east of England.

By contrast, finally, the environmental issue took longer to get off the ground. One academic critic of government policies drew on California's problems with oil spills and accused Britain generally of being 'hopelessly in love with North Sea oil'.[62] The issue came more sharply into focus and oil company exploratory activity moved further north and west in the British sector – outside, that is, areas where the immediate onshore region had at least the potential in terms of its infrastructure for providing required services. One correspondent to *The Times* declared: 'It would be scandalous if we were to allow Shetland to suffer a fate which would arouse every imaginable amenity group in Britain were we discussing the shores of Kent and Sussex or the civilisation of London.'[63]

*Scottish Politics and Offshore Oil Development.** Many of the economic issues raised in British political debates in the early 1970s had particular force for Scotland. Offshore oil development, moreover, gave an impetus to the articulation of latent discontents, and hence contributed in a decisive fashion to the atmosphere in which the Scottish National Party could achieve significant electoral victories. While oil was the crucial factor, the distinctive character of Scottish politics within the United Kingdom should not be overlooked.[64]

Although the electoral successes of the SNP parallel the discovery of large fields offshore, the Party had begun to enter the mainstream of Scottish political life in the General Elections of 1964 and 1966. In the municipal elections of 1968 the SNP outpolled every other party and group in Scotland, gaining over 100 council seats and the support of more than 30 per cent of the total electorate. Since the 1970 General Election the almost continuous series of successful strikes of oil has averted serious setbacks to this progress. The SNP took its share of the poll in the February 1974 General Election to 21.9 per cent of the Scottish electorate; in that of October, this figure increased to 30.4 per cent, and the Party returned eleven MPs to the House of Commons. Oil was presented as the major rebuttal of the argument that Scottish independence would necessarily entail loss of employment, a lowering of living standards and a general economic malaise. Without offshore oil, the point would have been seen as lacking much credibility. Nationalism has traditionally found support in times of prosperity, or of expectations of prosperity, but had been unable to sustain this backing during periods of economic decline. The SNP has consistently in the 1970s linked offshore oil policy with the issue of Scottish independence. In a manifesto of August 1974, for example, it pointed out that under existing United Kingdom legislation, the boundaries of Scotland's continental shelf were already defined – as a result of the

* This section was written in collaboration with Greig Macleod.

1968 Order mentioned earlier in the chapter – and that Scots law was already being applied within this area. Its position was stated as being that: 'The seabed and its subsoil in the submarine areas round the coast of Scotland shall be subject to Scottish sovereignty in respect of the development and exploration of natural deposits, to such an extent as the depth of the sea permits irrespective of any other territorial limits at sea, but not beyond the median line in relation to other states as agreed internationally.'[65] The general argument that London's revenue and taxation policy and existing planned rates of depletion of reserves worked to the detriment of Scottish interests has similarly been one to which public opinion has been responsive. In a poll published in *The Scotsman* in October 1974, 58 per cent of those questioned agreed with the statement: 'The oil in the North Sea belongs to Scotland, and the tax revenue from it should be used for the benefit of the Scottish people.' Comparable percentages were found in support of the views that 'Scotland will probably get very little benefit from the North Sea oil discoveries, it will all go to the oil companies and the British Government;' and that 'the Government is rushing through the development of the North Sea oil finds so that it can borrow money to pay off Britain's debts abroad.'[66]

The SNP has been able to move outwards from this central stand to elaborate more detailed policies for offshore oil development. In doing so, it has frequently taken the initiative in public and party political debate within Scotland on these questions. Thus it has called for a much lower extraction rate – of 40–50 m. tons per annum, rather than 130–150 m. – than have both major political parties in Britain. Such a policy, it argued in its 1974 manifesto, would extend the life of the resource to about a century and facilitate diversification of the Scottish industrial base. Second, and in line with Labour Opposition thinking during the early 1970s, it has called for a greater state role in offshore development. The approach of the Norwegian Government has been cited with approval because of its inclusion of such features as limited extraction rates, mandatory government participation in commercial oil fields, and obligatory quotas of Norwegian nationals and companies in oil exploration and exploitation. Third, it has emphasized the need for planned rates of growth with due regard to the environmental and social impact of oil. The effects of oil development, for example in the city and environs of Aberdeen,[67] were already marked by the mid-1970s. Concern had been voiced much earlier about the impact of similar kinds of development in Shetland or the Western Isles. Yet the complexity of the issues involved meant that no sharp confrontation arose between proponents of either oil development or environmental protection. In 1972 the chairman of the Highlands and Islands Development Board said that he wished 'people would stop reacting to the building of towns and houses and schools as if it were a curse. . .The development for oil will be a curse only if we mishandle it – if we allow ribbon development, traffic pollution, ugliness, and shoddy building, instead of taking the opportunity to show the world an example of forward thinking and good planning.'[68]

The argument in Scottish political debate hinged, however, on the economic potential of offshore reserves. One 1975 estimate of 1980 revenues from royalties and taxation, assuming production levels of 150 m. tons, was put at £3343 m. per annum. This figure, it has been pointed out, is equivalent to 68 per cent of the Scottish Gross Domestic Product in 1973.[69] Outside the SNP, there has been scepticism among some informed circles about the capacity of oil to act as a panacea, given, more particularly, the degree to which offshore oil development interests were non-Scottish or even non-British. The 'harsh fact' was, one writer observed in *The Scotsman* in 1975, that 'the main work of offshore oil production – the design, manufacture, and installation of systems to bring oil and gas ashore – is still dominated to a large extent by United States and continental interests.' There was 'still no major British – let alone Scottish – interest in the ultra-sophisticated fields of pipeline laying and platform installation.'[70]

The political repercussions of oil within Scotland have been widely felt. Each of the other Scottish political parties has been forced on the defensive; in the case of the Conservative Party in Scotland this has amounted to a difficult rearguard battle aimed at retaining a significant portion of its traditional support in Scotland. The Liberal Party in the early 1970s tried to channel nationalist sentiment towards its platform. In 1972, Jo Grimond, MP for Orkney and Shetland and a former party leader, called for more oil revenue to be diverted to local authorities in Scotland, adding that this revenue should not be used by the British Government in order to subsidize the *Concorde* supersonic airliner project.[71] Labour, itself threatened electorally by the SNP, especially after the Glasgow (Govan) by-election of 1973, responded by emphasizing the potential of offshore oil for creating employment in Scotland, provided that the constitutional framework of the United Kingdom remained intact. It did, however, move during Opposition in 1970–74 towards a commitment to create some form of Scottish assembly.[72]

The EEC's Energy Policy and Offshore Oil. A second challenge to British governmental autonomy in relation to continental shelf reserves, though of a far more muted and very different kind, arose out of British membership of the European Community. But in a somewhat similar way, oil triggered political activity which brought into question accepted norms and relationships. In law, the products of the seabed, and especially oil, and their exploitation, fall under the jurisdiction of the coastal state; the politics of the situation have been more complex. Popular indignation at the North Sea régime established in the 1960s has erupted occasionally in France, whose share of the shelf, as determined by the 1958 principle, was a mere 0.8 per cent of the North Sea area. The demarcations were denounced in strong terms by one writer in 1974: 'L'injustice de cette répartition est flagrante. Elle ne tient compte ni de la population ni des besoins. Elle constitue un déni de l'idée européenne. Elle consacre la monstruosité juridique qu'est l'appropriation de toute une mer. Les Francais qui ont accepté de signer cet accord sont de grands coupables. L'excuse de l'incompréhension ne suffit pas à les absoudre.'[73]

Questions of Western Europe's dependence on Middle East supplies have been discussed at the intergovernmental level since the 1950s.[74] The EEC itself began to take an active interest in the question at about the time that the ground rules for a common fisheries policy were under discussion. Since 1964, when the objectives of a common EEC energy policy were defined, it has been broadly accepted among the Commission's specialists that, 'L'intérêt de la Communauté requiert avant tout un approvisionnement sûr à des prix relativement stables et aussi bas que possible'; and that 'la dépendence naturelle de la Communauté à l'égard des importations revêt une importance plus grande que dans d'autres secteurs.'[75] The Community's continuing interest in this area has been reflected in a number of measures. A Council directive of 1968 imposed the obligation on member states to maintain minimum stocks of crude oil and/or petroleum products equivalent to at least 65 days' average daily internal consumption in the preceding calendar year.[76] It has also been involved in aspects of oil and gas policy as a by-product of work in other fields. For example, the Council in 1969 issued a directive on the attainment of freedom of establishment and freedom to provide services in respect of the activities of self-employed persons engaging in exploration for petroleum and natural gas.[77]

The Commission has occasionally shown an interest in taking the initiative in more significant ways. Criticism of the EEC's lack of an effective common energy policy arose even before the crisis brought about by Arab price increases in 1973–4.[78] The theme was developed on a number of occasions by Fernand Spaak, of the Community's energy directorate. Speaking in 1972, he argued that, while the attitude of Norway in wishing to develop her own offshore resources primarily in the interests of her own nationals was understandable, nevertheless 'maximum consideration' should also be given by producer countries to the interests of the Community as a whole. For example, there should be no restrictions on the freedom of establishment or on the freedom to supply services. With regard to exploration and production laws, he expressed the view that there 'might be some attraction in harmonizing what may seem excessive differences in the rights and obligations of licensees', and there might in general be a case for making exploration more attractive. In so far as rights of pre-emptive purchase existed in Community countries, they should be exercised in favour of the Community, and not in favour of any member state. Spaak also emphasized the need for efforts to be made to encourage the most rational and economic methods of transporting oil and gas from the source of extraction to the consuming area. The Community, for its part, should formulate its common energy policy in such a manner as to make the greatest possible contribution to the development of North Sea resources, to the balanced benefit of all concerned – the regions, industry, and energy consumers.[79] That the Community was moving cautiously in relation to North Sea shelf reserves is also evident from a 1974 study of Community energy demand in the 1975–85 period; the total requirements of the Community were expected to increase by about 5 per cent per annum during this period, with petroleum products satisfying the major part of new requirements by 1985. However, the part played by North Sea finds in these projections was not discussed, since it was 'premature to put forward an estimated amount of the effects – no doubt favourable – that the resources of hydrocarbons from the North Sea might have on the degree of energy dependence in the future of the enlarged Community.'[80]

Progress has continued to be made in the Community's energy policy. In 1973 the 65-day stockpile was increased to 90 days; and at the end of the following year the Council approved a variety of measures of conservation and diversification of supplies which, it was hoped, could reduce projected Community consumption by 15 per cent, and cut dependence on external supplies from the 1973 level of 63 per cent to between 40 and 50 per cent by 1985.[81] But developments have also been hampered by a number of factors. Britain's status in relation to the Community was not finally clarified until the result of the 1975 referendum had become known. The threat to British North Sea oil posed by EEC membership was raised by critics, including Anthony Wedgwood Benn, in the campaign preceding this vote;[82] a more dynamic stand by Brussels would thus have run counter to the goal of securing unequivocal British accession. The Community was further constrained by the importance assumed by energy questions in exchanges between Western countries in the mid-1970s. The response of Western consumer nations to Arab producers was directed through the OECD and the new International Energy Agency, rather than through the European Community's more restricted membership.[83] And Western European conflicts over energy policy during this period highlighted the many difficulties in the way of a common approach.

For its part, the British Government's interest both in sustaining public support for Community membership in 1974–5, and in establishing a strong bargaining position in the event of future negotiations on oil with other Western nations, dictated firm adherence to the letter of the law. In its White Paper on the renegotiated terms of entry arrived at during this period, the Government stated: 'The Community has started to establish a common energy policy. The Government welcome this work provided that it is conducted in a realistic fashion. They will never allow it to develop in ways which could threaten our own ownership or control over our own natural resources – North Sea oil and gas, for example – and the Commission have made it quite clear that this is no part of their purpose.'[84]

4. Western Europe: Emergent Régimes and Political Behaviour

The limited scope of this chapter was noted at the beginning, but the extent of this restriction can now be seen more clearly. The two functional areas discussed give only a partial picture of West European ocean politics, even discounting the emphasis on British and European Community politics. There is, for example, an evolving network of rules relating to pollution, particularly in the context of North Sea and tanker oil spillage. The Norwegian and British governments have been engaged for some time in rounds of talks on questions, such as pollution and safety, related to North Sea oil rigs. Shipping and transport, and the maritime aspects of defence, are also areas of more than marginal significance for the ocean politics of the region. Other, more specific, issues vary from the impact of the European Community's developing interest in the field of beach management, to the problems associated with activities such as seabed tin-mining off the coast of Cornwall or fish farming, and questions of the physical defence of North Sea oil rigs and onshore installations against sabotage from politically motivated groups. Finally, we have noted only in passing the global context. European Community member states made efforts to establish common positions for the Caracas, Geneva and New York sessions of the Third UN Conference on the Law of the Sea. Though in general it would appear that greater importance is attached to regional developments, the two levels are clearly closely interrelated.

The politics of oil and of fisheries display many points of difference, in terms of the sizes of the respective industries, the perceived importance of the issues at stake, the level at which intergovernmental exchanges are habitually conducted, the range and type of domestic and transnational organizations involved in political processes, the extent to which non-specialist publics have been sucked into political debate in these areas, or the constraints operating against the more severe forms of interstate conflict. In both cases, however, ocean activities influenced political behaviour in important ways. In the case of Britain, offshore oil became the carrot beyond the stick of the government's anti-inflation measures of 1975–6; even before the first flow of oil ashore in 1975, party politics had begun to adjust to the evident fact that beneficial electoral payoffs could be gained by whichever party was in office at the time the full impact of the new energy resource began to be felt. Fisheries too became a much more intensely and widely debated topic in the 1970s, and only partly because of continuing uncertainty over Britain's relationship with the European Community. In Scotland both issue-areas combined to bring into existence a significant regional challenge to the constitutional framework of the United Kingdom and the link with Brussels. Because of the prospect of conflict over ocean uses, there have been periodic discussions of the need for greater policy co-ordination at the national or European Community levels. The establishment of new ministries or agencies responsible for overseeing ocean policies might have the effect of increasing the monitoring and predictive capabilities of governments, but in the present circumstances it is difficult to see such bodies contributing usefully to the network of interdepartmental and intergovernmental consultation that already exists.

The states of Western Europe have been involved with ocean politics for as long as the seas have been used. The pattern of more recent developments falls neatly into this historical perspective. Yet the ocean politics of the 1960s and 1970s have been a more intensive affair than hitherto. There has been a trend towards the politicization of ocean activities and issues. To the degree that world politics during the next decade focuses increasingly on questions of resources, this trend can be expected to continue.

Notes

1. Elizabeth Young, 'Why Britain Needs a Ministry to Rule the Waves', *The Times*, 18 April 1975.
2. London, Robinson, 1750.
3. Haldor Laxness in the *Observer*, 27 May 1973; cited by William Wallace, *The Foreign Policy Process in Britain*, London, Royal Institute of International Affairs, 1976, p. 233.
4. Harold D. Lasswell, *Politics: Who Gets What, When, and How*, New York, McGraw-Hill, 1936.
5. Leon N. Lindberg and Stuart A. Scheingold, *Europe's Would-Be Polity: Patterns of Change in the European Community*, Englewood Cliffs, New Jersey, Prentice-Hall, 1970.
6. See for example the contributions to Georg Borgstrom and Arthur J. Heighway (eds.), *Atlantic Ocean Fisheries*, London, Fishing News, 1961. Studies of Britain include Trevor D. Kennea, *Changes of the Sea Fishing Industry of Southern England since the Second World War*, University of London, Ph.D. thesis, 1968; and W.C. Hodgson, *The Herring and its Fishery*, London, Routledge and Kegan Paul, 1957.
7. Michel Voelckel, 'Aperçus sur l'application de la Convention Européenne des Pêches', *Annuaire Français de Droit International*, 1969, pp. 763–4.
8. Daniel Vignes, 'La Conférence Européenne sur la Pêche et le droit de la mer', *Annuaire Français de Droit International*, 1964 pp. 671–2.
9. Albert W. Koers, *International Regulation of Marine Fisheries: A Study of Regional Fisheries Organisations*, London, Fishing News, Books, Ltd., 1973, pp. 90–2. See further: C.E. Lucas, 'Regulation of the North Sea Fisheries under the Convention of 1946', in *Papers presented at the International Technical Conference on the Conservation of the Living Resources of the Sea, 1955*, Rome, 1955, pp. 167–83.
10. See for example Herbert A. Smith, 'The Anglo-Norwegian Fisheries Case', *Yearbook of World Affairs*, 1953, pp. 283–307; Sir Humphrey Waldock, 'The Anglo-Norwegian fisheries case', *British Yearbook of International Law*, 1951, pp. 114–71; Richard O. Wilberforce, 'Some aspects of the Anglo-Norwegian fisheries case', *Grotius Society: Transactions for the Year 1952*, pp. 151–68.
11. Morris Davis, *Iceland Extends its Fisheries Limits*, Oslo, Universitetsforlaget, 1963; Lewis M. Alexander, *Offshore Geography of North-Western Europe*, Chicago, Rand-McNally, 1963, pp. 107 ff.; D.H.N. Johnson, 'Icelandic Fishery Limits', *International and Comparative Law Quarterly*, 1952 pp. 71–3 and 350–4; L.C. Green, 'The Territorial Sea and the Anglo-Icelandic Dispute', *Journal of Public Law*, 9, 1960, pp. 53–72; and for a more recent discussion of this and the later periods, see Stephen R. Katz, 'Issues Arising from the Icelandic Fisheries Case', *International and Comparative Law Quarterly*, 1973, pp. 83–108.
12. D.W. Van Lynden, 'The Convention on Conduct of Fishing Operations in the North Atlantic, London, 1967', *Nederlands Tijdschrift voor International Recht*, 14, 1967, p. 246; J. de Breucker, 'L'extension des limites de pêche et

le régime juridique de la pêche dans la mer du Nord', *Annuaire de Droit et Sciences Politiques*, 1963, pp. 115–31.
13. Van Lynden, op. cit., p. 247.
14. Ibid., pp. 248 ff. See further M. Voelckel, 'La Convention de 1er juin 1967 sur l'exercice de la pêche en Atlantique Nord', *Annuaire Français de Droit International*, 1967, pp. 647–72.
15. *Arrangement relating to fisheries in waters surrounding the Faroe Islands. Copenhagen, 18 December 1973,* Cmd. 5930, London, HMSO, 1975.
16. *Agreement ... on the regulation of the fishing of North-East Arctic (Arcto-Norwegian) Cod. London, 15 March 1974,* Cmd. 5615, London, HMSO, 1974.
17. *Exchange of Notes ... concerning the creation of certain trawler-free zones in areas adjacent to the present Norwegian fishery limit. Oslo. 30 January 1975,* Cmd. 5893, London, HMSO, 1975.
18. *The Times*, 1 July 1975.
19. Also Annex II of the Treaty. See Hans Peter Ipsen, *Europäisches Gemeinschaftsrecht,* Tübingen, J.C.B. Mohr, Paul Siebeck, 1972, pp. 830 ff.: Stanley Andrews, *Agriculture and the Common Market*, Iowa State University Press, 1973. The preamble to 2141/70 on the Common Fisheries Policy refers to Articles 7, 42, 43 and 235 of the Treaty (see below, note 24). For a discussion of the juridical basis of the Common Fisheries Policy, see D. Vignes, 'La réglementation de la pêche dans le Marché Commun au regard du droit communautaire et du droit international', *Annuaire Français de Droit International*, 1970, pp. 832–5.
20. Ibid., p. 836. The practice of Community organs is discussed in Y. Van der Mensbrugghe, 'La mer et les Communautés Européennes', *Revue Belge de Droit International*, 1969, esp. pp. 87–8, 104. The author cites as an example the Council regulation of 27 June 1968 (802/68) on the definition of the origin of goods; goods from one country include 'les produits de la pêche maritime et autres produits extraits de la mer à partir de bateaux immatriculés ou enregistrés dans ce pays et battant pavillon de ce même pays.'
21. 503/64; see *Official Journal of the European Communities*, No. 93, 1964, p. 2293.
22. Alan Campbell, *Common Market Law*, Longmans/Oceana, 1969, Vol. 1, p. 125, and Vol. 2, pp. 601–3; and 'Basic Principles for a Common Fisheries Policy', *Official Journal of the European Communities*, No. 58, 29 March 1967.
23. 252/68; see *Official Journal of the European Communities*, No. 32, 1968, p. 9.
24. 'On the establishment of a common structural policy for the fishing industry', 2141/70, *Official Journal of the European Communities*, No. 236, 27 October 1970, pp. 1–7; and *European Communities. Secondary Legislation*, London, HMSO, 1972, Part 24.
25. On the somewhat cumbersome phrase 'coming under the sovereignty or within the jurisdiction' of a state, see D. Vignes, 'New Tendencies in Respect of the Law of the Sea: Attitudes and Practices in the European Economic Community' p. 6: ' ... what the Community had in mind was the waters adjacent to the territorial sea, the access to and the use of which a member state, in virtue either of a treaty or of a national legislative provision, had reserved to its own nationals.'
26. In addition, Article 12 provides for the setting up of a Permanent Structural Committee for the Fishing Industry within the Commission, with representation from each member state.
27. Commission of the European Communities, *The Enlarged Community:*

Outcome of the Negotiations with the Applicant States, Luxembourg, Office for Official Publications of the European Communities, 1972. pp. 31–2. The document also acknowledged 'the very great importance of the fishing industry for Norway in consequence of Norway's special geographical situation.' On this see also Nils Vogt, 'EEC Enlargement: a Scandinavian Viewpoint', in *Britain and Europe Now*, London, Federal Trust, 1970.

28. The coastline of the United Kingdom specifically referred to consisted of the Shetlands and Orkneys; the north and east coasts of Scotland from Cape Wrath to Berwick; the north-east coast of England, from the river Coquet to Flamborough Head; the south-west, from Lyme Regis to Hartland Point (including 12 miles around Lundy Island); and County Down.
29. *The Enlarged Community*, loc. cit. On the general context, see P.J.G. Kapteyn and P. VerLoren van Themaat, *Introduction to the Law of the European Communities after the Accession of new Member States*, London, Sweet and Maxwell, 1973.
30. Wallace, op. cit.; Uwe Kitzinger, *Diplomacy and Persuasion: How Britain joined the Common Market*, London, Thames and Hudson. 1973, p. 170; Simon Z. Young, *Terms of Entry: Britain's Negotiations with the European Community, 1970–72*, London, Heinemann, 1973, p. 99.
31. Wallace, op. cit. On the background, see *Fisheries Dispute between the United Kingdom and Iceland*, Cmd. 5341, London, HMSO, 1973; Pierre-Marie Martin, 'L'affaire de la compétence en matière de pêcheries ...', *Revue Générale de Droit International Public*, 78, 1974, pp. 435–58; Louis Favoreu, in *Annuaire Français de Droit International*, 1972, pp. 291 ff.; and Katz, cited in note 11 above.
32. Young, op. cit., p. 100.
33. Kitzinger, op. cit., pp. 183–5. The author gives one common reaction of observers at the time; after listing five of the six key issues in the negotiations he adds, 'and finally, ludicrously, fish' (ibid., p. 97).
34. 'They remember the days of the 3-mile limit before 1964, when the Minches were scraped bare by big Fleetwood trawlers, Hebridean lobsters plundered by Bretons, spawning grounds in the Moray Firth destroyed by other big British and Belgian trawlers and boats from Flushing and Zeebrugge fished impudently up to the shorelines of the North Irish Sea and Firth of Clyde' (Neil Usher, writing to *The Times*, 5 April 1975).
35. *The Times*, 2 April 1975, quoting officials of the British Trawlers' Federation. In the referendum two months later on the renegotiated terms of entry of British membership of the European Community, the Western Isles and the Shetlands voted against acceptance; the effects of Brussels policies on fishing and crofting were major issues in the political debate preceding the vote (*The Times*, 7 June 1975).
36. *The Times*, 31 May 1975.
37. *The Times*, 1 July 1975.
38. Cited *The Times*, 25 March 1975. On the terms themselves, see *Renegotiation of the Terms of Entry into the European Economic Community*, Cmd. 5593, London, HMSO, 1974.
39. *The Times*, 3 April 1975. The Council of Ministers later produced a package of measures designed to alleviate the depressing effects on the industry of frozen fish imports (*The Times*, 1 July 1975).
40. *The Times*, 20 October 1970.
41. British Petroleum Co., Ltd., *The Oil Fields of Britain: An Account of the Search for Indigenous Petroleum and the Discovery and Development of the British Oilfields by the British Petroleum Exploration Company, Ltd.*, London, British Petroleum, 1956.

42. For a useful summary to that date, see Adrian Hamilton, 'What the Search has Shown So Far', *Financial Times*, 16 March 1972; and the later account in the Department of Energy's *Development of the Oil and Gas Resources of the United Kingdom*, London, HMSO, 1975, pp. 27–9.
43. *Petroleum Press Service*, July 1970, pp. 239–40.
44. Roger Vielvoye, *The Times*, 20 October 1972 ,Special Report on North Sea resources.
45. Sir Andrew Gilchrist, *Financial Times*, 14 December 1972.
46. Lord Balogh, 'The Scandal of the Great North Sea Give-away', *Sunday Times*, 13 February 1972. For a rebuttal, see Frank McFadzean, chairman-designate of Shell, ibid., 27 February 1972. William Hamilton, Labour MP for West Fife, said there seemed to have been a 'deliberate conspiracy' to undervalue the potential assets of North Sea gas and oil (speaking in an adjournment debate in the House of Commons, reported in the *Guardian*, 19 June 1972). Criticism of official underestimates has been formulated most persistently by Professor Peter Odell and his colleagues in Rotterdam; Odell has argued that North Sea oil potential may be up to five times greater than British Government forecasts. For a summary of some of these conclusions, and the reasoning behind them, together with responses by officials, see Jack McGill, *Investing in Scotland: The Fifth International Forum of the Scottish Council (Development and Industry)*, Glasgow, Collins, 1975, pp. 53 ff.
47. Sir John Eden, *The Times*, 16 March 1972. Cf. Tom Boardman, Minister for Industry, cited at *Petroleum Press Service*, June 1973, p. 204.
48. G.F. Ray, 'Medium-term Forecasts Reassessed: III. Energy', *National Institute Economic Review*, November 1972.
49. John Smith, *The Times*, 15 April 1975. This statement is elaborated in *Development of the Oil and Gas Resources of the UK*, op. cit. Cf. Boardman's May 1973 report to Parliament in which a 70–100 m. ton range by 1980 was envisaged (*Petroleum Press Service*, June 1973, p. 204). In 1974 estimates, the top end of the 1980 range was increased to 140 m. tons; however, interim production figures had by then begun to fall because of continuing delays in the offshore development programme, so that 1975 was the third year running that the government had been obliged to downgrade its estimates (see further in *The Times*, 15 April 1975).
50. *Great Britain, Acts and Bills. Continental Shelf Act, 1964*, London, HMSO, 1964; Uggi Engel, 'The case of the delimitation of the North Sea continental shelf before the International Court of Justice', *Nordisk Tidsskrift for International Ret*, 38, 1968, pp. 18–25; E.D. Brown, *The Legal Regime of Hydrospace*, London, Stevens & Sons, 1971, Ch. 2, pp. 41 ff. On the 1971 agreements between Britain and, respectively, Denmark, West Germany, and The Netherlands, see Cmds. 5193, 4881 and 4875, London, HMSO, 1971.
51. D.I. MacKay and G.A. Mackay, *The Political Economy of North Sea Oil*, London, Martin Robertson, 1975, p. 24.
52. Gordon Campbell, *Guardian*, 15 June 1972.
53. Speech in Inverness, *The Times*, 9 September 1972.
54. For a comprehensive discussion of official policy, see MacKay and Mackay, pp. 24–5, and Ch. 2 *passim*; and Ch. 7 *passim* for government policies on land. Licensing policy is assessed in K.W. Dam, 'Oil and gas licensing and the North Sea', *Journal of Law and Economics*, 1964. The background to all this is the transition from a coal-based economy, in which coal accounted for as much as 90 per cent of energy requirements even in 1950, through to a four-fuel economy (coal, oil, natural gas and nuclear power) postulated in the 1967 White Paper on the subject (Cmd. 3438). See further J.E. Hartshorn, *A Fuel Policy for Britain*, London, PEP, 1966.

55. For criticisms, and summaries of points made by the government's critics, see Lord Balogh, 'The Scandal of the Great North Sea Give-away', *Sunday Times*, 13 February 1972; James Poole, 'The Wrong Decisions Every Time', *Sunday Times*, 14 May 1972; 'North Sea Fact and Fiction', *Petroleum Press Service*, August 1972, pp. 278–80; and Adrian Hamilton, *Financial Times*, 18 July 1972. This debate took place in the context of changes in government policy during 1972 and 1973. Criticisms of taxation and licensing policy and procedures were also a feature of the *First Report from the Committee of Public Accounts, Session 1972–73. North Sea Oil and Gas*, London, HMSO, 1973. Changes in taxation policy were also an important part of Labour Government thinking after the 1974 General Elections.
56. James Poole, 'The Wrong Decisions Every Time', *Sunday Times*, 14 May 1972.
57. MacKay and Mackay, op. cit., pp. 24–5.
58. See for example the report on steps taken by the Home Policy Committee of the Labour Party (*The Times*, 13 February 1973); and by the Labour Party's Scottish Council (*Financial Times*, 10 February 1973). For a convenient summary of Labour's plans on returning to office in 1974, see Jack McGill, *Investing in Scotland: The Fifth International Forum of the Scottish Council (Development and Industry)*, Glasgow, Collins, 1975, pp. 87 ff.
59. The *Guardian* expressed support on the second point: 'Much as one welcomes Conservative conversion to state enterprise, one cannot immediately see either civil servants or a state corporation providing the knowledge, skill and enterprise required of a big oil company' (17 June 1972). Balogh attributed the last point, which he dismissed as 'ridiculous', especially to the Foreign Office ('The Scandal of the Great North Sea Give-away', *Sunday Times*, 13 February 1972).
60. Sir William McEwan Younger, *Guardian*, 15 June 1972.
61. *The Times*, 9 September 1972. Cf. the remarks of the Minister for Industry, Tom Boardman, reported in the *Financial Times*, 21 September 1972.
62. *The Times*, 29 August 1972.
63. *The Times*, 29 September 1972.
64. This has only belatedly received serious study. As a result, political scientists are 'beginning to realise that the British political system fits rather uneasily into the conventional categories by which it is usually described': James G. Kellas, *The Scottish Political System*, Cambridge University Press, 1973, p. 1. For an earlier study on this theme, see Ian Budge and D.W. Urwin, *Scottish Political Behaviour: A Case Study in British Homogeneity*, London, Longmans, 1966.
65. *Scotland's Future: The Manifesto of the Scottish National Party. An Introduction to a Practical Programme of Social Justice for the People of Scotland*, SNP, 1974, pp. 13, 19. Kellas notes that the distinct legal system of Scotland is one of the strongest clues to the existence of a Scottish political system (op. cit., p. 3). The SNP later criticized as a *reductio ad absurdum* the argument that Shetland should, on similar grounds to those put forward by the SNP for Scotland, lay claim to sovereignty over its own continental shelf (*SNP Research Bulletin*, Vol. 4, No. 4, October 1974, p. 1).
66. ORC poll data, published in the *Scotsman*, 4 October 1974. At the same time, however, 68 per cent supported the view that the benefits flowing from North Sea oil should be shared with the rest of Britain (ibid.)
67. See for example, Harry Dunn, *The Times*, 20 October 1972, Special Report on the North Sea; Duff Hart-Davis, 'North Sea Oil: Winners and Losers', *Sunday Times*, 13 August 1972; David Taylor, 'The Social Impact of Oil', in Gordon Brown (ed.), *The Red Paper on Scotland* (EUSPB 1975), pp. 270–81.

68. Sir Andrew Gilchrist, *The Times*, 20 October 1972. For a critical view, see G. Rosie, *Cromarty: The Scramble for Oil*, Edinburgh, Canongate Press, 1974.
69. MacKay and Mackay, p. 173.
70. Alistair Balfour, *The Scotsman*, Oil Supplement (January, 1975), p. 2, cited by Taylor, op. cit., p. 271.
71. Cited by Duff Hart-Davis, 'North Sea Oil: Winners and Losers', *Sunday Times*, 13 August 1972.
72. For a short discussion, see further Greig Macleod and Robert Boardman, 'Scottish Nationalism and Oil', *International Perspectives*, March/April, 1975, pp. 36–9.
73. Sydney Smith, 'Miraculeux Pétrole des Mers', *Paris Match*, 21 September 1974.
74. See for example, Richard L. Gordon, *The Evolution of Energy Policy in Western Europe: The Reluctant Retreat from Coal*, New York, Praeger, 1970; Harold Lubell, *Middle East Oil Crises and Western Europe's Energy Supplies*, Johns Hopkins, 1963; OECD, *Energy Policy: Problems and Objectives*, 1966; ECE, *The Price of Oil in Western Europe*, 1955; W.G. Jensen, *Energy in Europe, 1945–80*, London, Foulis, 1967; OEEC, *Europe's Growing Needs of Energy: How Can They be Met?*, 1956; OEEC, *Europe's Need for Oil*, 1958; and OEEC, *Towards a New Energy Pattern in Europe*, 1960.
75. Commission des Communautés Européennes, *Première Orientation pour une Politique Energétique Communautaire*, Brussels, Services des Publications des Communautés Européennes, 1969, pp. 11, 12. For an earlier discussion, see J.E. Hartshorn, *An Energy Policy for EEC?*, London, PEP, 1963.
76. 414/68, and 416/68; see *Official Journal of the European Communities*, No. 308, 1968, pp. 14, 19; and *European Communities: Secondary Legislation*, London, HMSO, 1972, Part 7, pp. 1, 7.
77. 82/69. Cf. the remarks of Spaak, note 79 below.
78. See for example Bastiaan van der Esch, speaking at the Fifth Congress of the International Federation for European Law, Berlin, September 23–26, 1970; cited at *Common Market Law Review*, 8, 1971, p. 272.
79. F. Spaak, 'EEC Energy Policy and the North Sea', summarized at *Petroleum Press Service*, October 1972, pp. 377–8; and the report of the first North Sea conference (*Financial Times*, 21 September 1972), and the second (*Financial Times*, 14 December 1972).
80. Commission of the European Communities, *Prospects of Primary Energy Demand in the Community, 1975–1980–1985*, Luxembourg, Office for the Official Publications of the European Communities, 1974, p. 57 n., and also pp. 21, 31, and 54.
81. *The Times*, 18 December 1974; Adrian Hamilton, 'Oil in Europe', *Financial Times*, 4 July 1973.
82. *The Times*, 14 April 1975.
83. See *Agreement on an International Energy Programme. Paris, 18 November, 1974*, Cmd. 5826, London, HMSO, 1975.
84. *The Times*, 15 April 1975. The Home Policy Committee earlier said that it 'totally rejected' the views of Spaak: 'Oil and gas found off our shores belong to the British people as surely as do our other mineral resources' (*The Times*, 13 February 1973). Cf. the remarks of Eric Varley, Secretary of State for Energy, on EEC suggestions for a common market in energy products (*The Times*, 18 December 1974).

Further Readings

1. M.W. Janis, 'The Development of European Regional Law of the Sea', *Ocean Development and International Law,* 1973, pp. 275–89.
2. M. Hardy, 'Regional Approaches to Law of the Sea Problems: the European Community', *International and Comparative Law Quarterly,* 24, 1975, pp. 336–48.

9 MARINE RESOURCE CONFLICTS IN THE NORTH PACIFIC*

Choon-ho Park

This chapter attempts to analyze the impact of the law of the sea on the major marine resource conflicts in the North Pacific region. For the purpose of this study, the term North Pacific will encompass the East China and Yellow Seas, the Sea of Japan, the Okhotsk Sea and the Bering Sea. Under this definition, the coastal communities concerned include China, Korea, Japan, the Soviet Union, Canada and the United States.

In this group six coastal states are countries of great variation in size, degree of development, economic, political, maritime and military power and extent of utilization of the sea. Among them are also the world's largest fishing states and most advanced ocean-mining states. This is a rare combination that makes the North Pacific unique as a maritime region, especially as it relates to the extractive use of the sea.

Conflicts over marine resources in this region, as everywhere else, arose originally from rival claims which adjacent or opposite countries placed on some species of fish found in their coastal areas. Eventually, such conflicts evolved into general problems of fishery jurisdiction between the claimants and were further complicated when distant-water fishing vessels of some coastal states began to frequent the offshore fishing grounds of others.

Consequently, some fishery disputes in the North Pacific severely strained the political relations between the parties involved, but were usually settled in the form of a negotiated agreement. One of the earliest examples of such a settlement may be seen in the fisheries treaty concluded between Japan and Korea in 1442 to regulate Japanese fishing in Korean coastal waters. A somewhat more recent one, which happens to be still in force, was the Bering Sea fur seals agreement concluded between Russia and the United States in 1824.

From the viewpoint of the law of the sea, however, there are four

---

* The author is indebted to Prof. Jerome A. Cohen, Director, East Asian Legal Studies, Harvard Law School, for his advice on this article, and to Mr. Michael R. Moyle and Miss Jamie P. Horsley of Harvard Law School for reading the manuscript. The views expressed in this article are those of the author.

major fisheries agreements in the North Pacific which are of basic importance in understanding the conflict of fishery interests among the coastal states. They are the Canada–Japan–United States agreement of 1952, the Japan–Soviet Union agreement of 1956, the Japan–South Korea agreement of 1965 and the China–Japan agreement of 1975.

On the issue of mineral resources in the North Pacific, the only serious confrontation arose over the East China and Yellow Seas. In these two adjoining seas, five governments of the three coastal states – China, Japan and Korea – argued over a patch of continental shelf believed to contain oil. Because both the two Chinese and the two Korean governments share common interests on this issue relative to other coastal states, the controversy here consists of three bilateral disputes which are closely interlocked with one another.

The conflict of interests over seabed oil here is characterized by the fact that it has almost every factor that makes shelf boundary delimitation a difficult undertaking. With the law of the sea itself still in the process of reform, none of the three disputes is likely to be settled independently of or differently from the others, certainly not in the near future.

Given the ocean development capabilities of the other coastal states – Canada, the Soviet Union and the United States – and the magnitude of the North Pacific Ocean as a potential source of mineral resources, it is quite possible that conflicts will eventually also arise in other parts of the North Pacific. At the present time, however, Japan happens to be the most involved nation, being a party to all four major fisheries agreements as well as to two of the three oil disputes in the region.

1. Fishing Rights Conflicts

(i) Between China and Japan[1]

The Yellow Sea and most of the East China Sea are relatively shallow and have abundant living resources, with the seabed ideally smooth for trawling. Because of this favourable natural condition, the offshore fishing grounds of China and Japan have always been highly attractive to fishermen, especially those of western Japan who found these grounds conveniently close to their own coasts. Whenever fishermen of different countries compete to share a common stock of resources, however, disputes over fishing rights usually arise, and the case of China and Japan was no exception.

The first clash between China and Japan over problems of fishing rights took place in December 1950, when a total of five Japanese fishing vessels were seized by China in the East China Sea allegedly for violations of what China regarded as its own fishing grounds. In the following years, China continued to seize Japanese vessels under similar charges. To Japan, which maintained diplomatic relations with Taiwan but had none with the new régime in Peking, the reason for the seizures seemed to be primarily political, but there was virtually nothing that the Japanese Government could do except informally protest against the Chinese activities.

Under such circumstances, it was the Japanese fishing industry that took the initiative to seek the safety of its operation in the East China Sea. A movement was started among Japanese fishermen's organizations in September 1952 which finally led to the formation in November 1954 of the so-called Japan–China Fishery Association of Japan, a private endeavour devoted to the promotion of peaceful fishery relations with China. In the meantime, the cease-fire in Korea the year before had helped to ease the regional tension, so that a non-governmental contact between China and Japan was thought to be possible.

Consequently, through the good offices of the Chinese People's Institute of Foreign Affairs, a series of negotiations were held in Peking in January 1955 between the above Japanese organization and its Chinese counterpart, resulting in the conclusion on 15 April 1955 of a non-governmental fisheries agreement with respect to the Yellow and East China Seas. When this agreement came into force in June 1955, China stopped harassing Japanese fishing vessels operating in its offshore waters.

On balance, however, the safety of operation which Japanese fishermen so ardently sought and finally secured by virtue of the agreement was a mixed blessing, as they had to agree to various restrictions which China pressed on them in the name of resource conservation. In the seven fishing zones established in the Yellow and East China Seas, Japanese fishing would be regulated in terms of season, gear and size of fleet. In three other zones which China had proclaimed for military purposes in 1950, fishing by Japanese vessels was practically forbidden. No less exclusive than any of these fishing or military zones was the so-called East China Motor Trawl Prohibition Line, sometimes called the Mao Tse-tung Line, drawn along Chinese coasts in 1950 to prevent Chinese and foreign motor trawling.

The agreement was to have expired in June 1956, but was extended twice up to June 1958 when, partly due to the deterioration of political relations with Japan and partly to increasing violations by Japanese fishermen, China refused further extension but continued the seizure of Japanese vessels violating the security and conservation measures set down by the agreement. In the following years, Japanese fishermen operating in the offshore waters of China tended to assume an attitude of self-restraint until 1963, when a second agreement was signed with some minor changes, to remain in force for two years. This one was reinforced in the form of a third agreement in 1965 with further restrictions in favour of China. A seine fishing regulation was also incorporated into it in December 1970 in order to limit Japanese seining in the western half of the Yellow and East China Seas. It is this third agreement that has been extended seven times up to December 1975 by which time, as noted below, a formal fisheries agreement signed between the two governments on 15 August 1975 is expected to come into force.

The initiative for a formal fisheries agreement was first taken in September 1972 when Japan and China normalized their diplomatic relations, although it was not until August 1975 that the final agreement was signed. Japan was strongly opposed throughout the negotiations to what China had regarded from the beginning as an indispensable element of the new agreement, namely, Japanese recognition of China's military and conservation zones. Particularly unacceptable to Japan was the so-called Military Warning Zone, which extended from 30 to 100 miles offshore in the north-western Yellow Sea, into which Japanese fishing vessels were forbidden entrance. Another point at issue was the horse-power regulation line which varied in distance from 100 to 150 miles off the Chinese coasts, and which was proposed by China as a new restriction on Japanese trawlers over 600 horse-power. When major differences had finally been accommodated in the form of a compromise, the new agreement turned out to be simply another version of the old, slightly modified in form but generally more restrictive of Japanese interests.

At this point, it is important to take note of the legal formality by which differences relating to the three (originally four) unilateral demands of China were resolved in the final agreement. In brief, Japan agreed to respect the Chinese position without formally recognizing it. The technicality used was the same as in the case of the non-governmental agreement, i.e. the zones were not referred to in the principal text of the agreement. Thus, in correspondence exchanged separately upon the signing of the agreement, Japan reserved its position to the extent that while it would not formally recognize the Chinese position, in consideration of the need of resource conservation,

Japanese fishermen would refrain from operating in the Military Warning Zone and the East China Motor Trawl Prohibition Zone. This evidently reflected Japan's desire not to create a precedent which might bear on its future negotiations not only with China but also with other countries in whose offshore waters Japanese fishermen are operating.

Apparently this is a mutually convenient arrangement, but is not without its negative aspects. First, legal formalities aside, Japan has already observed China's prohibitory zones for the past twenty years and has agreed to do so in the future. As a result, the question can arise in time as to whether, by virtue of the above expedient (i.e. allowing continued Chinese enforcement of the arrangement with passive Japanese acceptance), Japan has effectively recognized the validity and precedential character of the Chinese position. Second, even if a Japanese pledge made through a less formal mechanism than the principal text of the agreement would be less binding, any restrictions on China would be equally unenforceable.

In the final analysis, however, arguments for or against China's unilateral measures have to be viewed with reference to the emerging concept of a 200-mile economic zone. The security and conservation zones in question are all situated within 200 miles of the Chinese coast or on the Chinese side of the median line between China on the one side and Japan and Korea on the other, so that within the theory of the 200-mile economic zone, China would not have to rely on the pretext of security or conservation in order to assert exclusive jurisdiction over the resources in question. Furthermore, with regard to the horse-power regulation zone, the economic zone theory implies that future access of Japanese fishermen to the zone would be by permission of the Chinese rather than by virtue of the exercise of an historic right of fishing, a concept which is rapidly losing support. Thus the provisional character of the new agreement may be seen partly from the proviso that, upon expiry its three-year duration, either party may abrogate the agreement with three months' notice.

Finally, it is necessary to consider the impact which this agreement is likely to have on the relations of the parties with North and South Korea. From the standpoint of both Koreas, it would appear that the agreement has been concluded in disregard of the interests which they hold as coastal states on the Yellow Sea. In this connection, it may be recalled in passing that, when Japan and South Korea concluded an agreement on the joint development of the East China Sea continental shelf in January 1974, China strongly protested, arguing that: 'The question of how to divide the continental shelf in the East China Sea should be decided by China and the other countries concerned through consultations'. During the protracted negotiations between China and Japan for the present fisheries agreement, both Koreas remained conspicuously silent, but their subsequent actions – whether they were in response to the agreement or not – may be noted with interest.

North Korea seized a Japanese fishing vessel, the Shosei Maru, in the Yellow Sea on 2 September 1975, for an alleged violation of its territorial waters. This incident, in which two Japanese fishermen were shot dead and two others wounded, took place within three weeks of the signing of the Sino–Japanese agreement. Soon afterwards, it was reported that Japan had proposed a non-governmental fisheries agreement to North Korea. It remains to be seen how the agreement, if concluded, is going to be patterned – after the China–North Korea fisheries agreement of August 1959 or the current China–Japan non-governmental agreement. It may be added that this is, in fact, the second attempt by Japan and North Korea to enter into such an arrangement, the first one having been made in vain in April 1955.

South Korea responded on 2 September 1975, by making a statement in which it expressed its disappointment at having been ignored as one of the coastal states. Shortly afterwards, Japan was asked to observe 'the special conservation zones' which South Korea had set up in the Yellow Sea and the Sea of Japan. Japan objected on the grounds that the South Korean measures were in violation of the Japan–South Korean fisheries agreement of 1965. Both Koreas are aware that, while a multilateral fisheries agreement would be highly desirable and necessary, it will not be possible until political relations between the coastal states have improved. Under these circumstances, a more practical South Korean reaction is likely to eventually result in the form of a proposal to Japan to revise or even to abrogate the fisheries agreement of 1965, which is seen as basically detrimental to South Korean fishery interests, as discussed below.

(ii) Between Japan and Korea[2]

Fishery relations between Japan and Korea have always been volatile and, at times, extremely hostile. Up until very recently, Korean fishermen seldom visited the coastal waters of other countries, whereas their own fishing grounds in the south have been frequented by Japanese fishermen for centuries. Regulation of Japanese fishing in Korean coastal waters dates back to 1426, when Korea agreed to permit Japanese fishermen to settle in three Korean ports, and to 1442 when the two countries concluded a fisheries treaty for the first time.

By virtue of these arrangements, the number of Japanese fishermen visiting Korean ports and fishing grounds began to increase rapidly, often causing serious conflicts with Korean fishermen. The ever-worsening situation culminated in what Korean history regards as the 'Japanese Fishermen's Uprising' of 1510, which resulted in relations being broken off between the two countries. Their feud over fishing in Korean coastal waters continued to affect their political relations sporadically until 1910, when Korea was annexed by Japan.

Japanese rule of Korea ended in 1945, but, during the Allied Occupation of Japan (1945–52), the so-called MacArthur Line confined the operation of Japanese fishing vessels to limited areas around Japan. The Line was abolished in April 1952, when Japanese sovereignty was restored by the San Francisco Peace Treaty. In anticipation of this abolishment, South Korea sought to foreclose the return of Japanese fishermen to its coastal waters by declaring 'The Presidential Proclamation of Sovereignty over the Adjacent Sea' in January 1952. The Korean claim was symbolized by what was commonly called the Peace Line or the Rhee Line, which extended from 20 to almost 200 miles at some points and within which any Japanese fishing vessel was liable to be seized. Thus began one of the most acrimonious fishing rights disputes in history, which lasted for fourteen years before it was settled in the form of a negotiated agreement in 1965.

The fisheries agreement of 1965 has practically superseded the Peace Line, although it has never been formally withdrawn by South Korea. The agreement was concluded as part of a package deal by which the two countries normalized their relations, and their fishery relations have since entered a period of co-operation instead of confrontation. It is noteworthy that, for the first time, Japan has formally agreed to recognize the 12-mile fisheries zone of a foreign country. From the standpoint of South Korea, however, the agreement was essentially a retreat from its previous stand. The fishery jurisdiction of South Korea was confined to a zone up to 12 miles from its coasts, and, in the adjacent joint control zone, seizure of Japanese fishing vessels was not possible even for actual violation of the agreement. The Japanese catch in this second zone was to be measured, based on quarterly reports submitted by Japan. Additional baselines along the Korean coasts would not be drawn except by consultation with Japan. Aside from a series of such stipulations not commonly seen in most other such agreements, however, it is important to note that, under this agreement, the fishermen of both parties could have been able to operate peacefully in waters where earlier they could hardly stand the sight of one another.

In the meantime, the law of the sea itself has undergone some basic changes. When the Peace Line was declared by South Korea in 1952, the maritime jurisdiction of a coastal state was not regarded as expansively as it is now. With the emergence of the 200-mile economic zone concept, such jurisdiction is becoming increasingly exclusive. As a consequence of these new trends, there is doubt as to whether the fisheries agreement of 1965 between Japan and South Korea will survive. With the recent developments on the international scene, both Koreas may seek a new course in regulating foreign fishing in their offshore waters, perhaps following the Chinese model as embodied in the Sino-Japanese fisheries agreements of 1975.

(iii) Between Japan and the Soviet Union[3]

Fishery relations between Japan and the Soviet Union have been as complicated as those between Japan and Korea. Japanese fishermen began to frequent the coastal waters of Sakhalin in the early eighteenth century and gradually extended their operations to other areas off the Maritime Province of Siberia. Regulation of Japanese fishing around Sakhalin dates from the middle of the nineteenth century when, in February 1855, the Poutiatine's Treaty was concluded, concurrently opening Russo-Japanese diplomatic relations and settling the Kurile border issue. Since fishery problems between Japan and Russia were closely related to territorial issues, it was necessary to settle them by means of supplementary provisions in their territorial arrangements. This characteristic practice continued up until 1907, when they concluded a formal fisheries agreement.

Russo-Japanese fishery relations were also characterized by a series of controversies that arose from their different notions of territorial sea limits; Japan has been consistent in its application of a 3-mile limit since 1870, while Russia was not particularly specific up until 1909, when its 12-mile limit was formally put into practice. When Japan expanded its crab fishing in 1921 and salmon and trout fishing in 1927 and sent its fleet to the north-west Pacific, the Soviet Union responded with unilateral measures that included seizure of Japanese vessels violating its territorial sea. However, the Soviet Union concluded agreements with Finland in 1920 and with Britain in 1930 allowing the fishermen of those countries to operate within its territorial sea, and it eventually acquiesced in granting similar privileges to Japanese fishermen as well.

During the post-war period, Japan's north-west Pacific fisheries encountered basically different problems. When the MacArthur Line was abolished in 1952, Japanese fishermen immediately resumed their salmon and trout fishing off Russian coastal waters. In 1955, the Soviet Union reported a sharp decline in the population of these species in the north-west Pacific and placed the blame on Japanese overfishing. In March 1956, when negotiations with Japan on a territorial issue deadlocked, the Soviet Union surprised Japan with a proclamation establishing a fishery conservation zone in the north-west Pacific. Japanese salmon and trout fishing in the area was to be greatly restricted in terms of catch, season, gear and sphere of operation. The line enclosing the zone was commonly called the Bulganin Line, in the fashion of other such devices like the Mao Tse-tung Line of China and the Rhee Line of South Korea. Japan's persistent request for the return of its northern territory was answered by the Soviet Union with a lightning blow to its fishing in the very area in which the territory was situated. Japan was thus compelled to negotiate for a fisheries agreement, which was signed in May 1956 and came into force in December of that year. Consequently, the Bulganin Line was not applied at all, but was superseded first by a provisional measure and subsequently by the North-West Pacific Fisheries Convention of 1956.

This convention regulated Japanese salmon and trout fishing in the north-west Pacific through a powerful fisheries commission, which meets annually to adopt various conservation measures covering fishing for the year. The commission is authorized to determine not only the size and location of the area to be closed to Japanese operation but also to limit Japan's annual catch. Ever since the commission's first meeting in 1957, the closed area has steadily expanded and the tonnage allotted to Japan has gradually decreased, from 180,400 tons in 1957 to 87,000 tons in 1975.

The convention also regulated Japanese crab fishing in the north-west Pacific. Crab fishing represents one of the most important Japanese fishing enterprises, so much so, in fact, that Japan has been reluctant to ratify the Geneva Convention on the Continental Shelf, partly because, according to the Convention, crabs belong to continental shelf resources rather than to ordinary fishing resources. In contrast, the Soviet Union sharply disagreed with Japan on this definition and even incorporated its version into Soviet domestic law in February 1968. Subsequently, in the face of Japanese objection, regulation of crab fishing was written into a separate agreement in April 1969 along the pattern of the Japan–United States agreement of 1964. The conservation measures for crabs are now much more extensive and restrictive than in the original agreement and, as in the case of salmon and trout fishing, the tonnage allotted to Japan has also steadily decreased. In recent years, either side of the Kamchatkan Peninsula occasionally has been closed entirely for the season.

In a legal context, the conflict between Japan and the Soviet Union over north-west Pacific fishery resources arose originally from their different delimitations of territorial sea but was greatly complicated in addition by their disagreement over the concept of the so-called historic fishing rights. Since this concept is now losing force, a significant point related to their territorial sea limits remains to be considered. Until very recently, the dispute between the two countries was confined to fishing that took place in the offshore waters of the Soviet Union, not those of Japan. Between late 1974 and early 1975, however, a dramatic reversal of circumstances took place when a mammoth fleet of nearly 100 Russian fishing vessels, most of them large trawlers served by huge mother-ships, suddenly appeared close to Japanese coasts and started raking the fishing grounds immediately outside the 3-mile limit. Russian fishing in Japanese coastal waters began in the mid-1960s, but on a virtually negligible scale. This grand expedition, therefore, deeply shocked Japanese coastal fishermen. Amid their cries for immediate extension of the Japanese territorial sea limit up to 12 miles, the Government was compelled to seek an agreement with the Soviet Union. In September 1975, Japan was greatly relieved when an operational procedure to regulate Russian fishing in Japanese coastal waters was agreed on. Japan itself is now ready to follow the general fashion of the 12-mile limit. Until this actually has been done, however, its coastal fishing grounds will continue to remain vulnerable to foreign fishing.

In the final analysis, the future of fishery relations between Japan and the Soviet Union will also depend largely on what the Third United Nations Conference on the Law of the Sea will decide with respect to the 200-mile economic zone proposal, which Japan is reluctant to accept. It now remains to be seen how rigidly or flexibly the Soviet Union, itself one of the major distant-water fishing states as well as a supporter of the proposal, would apply it to protect its own coastal fisheries on the one hand and its distant-water fisheries on the other.

(iv) Between Japan and the United States[4]

Fishery relations between Japan and North America began with a dramatic controversy in 1936 when, under a three-year plan, Japan launched an expedition to Bristol Bay for the purpose of surveying Alaskan salmon fisheries. The arrival of Japanese fishermen in the

North Pacific instantly touched off an angry protest from the Pacific fishermen of the United States and gave rise to legislative activity in Congress. In 1937 alone, three Bills were introduced purporting to restrict Japanese fishing in the North Pacific. In the face of this strong reaction, the Japanese surveyors withdrew from the troubled waters in 1938. The Pacific fishermen sought to foreclose any return of Japanese fishermen so persistently that, even during the War against Japan, three more Bills were submitted in Congress, making a total of ten by 1943. Although none of the Bills passed, the efforts succeeded in sustaining concern over the issue until it was finally given a place in one of the two Truman Proclamations of September 1945.

During the post-war years, Japanese fishing was restricted by the MacArthur Line, and the Pacific fishermen of North America relaxed their concern over the issue. However, when preparations were under way in 1951 for a peace treaty with Japan, a strong demand arose not only in North America but also in Europe and Oceania to ensure that, upon restoration of its sovereignty, Japan would respect the conservation measures for high-seas fisheries taken by other countries. Thus, Article 9 of the treaty obligated Japan to 'promptly negotiate with the Allied Powers so willing for the conclusion of fisheries agreements'. It was pursuant to this provision that, in November 1951, Canada, Japan and the United States held negotiations in Tokyo leading to the conclusion of the North Pacific Fisheries Convention, which came into force in June 1953.

By the terms of the convention, Japan agreed to abstain from fishing for halibut, herring and salmon in specified waters off the coasts of North America. In the case of salmon, the scope of specified waters was supposedly determined on the basis of their migratory range from United States coasts. This was the origin of what has come to be known as the principle of abstention, a new device by which major fisheries of the North Pacific have been largely pre-empted to date in favour of the two coastal states. In the course of the negotiations which took place before Japanese sovereignty was restored, the Japanese delegation was accorded 'a sovereign status', but Japan deeply resented the circumstances under which the principle had to be accepted. Japan was also concerned about the probable impact which its first post-war fisheries agreement would have on its fisheries relations with other countries. Japan has since tried a number of times to revise the convention, but in vain; for obvious reasons, it was not possible to obtain the required unanimity of Canada and the United States.

On its part, the United States has sought on a number of occasions to incorporate the abstention principle into universal conventions, relying on the particular ecology of the anadromous species represented by the salmon. An initial attempt was made at the First Law of the Seas Conference in Geneva in 1958. Failing in this, the United States ratified the Geneva Convention on the High Seas Fisheries with the understanding that the applicability of this principle should not be impaired by its ratification. In the current Third Law of the Sea Conference, this principle of abstention has again been advocated by the United States as the 'species approach'.

For two reasons, this convention is by far the most important of all the arrangements concerning North Pacific marine resources that are being shared by Canada, Japan and the United States. First, resources other than halibut, herring and salmon are of lesser importance to Canada and Japan and hence have not required bilateral regulation. Second, Japan and the United States currently have nine bilateral agreements, including one related to whaling in the North Pacific, most of which have directly or indirectly supplemented the present three-party convention as US–Japanese fishery relations became increasingly complicated. Three of these arrangements deserve to be noted because of their importance in Japan–United States fishery relations. One is the agreement of 1964 concerning king and tanner crab fisheries in the North Pacific. In this agreement, the United States describes crabs as continental shelf resources rather than fishing resources, as does the Soviet Union. It may be assumed, therefore, that the Japan–Soviet Union agreement of 1969 was patterned after this one. The second agreement of interest is that of 1967, which was concluded as an adjustment made necessary by the 12-mile fishery zone declared by the United States in 1966. The third one is the salmon fishing agreement of 1974, which supplemented that part of the three-party convention of 1953 concerning only Japan and the United States.

The number and content of all these arrangements between Japan and its North American counterparts since 1953 demonstrate how complicated their fishery relations have been. As in the case of Japan's fishery relations with other countries, future relations will hinge on the prospect of the 200-mile economic zone régime, as discussed later.

2. Continental Shelf Conflicts[5]

The Yellow Sea and the East China Sea are only a small area of the sea enclosed by the territories of China, Japan and Korea. The water is mostly so shallow that the entire seabed consists of a single piece of continental shelf with a narrow trench lining the west coasts of Japan's Kyushu and Okinawa. This means that the shelf may be delimited simply by drawing a set of three bilateral lines converging to a trilateral boundary somewhere in the East China Sea.

Nevertheless, a boundary dispute over this area started in 1969 when the coastal states became overly excited by the exaggerated promise of oil in their own offshore areas and began to make unilateral claims to what should have been divided by agreement with one another. The dispute has now become a major problem of the region, and it shows no prospect of settlement in the immediate future. There are various reasons for holding this rather pessimistic view.

Politically, North-East Asia has too many governments. Although the region has only three countries, those three countries contain five governments, China and Korea each having two. In other words, the seabed controversy is being argued by five parties over what should normally require only three to settle. In the present circumstances it is difficult for the parties merely to get together, far less successfully negotiate boundaries for the sea area.

Economically, North-East Asia has always suffered from a poverty of oil. Only China has recently become an enviable exception, while Japan and Korea still remain as poor in oil as ever. The price of oil has gone up four times since the energy crisis of 1973 and shows no sign of decline in the near future. As a result, the importation of oil now represents a major drain in the balance of payments of Japan and Korea. As a matter of fact, few other economies are so helplessly vulnerable to the politics of oil. This is a really crucifying situation to both of them and compels each to secure every square inch of the continental shelf to which it believes itself to be entitled. Furthermore, China's self-sufficiency in oil cannot lead either of them to expect her to be more flexible in negotiating for the boundaries, especially when the world is becoming increasingly conscious of the importance of natural resources and their development.

Geographically, the Yellow Sea and the East China Sea are highly complicated as far as the delimitation of shelf boundaries is concerned. First, the coastlines are so irregular at many points that the drawing of straight baselines alone will create a series of controversies among the parties involved. Second, there are uninhabited offshore islands which many would argue do not really deserve to be given full effect as base points for the measurement of distance. Third, there is a trench along the coast of Japan, with depths ranging from 400 to 2,500 metres which, unless ignored as a limiting factor, will cause Japan to claim great inequity in the division of continental shelf. Fourth, a serious territorial dispute has even emerged between China and Japan over the ownership of the Senkaku-Tiaoyutai islands, which has to be settled as a prerequisite to the solution of the boundary problem. The 1958 Geneva Convention on the Continental Shelf is a very limited help to the parties that confront this combination of complexities, a combination rarely found elsewhere.

Indeed, the present international legal dispute over the shelf originates, in large part, from the inevitable ambiguities of the Geneva Convention in relation to the delimitation of continental shelf boundaries, and has been further complicated by what the International Court of Justice invented in the course of its deliberations on the North Sea Continental Shelf Cases of 1967 to 1969. The judicially created concept of the so-called natural prolongation of land territory as an alternative basis for determining shelf boundaries between opposite or adjacent countries has emerged to undermine much of the foundation for the median-line principle, according to which neighbours should divide disputed shelf areas on an equal basis. To make matters more complicated, with the Third Law of the Sea Conference of the United Nations currently in progress, the natural prolongation principle and the median-line principle are now open to the danger of being partly superseded and partly modified by yet a third concept – that of an exclusive economic zone up to a limit of 200 miles from the coastal baseline. Pending the outcome of the current law-making conference of the United Nations, however, the parties to the present dispute have temporarily suspended the regional controversy, and will resume it upon conclusion of the conference.

The dispute has led to confrontation. In search of a breakthrough from what would otherwise remain an endless legal scramble, Japan, South Korea and Taiwan have made serious attempts to develop oil by joint efforts, leaving the boundary issue aside for further negotiation. The first attempt was made in late 1970, but the People's Republic of China came forward with a strong protest that frustrated the effort. A second attempt was made between Japan and South Korea alone and they signed two agreements in January 1974. One concerns the shelf boundary in the Korean Strait areas, which is not particularly problematic. The second, however, has become controversial, since Japan and South Korea decided, despite Chinese objection, to develop oil from heavily overlapping areas of the East China Sea, again suspending the boundary issue for further negotiation. South Korea ratified the agreements in December 1974 and is pressing Japan to do the same. Though the prospect of its success remains unpredictable, the significance of this endeavour deserves to be noted, and it may indeed prove useful for the settlement of disputes elsewhere. However, it has to be pointed out that from a legal point of view joint development does not settle but simply postpones the issue and that, unless all the claimants agree, it will possibly create additional difficulties in settling the basic issue of boundary delimitation.

The legal aspect of the present dispute can be summarized as follows: the argument essentially hinges on which principle of international law to apply. China invariably adheres to the natural prolongation of land principle, while Japan persists on the median-line principle. South Korea expediently relies on a combination of both. The innovation of an exclusive 200-mile economic zone would, however, help to eliminate as a limiting factor the legal status of the Okinawa Trench, or any other submerged areas exceeding 200 metres in depth, as well as override the natural prolongation of land territory principle because of its exclusivity. As boundary problems are confronted, the principles in the sea resources controversy are at this very moment undergoing an evolution. The median-line principle was seriously undermined by the natural prolongation theory, which, in turn, is open to a similar fate before the economic zone régime. Yet this reversal is likely to give the median-line principle greater applicability once again, since it is the only alternative easily assimilated into the 200-mile scheme because of the geography of the area. Korea, China and Japan are all within 400 miles of each other, thus making applicability of the 200-mile zone for each of the neighbours an impossibility and requiring some reasonable means of meeting the situation. The expectation is that in these circumstances the median-line principle will be the basis for the negotiations that will ultimately settle the problem. This trend will be definitely advantageous to Japan.

3. Conclusion

Up until the late 1960s, marine resource conflicts in the North Pacific were caused solely by problems of fishing on the high seas. Each of the fishery disputes discussed above had its own characteristics, arising from different historic backgrounds. But when, during the first two post-war decades, the maritime jurisdiction of coastal states began to be extended with respect to fishing in their adjacent waters, the traditional concept of a non-coastal state's historic fishing rights came into conflict with the newly emerging concept of a coastal state's preferential rights. In few other areas of the world was this conflict so dramatically realized as in the North Pacific. Since Japan was the only country that was involved in all the four major fishery disputes in the North Pacific, the regional controversy was being argued, in a sense, between Japan on one side and the rest of the coastal states on the other.

Furthermore, while the North Pacific region was thrashing out fishing right problems, the law of the sea itself was undergoing basic changes. To cope with the changing circumstances, the coastal states relied on what may be called an 'annual review' approach which offered two options. One was to enter into short-term arrangements, such as the China–Japan agreement of 1955–74 which had a mandatory life of one or two years but was renewed upon the expiration of each extension. The other option was to undertake long-term arrangements such as the Canada–Japan–United States convention of 1952 and the Japan–Soviet Union convention of 1956, which stipulated clauses allowing regular review of the operation. In this case, the regulatory organs were, of necessity, commissioned with stronger decision-making authority. Both methods also served to encourage more faithful observance of the arrangements on the part of the non-coastal state party – which was, in the present context, Japan.

As noted earlier, the future of the marine resource conflicts in the North Pacific, as everywhere else, is going to depend greatly on that of the 200-mile economic zone régime. In this connection, it is important to take note of an extraordinary geographical factor; Canada, Japan, the Soviet Union and the United States would be four of the seven largest beneficiaries of a 200-mile limit, since as much as 45 per cent of the submarine areas within that limit fall under their (the seven) jurisdiction. It is therefore necessary to consider the current attitudes of the North Pacific coastal states to this new régime, which appears likely to be adopted.

The coastal states of the North Pacific have made their positions on a 200-mile zone reasonably clear, with the exception of Japan whose support appears to be contingent on the degree of its exclusivity. This is understandable, as nearly half of Japan's annual catch of fish comes from distant-water fishing within 200 miles of other countries – in particular, Canada, the Soviet Union and the United States. South Korea assumes a similar attitude on this point. Geographically, China and North Korea would not greatly be affected by a 200-mile limit and will therefore support it in the name of what they fondly call the Third World interests. As maritime, naval and technological superpowers, the Soviet Union and the United States appear to find their own coastal fishing interests in heavy conflict with their global maritime interests and would therefore seek to make the zone selectively exclusive. Canada appears to be a more ardent supporter of the régime than any of the others.

In sum, the marine resource conflicts in the North Pacific are likely to be further complicated once seabed oil and other mineral resources are found in commercial quantities, while the fishing rights problems will probably be simplified if a 200-mile economic zone is applied.

Notes

1. Z. Ohira and T. Kuwahara, 'Fishery Problems between Japan and the People's Republic of China', 3, *Japanese Annual of International Law*, 1959, pp. 109–25; C.H. Park, 'Fishing Under Troubled Waters: The North-East Asia Fisheries Controversy,' 2, *Ocean Development and International Law*, 1974, pp. 110–22.
2. C.H. Park, ibid., pp. 98–110 and p. 123.
3. Z. Ohira, 'Fishery Problems between the Soviet Union and Japan', 2, *Japanese Annual of International Law*, 1958, pp. 1–19.
4. W.W. Bishop Jr., 'The Need for a Japanese Fisheries Agreement', 45, *American Journal of International Law*, 1951, pp. 712–19.
5. The Sino–Japanese–Korean disputes are so closely interlocked that they are treated in one section here instead of three. An earlier version of this section was presented at the 27th Annual Meeting of the Association of Asian Studies at San Francisco, 24–26 March 1975; C. Bethill, 'People's China and the Law of the Seas', 8, *International Lawyer*, 1974, pp. 724–41; C.H. Park, 'Oil Under Troubled Waters: The North-East Asia Sea-Bed Oil Controversy', 14, *Harvard International Law Journal*, 1973, pp. 212–60.

References

Butler, W.E., *The Soviet Union and the Law of the Sea*, Johns Hopkins University Press, 1971.

Cohen, J.A. and H. Chiu, *People's China and International Law*, Princeton University Press, 1974.

Johnston, D.M., *International Law of Fisheries*, Yale University Press, 1966.

Kashara, H. and W. Burke, *North Pacific Fisheries Management*, Resources for the Future, Inc., the Program of International Studies of Fishery Arrangements, Paper No. 2, 1973.

Oda, S., *International Control of Sea Resources*, A.W. Sijthoff, 1963.

Reiff, H., *The United States and the Treaty Law of the Sea*, Minnesota University Press, 1959.

Weissberg, G., *Recent Development in the Law of the Sea and the Japanese–Korean Fishery Disputes*, Martinus Nijhoff, The Hague, 1966.

Food and Agriculture Organization, *Papers Presented at the International Technical Conference on the Conservation of the Living Resources of the Sea*, Rome, 18 April – 10 May 1955, United Nations, 1956.

United States Senate, Committee on Commerce, *Treaties and Other International Agreements on Fisheries, Oceanographic Resources and Wildlife to Which the United States Is Party*, US Govt. Printing Office, 1974.

United States Dept. of State, *Limits in the Seas, No. 36, National Claims to Maritime Jurisdiction*, 2nd rev., 1974.

Further Readings

1. C.H. Park, 'Fishing under Troubled Waters: The North-East Asia Fisheries Controversy', 2, *Ocean Development and International Law,* 1974, pp. 93–136.
2. C.H. Park, 'Oil under Troubled Waters: The North-East Asia Sea-Bed Oil Controversy', *Harvard International Law Journal,* 14, 1973, pp. 212–60.
3. L. Wells II, 'Japan and the United Nations Conference on the Law of the Sea', *Ocean Development and International Law,* 2, 1974, pp. 65–91.
4. H. Chiu and C.H. Park, 'Legal Status of the Paracel and Spratly Islands', *Ocean Development and International Law,* 3, 1975, pp. 1–28.
5. D.M. Johnston, 'Marginal Diplomacy in East Asia', *International Journal,* 26, 1971, pp. 469–506.
6. M.W. Janis and D.C.F. Daniel, 'The USSR: 'Ocean Use and Ocean Law ', Law of the Sea Institute Occasional Paper No. 21, Kingston, Rhode Island, 1974.
7. C.H. Park and J.A. Cohen, 'The Politics of China's Oil Weapon', *Foreign Policy,* 20, 1975, pp. 28–49.
8. C.H. Park, 'Sino-Japanese-Korean Sea Resources Controversy and the Hypothesis of a 200-mile Economic Zone', *Harvard International Law Journal,* 16, 1975, pp. 27–46.

PART IV: THE COASTAL COMMUNITY

10 THE SMALL MARITIME COMMUNITY AND ITS RESOURCE MANAGEMENT PROBLEMS: A NEWFOUNDLAND EXAMPLE

Geoffrey Stiles

1. Introduction

It is a disturbing commentary on our attitudes toward marine resource management that few if any of the solutions put before international bodies during the past few years of intensive negotiation have contained a clear-cut statement of the rights of the coastal *community*. Although it is readily apparent that many of the world's ocean fisheries are ultimately community-based, even in the highly industrialized countries of the North Atlantic, the community itself is almost never recognized in legal statute or in international agreement as a possible basis from which fishery management strategies should originate.[1]

Nor is this particularly surprising. Given the marked tendency during the past fifty years toward centralization of government services in most nations, and the tendency to use biological and macro-economic criteria, rather than sociological ones, in fisheries management, it would require nothing short of a bureaucratic revolution to shift the focus back to the community level in this area of concern. Yet it is the very absence of community-level inputs in resource management which may prevent the world's fishing nations from maintaining management systems that are biologically sound, economically efficient, *and* socially equitable. Not all forms of marine resource exploitation are amenable to management at the community level, but offshore oil exploration and distant-water fisheries are two exceptions which come immediately to mind. The usefulness of community-level management is especially evident in the case of artisanal fisheries, where the location of small coastal communities is a critical factor in the enforcement of specific conservation measures. Traditional community-level approaches to *self-management* of the local resource-base could supply useful insights for the planner, politician, or negotiator attempting to develop better management systems at the world or macro-regional level.

The major difficulty in this idea – aside from its political implications for strongly centralist nations such as the US or Great Britain – is the lack of systematic information available to community-level management systems. The purpose of this paper is to consider how this deficiency might be corrected. In focusing specifically on the relationship between coastal *communities* and marine resources, it differs from the few other attempts to grapple with the effects of self-management systems among fishing peoples.[2] Yet it deals only in a limited way with the effects of imposing limited-entry schemes on the local community although such schemes are not without importance in the region to be discussed here. The conclusions are drawn from the examination of a single area, the Canadian province of Newfoundland, in which the author has worked personally. The Newfoundland experience is one of the more interesting examples we have of the clash between community-level initiatives and centralist government regulations, and of the ultimate defeat of these initiatives through government ignorance of the way in which community-based inshore fisheries are sustained.

2. The Setting: Canada and the Coastal Community

Canada is indisputably one of those nations which would benefit most from current diplomatic efforts to extend coastal state authority. Its extensive coastline, the socio-economic importance of its fisheries, and its geographical position astride the once bountiful offshore 'banks' of the north-west Atlantic, all combine to give this nation a vital stake in the outcome of the negotiations on the law of the sea. In stating its position on fishery jurisdiction, the Canadian Government has expressed not only its concern for the conservation of the resource, but also its determination to preserve it for exploitation by Canadian fishermen.[3]

From the viewpoint of the intended beneficiaries, particularly the inshore and community-based fishermen, Canadian Government policy over the past twenty years has been an exercise in deception. In the worst light, it might even be construed as a calculated effort to eliminate the inshore fishery entirely. This policy has been accomplished, broadly speaking, in two ways: first, by subsidizing the movement of fishermen and their families from rural locations to more urban ones; and second, by spending the largest proportion of 'development' funds on offshore fishing. More specifically, these funds have been expended on the construction of centralized processing facilities, integrated (in all but a few cases) with mid- and distant-water trawler operations owned by the processing companies themselves.[4] From these policies one might project a bleak future for the small coastal communities of Newfoundland: a gradual reduction in the number of communities participating in the inshore fishery, coupled with increasing employment in processing and other support industries tied to the growth and maintenance of the offshore sector.

The rationale for this policy is, in fact, rather clearly stated. As one government report of the 1960s put it, the major aim of fisheries policy in Canada during the preceding decade had been the

> encouragement to mobility out of the industry for *surplus labour*. This means abandonment of the concept that this industry is a *residual rural subsistence sector* which has unlimited power to absorb unemployment or underemployment ...[5] (italics mine)

In short, the government's approach was to depict the inshore, community-based fishery as wasteful of labour, relatively inefficient with respect to catch potential (compared with the offshore sector, at any rate), and generally difficult to manage because it tended to act as a kind of residual catchment for men who were unable to find full-time employment elsewhere.

The result of this policy was a series of programmes, beginning in the mid-fifties and still in force today, to redistribute gradually the rural populations as a means of encouraging them to engage in other industries than the inshore fishery, to enforce more 'professional' standards for recruitment into the industry, and to limit access to some kinds of inshore fishing, particularly those dealing with the more vulnerable shellfish and pelagic fish populations. Limited access was apparently designed both as a means of ensuring the conservation of the resource and as a way of forcing 'marginal' operators out.[6] Although these programmes have not always been successful in achieving these ends, they have certainly resulted in a gradual reduction in the size of the inshore fishing labour force and, more significantly from the viewpoint of this paper, they have greatly compromised the economic and political role of the small coastal fishing community by reducing its participation in the Canadian fishing industry as a whole.

The effects are, of course, variable: the policies have had greater impact in some areas than in others. Nowhere has the impact been more disruptive than in Newfoundland, where the inshore fishery has always played a highly significant role in the total economy. Nevertheless, the continued implementation of these policies, signalled by the recent decision of the federal Government to begin licensing inshore *groundfish* operators and crews,[7] suggests clearly that the Canadian Government's goal is to *centralize* and *formalize* the administration of the inshore fishery, so as to limit community involvement in the development of an overall resource-management régime.[8]

3. Newfoundland: a Unique Case?

If this trend continues, it will certainly have its most critical effects on the province of Newfoundland. From the economic (centralist) point of view, Newfoundland seems to have provided the most extreme example of fishery mismanagement; whereas from the sociological (communalist) viewpoint, this province is seen to provide unusual opportunities for decentralized and even community-oriented management. The Newfoundland example may not be unqiue; but it does provide at least one model of how such a decentralized system might work. The Newfoundland experience shows that present efforts to limit entry to the fisheries will fail unless they are reinforced by local involvement in the key decision-making processes.

The early settlement of Newfoundland was in fact partly the result of disputes over access to coastal space. The earliest planned settlement, chartered in 1610 under the leadership of Englishman John Guy, was expressly prohibited by the terms of its charter from asserting jurisdiction over the fishery,[9] apparently because the British Crown anticipated objections from the merchant adventurers of the West Country, who wished to have Newfoundland's settlement limited or even prohibited because of its potential ability to interfere with their own operations. The West Country merchants at this time operated a system of English-financed ships which prosecuted the fishery in Newfoundland coastal waters, 'made' the fish in special shore stations, then returned to their home ports with the finished product. This system was relatively easy to control and had the important secondary benefit of training men in the rudiments of seamanship, so that they could later be employed in the navy and merchant marine with little further preparation. The fishery thus became a linchpin in English mercantilist policy,[10] and for many years the arguments of the 'fishermen' (that is, the employees of the West Country merchants) were given precedence over those of the 'settlers' (that is, the people resident in Newfoundland), in determining the administration of the colony as a whole.

These facts notwithstanding, Guy's colonists seem to have been firm in setting their own standards of coastal jurisdiction:

> In spite of the reservation, Guy issued orders shortly after his arrival which he expected the fishermen to observe, wherein he

> asserted his right as governor to jurisdiction over the fishery ... With the arrival of ... permanent settlers, there were ample grounds for defining and limiting the activities of the fishermen, who heretofore had freely enjoyed all the facilities which the island offered.[11]

Previous to Guy's arrival, the only laws regulating the activities of itinerant fishermen and their rights to exploit the coastal waters were the customary arrangements by which the first captain to arrive in a given harbour each year could have first choice over grounds, stages, and other equipment – the so-called 'law of the fishing admirals'. At this time, the distinction between inshore and offshore jurisdiction had certainly not been thought of, and the conflicts that arose were between 'settlers' and 'fishermen' concerning the prerogatives of the former, such as their right to use the best grounds before the fishermen arrived each spring from England, and to appropriate equipment left behind by the fishermen over the winter.

The designs of these early settlement companies – a few weaker examples, such as George Calvert, excepted[12] – were decidedly monopolistic. In lobbying for an end to unrestricted fishing they were motivated not by concern about the overexploitation of stocks or by consideration for the individual settler, but rather by their determination to replace the West Country interests as exclusive beneficiaries of a lucrative resource. For the most part they failed in this purpose, although Guy himself was able for some time to control access to the fishery of Conception Bay, the location of his own colony.

Jurisdictional problems were, at this time, informally administered by the parties concerned, and not by a government agency. Although efforts to bring about statutory enforcement persisted through the early seventeenth century, it was not until 1634 that the first clear statement of principles for administering the fishery was promulgated: the so-called 'First Western Charter', which briefly but effectively legitimized the claims to priority of the West Country fishermen. In this charter, the customary rights of the 'first skipper in port' were firmly established for the first time. These 'fishing admirals' not only had first choice of grounds, stages, and harbour space, but could effectively regulate the space available to later arrivals, and indeed serve as final arbiters of disputes over these matters, even where settlers were involved! Perhaps more important, for the present discussion at least, they were given control over the management of the fishery itself:

> The regulations ... were designed to insure the prosperity of the fishery by preventing such practices as throwing ballast and press-stones into the harbours, casting anchor where it might interfere with seining, defacement or injury to the equipment used in the catching and curing of fish and the making of [cod] oil.[13]

Although it may seem that regulations of this sort would have had considerable impact on the conduct of the fishery, and on rights of access in particular, the truth is that the charter was so limited in its powers as to be virtually ineffectual. The disputes between settlers and the West Country fishermen in fact continued, and the need for settlement did not suddenly abate. Nor did it cease after the more emphatic charter of 1676 was promulgated, renouncing the settlers' claims and ordering the forcible removal (or retreat to a point six miles inland) of all the resident population of the island. Indeed, during the next hundred and fifty years the island shows a slow but nevertheless steady increase in population, and a more or less continuous development of basic institutions, contrary to some historians' view that the Crown's policy of removal was remorselessly effective.[14]

This continuing conflict between settlers and fishermen seems to have centred, as before, in several related issues: access to shore facilities, alleged loss of fishing crews to settlers, and encouragement offered by settlers to foreign interests, such as the French. The issue most relevant to the present inquiry was, however, the question of access to fishing space, reflecting a gradually increasing recognition on the part of the West Country fishermen that their productivity was suffering as a result of losing control over the Newfoundland fishery. Reports of poor catches occur intermittently during the seventeenth century, but are particularly numerous after 1660. Although these shortfalls are attributed to a variety of causes, it seems clear that a major reason was the extraordinary congestion of critical fishing areas. It should be noted here that the early British fishery in Newfoundland was essentially an inshore fishery, the offshore banks being exploited at that time mostly by Spanish and Portuguese boats, which stored their fish 'wet' (that is, in salt bulk and without drying), and had little to do with the coastal areas of the island, save for occasional stop-overs to weather a storm. Moreover, the space available for the British fishery was further limited by French control of both the entire south coast, from Cape Race west, and the area northward above Cape Bonavista. Later, the French claims to these areas would be challenged and then abrogated by treaty, but in the beginning the French presence drastically restricted the access of British fishermen to the inshore resource.

In short, then, the early fisheries of Newfoundland, including both community-based and West Country participants, were acutely troubled by the problem of access to the resource, as well as by a variety of secondary problems stemming from this, such as access to shore facilities, stability of the labour force, and jurisdiction over fishing disputes. Although the access problem would be expressed officially in terms of competing mercantile groups,[15] the problem was usually described quite differently at the local level, namely as a question of 'settler's rights'. To the planter and his compatriots, the debates over how to utilize the colony most effectively, whether as a fishing station or as a dependent settlement, were probably much less important than the mundane but economically more critical issue of how much of the settlement's local resource-base was included in its charter. Certainly, most planters felt strongly that their rights should extend beyond the land itself and even the landwash, to include those marine resources which could be effectively exploited from the community itself.

For Newfoundland, the final decision on this matter was postponed until after settlement became, once again, a legitimate policy objective. The establishment of a final settlement policy can be dated from the appointment of the island's first resident Governor (1729), the first formal recognition by the Crown that the island should be treated the same as other colonies in the Empire. Legitimacy brought with it the usual efforts at enforcement, principally through the appointment of magistrates with authority over local disputes. As one might predict, the initial encounters of the magistrates with customary forms of local authority in coastal Newfoundland were fraught with difficulty. In most harbours, the rule of the 'fishing admirals' was still absolute, and the initial design of the new colonial government was to limit magisterial authority to the period between fishing seasons, thus avoiding potential conflict with the admirals. But in the end, the arbitrariness of the latter in applying the law, particularly to settlers, compelled the magistrates to attempt to apply their authority more comprehensively, and to interfere directly with the admirals' decisions.[16]

Even with this effort, the settlers gained little real ground in their battle to achieve exclusive riparian rights or priorities. As West Country interests had gradually withdrawn from the fishery, due mostly to the effects of the war with France, the settlers had gradually become dominant in the local fishery, so that by 1713 they were catching most of the fish. Yet their legal status in the coastal area did not improve by virtue of this change, and it did not even alter significantly when the West Country merchants as well as some resident companies in Newfoundland shifted their interests to the Grank Bank fishery further out, apparently because of persistent failures in the inshore fishery. This occurred mostly after the Treaty of Utrecht, which gave the south coast of the island back to the British. Accordingly, at the same time as local stock failures generated this renewed interest in the offshore fishery, they also compelled Newfoundlanders to move westward along the south coast, which had previously been inhabited primarily by French-speaking settlers and by the representatives of the French mercantile and fishing fleets.

This population movement, which extended eventually to the west coast as well, brought a temporary diminution of pressures on the resource in the area from Cape Race to Cape Bonavista, the former 'English shore'. Though the south coast remained, and remains today, less populated than the eastern portions of the island, it provided the basis for a more complex and ultimately more independent fishery. This was due both to its isolation from the colonial government, and to its ice-free conditions, which meant that winter and early spring were the most productive fishing seasons. As we will see in the examples given later in this paper, the absence of a close relationship with government in this area proved a disadvantage in the administration of the local fishery.

The first complete and accurate picture of the state of the fishery on the island comes from the reports of fishery officers delegated by the colonial government to tour the major coastal areas under British jurisdiction. These reports are not regularly published until *c.* 1833, about eight years after Newfoundland gained its first representative, though still colonial, government, and more than a hundred years after the major dispersal of settler populations began. We have no detailed knowledge of what happened to the settlers' jurisdictional problem during this rather lengthy period, but the comments of the earliest officials to visit these areas indicate clearly that most settler populations were well in control of their inshore fisheries – though the exact form of the adaptation varied substantially from one part of the island to another – and that these fisheries were already, to some extent, self-regulating.

There were, of course, issues to be resolved. One which is perennially evident in the fishery officers' reports is the matter of the 'bait fishery' arrangements whereby French and American 'bankers' relied on the settlers for capelin, herring and squid, the principal bait species used by the 'bankers' in the offshore fisheries. This was the chief issue on the south coast, which was closest to the Banks, and also seems to have had the most prolific and varied supply of baitfish. Yet it epitomizes the independence and aggressiveness of the settler who, accustomed to government indifference to his plight (or indeed to the absence of any government at all), sought solutions which he saw as necessary for his survival. The bait fishery, from the settler's viewpoint, was part of the basic fishing cycle. Since he had to supply his own bait, and had to set nets and bar-seines for this purpose, it seemed only reasonable to set additional nets and sell the surplus catch for cash to passing 'bankers'. What is more, this practice nicely complemented the other aspects of the yearly cycle: on the south coast, both capelin and squid arrived after the most important fishery of the year, the winter–spring cod fishery, was over, and it therefore provided work during that season when there was little work elsewhere, beyond sporadic agricultural activities.

Nevertheless, the reports of officers from the 1870s and 1880s are filled with references to the deleterious effects of the bait trade–effects on the bait stocks themselves, as well as on the disposition of local fishermen to fish the food stocks, such as cod and salmon. The officers are frequently at odds with the local population in these matters. They speak of the 'inducements held out to the fishermen ... to take the herring indiscriminately, and by the lucrative but illegal method of barring.'[17] They also lament the impoverishment of some fishermen, who seem to have given up other aspects of their subsistence in the unrelenting pursuit of cash remuneration from the 'bankers'. In effect, from the government's point of view, these fishermen were the victims, rather than the victors. They were being monopolized by a substantial and ever-increasing demand for bait at low cost, which would ultimately prove disastrous to their maintenance of the other fisheries. Although they were not being directly challenged for the inshore resource, as was the case in the days of the West Country's domination, the effect was much the same: a decline in catches, at least of cod and salmon.

In this situation, the basically protectionist policy of the Newfoundland Government towards the coastal community was often severely modified: the fishery regulations were used to prohibit the sale of baitfish to foreign interests, and the more rapacious methods, such as the bar seine, were directly prohibited – all at the insistence of fishery officers, though not of the communities concerned. The difficulty of enforcing such measures, however, meant in effect that the local population could safely ignore those regulations which did not appear to serve its own interests, while using government officers to enforce those which did. This situation was altered somewhat over the years as the scale and intensity of government surveillance in these areas increased; but the cumulative effect of local-level interaction between settler and fishery officer has been to foster a surprisingly decentralized and producer-oriented, albeit *ad hoc*, system of *access-management.*

This system is by no means uniformly evident across the province. Indeed, there are many areas where fishery officers have never been regularly stationed, and where the possibilities of using the officers as a medium for transmission of local-level demands have gone unrealized. There are, on the other hand, areas of intensive use, mostly on the Avalon Peninsula near St. John's, the capital city, in which a considerable variety of gear- and spatial-limitations have been invoked over the past century. In a later section, the workings of this process will be described in somewhat greater detail, based primarily on evidence gleaned from research on the Avalon Peninsula itself.[18]

4. The Newfoundland Fishery Regulations and the Development of Access-Management

It should be emphasized that it was not simply the technology itself – although this was a principal focus of debate – but rather *its effect on the distribution of fishing space* that was at issue in the earliest years of government involvement with fisheries. After the bait fishery was placed under control,[19] fishery officers were often called upon to arbitrate local disputes over the use of a particular kind of gear – for example, bar-seines, or bultow in some areas – usually because residents saw them as incompatible with the use of other kinds of gear *in a particular space*, and also because some kinds of technology were seen as a threat to the stocks.[20] A community where a large number of residents used hand-lines (baited hook-and-line) might, for example, take offence at a nearby community whose fishermen were using a space-consuming technology such as the bultow, and thereby infringing on the first community's fishing space. (The same kind of dispute could equally well take place *within* community boundaries, although it was the inter-community sort which usually reached the ears of the officer.) Their complaint to the local legislative member would usually feed back to the fishery officer, who would meet with the fishermen and attempt to reach agreement on which areas should be set off for hand-lining purposes alone; and this new 'sanctuary' arrangement would then, following verification by the legislative assembly, be incorporated directly into the Newfoundland fishery regulations as a new article.[21]

The first set of such regulations, applying both to inland and coastal fisheries, was promulgated in 1890. Since then it has been amended almost as often as complaints were received: that is, as often as coastal communities have bothered to manifest a collective concern for the management of local fishing space. In this long and continuous process of adjudication and amendment, a kind of 'common law' of coastal management has emerged, based on the unstated principle that communities have the right to seek protection under law for their own systems of access-management. In the regulations themselves, these efforts appear for the most part as restrictions on the use of a particular fishing method, but in many cases a provision of this kind reflects the concern of local communities at threats from outsiders as much as with the possibly damaging effects of a particular type of gear, such as gill nets in the present day. In so far as they legitimize the process of allocating the 'berths' used for certain kinds of fixed technology, the regulations are also representative of the community's system of *social control*, its informal means for ensuring the equitable distribution of resources. This function is particularly evident in the case of the summer cod-trap fishery. It is less evident, as we shall see, in the case of government efforts to restrict certain kinds of pelagic fisheries.

5. The Cod-trap Fishery

The cod trap is a type of gear extensively used in Newfoundland communities to exploit cod during their early summer migration from offshore banks to inshore waters. The cod follow the rise of the warmer layers in pursuit of capelin, a small baitfish which spawns on the beaches during this season. The trap, a large net-like device which blocks the cod as they swim along the shoreline and forces them into a 'box' of small-mesh netting, must be anchored to the bottom at favourable points along the shore. Indeed, not all coastal areas of Newfoundland have sufficiently smooth bottoms or are shallow enough for placing such traps; and for those that do, the availability of favourable spots is usually quite limited, and the returns from these quite variable.

One consequence of this variation is that communities have developed locally administered systems of allocating trap 'berths'. Berths are well known and are usually given a name derived from their geographic or hydrographic location: for example, 'Black Point' or

'Job's Rock'. In some areas the method of allocation is simple familial inheritance, and the berth names may in fact be those of the family of ownership. Elsewhere allocation is based either on a draw system, often administered by local fishery officers, or, in a very few cases, on a first-come first-served basis, with the competition for berths set for a particular day. The Newfoundland fishery regulations contain, in fact, a specific procedure for berth allocation, based on the principle of drawing lots annually, though contingent on community initiative in setting up a 'local codfishery committee'.[22]

The trap-berth phenomenon, whatever its method of allocation, is quite specifically based on a land–sea relationship; but unlike, for example, the territories of Maine lobstermen analyzed by Acheson,[23] trap-berth locations are not seen as an extension of land *ownership*, even in those cases where the berths are owned by families in perpetuity. Indeed, they could not be, since many of the berths are located outside the community proper; and in Newfoundland, private ownership of land, to the extent that it exists at all, is usually restricted to small 'gardens' on which the house is set, and occasionally to outfields for grazing.[24] Even in the few cases where individuals do own land adjacent to their trap-berth, it appears that they do not associate the two kinds of ownership in any formal or explicit way.[25]

The berths are land-oriented, then, only in the sense that they are located close inshore, must be fixed to a rock or staked to beachland at one point, and are locatable by land references. The resource in this case, cod, is really a highly mobile species, much more so than lobster, but its mobility is relatively predictable during the capelin 'spawn', and the trap fishery is based on that predictability. Trap locations are in fact very precisely known, as are the advantages of one berth over another. Where competition or drawing for berths is preferred, these advantages may produce a highly politicized atmosphere in the small community – and correspondingly, the community's 'right' to a certain range of berths may be quite aggressively defended, as shown by Martin in his analysis of this phenomenon in two Avalon Peninsula communities.[26]

6. Other Fishing Methods

Generally speaking, the more mobile methods used in Newfoundland, such as most forms of long-lining, gill-netting, and seining, lend themselves to more flexibly defined locational systems, hence to a somewhat less rigid approach to access-management. These systems are often focused on the fish-finding abilities of the individual boat skipper, who searches for a productive 'spot' of fish, and having located it, attracts other skippers, each maintaining an informally prescribed distance from the original finder and from each other. Spacing systems of this sort were, in fact, described over seventy years ago by Rudyard Kipling in *Captains Courageous*, which dealt with life among the schooner fishermen of the Grand Banks.[27] More recently, Andersen has provided detailed descriptions and analysis of the activities of modern steel trawlers, whose skippers are perennially involved in an information-management competition, entailing systematic efforts to distort both catch figures and vessel location.[28]

Such systems are not, of course, community-based. The fishing units in question may originate from communities, but they are usually owned by large business enterprises and they are operated far from shore, not only beyond community influence, but often in international waters. Nevertheless, the need both to locate the catch species, and simultaneously to avoid encroachment from other boats having competing interests, generates spacing mechanisms not unlike those which operate in relatively mobile community-based fisheries the world over. In coastal areas of Newfoundland where 'trawls' (long-lines) are employed, the rights of a given community to its grounds are often quite carefully delimited. Yet this delimitation is relative, not absolute, for long-lines are more often set and retrieved on a daily basis, and each day may generate an entirely different set of locational choices. The rights over 'grounds', then, are simply a matter of determining first where community A's boats are fishing on a given day, and then following the convention (say) that one's own boats generally fish *west* of the community A boats. In this way, massive gear entanglements are usually avoided, and at the same time the boats are distributed over available ground space as equitably as possible.[29]

The informal conventions which govern such spacing between communities apply also to spacing between boats of the same community. Men who fish 'gunnel to gunnel' with another boat, even that of a close relative, are looked upon as encroachers; and while this does not often lead to public confrontation or reprisal, comments among crew members about the encroachers' indifferent attitude toward safety, or the likelihood of entangling gear, or the possible effects on one's own 'catch', are quickly heard. It is thought to be self-evident in fact, that when using mobile techniques as long-lines or seines, the possibilities of running afoul of another boat's gear, or being suspected of intruding on another's spatial preserve, and thereby risking accusation as a usurper of limited resources, are far greater than with stationary gear.[30]

Spacing systems of this sort preserve, I believe, a relatively equitable basis for resource allocation. That is, they ensure that individuals do not encroach on one another's fishing space to an unreasonable extent, and they tend to randomize the problem of access for the eligible fishing population. As suggested above, access is often linked formally to the type of technology used. Communities may petition the provincial or federal government to restrict certain areas to the use of a specific kind of gear, if it can be demonstrated that competition from other methods is seriously endangering the rights of certain individuals to catch fish, or, alternatively, if it can be shown that fish stocks are being too rapidly depleted in the area concerned as a direct consequence of the use of this gear.

The only qualification which might be noted here is that the 'equitability' of systems such as this is inextricably tied to the complicated question of community 'membership'. Exactly what constitutes membership in communities such as these – where, for example, men from outside the community may marry women from within it, and take up residence there – is generally a difficult question. Indeed, at least one major confrontation between fishing communities over the use of traditional cod-berths was resolved, ironically, in exactly this way: namely, when the 'outsider' established residence through marriage in the community to which he wished to gain access.[31]

7. Conclusions: Community Autonomy and the Prospects for Resource Management

The Newfoundland case illustrates, I think, the possibilities as well as the difficulties inherent in administering access to marine resources on the community level. It is important to recognize that the processes described above do *not* constitute 'resource management systems' as such. They do not entail estimates of the impact of exploitation of the resource itself on a regular basis, followed by efforts to redirect effort accordingly. On the contrary, they are really *access*-management systems, based as they are on the assumption that individual communities should have a say in determining *who* gains access to immediate coastal resources, and by what *means*.

This fact notwithstanding, the opportunities for enforcing local perceptions about resource depletion are considerable in such a system. By maintaining formal linkages with government officials, who themselves acknowledge the validity of local-level opinions in this process, even if only for political reasons, the small community can react quite effectively to a perceived threat to its resource base. Although this reaction may be expressed officially in technological terms, against a 'threat' from a too-efficient technology, rather than as an intrusion from the 'outside', there is evidence that *informal* controls are operative in traditional spacing mechanisms, the recognition of community grounds, and lottery and other allocative systems for the awarding of fixed berths.

The problem with such systems is, of course, that they are largely extra-legal and unenforceable, with the exception of technological restrictions, seasonal limits, and, more recently, entry limitations. But this is a 'problem' only in so far as governments are unwilling to accept local or community jurisdiction in such matters. Although it is by no means easy to imagine government moving towards such a decentralized mode of administration, there is certainly no reason why these possibilities could not be tested in concrete situations, perhaps by allowing certain communities to experiment with their own limitation formulas and then gauging the effects in terms of catch returns, distribution of income, and so forth.

In Newfoundland there has been a considerable, and growing, reaction against recent attempts by the Canadian federal Government to impose a licensing boat registration programme. This reaction is explained, I think, by the very facts which this paper has presented: namely, that in this province, a somewhat unique set of historical circumstances has produced an unusual degree of informal autonomy among coastal communities, with respect to the determination of who fishes where, and with what kind of gear; and also who is *entitled* to fish, that is, to call himself a fisherman. The licensing programme, by contrast, proposes to supply each fisherman with a licence, authenticating his status from an official point of view; and to register each vessel, taking note of its pattern of utilization (whether it is engaged in the groundfishery, or in pelagic fisheries, what kinds of gear it uses, and so on). Although the programme does not at present entail a scheme of limited entry, it does unquestionably provide a *sound factual basis for the administration of such a scheme*. The past actions of the government do not give the fisherman much hope that such restrictions will not eventually be forthcoming.[32]

Indeed, two such programmes are presently in effect in eastern Canada, in the lobster and salmon fisheries, both of which are now restricted to 'bona fide' (full-time) fishermen.[33] A third has already resulted in the eventual shut-down of a fairly specialized fishery, drift-netting for salmon in New Brunswick and south-west Newfoundland. The drift-net case is a particularly instructive one, for it involved (in Newfoundland) all three kinds of restriction above, beginning with a declaration of exclusive grounds, followed by restrictions on the kinds and amount of gear which could be used, and finally by restrictions on who could fish. The latter phase was reached in 1968, when the federal Government imposed a freeze on the issuance of licenses for drift-netting. After this proved ineffective because of difficulties in dealing with marginal cases,[34] the Government tried to accommodate local values concerning equitability by expanding the category of eligible fishermen to include many who had fished previously but had inadvertently failed to engage in drift-netting in the 'base' year, 1967. The adjudication of these marginal cases in turn opened the flood gates to another series of considerations, in this case having to do with the question of whose definition of 'bona fide' would be applied in these judgements: the fisherman's, the community's, or the Government's? Perhaps the chief complaint heard from full-time fishermen in this respect was that men earning sizeable incomes from work, such as the railway or coastal steamers, which permitted extensive leisure time, were being allowed to retain licenses for drift-netting because they had had them previously, while unemployed fishermen were being refused them on grounds that they did not have them!

These controversies reached new heights when the Government announced in 1972 that it was ceasing its policy of restrictions and replacing it with a policy of elimination: namely, an immediate termination of *all* drift-netting for salmon, followed by a negotiated programme of subsidies to those fishermen who were affected by this. The impact was tempered somewhat by a parallel announcement that the amount of the subsidies would be decided by local committees meeting in close consultation with fishermen. The final policy which emerged from these meetings was, although generally satisfactory to the fishermen, encumbered by numerous misconceptions about the role of such a fishery in the community economy. Only now, several years after the initial decision, these misconceptions are beginning to cause problems for the fishermen concerned. The key misconception relates to the nature of crewing. A major condition of the Government's willingness to provide monetary compensation to those who were disqualified was that the compensation go only to the *existing* crew of the boats fishing in 1972. Since crews often vary from year to year, and even from season to season, this meant in effect that in future years not all the members of a given boat's crew would receive their compensation grant during the period when they would formerly have been drift-netting, unless they were on the *original* grant list. From the viewpoint of the skipper, who was initially expected to disburse the grant to his crew, this proved difficult indeed. It meant that he might be forced to give the compensation money to men who had since left his boat, while not giving it to some who had joined since!

This rather minor point was, of course, partially resolved by taking disbursement out of the hands of the skippers. But it serves to emphasize the difficulty of making decisions about limited-entry programmes outside the community context itself. Here, of course, the government made the minimal gesture of allowing local opinion to influence the form of the original programme, as well as the modifications which ensured. But they failed in the first instance to appreciate the way in which this particular fishery – a brief, seasonal one at that – related to broader issues in the management of the community's resources. It is little wonder that programmes of this sort so often run afoul of local sentiment, and so often fail the test of equitability!

But what real alternatives are there, when the sea's resources are being so rapidly depleted? Putting aside for the moment the broader question of whether small communities should bear the brunt of limitation programmes, when in fact the ultimate cause of resource depletion is not their fishing activities but those of the offshore fleets, we can, I believe, find much of an instructive nature from studying and analyzing the conduct of small communities in their own efforts to achieve management of the local resource base. Even if the systems described here would not pass muster from a biologist's point of view, based as they are on *perceptions* of the resource base rather than on systematic measurement of it, they do seem to demonstrate that a decentralized and fisherman-oriented management régime is infinitely preferable to one which filters down from 'above', that is from scientists and bureaucrats living far away from the realities of fishing as a form of livelihood. If nothing else, such a decentralized system would avoid the inefficiencies which result from a failure to understand the *consequences* of limitation; and it might incidentally provide greater local political support for the international negotiation process, which now seems altogether too distant and arbitrary to those who gain their living from the sea.

Notes

1. There are apparently only a few exceptions. Norway, perhaps the best example of a modern nation state which attempts consistently to localize or decentralize the decision process, made efforts in the 1940s to have the jurisdiction of coastal communities over their own resources recognized in international law. More recently, the American state of Maine has decided to allow coastal communities to make their own decisions regarding the zoning of coastal space – an indication that government in this area is at least sensitive to the possibility that coastal communities may have a better understanding of this issue than government itself! The Maine case is somewhat qualified by the fact that the procedures and criteria for zoning are set by the state itself, and by the fact that the state has not granted this right in perpetuity, but only on the condition that action be taken within a two-year period.
2. R. Andersen, 'Public and Private Access-Management in North Atlantic Fishing' (tentative title), in *Northern Maritime Europeans*, R. Andersen (ed.), Mouton, 1975. On the impact of limited-entry schemes on Newfoundland, see Alexander, Storey *et al.*, *Report of the Committee on Federal Licensing Policy and its Implications for the Newfoundland Fisheries*, Memorial University of Newfoundland, 1974.
3. In interviews with local representatives of the federal Fisheries Division, Department of the Environment, it has been emphasized that Canada can not simply offer itself as the *protector* of the resource, but must also make a strong case for being the *exploiter* as well.
4. For criticisms of this two-pronged 'development' programme, see Brox, *Newfoundland Fishermen in the Age of Industry*, Institute of Social and Economic Research, St. John's, Newfoundland, 1972.
5. This quotation is taken from a restricted in-house document of the Department of Fisheries of Canada (Economic Services), entitled 'Trends in the Development of the Canadian Fisheries: Background Document for Fisheries Development Planning', April 1967. While not the same as the public pronouncements on this issue made by the department concerned, it is certainly a good indication of the underlying assumptions which produced the public policy.
6. The sense in which entry limitations might force 'marginal' operators out of the fishery is discussed later in the paper in relation to the restrictions imposed on salmon drift-netting. Speaking generally, the problem centres on the definition of '*bona fide*': in Canada, limited-entry programmes have usually meant restricting fishing to those who could claim to be full-time fishermen, that is, whose income was derived mostly from this source. This has the immediate effect of limiting the entry of individuals who may wish to supplement other sources of income with certain kinds of seasonal fishing – and since these men are as much a part of the potential labour pool as so-called 'full-timers', the final consequence of such a policy may be to restrict the flexibility of fishing as a small-scale enterprise. For an elaboration of this point, see Alexander, Storey *et. al.*, op. cit. pp. 32–5.
7. As noted again below, this new programme has two phases: enumeration and registration of *vessels* involved in the groundfishery; and enumeration and licensing of *fishermen*, including both boat-owners and all crewmen.
8. This is, admittedly, a value judgement; but it is a value judgement reinforced by experience! Centralized and formalized administration of such programmes need not imply a lack of local participation in planning and decision-making, but this is more often than not the result. In the Canadian case, fisheries management presents a very special problem, since fisheries fall entirely

within federal jurisdiction; so that for Newfoundland, a member of the Canadian nation only since 1949, with several centuries of experience in administering fisheries – an experience which, as this paper argues, has had the cumulative effect of *strengthening* local-level inputs – now feels the impact of a system which by comparison is highly centralized and bureaucratized in this area.

9. Lounsbury, R., *The British Fishery at Newfoundland, 1634–1763*, Yale University Press, 1934, p. 39.
10. Ibid., pp. 144–5.
11. Ibid., p. 40.
12. Lounsbury notes that Calvert, who colonized Ferryland on the southern shore of the Avalon Peninsula in the 1620s, was different from other planters in his desire to maintain peaceable relations with the fishermen – in part because he had intended to create an agricultural and not a fishing settlement, and in part because he disagreed with some of the policies of the London merchants, arch-rivals of the West Countrymen. Ibid., pp. 47–8.
13. Ibid., pp. 74–5.
14. K. Matthews, 'Historical Fence-building; a Critique of Newfoundland Historiography', Paper delivered to annual meeting of Canadian Historical Association, St. John's, Nfld., June 1971.
15. The 'competing mercantile groups' in this case were that of the West Country in England, the major source of financing for the fishery, and London, where many of the merchants favoured the plight of the residents, hoping to gain their allegiance and out-flank their West Country rivals.
16. Lounsbury, op. cit., pp. 280–2.
17. This quote is taken from reports contained in Colonial Office document series 880, Memorial University Library. I am indebted to Chris Balram for his work in reviewing this series of documents for me during the summer of 1974.
18. The work described here is taken largely from Kent Martin's analysis of this phenomenon as it occurs in two southern shore communities in Newfoundland. Kent Martin, *The Law in St. John's Says ... Space Division and Resource Allocation in the Newfoundland Fishing Community of Fermeuse*, unpublished M.A. thesis, Memorial University of Newfoundland, 1973.
19. For an early legislative attempt to limit the bait trade, see *Consolidated Statutes of Newfoundland*, 1892, c.129.
20. The earliest perception on the part of fishermen that their resources were threatened by a particular method of fishing appears to have been in the case of the 'bultow', or long-line trawl, first employed by French boats on Newfoundland's south coast and on the Grant Banks. As one informant told it to me, this had 'all the old fellas convinced there'd never be a fish left in the sea, if the French boats was to keep on usin' the trawl.' Ironically, the trawl is now viewed by these fishermen and by many authorities as the *most* conservative and efficient gear available, because it keeps the fish 'alive' before being brought aboard, minimizes losses due to spoilage, and is ineffective in catching fish if lost unlike the gill net.
21. For example, Sec. 59 of the Fishery Regulations states: 'No person shall set any cod trap within 300 fathoms of Clears Cove Rocks on the N.E. of Fermeuse or the Sunken Rocks on the S.W. of Fermeuse.' Other regulations may specify the seasonal limits for certain kinds of fishing, the areas available to, say, traps as opposed to hand-lines, and so forth.
22. See *Newfoundland Fishery Regulations*, p. 12.
23. See James Acheson, 'The Lobster Fiefs: Economic and Ecological Effects of Territoriality in the Maine Lobster Industry' (tentative title), in *Human Ecology* (forthcoming issue).

24. The best discussion of land ownership and inheritance in a Newfoundland community is found in J. Faris, *Cat Harbour: a Newfoundland Fishing Settlement*, Institute of Social and Economic Research, St. John's, Nfld., 1972.
25. The same lack of association between land areas and berths is evident in the oyster fishery on the Bras d'Or Lakes of Nova Scotia. The traditional berths often *appear* to be associated with land owned by the same person, but closer examination reveals that the association is purely accidental, and that there is no local acceptance of the possibility that such an association *should* occur. Compare with Acheson's lobster territories (op. cit.), in some of which there is a very clear, albeit extra-legal, association between land ownership and seabed ownership.
26. Martin, op. cit.
27. Rudyard Kipling, *Captains Courageous*, New York, 1894.
28. Raoul Andersen, 'Those Fisherman Lies', in *Ethnos*, Vol. 7, 1974.
29. This is not to say that entanglements do not occur. Particularly when a long-line 'trawl' is used, the possibility of crossing over another man's gear is quite high. For example, if some fishermen leave it overnight and others engage in 'day-setting' only, the risk of entanglement is quite high.
30. Nevertheless, some men fish close to one another on a fairly regular basis. Where I have witnessed this kind of situation, however, it has almost always involved a dependency relationship of some kind; and it rarely results in accusations of intrusion, unless the resource is an exceptionally scarce one, such as salmon.
31. The example in question involved a community near St. John's, where most families had ceased to use fishing as even a residual basis of income, and where the local trap berths had not been fished in years. The problem occurred when fishermen from a community 'across the bay' (c. 30 miles distant) entered the first community's fishing space and began to use their berths regularly. The reaction was instantaneous and direct; the intruders were told to leave, and when they refused, the Dept. of Fisheries was asked to make a ruling. The ruling was as expected by the local population: berths belong to a community in perpetuity, whether in use or not. (It is interesting to contrast this attitude with the statement about 'residual employment' given in the fisheries document quoted earlier.) In the end, the intruding fishermen partially circumvented the ruling by arguing that, since one of the crewmen was married to a local girl, and had established residence there, he could properly use the 'community's' resources, though not a native.
32. Cf. Alexander, Storey *et. al.*, op. cit., p. 15.
33. See note 6 above. The definition of '*bona fide*' in the case of lobster and salmon fisheries is based on: (a) time spent fishing in each year; and (b) income status. The most recent limit for (a) is eight months per year minimum; while (b) is relatively undefined, the '*bona fide*' fisherman being one 'all or most of whose income is derived from fishing'.
34. The most common kind of 'marginal' case was the individual who had been alternating fishing with construction employment in the area – a common pattern among men under 25 – and who had decided not to participate in the drift-net fishery in 1967 because of the extraordinary amount of construction work available. Other 'marginal' cases included men who had not had a licence themselves, but relied on a crewman's licence and then found that the crewman no longer intended to fish with them; and men who had relied on a father or other relative to hold the licence, and who wished to strike out on their own despite the lack of a previous licence for themselves.

11 THE SMALL ISLAND SOCIETY AND COASTAL RESOURCE MANAGEMENT: THE BERMUDIAN EXPERIENCE[1]

Raoul Andersen

1. Introduction

The purpose of this essay is to acquaint the reader with some of the human problems encountered by many small volcanic and coral island societies of the mid-Atlantic, Pacific and Indian Oceans, when their people undertake to manage their offshore – and particularly fish – resources.

The discussion is general and exploratory in nature, but draws upon a study, begun in January 1975, of the comparatively highly developed coral reef commercial fishery of Bermuda.[1] To some extent it also draws upon the author's experience gained over several years while observing the fishery of Newfoundland, a coastal province within a large, although not uniformly developed, industrial state.[2]

There are two principal reasons for this study. First, many of us are inclined to misconstrue, or even overlook, the special nature of fishery resource management and development problems faced by the smallest coastal societies. The likelihood of neglect or misunderstanding is especially high just now during the current inter-state law of the sea negotiations and during current exchanges of threats of unilateral action by the major coastal states.

Second, fishery management has to be worked out eventually in local and micro-regional settings where the key elements shaping the outcomes of management programmes are resources, fishermen, the social and economic structure of their communities, industries, markets, governments and their fishery specialists. The complexity of the problems of institutionalization posed by these variables is in stark contrast against the seeming simplicity of the small island society.

These points suggest many possible lines of enquiry, but this paper is restricted to a consideration of two aspects of small island coastal fishery management: (i) customary tenure practices in the context of the changing Bermuda fishery; and (ii) some sociological implications flowing from different types of candidates for the crucial role of fishery officer in such settings.

Although this study is confined to the Bermuda Islands, one would like to extend this kind of enquiry to less well-documented situations in other island societies, such as the Cape Verde Islands, St. Vincent and the Seychelles. Many of the Atlantic, Indian Ocean and Pacific island societies have become or, like Bermuda, are becoming nominally independent states, or units within island confederations. Most retain some form of colonial status linking them in a continuing dependency relationship with a larger power which, at least theoretically, underwrites the small state's territorial integrity. Sometimes their fisheries are protected from foreign competition; sometimes they are not. Because of the lack of data, it may be difficult to demonstrate the biological effects of foreign fishing in their stocks, however direct these effects might be on market prices.[3] In any event, the fisheries will apparently be little altered in the immediate future, regardless of the outcome of current law of the sea negotiations.

Bermuda is of special interest as possessor of a coral reef fishery which has grown to the limits of renewability in response to native and tourist market pressures. It is a modern, not a traditional fishery, in that both commercial and subsistence fishing are carried on today under motor power, bait and catch are often refrigerated, catch is wholly marketed on a cash basis, and most of it is trucked from dockside to hotels and restaurants. Notwithstanding its modern aspects, the Bermudian case is instructive in revealing some of the implications of modernity for those fisheries closer to the traditional end of the spectrum of small island societies.

2. The Bermuda Fishery

Bermuda is a British dependency composed of about 150 islands clustered in a chain about 22 miles long (Map 1). It has a surface area of about 20 square miles. About 20 of its islands are inhabited and linked together by causeways and bridges. Its resident population numbers about 55,000.

The first colonists attempted to develop a plantation economy on the Bermudas but the land proved unsuitable. Instead, they developed various kinds of maritime enterprise, such as shipping, privateering, whaling, ship-building and repair. These activities remained central to their economy from the mid-seventeenth until the nineteenth century. Following World War Two income from tourism and 'exempted companies' – foreign corporations that use Bermuda as a base for their international financial transactions – have become the mainstays of the Bermuda economy (Manning, 1973:3–26).

For our purposes, the Bermuda fishery is divisible into two phases (cf. Watson *et al.*, 1965):

(i) Traditional hook and line fishing primarily for rockfish and grouper, 1612 to *c.* 1935.
(ii) Modern pot fishing for rockfish, grouper and spiny lobster, *c.* 1936 to date.

The Traditional Fisheries: The history of the Bermuda fishery and its development from the period of initial settlement to the displacement of sail-powered fishing sloops by the introduction of motor power in the mid-1930s has yet to be written in detail. Scattered accounts suggest the first settlers discovered virgin stocks of fish, whales and turtles in great abundance and fished them with remarkable ease. Their technology included oar- and sail-powered small craft; seine and cast nets; spears and prongs; hook and line; and small wooden traps.

Some commercial interests in Bermuda had reportedly developed a distant water sailing sloop fishery which exploited the Grand Banks for cod in the latter part of the eighteenth century, but it was apparently soon terminated as it contravened the Treaty of Paris of 1763 (McCallan, 1948:110). Shore and distant-water whaling also played a role in the Bermudian economy from the seventeenth century to the close of the nineteenth century (McCallan, 1948:101–110).

Subsistence fishing by members of scattered households has prevailed traditionally throughout the year, and it continues to some extent around the islands today. By the eighteenth century some part-time specialists seem to have appeared on the scene, providing farm or 'plantation' families and growing town populations with their fish requirements, perhaps initially on a cash-in-kind basis, and later on a credit and cash basis.

The people of St. David's Island in particular in eastern Bermuda have long been involved in various kinds of maritime enterprise: for example, whaling, turtling and piloting. The island became an important centre for year-round sloop hand-line fishing at least as early as 1900, when about 15 open-decked well-boats averaging 30 feet in length were regularly supplying markets in St. George's and greater Hamilton parish. An account of this sloop hand-line fishery is given elsewhere (Andersen, forthcoming). It will suffice here to indicate some of its important features.

Between 1900 and 1910, St. David's Island had a population estimated at about 150 to 200. It formed a community of fishermen, farmers, pilots and pilot-boatmen, carpenters, boat-builders and masons who drew their livelihood largely from the business and markets of nearby St. George's and Hamilton. Most family heads owned their own

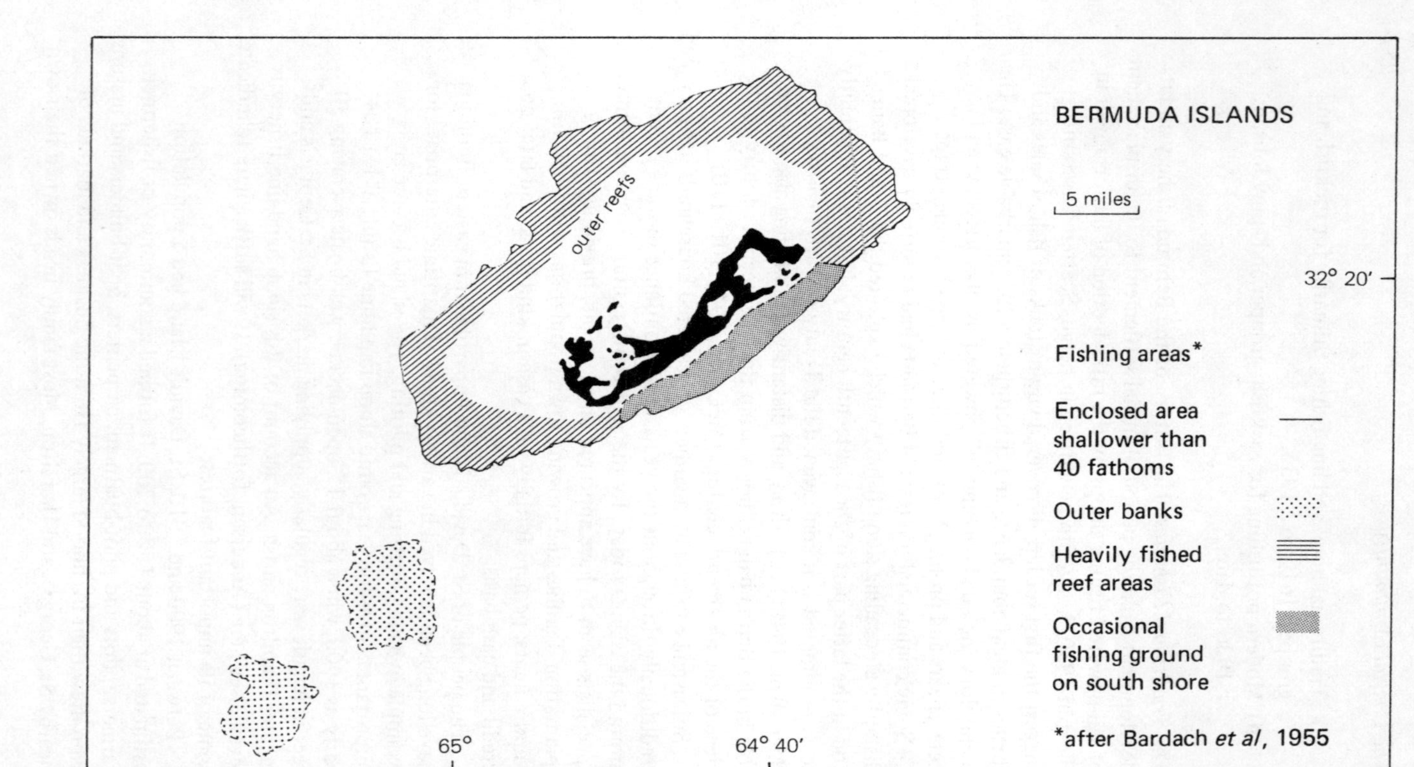
BERMUDA ISLANDS
5 miles
outer reefs
32° 20′
Fishing areas*
Enclosed area shallower than 40 fathoms
Outer banks
Heavily fished reef areas
Occasional fishing ground on south shore
*after Bardach et al, 1955
65°
64° 40′

houses and all commercial fishermen their own boats. The typical commercial fisherman was pluralistic: that is, he included a variety of activities and skills, such as farm work and gardening, vessel construction and repair and ship piloting in his total work adjustment. Moreover, most workers identified as specialists in some line of work, such as shipwrights and harbour pilots, pursued subsistence fishing as off-time permitted.

The 15 St. David's Island sloops and their crews of two or three men exploited the reef grounds roughly east and east by south of St. David's and St. George's Islands. Baitfish, such as fry and pilchard, were integral to the conduct of hand-line operations, and bait was seined and captured in the shallow waters of lagoons and beaches by individual crews each morning before making for the fishing grounds. These crews frequently assisted each other and shared their bait catch when it was large.

The sloops occasionally ranged beyond 5 miles offshore, but most fishing was done around reefs in depths between about 10 to 25 fathoms. This is particularly true where it was possible to take accurate positional co-ordinates by triangulation using fixed landmarks.

Preliminary information suggests that the fishermen in question had a virtual monopoly over these fishing grounds – a *de facto*, if not *de jure*, common – by dint of an advantageous position in proximity to the reef grounds and the other economic activities of inhabitants in other parts of the island group. Moreover, a system of customary positional tenure prevailed in areas less than 25 fathoms in depth: individual fishing boats had a customary right to the usufruct of fishing 'places', which they might hold for days or weeks.

Usufruct here is based upon the understood relationship between baiting or bait investment as a means to lure fish on a given day *and* the accepted 'right' to hold fish at the location over a period of days. As one retired fisherman put it:

> I've been there in 10 to 12 fathoms. You could see bottom. You take the glass and look through it, and you'd see the fish on the bottom. And many a time I'm seen six and eight big rockfish – they would weigh at least 50 to 100 pounds. And you may not catch 'em today, but you'd put a lot of bait there and hold the fish there and eventually you'd catch 'em. You may go there tomorrow and catch three to four hundredweight.

Another fisherman wouldn't go to that place at any time if you

> baited it. If he saw you there baiting the place, he could take your marks. It's no trouble for him to take your marks and get there. But he wouldn't do it. He wouldn't go to that spot. He'd ... make a spot of his own. And another fellow ... a place of his own. Sometimes you wouldn't be far apart, sometimes only hailing distance. But they wouldn't go where you was fishing. And that fish, if you baited there, it would stay there.

According to this same fisherman, one fished 'anywhere' in the deep water beyond 25 fathoms depth. Fishing 'places' did not obtain in this zone, and we may make the assumption that there were fewer restrictions on competition in these waters.

The live wells were used to bring the rockfish and groupers ashore alive. Rockfish were generally disposed of within about 24 hours or less, and when the groupers could not be marketed immediately they were held in 'ponds' (or pounds) built along the shore of a sheltered bay. Each of the 15 boat-owners reportedly had his own pond that held from 400 to 1000 pounds where the catch might be held without harm for weeks or months if need be.

Marketing in this period was little organized. Each fisherman was his own entrepreneur. Some fish were sold for cash at dockside to consumers; some sold wholesale to retail stores and hotels; and some by horse-drawn cart run through settlements as far as Hamilton. Always, there was the prospect that the commercial fisherman might have to compete against the many occasional or part-time subsistence fishermen scattered around the island chain who might come home with a good catch and market their excess at cut-rate prices. And so it remains today.

From the perspective of coastal fisheries what level of development does this fishery represent? If viewed against the many contemporary island fisheries of the Atlantic and beyond, we may crudely pigeon-hole it as a 'traditional', unmechanized commercial fishery. By choice or chance, these fishermen are advantageously located to exploit fishing grounds and markets. Their island is not strictly and solely a 'fishing community', although they have a 'community' by virtue of common residence and participation in the exploitation of what appears to be 'their' traditional grounds. They share a common body of environmental knowledge gleaned through years of practical experimentation and inherited lore, and a body of rules and understandings about the conduct of operations in the marine common.

Above the level of the small fishing unit, these fishermen are essentially unorganized in the corporate sense. Economic reciprocities occur among them while obtaining bait and fishing, and doubtless in other spheres, but individualism and self-reliance are prevalent values. The unorganized individual marketing practices reflect these values and, presumably, have resulted in losses due to spoilage and forced sales below cost.

Even if we characterize the St. David's Island marine common as a system of tenure over reef fishing space, we may question its value in the management of reef fisheries. One would like to think that the 15 sloops were part of a marine community ecosystem representing a balance between fishing effort and fish resources. But it is equally likely that this situation merely reflects the market interest in the fishing occupation, and other factors.

We meet here a pervasive problem for the manager of fisheries in island reef settings: the man-sea ecosystem relationship is only beginning to be understood. A marine biologist who specializes in atoll fisheries (Johannes, 1973) writes of reef and lagoon tenure in such settings:

> ... whereas one can glean from the literature various brief acknowledgements that such a thing ... exists on many Pacific islands, the details are lamentably few. Most of the information is anecdotal, for the interest is often clearly peripheral to the main interest of the writer – which, often, is land tenure.

This informational shortcoming exists even in settings where colonial archives permit documentation in considerable depth. Bermuda is illustrative: as early as 1620 concern about the abuse and overexploitation of various stocks moved the Bermuda Assembly to pass the first protective regulatory measures concerning the green turtle, and other regulations were tabled in 1627 concerning pilchards and 'frye' (LeFroy, 1876, Vol. 1: 411–12). Despite this early and, it seems, continuing awareness of environmental damage and the need for management restrictions, nearly three centuries later Verrill (1901–2: 699) was moved to observe:

> The fishes have contributed largely to the food of the Bermudians, ever since the first settlement, and therefore it is not strange that they decreased both in number and size. But it is difficult to determine definitely how much they have decreased, for accurate records and statistics are lacking. Moreover, it is possible that

natural physical causes ... caused the death of multitudes of fishes.

The relationship between past and present fishing effort, stocks and productivity, and customary tenure systems and conservation practices remain largely unrecorded and undefined in most small island settings today.

Rise of the Modern Pot Fishery: Auxiliary gasoline engines had begun to displace sail power in the Bermuda fishery by the 1930s, but it was not until about 1939 that the first intensive use of fish pots or traps for rockfish and groupers began. Pots had been in use perhaps since the earliest settlement of the islands, but they were comparatively small and used primarily for subsistence purposes. Between *c.*1900 and 1939 only one East End fishing family used pots extensively and that was for lobsters; and this family was also unusual in having developed a specialization in turtle fishing. Otherwise, hand-lining had remained the prevalent method for taking large rockfish, apart from seine and cast nets used when fishing close inshore. Pot use gradually expanded in number and pot size to dominate commercial production, although it did not wholly supplant hand-lining. In fact, hand-line fishing is still the principal method used by charter boat fishermen when engaged in commercial fishing in their seasonal 'inactive' periods. The ostensible reason is that the use of large wire pots tends to damage the sides and decks of their vessels thus endangering their appearance in the charter trade.

By the 1930s, commercial fishing from several points at the west end of Bermuda (for example, from Somerset and Mills Creek near Hamilton) had developed to some extent, but to what level is yet unclear. It seems that the onset of the Second World War interrupted the offshore fishery around the islands, and good quality fish was extremely scarce in the markets. Between 1939 and 1946 only one St. David's fisherman continued intensive fishing of the reefs off St. George's and St. David's Islands, the putative St. David's commons. Most of the other fishermen were drawn away by more attractive wage-labour opportunities, especially around the construction and maintenance of wartime military installations, and, doubtless, fishing was viewed as hazardous under war conditions. The St. David's fisherman in question chiefly supplied the islands' artillery batteries, especially at the east end.

After the War, men from other parts of Bermuda entered the pot fishery and catches from near offshore grounds began to decline under growing fishing pressure. It seems that no formal organized attempt was made to preserve St. David's commons and given the greater mobility made possible by engine power, men felt freer to set their gear wherever convenience and prospects indicated. Relations among fishermen became extremely competitive on the fishing grounds all around Bermuda as the years passed. Today, former pot fishermen speak of having been 'driven out of the fishery' by endless destructive assaults upon their fishing pots, and such spatial management as now obtains upon the fishing grounds results from a continuing see-saw struggle waged among fishermen to maintain their lines of pots against encroachment and to drive back competitors. Simultaneously, a government fishery authority has grown more active in regulation and enforcement.

Perhaps in response to concerns for the fishing industry's ability to supply a growing domestic and tourist demand for fish, the Bermuda fishery was made the subject of a special Fisheries Research Program in the mid-1950s (Bardach *et al.*, 1955, 1958). Findings from this research indicated Bermudian fish landings of about 1,250,000 lb.,[4] while another 600,000 lb. were imported (Bardach *et al.*, 1958:1). The productive coral reef environment for rockfish and groupers was estimated to be about 450 square miles.

In addition to their biological findings, Bardach and his colleagues (1958:30–5) made several important observations and organizational recommendations for improvement of the fishery. These recommendations called for the government to impose an organizational structure upon the fishery and its fishermen, create a substantial subsidy for the industry on a par with agriculture; appointment of a fishery officer or adviser and an administrative assistant; development of more scientific and statistical information on all species caught; creation of fishing centres and improvement of storage and marketing practices; gear modernization; and creation of a government loan scheme to assist fishermen to modernize their boats and gear (cf. Hess, 1966).

Common sense tells us that before their introduction such innovations must be assessed in terms of their 'fit' with and effects upon the existing ecology and social and economic structure, especially as regards income and employment. Yet the literature of development, modernization and westernization is replete with cases of directed change failure where innovation occurred before or without rigorous study of existing or native economies and concepts of social organization (e.g. Foster, 1962; Arensberg and Niehoff, 1964; and Cochrane, 1971). Development problems in the agricultural industries, which dominate this literature, are even more critical in the case of fishery development because of the much greater difficulty in predicting output, because of higher operational risks, and the extreme perishability of the catch, especially in settings lacking marketing, storage and transport facilities (Alexander, 1972:4, and *passim*).[5] Present purposes and insufficient preliminary data do not permit me to add a detailed account of Bermuda experience in implementing change along lines advanced primarily by Bardach and his associates, but some observations about the present status of the fishery are in order.

Most, but not all, Bermuda commercial fishermen are now organized into associations of full-time commercial fishermen. They feel that their fish sales and income are threatened by both the commercial charter boat and the part-time fishermen who are viewed as being in a position to 'dump' fish on the market at cut-rate prices. After all, 'the charter boat man can afford to sell his fish cheaper because he's already been paid under charter.' According to this thinking also, the part-timer does not have to worry about how irresponsibly he fishes or how cheaply he sells his surplus catch; he already has a job. All three classes of fishermen are convinced they have to fish to live and that the fishery needs more effective management. The full-time commercial fishermen dominated the industrial fishery catch in 1974, but in the eyes of the other two groups, much of it is taken by systematic violation of fishery regulations. Thus the level of co-operation within and between these associations leaves much to be achieved.

In accordance with the Bardach recommendations, a fishery officer and an administrative assistant have been appointed with their offices based at the Bermuda Aquarium, The Flats, roughly equidistant between the most active bases of commercial activity. The level of government subsidy for fishery administration is disproportionately small by comparison with agriculture, although fishermen have been assisted in the modernization of their vessels and gear. Marketing remains individualistic and underorganized. There is a fear among all fishermen that their stocks are seriously overfished, but catch levels and the status of most stocks are only now being well defined. Registration, licensing and entry restrictions are now being formulated.

In this shift toward a modern fishery under government regulation, there is no indication that serious thought was given to community-level regulation. The supposed St. David's common mentioned earlier seems not to have been considered as a base for development of a modern reef management system. Is this a significant oversight? Or do I read more regulatory potentiality into this customary organizational structure than is merited?

Put in more general terms, what is the modern management potential of customary coastal resource practices? There is no easy answer to this question. The Bermuda case is simply uninformative, although its development exemplifies the typical path of rapid, largely undirected growth of modern fisheries in many, if not most, small island and other coastal settings. This growth has been facilitated in large part by advances in vessel and gear technology which have promised greater certainty of catch, higher mobility and an expanded productive environment. In fact, the prospect of full utilization of this technology has encouraged development which largely, if not wholly, ignores customary tenure, and fosters the view that the domestic commons are a fishery that can remain unregulated.

Anthropologists and others familiar with fishing societies have often lamented official inattention to customary tenure systems and conservation practices in traditional fisheries as a possible basis for modern coastal management systems designed to minimize social and economic disruptions and reduce the prospect of overfishing local resources. Traditional tenure arrangements around the world range from reef and lagoon ownership by families and chiefs to exclusive community marine commons. The St. David's commons may be of marginal significance because of their relatively unorganized character, and it is not yet possible to show their contribution to a stable and productive local fishery at an earlier stage of economic history. While the matter is open to speculation, it is relevant to note the similar experiences elsewhere.

Johannes (1973) shows that reef ownership by families and chiefs is still common in Micronesia and that 'reef and lagoon resources are generally viable except around population centers'.[6] In Western Samoa and the Cook Islands, by contrast, reefs and lagoons are largely common property and the fisheries resources are seriously overexploited. Johannes cites Japan and Korea as two coastal states with 'extensive and elaborate systems of dividing up coastal fishing rights' derived partly from traditional tenure practices similar to those of Micronesia. Although the case for these practices remains somewhat uncertain, their role in traditional fisheries and their potential significance for modern coastal management merit consideration. The fishermen's co-operative, which often emerges along with planned economic development in a local community setting, may be the best vehicle for the continuation and enhancement of desirable tenure practices. Here, the owners might 'police their resources energetically at no cost to the taxpayer – a job that cannot be done effectively by the chronically understaffed and underequipped fisheries departments of the Pacific Islands' (Johannes, 1973). Although supporting evidence is lacking on this point, Hess (1966:9), a fishery researcher and fishery officer, argued for the development of fishermen's co-operatives in Bermuda on the grounds that they were the 'best tried methods of discouraging illegal hauling and/or theft of fish posts' in the Caribbean area.

Johannes' remarks about the chronic problems of fishery administration may be taken as characteristic of small island fisheries. This point returns us to the basic reason for this exploration: coastal fishery management and development is rather more problematic for the small tropical and sub-tropical island society than it is for the larger, economically and scientifically developed state. The former generally have a comparatively limited natural resource base. The situation of island states in the Lesser Antilles is illustrative. Rodriguez (1974:58–60) characterizes their reef fisheries as:

> ... surrounded by deep ocean waters, and concentrations of fish in such waters are not dense. For this reason most of the fisheries in the area are inshore reef or hard bottom fisheries. There are practically no trawlable bottoms, and catches depend almost entirely on fish traps and lines. It should be stressed that these methods ... are well suited to the natural conditions under which the fishermen operate. The catch consists of a variety of demersal fish, mainly snappers and groupers.

We must add spiny lobster to this short list. In most cases, we may not reasonably expect their fishermen to range the high seas in search of new fishing grounds, although some will undertake to exploit high-seas pelagic species, capital and marketing wherewithal permitting. They have little prospect of industrial development; consequently, small government revenues, limited administrative resources, and few trained personnel. Little improvement may be expected, notwithstanding some economic growth around sun-travelling tourists, agriculture, and offshore mineral resource development (cf. Rapaport *et al.*, 1971: 148–62).

The situation of developed, and particularly northern industrial, states is radically different and more favourable. They have the revenue base, and the scientific and administrative apparatus necessary to meet most environmental and economic challenges. The widely publicized fishery management difficulties faced by these states in the North Atlantic and North Pacific are within their means to resolve despite the heavy costs in additional administrative, scientific and organizational effort. Only whether they will do so, when and how remain to be decided. (How these important decisions are achieved is a study in itself and of no immediate relevance here, although the decisions themselves may well prove fateful for the future of fishing industries in many of the small societies of concern in this essay.)

3. The Fishery Officer

Roles and Requirements

Achievements in the Bermuda fishing industry since the mid-1950s are in large part attributable to the efforts of individuals who served in the capacity of fishery officer and, since 1973, assistant fishery officer. At this point, therefore, some consideration should be given to the social structural problems to be expected by the different kinds of persons who might assume this role. These ideas are admittedly speculative, but this consideration is important to the degree that expert advisers are needed to guide and monitor fishermen's organizational efforts, assess their resources, production and markets. In many small island fisheries these requirements are crucial.

Serious fishery management efforts may be expected to begin with the appointment of *one* individual to a full-time or part-time post as fishery officer. In some countries this official is established as an autonomous 'department', but more commonly he is attached to another government ministry, such as Agriculture in the case of Bermuda. Government may have established the role in response to pressures brought to bear by fishing interests, or as a result of its independent perception of need. Either way, the terms of reference at the beginning are usually broadly defined, conveying general responsibility to 'manage' the fishery and its developments. It is generally understood that this includes major responsibility for the formulation and enforcement of regulatory measures and for the gathering of relevant information.

It should be stressed, however, that the fishery officer's task is far more complex and multi-faceted than the above terms of reference suggest. At various times, even simultaneously, the officer will be expected to function as administrator, legal and development adviser, scientist, arbitrator, middleman and enforcer. In some cases it may prove necessary to act as 'lobbyist' to move government to action. It will almost certainly be necessary to campaign regularly for financial support from government for his department's and the industry's needs, and to adjust to resultant allocations below actual requirements.

This multiplex role is played in an administrative environment that is intimate and intensely personal, in which government is highly proximate to the citizen. There is an especially heavy pressure of personal commitments upon administrators in a small and close-knit society. Rapaport *et al.* (1971:151–3) observe: 'Pressure from family, friends and politicians will be brought to bear on ministers, senior administrators, and in fact on all civil servants far more so than in larger societies, where the decision-making process is more systematized and impersonal.'

These many expectations and conditions underline the seriousness of the recruitment and selection of the fishery officer. In the small island setting, he carries a great burden. With the right person, management and development may proceed reasonably well. With the wrong person, there may be little improvement and much damage to existing resources and operations. What kinds of expertise should the individual bring to such a role? Should this include previous experience in some phase of fishery production and, where it obtains, marketing? Perhaps a fisherman or middleman? Or might it be wiser to have someone experienced in fishery science, or the management of some other renewable resource? Or perhaps financial resources or administrative aims only permit appointment of a young person with a sufficient level of education, perhaps in business or commerce, to provide reasonably competent administrative ability?[7]

Given these options, what kinds of social structural factors might influence the ability of such appointees to speak and act effectively in their capacity of fishery officer? Effective performance in the role, particularly for the fisherman, merchant, and the student with administrative capabilities, assumes that he is able to draw upon the scientific expertise of others for sound management assessments and regulatory guidelines, or at least that the officer has the opportunity to develop the minimal necessary skills over a period of time. International development agencies of the United Nations and various developed nations have a long history of providing the professional expertise needed for rigorous stock assessment and fishery development advice on a short-term basis, and various fishery technical schools and colleges offer specially designed training programmes to provide the practical know-how for persons like fishery officers, although differences in scale and specialization may make it difficult to apply the training experience at home (Gerhardsen, 1966; cf. Rapaport *et al.*, 1971: 154–6).

The political-economic structure of many small island societies doubtless continues to reflect recruitment practices which derive from their traditional-colonial and plantation histories, where government functionaries issue from a landed, mercantile or political élite. Their offspring have characteristically had the economic resources, education and experience that prepare and enable them to function in entrepreneurial and public positions.

Fisherman as Fishery Officer

Fishermen, on the other hand, are generally at a competitive disadvantage. They have not had such resources and opportunities. Typically, they belong to a peasant client–élite patron type of relationship or are, at best, petty entrepreneurs. In consequence, the island society which seeks to recruit its fishery officer from the ranks of the fishermen themselves, perhaps to broaden or democratize the basis of appointment or simply to have the best informed person in a position of authority, may expect some stresses to appear in his relationship with government officials with élite identity, unless the social structure of the particular society has been radically altered to reduce or eliminate traditional influences.[8] Merely being a fisherman in some class and caste societies may be sufficiently stigmatizing to create serious communication and co-operation problems for the officer no matter how high his reputation in fishing circles. Such stresses may be reflected in a resentful attitude that the better-educated functionaries are 'sharkies always looking for you to break down' or trying to 'put me down' or 'cut me to pieces because I do not have the right words' when engaged in the give-and-take of decision-making.[9]

Despite the advantages flowing from his professional experience with other fishermen and their problems, the fisherman-appointee may find his work seriously hampered by established inter-community, corporate and individual rivalries and jealousies. He may have to contend with the fact, or his own suspicion, that his post is coveted by other fishermen, who see themselves equally, if not better, qualified, and resort to back-biting in one form or another. He may expect other fishermen to 'pick him to pieces' for his own previously established reputation for cunning violation of enacted and customary regulations while engaged in fishing, and thereby undermine his efforts to secure compliance.[10]

These problems may seriously hinder the officer in discharging his responsibilities effectively at least in the early stage of his career; and within the context of a small society they may be sufficient to generate a high 'mortality' rate among the occupants of this position. Practice shows, fortunately, that these are not insurmountable problems.

'Merchant' as Fishery Officer

Appointment of someone identified locally as a middleman-merchant may prove especially problematic, depending very much upon the candidate's reputation for fair and objective transactions with the fishermen and on the extent of the socio-economic and cultural gap between them. It may be a sound appointment in some cases, but one cannot ignore trends in what seems an era of burgeoning anti-capitalistic sentiment. A merchant-appointee seems increasingly anachronistic and generally evocative of suspicion. Fishermen may view such an officer's efforts at management and development with suspicion because of the possibility of underlying economic motivations. Whether or not justified, an unco-operative attitude so caused may vitiate the best efforts of the officer. As a result, the potential value of the merchant-appointee's market skills for fish resources may not be realized. In fact these skills may be better used in the capacity of government adviser within the same or some other department.

The merchant appointee may also encounter problems in maintaining a flow of adequate information from fishermen to policy-makers. Such an appointment may perpetuate a traditional patron-client linkage in the guise of a modern administrative structure. This is not likely to be desirable, if it denies fishermen an effective voice and role in decision-making for the fishery and themselves – a particularly important consideration where fishermen are industrially unorganized. Contemporary thinking in fishery administration seems to favour placing decision-making powers and responsibilities in the hands of the primary producer himself, wherever this is possible, over take-hold and highly centralized administrative decision-making which tends to try to do almost everything for them. The centralist orientation, it is believed, tends to discourage the self-reliance and initiative which are essential to successful enterprise, especially where vigorous market-oriented production is the goal. A (patron-) merchant-candidate is generally not conducive to these ends, although the answer in each case lies in the candidate's attitude, as an individual, to fishery administration and development, and in the circumstances of each community and state.

Scientist or Technician as Fishery Officer

A scientific input from marine biology is obviously necessary at some point in effective fishery planning, but there seems to be no special advantage in recruiting the fishery officer from scientifically qualified persons – whether the 'scientific' is a high-level professional or merely a capable technician without a specialist.[11] To the extent that such a person is chosen as officer because of his expertise and skills in fishery investigation, fishermen may have such high regard for his scientific knowledge or technical skill that their expectations exceed what can be delivered at least within a short span of time, particularly in the case of an island reef fishery. Johannes (1973) writes:

> ... coral reef fishes present biologists with the most complex fisheries management problem in the world. Age, growth and population statistics, all central to rational fisheries management, are exceptionally difficult to obtain. Many species have planktonic larval stages which are at the mercy of the currents and may drift for weeks or even months at sea before moving into a reef community. Thus the genetic and geographic origins of reef fish populations are generally not known, nor the localities in which their progeny will ultimately reside. In addition, unlike most populations of major commercial species in higher latitudes, reef fish populations are highly fragmented into small circumscribed groups and mating is not random. These circumstances greatly complicate the study of population dynamics. The inability of biologists to determine ages and growth rates of many reef fish, because of the absence of well defined seasonal growth rings in scales or bones, adds further to the problem, as does the uniquely large number of species involved.
>
> At present, therefore, resources management schemes (such as they are in Oceania) have to be constructed largely on the basis of intuition and good intentions. Pity the poor resource manager in such circumstances. It is his job to institute conservation measures – but when he does so, he is generally not in a position to defend them with hard evidence that they will work. His regulations are thus often ignored, and his motives, and even his ancestry, are often questioned by the people he is trying to help.

In consequence, the scientist-officer may have much of his time taken up in disillusioning the people he serves, and others, with respect to the depths of his knowledge and the ability of his technology to provide ready solutions to exceedingly difficult man-environment problems.

The role as *enforcement* officer is always likely to be a source of difficulty in the officer's performance of advisory duties, but perhaps especially for the official with scientific credentials. For example, when listing their general recommendations for the future development of the Bermuda fisheries in their second Progress Report, Bardach and his associates (1955:87–9) called for the appointment of a permanent fisheries biologist *and* an administrative assistant for him. The latter was to be a Bermudian who would act as a 'liaison officer' to aid the 'obviously ... imported' scientist and help him overcome his unfamiliarity with local conditions. It was suggested that the scientific official *not* be called 'Fisheries Officer, because of the obvious opprobrium that accompanies this title, and the suggestion of law enforcement which is not necessarily intended.' This proposal was dropped in their Final Report (1958), however, in which they call for appointment of a 'fishery officer or advisor'. Judging from observations during a short visit in January 1975, the Bermuda fishery officer and his assistant devote a considerably greater amount of time and effort to enforcement than is desired. What impact their prosecution of various violators will have upon their relations with fishermen, and overall fishery management, remains to be established.

Unless he is one of the rare persons with prior experience on the practical side of commercial fishing, the scientist officer will suffer criticism for not *really* knowing much about the business of making a living from fishing. This criticism will be further fuelled by the unpopularity of subsidy programmes, regulatory measures and other administrative actions.

The need to be highly visible among fishermen while also fulfilling the scientific requirements of his role may create a difficult problem in the allotment of the officer's time. Although it may not dramatically improve the value of his stock assessments and growth calculations, time spent learning about subsistence and commercial fishing as integral components in a way of life improves the chances for co-operation on the part of fishermen and, thereby, successful resource management and development. The individual officer must find a middle road, of course.

To the degree that his role requires a common-sense political expertise in negotiating with people, and other departments of government, his professional training and scientific credentials do not guarantee success. This raises the general question of communication across class, caste and national status boundaries in the fishery officer–fisherman relationship. Despite professional or semi-professional status, problems may be encountered in communicating those fishermen viewpoints with which he agrees to administration, especially where it is dominated by a traditional élite with archaic notions of government authority and scepticism, regarding the fisherman's ability to appraise their situation in accurate and realistic terms.

The scientist-officer may find it necessary to develop two languages (but not a 'forked-tongue'): one for policy-making administrators and another for those fishermen with little formal educational experience. The professional mode of discourse may have little place in conversations with fishermen, though one may be surprised at how quickly the scientist's jargonized 'mysteries' are comprehended if put across in a straightforward manner. Many public administrators have experienced embarrassing difficulties and failures, and members of the community suffered unnecessary frustration and disillusionment because government plans and intentions were not understood. The individual who cannot communicate comfortably in both directions in this relationship probably ought not to be in this critical front-line post. The alternative is a supportive research post.

The appointment of someone with administrative experience or potential, but without knowledge of fishery science or the fishing industry, is not likely to create new social problems that would impair his performance of the role of fishery officer. If there is any pressure upon his Ministry or department to increase fishery production or earnings, he will probably experience the same broad range of expectations encountered by his predecessors; and he will be given an opportunity to prove himself despite any initial criticism of government for having appointed a 'dummy' to the post. No matter what kind of person is selected for the role, all will undergo a period of socialization-enculturation in which fishermen (and others) 'try the green man' to fathom his understanding, sincerity and intelligence.

We should also ask who will set the criteria and choose the individual appointed. Fishery decision-making ought not to be viewed as a 'purely governmental' matter, unless of course fishermen already have such clearly discernible roles in government that no further involvement of the fishermen is required. Generally, however, fishing communities do not exercise preponderant influence within the national political system.[12]

Since most small-state fishermen tend to be occupationally pluralistic with dispersed independent producers, and frequently lack an established tradition of collective organization, almost any form of fishermen-representation in the decision-making process, for example on fishery advisory committees, may prove a difficult goal to attain. Even where fishermen have their own organization, for example, as with the Bermuda Commercial Fishermen's Association (full-time fishermen), Bermuda Charter-Fishermen's Association (seasonal commercial and charter fishermen), and Bermuda Fishermen's Association (part-timers), squabbling within and between groups makes for ineffective representation. Yet representation must be encouraged if fishermen are to co-operate and acquire the managerial awareness conducive to full and rational development of the resource. It is also necessary to help build confidence in the government's commitment to responsible policy formulation and decision-making, as opposed to seemingly uninformed, remote and arbitrary action (cf. Crutchfield, 1972).

4. Conclusion

This exploration has been undertaken within the limited sphere of preliminary field data on Bermuda and with special reference to island, and particularly reef, fisheries which are relatively heterogeneous ecological systems (Thomas, 1968). Whether in the Atlantic, Pacific or Indian Ocean, the pressure to modernize their subsistence and commercial fisheries appears to be ubiquitous and unavoidable. Within the framework of their typically small-scale and often traditional societies and economies there may be unrecognized assets for fishery modernization in existing marine tenure arrangements and local knowledge of the marine environment. Modernization is more likely to be carried out efficiently and equitably if fishermen play an active part in fishery decision-making and management. The path to such a goal is strewn with difficulties, only some of which have been mentioned here (see also Epple, 1975). But without the co-operation of fishermen, whether or not built upon pre-existing concepts of tenure and conservation, the prospects for successful coastal and fishery management in small states are dim indeed; and that fact must also concern the economically advanced nations with which many of these island societies are allied as dependents.

Since much of the responsibility for mobilizing effective fisherman organization often falls to the lone individual who assumes the role of fishery officer in these settings, some emphasis has been placed on the question of *who* that person might be. My discussion of this question is admittedly biased by observations in the Bermuda setting where there is little distance between the home office and the field, as all fishery participants are highly accessible and visible. In other island settings great physical distance between islands in a group makes for a highly dispersed effort between the field staff and the central office.

Another question requiring close scrutiny is *how* the officer fulfils the requirements of his role and promotes the growth of fishermen capabilities in organizational roles. Neither of these questions appears to have received close study in these societies to date. These problems assume increasing significance as we move closer to an era of new legal régimes resulting from the Third United Nations Conference on the Law of the Sea. It is unrealistic to expect radical increases in fishery production, let alone improvements in the distribution of income to fishermen, as a direct result of these new régimes (Knight, 1974:383 and *passim*), but we should ask how small island societies will respond to new opportunities and responsibilities under the new legal order.

Notes

1. Data upon which some of this discussion is based were obtained during a two-week preliminary field-work period in January 1975. This research was supported in part by a small Exxon Foundation Fellowship administered by the Bermuda Biological Station for Research, St. George's West. I am most grateful for their support.
2. For a further consideration of the problems encountered by Newfoundland fishing communities, see the previous chapter by Geoffrey Stiles, 'The Small Maritime Community and its Resource Management Problems: A Newfoundland Example'.
3. The fishery of a small coastal state of the kind in question may also be affected by foreign fishing to the extent that the migratory species upon which it depends for food or bait (e.g. pilchards, sardines, bonito) are significantly influenced by the marine fisheries of other nations. But the causal linkage between distant fishing effort and changes in the local stock may be difficult to establish, and in the absence of substantial scientific evidence it may be necessary to proceed on the false assumption that the two are ecologically independent.
4. In 1973 official Bermuda statistics report landings of 1,034,596 lb.
5. Alexander's recent work on fishery modernization in Southern Ceylon (1972), and particularly his mimeographed report 'Some Aspects of Southern Fisheries Development' (1972), is an excellent illustration of the questions raised about the implications flowing from alternative kinds of innovations. See also his chapter following, 'The Modernization of Peasant Fisheries in Sri Lanka'.
6. For example, Mason (1968:304) writes of the Onotoa, about 1,500 people living on a small (5.21 sq.m.) atoll in the southern Gilberts: The Onotoan is basically dependent upon his land and defends his title with great vigour. Real property is defined as parcels of land and associated with *babai* pits and fish ponds, as well as offshore reef and lagoon areas. Rights to property are normally inherited from either parent, although sons receive preference,

especially the eldest. Use of inherited resources is restricted by subordination to interests of his kin group. Trespass by outsiders is punishable by extreme action of the owner.'

7. Willson (1966) touches upon the question of personnel and selection criteria, although in the framework of relatively large-scale administrative units for developing coastal states. Fishery education programmes are explored at some length by Gerhardsen (1966), but his discussion is also framed in terms of an administrative capability considerably above that assumed in the present essay. The general discussion of public administration and other problems special to small states by Rapaport *et al.* (1971) is useful, although fisheries are not specifically discussed.
8. The search for recruits to government positions from outside a traditional élite may occur as a result of various kinds of developments: for example, as part of a process of democratization after national independence, within a programme of economic diversification and educational reform, or by virtue of more general policies explicitly formulated under Marxist or some similar populist inspiration.
9. These expressions come from one Bermudian commercial fisherman who has served on various fishery advisory committees which include lawyers and merchants.
10. Epple (1975:26), speaking of mobilizing an effective elected leadership for a co-operative organization among the fishermen of St. Andrew's, Grenada, observes: '... fishermen are reluctant to grant to a peer the right to exercise authority, or to acknowledge any attempt at leadership by a fisherman *vis-à-vis* his mates.'
11. As it turned out, both the scientifically trained Chief Fishery Officer and his assistant in 1974 were native Bermudians although the former was trained abroad.
12. Iceland is a special case. Because the fishing industry accounts for as much as 90 per cent of the GNP, the industry has enormous political influence.

References

Alexander, P., 'Some Aspects of Southern Fisheries Development', mimeographed, 1972.

——, '"Ethno-Accountancy": Local Level Management Systems in the Fishing Industry of Southern Ceylon', 1972.

Andersen, R., 'Bermudian Handline Fishing in the Sailing Sloop Vessel Era', forthcoming in *Studies in Fishing Culture*, Festschrift in honour of Holger Rasmussen, Bela Gunda (ed.), in preparation. Debrecen, Hungary.

Arensberg, C.M., and A.H. Niehoff, *Introducing Social Change*, Chicago, Aldine, 1964.

Bardach, J.E. *et al.*, *Bermuda Fisheries Research Program: Progress Report No. 2*, unpublished, 1955.

——, *Bermuda Fisheries Research Program: Final Report,* Hamilton, Bermuda, Bermuda Trade Development Board, 1958.

Cochrane, G., *Development Anthropology,* New York, Oxford University Press, 1971.

Crutchfield, J.A., 'Economic and Political Objectives in Fishery Management', in *World Fisheries Policy*, B.J. Rothschild (ed.), Seattle and London, University of Washington Press, 1972, pp. 74–89.

Epple, G.M., 'Technological and Organizational Factors in the Development of a West Indian Fish-marketing Co-operative', paper presented at a symposium on Technological Change and its Effects on Maritime Communities, Society for

Applied Anthropology Meetings, Amsterdam, 1975.
Foster, G.M., *Traditional Cultures and the Impact of Technological Change*, New York, Harper and Row, 1962.
Gerhardsen, G.M., 'Fisheries Education and Training in Growth and Development Programs', in Report of the Conference on Fishery Administration and Services, Rome, FAO Fisheries Reports, No. 43, 1966, pp. 80–114.
Hess, E., *Final Report* (The Bermuda Fishery Industry), Office of the Chief Fishery Officer, Bermuda Government Aquarium, The Flatts, Bermuda, unpublished, 1966.
van den Hoonaard, W.C., 'An Ethnographic Account of Relations Between Fishermen, Marine Biologists and Politicians' (The Icelandic Shrimp Industry), unpublished, n.d.
Johannes, R.E., 'Exploitation and Degradation of Shallow Marine Food Resources in Oceania', forthcoming in Proceedings of the Pacific Science Association Meetings, Guam, 1973.
Knight, H.G., 'Impact of some Law of the Sea proposals on Gulf and Caribbean Ocean Resource Development', in *Caribbean Study and Dialogue*, proceedings of Pacem in Maribus IV, Malta, International Ocean Institute, 1974, pp. 366–413.
LeFroy, J.H., *Memorials of the Discovery and Early Settlement of the Bermudas or Somers Islands 1515–1685*, 2 vols. (Compiled from the colonial records and other original sources), 1876.
Manning, F.E., *Black Clubs in Bermuda*, Ithaca and London, Cornell University Press, 1973.
Mason, L. (1959), 'Suprafamilial Authority and Economic Process in Micronesian Atolls', reprinted in *Peoples and Cultures of the Pacific*, A.P. Vayda (ed.), New York, Natural History Press, 1968, pp. 298–329.
McCallan, E.A., *Life on Old St. David's, Bermuda*, Hamilton, Bermuda, Bermuda Historical Monuments Trust, 1948.
Rapaport, J. *et al.*, *Small States and Territories: Status and Problems*, New York, Arno Press, 1971.
Rodriguez, G., 'The Living Resources of the Caribbean and Gulf of Mexico', in *Caribbean Study and Dialogue*, Proceedings of Pacem in Maribus IV, Malta, International Ocean Institute, 1974, pp. 43–66.
Thomas, W.L., Jr. (1967), 'The Pacific Basin: an Introduction', reprinted in *Peoples and Cultures of the Pacific*, A.P. Vayda (ed.), New York, Natural History Press, 1968, pp. 3–26.
Verrill, A.E., 'The Bermuda Islands', *Transactions of the Connecticut Academy of Arts and Sciences*, 11, part II, 1901–2.
Watson, J.W. *et al.*, *A Geography of Bermuda*, London, Collins, 1965.
Willson, F.M.G., 'Fisheries Administration and Development: an Introductory and Comparative Survey', in *Report of the Conference on Fishery Administration and Services*, Rome, FAO Fisheries Reports, No. 43, 1966, pp. 19–79.

12 THE MODERNIZATION OF PEASANT FISHERIES IN SRI LANKA

Paul Alexander

1. Introduction

The pressing need for the development of South Asian fisheries is apparent to even the most myopic investigator. About a quarter of the South Asian population do not get enough to eat and a considerably greater percentage suffer from a lack of high-grade protein (FAO, 1968). Development of the region's underexploited fisheries is the only possible internal solution to these problems, for many people are prevented from eating animal protein by dietary laws, and in any case the scarce land can be more efficiently used for grain production.

The basic dilemma in developing the fisheries – to increase production without decreasing employment – should also be readily apparent, but a glance at the history of fisheries development suggests it is seldom appreciated. Foreign experts, as well as local administrators trained in overseas universities, have avoided the most important problems by concentrating on industrialized fishing under the control of large private companies or government corporations. (Alexander, 1975a; Colombo Plan, 1958; Ceylon Fisheries Corporation, 1965). The point that the fish produced by these measures is too expensive for local consumers and that these 'developments' further impoverish the traditional fishing community are unrecognized or ignored. Consequently attempts to modernize peasant fisheries have proceeded on an *ad hoc* basis and are based on myths and prejudices about the peasant communities, rather than on planning and research (Klausen, 1968). Although research into such programmes is more often forced to explain failure than account for success, it does suggest that an increase in production need not imply a decrease in employment. A prerequisite, however, is that high degrees of technical skill in designing boats and gear for local conditions are combined with a detailed knowledge of the local community, particularly the indigenous economy (Hill, 1970).

The constraints on the development of peasant fisheries are to some extent identical with the constraints on peasant agriculture. In both situations factors such as the small-scale enterprises, the inefficient technology and poor marketing arrangements, the lack of finance for repairs and maintenance costs, and the incompatibility of high producer prices with very poor consumers, pose difficult problems. But as Firth (1966:2) points out, fisheries have some special features which make planning even more difficult. Firth was mainly concerned with distribution and stressed such difficulties as the marketing of a highly perishable product, the large capital factor combined with uncertainty as to when financial demands will occur, and the entrenched position of the middlemen. When we turn to the production we find another set of special problems: indigenous notions of sea tenure are difficult to codify and often encourage increased participation when the marginal product is diminishing, while fishing gear – unlike land – depreciates rapidly and is a poor avenue for saving.

This chapter discusses some of these problems through an historical analysis of a fishing village in Southern Sri Lanka. There are a number of reasons for concentrating on the village, rather than the regional or national level. The most important reason is that it is becoming increasingly clear that many of the indices hitherto used in macro-studies are inadequate as measures of development. As Seers (1970:3) has noted, the important question to ask about a country's development is: What is happening to poverty, to unemployment and to inequality? A discussion couched in terms of changes in GNP or *per capita* income will not provide an adequate answer. What is required is more empirical work in local communities and less application of supposedly normative rules of conduct derived from inadequate theory.

Empirical studies of village communities should also demolish the persistent belief that the sponsored introduction of new technology is the only, or even the major, source of social change in peasant societies. The tremendous changes in the economic and social life of most South Asian villages over the past three decades are only in small part due to technological innovations: internal population growth and national political developments have both been more important. It is to be hoped that the stereotyped and prejudiced notions which Apthorpe (1971) labels 'the social value theory of development' will also become a victim of village studies. Although the failures of co-operatives and the rejection of new technologies are often explained by referring to culturally based obstructive values supposedly held by the peasant population, such explanations seldom stand up to empirical investigation. Peasant villages are not necessarily conservative: some will always accept new methods that promise increased rewards, but all will reject methods that raise risks to an unacceptable level. (Cancian, 1972; Lipton, 1968).

I do not suggest that village studies should replace national surveys; the two are complementary. Each village is in some ways unique, and accurate generalizations presuppose national statistics. But, in turn, the adequate design and interpretation of national surveys requires a close familiarity with local rural communities.

2. The Village of Mawelle

The Setting

Mawelle – which means big beach – is a fishing community of 1031 inhabitants on Sri Lanka's southern coast. To the west a ribbon of densely populated settlement extends 120 miles to the national capital Colombo, while in the east settlement rapidly decreases through a series of small, isolated, poverty-stricken fishing villages to the uninhabited scrublands of a national game reserve.

Mawelle beach is an almost perfect setting for a peasant fishing village. A granite headland, 100 feet high, blunts the force of the south-west monsoon which blows from April to August, creating a sheltered anchorage for mechanized craft and making Mawelle one of the few villages where fishing is possible throughout the year. Two hundred yards of smooth, steep-sloping beach permit the operation of two beachseines simultaneously, while the submerged rocks in other parts of the harbour and the reef 1½ miles offshore shelter rockfish and lobsters. A four-acre lagoon separates Mawelle from the agricultural villages further inland, but the waters are very brackish and support only small bony carp and miniature prawns which are suitable only for bait.

The Population

The inhabitants of Mawelle, like those of the other coastal villages, are all Sinhala-speaking Buddhists of the *Karave* (fishermen) caste, a caste which is usually ranked second to the *Goigama* (cultivator) caste in national hierarchies, but whose members do not acknowledge caste superiors. At first sight Mawelle seems to be a good example of the stereotyped autonomous, conservative, homogeneous and inward-looking peasant village which is constantly depicted in the pages of the development literature. This impression gains weight with the knowledge that nearly all marriages are contracted with members of the three adjoining villages and that many people leave Mawelle only to visit the doctor or to make a pilgrimage. Nevertheless the impression is mistaken. Nearly all Mawelle people are literate and the newspapers and radio provide fuel for their burning interest in national affairs. Most of the small shopkeepers in other regions are *Karave*, for since 1910 Mawelle has been involved in an extensive network trading dried fish for rice. In fact, throughout Mawelle's history national political events have been the most important single influence on internal village developments.

The Economy

Today the Mawelle economy is overwhelmingly dependent upon fishing. Of the 240 employed males, only 17 do not draw their incomes from the sea, either directly as fishermen or indirectly in providing services for the fishermen. The estimated Rs. 330,000 earned by the fishermen in 1971 was the sole sustenance of 204 Mawelle families as well as another fifty households in adjoining villages. This gives an average annual household income of Rs. 1,170 which should be compared with the poverty line figure of Rs. 1,758 calculated by the Central Bank (ILO, 1972).

The majority of Mawelle families are even poorer than these figures suggest: social stratification is very marked and an élite of mechanized boat-owners and fish middlemen have incomes well in excess of Rs. 10,000 while other households earn less than Rs. 500.

Unemployment, a serious problem throughout Sri Lanka, is particularly high in the fishing villages, especially among high school and university graduates. Of the 33 Mawelle youth who have reached this level since 1964, only 10 have ever been in permanent employment. But despite the faint chances of obtaining a job commensurate with their qualifications, 19 Mawelle children are in their last two years of high school and four are at University. Men are increasingly turning to political contacts as a means of obtaining jobs in government organizations, but very few jobs are available. In the meantime, as the 1971 insurrection so dramatically demonstrated, the combination of educated, highly politicised and unemployed youth, plus an underemployed, poverty-stricken and increasingly dissatisfied peasantry, is a particularly volatile combination.

In 1971 three types of fishing were current in Mawelle: deep-sea fishing 10–20 miles offshore for sharks and tuna using 3½-ton mechanized craft; inshore fishing up to two miles from the coast using traditional outrigger craft and nylon driftnets for anchovies and sardines; and beachseining for anchovies and sardines. The comparative operating results of three technologies are set out in Table 1.

Although the mechanized craft produce the biggest proportion of

Table 1: Comparative Annual Operating Results: Beachseines, Mechanized Craft, Inshore Fishing

	Beachseines RS	Mechanized Craft RS	Inshore Fishing RS
Capital Cost of Equipment	383,625	302,500	48,100
Annual Catch[a]	173,571	279,720	36,800
Production Costs	66,330	74,000[b]	14,430
Interest (three per cent)	11,508	9,075	1,443
Nett Catch	95,733	196,645	20,927
No. of Men Employed	274	47	81
Return Per Man	349	4,184	258

a. Includes fish distributed for consumption without payment.

b. Includes fuel costs and repairs.

c. These figures include both men who work the gear and men whose income is derived solely from gear operated by others. Seven Mawelle men get the majority of their income from mechanized boats owned by them and operated by others, and approximately 70 men and women from Mawelle and elsewhere derive income from beachseines which they do not operate themselves. All 47 men associated with the mechanized craft are employed full-time, but 37 of the "bible" fishermen also participate in beachseine fishing. About 180 of the 274 men employed on the beachseines get the major part of their income from working these nets.

the annual Mawelle catch, they do not make the largest contribution to the village economy. Production costs for the mechanized craft are high and much of it goes to extra-village sources: approximately Rs. 74,000 for fuel and repairs and Rs. 111,000 in wage payments to crew members living in other areas. As all the fish taken by the mechanized craft are sold to middlemen from other areas, the total contribution to Mawelle's economy is about Rs. 100,000, most of which goes to twelve households. In contrast the production costs of the beachseines are mainly intra-village payments. The catch is sold to local middlemen and, assuming a 25 per cent clear profit by the middlemen, the contribution of the beachseines is Rs. 275,000 or 70 per cent of the village's income.

The data in Table 1 also makes it possible to discuss the economic structure of the three technologies. Although efficiency, calculated in terms of profit per man hour, is not very important in a village with serious underemployment, the comparative figures are: Mechanized craft Rs. 3.5, beachseines Rs. 2.8, inshore fishing Rs. 0.3. The mechanized craft provide the greatest profit per unit of capital (mechanized craft Rs. 0.64, beachseines Rs. 0.21, inshore fishing Rs. 0.48) but the extent of capital investment is considerably greater. Overall Rs. 7,500 are invested for each man employed on the mechanized craft, as opposed to Rs. 1,400 for the beachseines and Rs. 600 for inshore fishing. All the money for the mechanized craft was provided by the government and less than one in twenty applicants can obtain a boat or employment as a crew member.

The paramount position of the beachseines is clear; they provide two-thirds of the village income and at least part of the income of 300 men. Inshore fishing is mainly a subsistence activity for men without other employment and even during the annual flush period most of the catch is sold within the village. The mechanized craft are the only technology where the marginal product of both labour and capital is neither close nor equal to zero, but access is limited to men with boat-owning relatives or good political contacts.

It is evident to both outside observer and villager alike that the Mawelle economy is in serious trouble. Extra-village employment opportunities are almost non-existent (ILO, 1972) and the fisheries have been unable to absorb the annual 2.5 per cent growth in the population, with the result that the average household income is 25 per cent below the poverty line and is still falling. While all are affected by the population growth, each of the three fishing technologies has particular problems. Two-thirds of the mechanized craft issued since 1961 are wrecks and the remainder are often beached for long periods because of a lack of finance and facilities for repairs. There are about three times more inshore craft than the limited fishing area can support, with consequent internal factionalism, high production costs, low profits and maldistribution of the catch. The same is true for the beachseines, where the number of nets is so excessive that the average net is used only seven times a year. If the beachseines were reduced from their present 99 to the optimum of 18 the community's profits from this form of fishing would double to Rs. 143,000 per year.

To understand how this situation arose we must look at Mawelle's history over the past hundred years.

3. The History of the Beachseine Economy

Early Settlement

Mawelle village was founded in 1871 by a minor official in the colonial government who by using his official position was able to purchase 27 acres cheaply and begin a coconut plantation. His three sons, who later took different names, established the three families that are today regarded as the original founding families of the village. Actually a small community of fishermen, drawing a meagre living from fishing in the lagoon and off the rocks, had earlier settled on the land immediately behind the beach, but they lacked official title to their house sites and were soon herded into a small hamlet (now called Kandegoda) at one end of the beach.

The first of the large beachseines, which were to dominate Mawelle's economic history, was brought to the village around 1885 by one of the founding families. These nets (measuring half a mile along each wing) were much more efficient than the small Sinhalese beachseines and were brought to Sri Lanka around 1870 by migrant Tamil fishermen from the Madras coast (Wright, 1868). Their dispersal throughout the island in less than fifteen years makes nonsense of the belief that peasant fishermen are too conservative to experiment with new methods. The beachseines require a crew of at least nine and were probably initially worked by members of the Kandegoda fishing community, but a series of in-marriages quickly raised the 'founding family' section of the population, and by 1914 all of the beachseine labour was drawn from this group.

Overfishing

Examination of a wide range of historical documents suggests that Mawelle's history prior to 1939 can best be seen in terms of an intensification of trends already present at the turn of the century. The optimum number of beachseines – that is the number which will allow continuous fishing throughout the day – is 18 and this was reached well before 1920. The following twenty years are a classic illustration of what Hardin (1968) has described as the 'Tragedy of the Commons' and what economists more prosaically call the common-property resource problem.

Once the optimum number of nets was reached, additional nets did not increase the total catch and, because they increased production costs, actually lowered the community's profit. But while it was in the community's interest to limit nets to the optimum number, participation in beachseining was tied to ownership of nets, and thus newcomers (mainly sons of beachseiners) had to add additional nets if they wished to continue beachseining. A hypothetical example will make this clear. If there are twenty nets, a man who owns one net will receive 1/20th of the total catch. If his two sons merely take over his net they will each receive 1/40th of the catch, but if one constructs a new net they each receive 1/21st. Because additional nets increased the production costs without increasing the catch, their construction was clearly uneconomic from the point of view of the community as a whole, and this was recognized by the fishermen. But there were equally good reasons for individuals to continually add to their numbers. As there were no economic restraints on increased participation, and as the social restraints proved ineffective, nets continued to increase, reaching 36 by 1938.

Stratification

One consequence was increasing stratification among beachseining households. In the early years the beachseines were normally worked by the owners or their heirs, but as numbers rose, men unable to meet the heavy maintenance costs, and men whose fathers were unable to finance additional nets, dropped out of the net-owning group to become wage- or share-labourers. While this slowed the process of net expansion it also divided the beachseiners into two classes. Other events during the 1900–39 period accelerated the stratification process. As the population grew the coconut plantations were cut for house sites, depriving the village of the income from the nuts and from manufactured products such as coir rope. One of the richer men opened an arrack tavern and by foreclosing debts acquired control of much of the land and fishing equipment. These changes in the economic base were quickly followed by changes in the superstructure. The successful owners adopted honorific surnames and lifestyles based on Sinhalese feudal notions, and the kin-based unity of the beachseining families was destroyed (cf. Obeyesehere, 1967).

Market Development

By 1938 the proceeds from agricultural products were negligible and the Mawelle economy was almost completely dependent upon fishing. While men from Kandegoda had gained deep-sea experience in other villages and were now operating a small deep-sea fleet of traditional craft, and most villagers were using small traditional craft for inshore fishing, more than 80 per cent of the catch was from the beachseines. With the exception of small amounts of twine for the beachseines, and fish-hooks, all the fishing gear was produced within the village.

For the greater part of the year about three-quarters of the catch was consumed within the village; the remainder, plus the bulk of the catch from the short flush period, was dried or salted for later sale in the interior. The returns from the sale of this preserved fish, plus remittances from men working in other areas, provided a cash income, while the free government rations of the staple rice were taking on increasing importance. Mawelle's resources had thus actually diminished while the population grew from 468 in 1901 to 752 in 1931, and the long-term survival of the village depended upon the discovery of new resources or the development of more valuable products.

The latter did occur. With the onset of war fish prices more than doubled throughout Sri Lanka, but a more important factor in Mawelle's case was the improvement in market access. In 1940 a paved road connected Mawelle to the main Southern Province highway, an ice factory was built in a nearby town, and the government-sponsored Fish Sales Union made transport available at low cost. Mawelle fish could now be sold at low price throughout the heavily populated and protein-starved Southern Province and fish prices rose from Rs. 3 per hundredweight of dried fish to more than Rs. 15 for wet fish. Within three or four years Mawelle beachseining changed from a semi-subsistence activity to a fully commercial enterprise.

Net Ownership

A less desirable consequence was an immediate increase in the number of nets: from 36 in 1939 to 71 in 1945 and 108 in 1966. There were three main reasons for the initial spectacular increase. First, the higher fish prices made the beachseines a very profitable investment even when they were worked by wage labour. Although the marginal product remained at zero the amount of profit was very high and the return on capital was greater than 40 per cent. The beachseines were thus converted from a technology used by peasant fishermen for a subsistence living to a channel for very profitable investments by the rising class of Sinhala entrepreneurs. Second, there was much more money available in the fishing community. Although the benefits of the increased prices were not equally distributed, there were now several persons with large amounts of money and few alternative avenues for investment. Third, and perhaps most important, as nets were added, all individuals had to join in the race to protect their equity in the total catch. Thus the process of net construction took on increasing momentum as each individual strove to maintain, or if possible increase, his share of the catch.

The structure of net-ownership was radically altered; the owner-operators were replaced by entrepreneurs operating their nets on a hire basis. By 1945 the ten biggest net-owners owned 14 per cent of the total nets, as opposed to 6 per cent in 1938, and the extent of entrepreneurial domination was even greater for several registered their nets in the names of relatives so as to conceal the extent of their ownership. In these circumstances the poorer men found it increasingly difficult to retain their nets. The higher the number of nets, the fewer times a particular net was used and the smaller the chances of participating in the high catch period. Big owners could meet these risks by financing unsuccessful nets with the proceeds from successful ones, but small owners without access to additional finance were forced to sell their nets during bad seasons.

By 1945 the beachseine economy had taken on most of its present features: the nets were a very profitable investment even if the owner had to pay labour; the number of nets was far larger than optimum; the system of allocating turns in conjunction with the very short period of high catches gave a most unequal distribution of the catch among individual nets; and the peasants were being forced out by the capitalists. In 1966 the government prohibited additional nets, but by this time the numbers were far too high (108) and attempts to reduce them by amalgamating nets or forming a co-operative have failed. In 1971 there were few independent net-owners; the bulk of the nets were owned by members of three competing kin-based political factions and were worked by the political and economic clients of the faction leaders. Fights were common (9 nets have been burned since 1970) and at the end of my field work it seemed only a matter of time before a single faction took control.

4. The Introduction of New Technologies

The 'Bible' Nets

With the exception of the full moon period when large catches of small squid were taken, inshore fishing before 1962 seldom produced fish for sale. Each evening men rowed out to the rocks at the mouth of the harbour and the fish they caught with hand-lines or small throw-nets were consumed within their households or distributed without payment to relatives. In 1962, however, two of the beachseiners introduced a small-mesh nylon drift net which they had seen being used by Catholic fishermen north of Colombo – hence the name 'bible' net. Using the nets in the same area and in direct competition with the beachseines, the two men made more than Rs. 15,000 in three months before increasingly bitter conflict with the beachseiners resulted in the destruction of their net. The local police were alarmed at the fights that occurred and eventually prohibited the use of 'bible' nets within the harbour.

Other men immediately realized the possibilities of the new nets. Within two years 35 of the traditional craft used for inshore fishing were equipped with nets and in 1971 all 37 of the traditional craft had nets and there was sufficient unused netting to equip a further 10.

It quickly became apparent that the fishermen had been too quick to invest in 'bible' nets, for the area of the fishery is far too small for the number of craft involved. The area in which the nets can be laid is limited by three factors: the lack of propulsion other than oars limits fishing to within 4 miles of the beaching area, the nets and craft drift with the tide and thus cannot be laid too close to the shore, and there is a concealed reef 1½–2 miles offshore. Consequently the entire 'bible' fleet fishes in two sections, one at each side of the harbour mouth. A shoal moving down the coast is confronted by a series of parallel lines of nets, each about 400 yards long, and most of the shoal is taken by one or two nets.

From the point of view of the individual fisherman, the spot at which he lays his nets must meet two conflicting objectives: he wants his nets to be the first the fish reach, but most shoals will eventually pass across the harbour mouth so that laying the nets far down the coast requires considerably more effort for no more reward. Because of the excessive number of participants the fleet as a whole travels much further than is necessary for maximum catches.

These constraints, in conjunction with the fact that the inshore fleet, like the beachseiners, take about 40 per cent of their annual catch in a single flush period of approximately six weeks, divide the 'bible' fishermen into two groups. For ten months of the year only 11 of the 37 craft fish regularly. The 33 men manning these craft are mainly older men who derive very little income from other sources and must fish on every occasion, irrespective of the chances of a good catch, in order to provide fish for their households' consumption. In 1971 the average annual cash return per crew member was only Rs. 292 and about Rs. 150 worth of fish was consumed in their homes. If production costs are calculated on a basis which includes the repair and replacement of gear, the profit per fisherman (including the fish he consumes) is only Rs. 293. At present, however, no attempt is made to replace damaged gear and because the village has such an excessive amount of netting, gear can be readily borrowed for a mere token payment.

During the flush season all 37 craft are used on most nights. Catches are very heavy (my records show 16 nights where the cash sales exceeded Rs. 1,000) but there is also a severe maldistribution of the catch. On the most successful night one craft received Rs. 1,390, two others around Rs. 600, and 31 craft shared less than Rs. 400. The sixty-odd men who fish only during the flush period are beachseine fishermen and young single men without regular employment. The younger men are able to fish further down the coast and most get bigger annual incomes than the men who fish throughout the year.

Although it is clear that the same catch could be taken with far fewer craft, it is difficult to estimate the optimum number. However, if four craft were fishing at each side of the harbour mouth, incoming shoals would be confronted by a mile of nets and most would probably be taken. On the nights when the catch exceeded Rs. 200, 70 per cent was taken by the top three craft, in most cases craft fishing alongside each other. Allowing a 50 per cent margin for error, a reduction in the fleet from 37 craft to 12 would lower capital and production costs by two-thirds and would increase profits by Rs. 8,500. Even if this was distributed among all 81 men presently engaged in inshore fishing, it would raise their incomes by 40 per cent.

The 'bible' fishermen are caught in the same dilemma as the beachseiners. They are well aware that it is in the interests of the community as a whole to reduce the size of the 'bible' fleet; indeed this point was continually stressed to me during my first week of field work. But at the same time there are equally cogent reasons why each individual must continue to fish. In some senses the dilemma is more acute for the inshore fishermen because the ready availability of gear and the night fishing encourage extensive marginal participation during the short period of heavy catches. The maldistribution of the catch gives many of these marginal participants very heavy profits at the expense of the older men who must fish throughout the year.

The Mechanized Craft

The Sri Lanka Government's major attempt to develop peasant fishing has been focused on the introduction of a 28-foot, 3½ ton mechanized craft, powered by a diesel motor, to be used for driftnetting at the edge of the continental shelf. Since the craft were designed in 1962, more than 2,500 have been issued to peasant fishermen through a government-sponsored hire-purchase scheme A generous estimate made by the Sri Lanka fisheries department is that 75 per cent of these craft are still afloat; a more realistic estimate based on my field work in the Southern Province is less than half. The operation of this scheme throughout the Southern Province was discussed in another paper (Alexander, 1975c); here I will briefly summarize the conclusions of that paper and describe the history of the mechanized programme in Mawelle.

The mechanized craft were mainly responsible for lifting coastal fish production from 7,400 tons in 1961 to 21,000 tons by 1969, but the hire-purchase scheme which was designed to ensure that the craft remain in the hands of peasant owner-operators was a failure. Less than 20 per cent of the loans were recovered; the craft were beached for long periods because of a lack of facilities and finance for repairs; and the average boat life was very short. Successful boats soon became the property of a small élite of capitalists who, while drawn from the fishing community, no longer fished themselves. The main reason for its failure was the planner's implicit assumption that the values and attitudes governing the operation of the craft would be those of an urban mercantile community and that boat operators would have full access to the facilities available in such communities. This was not the case. Social pressures within the villages, in combination with the operators' own values, made it impossible to recruit crews on a wage-labour basis and catches were shared among the crew along traditional lines. This method of catch distribution gave insufficient weight to the heavy capital costs of the new technology. Repairs were expensive and often had to be financed from non-fishing resources because the banks and the Fisheries Department would not accept a lien on future catches as security for a loan. Even when finance could be arranged, repairs were very slow, for neither mechanical workshops nor skilled mechanics were readily available. The boat-owners quickly found that it was impossible under these conditions to meet the hire-purchase payments and still operate the craft at a profit.

In response to this situation a 'tied boat' system developed. As successful mechanized craft take high catches of very valuable fish and as there is a wide differential between beach and retail market prices, it was profitable for large fish wholesalers to advance considerable sums for setting-up and maintenance costs in return for the sole right to buy the catch at current market prices. Successful owners were able to make high profits under this system, especially as they were making only token loan repayments, and could spend their income without worrying about financing future repairs. Less skilful, or less lucky owners, however, quickly ran out of credit and were forced to sell their boats. As the sales were illegal, prices were very low. This contributed to the short operating life of the craft, for it was cheaper for successful owners to buy and repair these relatively new craft rather than continue to repair their own ageing boats, especially as the hire-purchase debt remained the responsibility of the original owner.

Consequently a small group of successful fishermen emerged, each of whom operated several craft. Running a fleet rather than a single craft, both reduced the risks and made the owner less dependent on finance from the middlemen, with the result that several of these men now own more than ten craft which are skippered by relatives. Rather ironically, as the craft fell into fewer hands and as unemployment became more intense in the fishing villages, owners began recruiting crew members (other than the skipper) on a wage labour basis.

In some ways Mawelle is an inappropriate village to examine the impact of the mechanized craft because it is not traditionally a deep-sea fishing village and the mechanized craft have not markedly affected the economy. However many of the villages to which mechanized craft were issued were not deep-sea villages and the fate of the 23 craft issued in Mawelle was duplicated in many other communities.

The first ten craft which were issued in Mawelle between 1962 and 1966 were allocated by ballot. The ballot appears to have been fairly organized, but because merely fishing (rather than deep-sea fishing) experience was required, all of the craft went to the more numerous beachseiners. The fishermen and middlemen of Mawelle were not sufficiently wealthy both to pay the initial Rs. 1,000 deposit and to provide a full complement of nets, so the craft were used for trolling rather than driftnetting. Their owners were thus using ill-equipped boats with inexperienced crews and it is not surprising that the catches were often lower than those of the Kandegoda men using the much cheaper traditional craft. Four craft were soon damaged beyond repair and the remainder were quickly sold to fishermen from the east coast.

Many of the initial owners were faced with heavy debts to the government and middlemen, even though they no longer owned their craft, and when a second ballot was held for eight boats in 1967 only Kandegoda men applied. These men were much more successful. They were able to establish 'tied-boat' arrangements with their relatives in a thriving deep-sea fishing village nearby, and with their previous deep-sea experience and well-equipped craft took large catches. Although only three of the craft were still in service in 1971, three of the other original owners had been able to purchase second-hand craft when their own were damaged. One of them was also able to obtain two new craft when two of his close relatives were successful in a later ballot.

In 1970, in an endeavour to recover more of the loans and to pursue its policy of village development, the government decided that future craft would only be issued to co-operatives. In Mawelle, as in other fishing villages, the policy was disastrous: three craft were issued and all were wrecked within three months. There were several contributing factors. Nets and other gear were stolen; there were accusations of embezzlement; and the co-operative was unable to obtain finance for repairs. But the major reason was that the co-operative had more than 70 members and it was impossible to arrive at an acceptable means of allocating a mere 12 highly-paid jobs among this large group of underemployed men.

5. Conclusions

Are there any lessons to be learned from this somewhat abbreviated account of the history of a single Sri Lanka fishing village, which are applicable to the entire South Asian region? As was noted in the Introduction, every village is unique and many of the particular problems mentioned are probably peculiar to Mawelle. Nevertheless, it is possible to draw two broad conclusions which, I feel, are of general relevance to the modernization of South Asian fisheries.

The first is that planners must give much more weight to the region's rapid and sustained population growth. In most South Asian countries the population is increasing at a rate which approaches 3 per cent per year. These high levels of growth are a recent phenomenon and are due mainly to the extension of medical facilities to the rural areas over the past three decades. Population control measures, such as government-sponsored contraception programmes and the increasingly late age of marriage, may eventually stem the rate of growth, but the population is very young and the labour force will continue to grow at a minimum of 3 per cent in the next twenty years (Wriggens and Guyot, 1973).

These high rates of population growth have very important consequences for the development of fisheries and other natural resources. It is not enough to plan employment for new people coming into the labour force. Attention must also be given to the effect of population pressure on existing employment. Mawelle beachseining and inshore fishing illustrate the extent to which traditional fisheries are becoming uneconomic because of increasing labour participation. Development plans therefore cannot be centred on industrialized fishing in the expectation that the traditional economy will continue to absorb most of the fishing population. If peasant fishing is to survive, there is an urgent need for modernization, especially through measures such as the mechanization of traditional craft, which increase the exploitable area of the fishery without radically increasing costs.

Although technologies which substantially increase production are already widely available, most were developed within the capital-intensive fisheries of the North Atlantic and Japan, and have deleterious social consequences when used unmodified in South Asia. If technological innovations are to benefit the bulk of the South Asian population they must be tailored for local conditions: production must not be increased at the expense of employment and the fish must be cheap enough for local consumers to buy. These objectives require small, relatively cheap, mechanized craft rather than large trawlers; and research into better methods of drying and salting fish, rather than the construction of expensive canneries and freezing plants. Many of the large trawler and cannery projects in the region foundered on inefficient management (Jayaratne, 1972), but even with the most efficient management they would have contributed little.

The second conclusion is that the successful introduction of even the relatively cheap innovations suitable for peasant fisheries requires very careful planning and a deep knowledge of the indigenous economy. This does not merely mean, as one development expert has claimed (Cochrane, 1970), that the planners should talk to local administrators so as to test the plans for 'cultural fit'. It requires a rigorous investigation of the local economy, the delineation of the ways in which the innovations may affect the economy, and the creation of new institutions to bridge any gap between the two.

While the agencies responsible for technological innovations have usually attempted to train peasants in their operation, it is rare to find even the most elementary training in management. It should be clear that the far larger and less predictable financial demands arising from these innovations pose tremendous difficulties for traditional forms of social organization, but the peasants are given little help in solving the problems. Unless technological innovations are accompanied by new forms of social organization, South Asian fisheries development, like the Green Revolution (Jacoby, 1972), will benefit mainly a small élite of rich producers and the urban middle class.

References

Research in Sri Lanka between February 1970 and August 1971 was funded by the Australian National University. Considerably more detailed accounts of the Sri Lanka rural economy, including aspects of fisheries development such as marketing which are not discussed here, can be found in the papers listed below.

Alexander, R.P., *Risks, Rewards and Uncertainty; Fishermen of Southern Sri Lanka*, Ph.D. Dissertation, Canberra, Australian National University, 1973.

——, 'Do Fisheries Experts Aid Fisheries Development', *Maritime Studies and Management,* July, 1975a.

——, *The Common Tragedy; Population Growth and Fisheries Development in Southern Sri Lanka,* MS., 1965b.

——, *Innovation in a Cultural Vacuum,* MS., 1975c.

Apthorpe, R., 'Some Evaluation Problems for Cooperative Studies', in P.M. Worsley (ed.), *Two Blades of Grass*, Manchester, Manchester University Press, 1971.

Canagaratnam, P., and J.C. Medcof, 'Ceylon's Beach Seine Fishing', *Bulletin of the Fisheries Research Station*, Colombo, Vol. 4, 1956.

Cancian, F., *Risk and Uncertainty in a Peasant Community*, Stanford, Stanford University Press, 1972.

Ceylon Fisheries Corporation, *Draft Ten Year Plan for the Development of the Fishing Industry*, Ceylon, Ceylon Government Press, 1965.

Cochrane, G., *Development Anthropology*, Oxford, Oxford University Press, 1971.

Colombo Plan, *Recommendations on Development of the Fishing Industry of Ceylon*, Colombo, Government Press, 1958.

FAO, *Fisheries in the Food Economy*, Rome FAO, 1968.

Firth, R., *Malay Fishermen* (2nd ed.), London, Routledge and Kegan Paul, 1966.

Geertz, C., *Agricultural Involution*, Berkeley, University of California Press, 1963.

Hardin, G., 'The Tragedy of the Commons', *Science*, 162, 1968, pp. 1243–8.

Hill, P., *Rural Capitalism in West Africa*, London, Cambridge University Press, 1970.

ILO, *Matching Employment Opportunities and Expectations: A Programme for Ceylon*, Geneva, ILO, 1972.

Jacoby, E.H., 'Effects of the "Green Revolution" in South and South-East Asia', *Modern Asian Studies*, 6, 1972, pp. 63–9.

Jayaratne, B.C.F., *Report of the Ceylon Fisheries Corporation Commission of Inquiry*, Colombo, Government Press, 1972.

Kirby, E.S. and E.F. Szczepanik, 'Special Problems of Fisheries in Poor Countries'. In R. Turvey and W. Wiseman (eds.), *The Economics of Fisheries*, Rome, FAO, 1957.

Klausen, A.M., *Kerala Fishermen and the Indo-Norwegian Pilot Project*, Oslo, Universitetsforlaget, 1968.

Lipton, M., 'The Theory of the Optimizing Peasant', *Journal of Development Studies*, 4, 1968, pp. 327–51.

Obeyesekere, G., *Land Tenure in Village Ceylon*, London, Cambridge University Press, 1967.

Seers, D., *The Meaning of Development*, A/D/C reprint, 1970.

Wriggens, W.H. and J.F. Guyot, *Population, Politics and the Future of Southern Asia*, New York, Columbia University Press, 1973.

Wright, W.D., *Report of the Commissioners Appointed to Inquire into The Sea Fisheries of Ceylon*, Colombo, Government Press, 1968.

13 EQUITY AND EFFICIENCY IN MARINE LAW AND POLICY

Douglas M. Johnston

1. A Bifocal Perspective on the Law of the Sea

The law of the sea has become something more than law. It might more accurately be characterized as 'international marine policy'. Yet it is still true to describe the law of the sea as a compartment of public international law, and no distortion is involved in so describing it provided international law is broadly conceived.

International law – and, therefore, the law of the sea – serves at the same time as a value system for regulating the conduct of international affairs and as a highly elaborate set of problem-solving techniques. It is made, developed, clarified, applied and reformulated in the process of authoritative decision at work in international society. This society can properly be referred to as a 'world community' to the extent that the nation states, and the other major actors in the international system, have a common need to comply with substantially similar or compatible norms and to resort to an accepted range of organized procedures. Current developments in the law of the sea should then be evaluated by reference both to what may be described as 'ideological' and 'technological' criteria. One wishes to know whether these developments are fair and are likely to work. In this bifocal perspective, the new law of the sea for the late twentieth century should accommodate all reasonable demands for equity and efficiency in the emerging world community.[1]

For the sake of equity, the new law of the sea should represent a sensitive response by the organized world community to an assortment of legitimate value demands. In this perspective the current revision of the law of the sea is conceived essentially as a law reform movement, the primary objective being a general improvement in human welfare. It is generally believed, as the ideological axiom of our times, that the well-being of the individual in national society is most likely to be bettered through the enrichment of his state. It is not surprising, then, that insistent wealth demands, consistent with the new ethic of resource allocation,[2] are a conspicuous feature of the Third UN Conference on the Law of the Sea (UNCLOS III). Applied to some issues, such as the extent of coastal state jurisdiction, the demand is for more autonomy or independence; in other matters, such as the functioning of the International Seabed Authority, the call is for co-operation, and attention is drawn to the fact of interdependence in the world community.

For the sake of efficiency, on the other hand, the new law of the sea should provide innovative and constructive techniques in the new applied science of 'ocean management'.[3] Most of the marine sciences are still in their infancy, but the arrival of impressive technologies has given rise to great expectations from new sources of wealth. Never before in history was it more important to organize human effort at the highest level of efficiency in the production of wealth for the betterment of all peoples. Efficiency in ocean use lies in the interest of all, since none can benefit from waste, incompetence or confusion. The demand is, then, also for an orderly and rational approach to the management of marine resources, the dissemination of oceanographic knowledge, and the development of maritime skills.

2. The New Equity in the Law of the Sea

(i) Introduction

Like other treaty documents produced in recent years, any final text approved at UNCLOS III is likely to be remarkable for the number and variety of references to categories of states intended to benefit preferentially under the new treaty law of the sea. This pattern of privileged treatment is becoming so familiar in many areas of law-making in international society, especially in economic or resource areas of law, that one almost discerns an evolutionary process in what might be described as 'international welfare law'.[4] What is especially striking about this trend is that it is designed to benefit a very large majority of subjects in the international legal system, and not just a limited number of small minorities as has been the case typically in the history of national welfare law. At the international level what emerges is a new set of rights or privileges extracted by the majority through a mixture of persuasion and will-power, rather than a special status conferred on a minority by favour of a sympathetic majority.

Although it is too early to predict the outcome of UNCLOS III in specific detail, it is not difficult to envisage the categories of states which the UNCLOS treaty is intended to treat preferentially under the new equity. To obtain a clear picture of this trend one can peruse the Informal Single Negotiating Text (ISNT) that emerged from the Geneva session in May 1975, although it must be emphasized that this document has no juridically binding character.[5] This document was drafted with the purpose of revealing the range of claims that are being made, rather than as a contribution to compromise language which might be acceptable to the conference. Yet the document does seem to be fairly accurate in reflecting the categories of states intended to benefit preferentially in the new treaty law of the sea. The emerging pattern of preferential treatment can be described most easily in two separate contexts: the extension of coastal state jurisdiction and participation in the International Seabed Authority.

(ii) Extension of Coastal State Jurisdiction

The most famous and most significant feature of UNCLOS III is the general concurrence in principle on a uniform and massive extension of coastal state jurisdiction out as far as 200 miles. This development is reflected in the concept of a multi-functional régime of coastal authority within a 200-mile 'economic zone' (EZ)[6] and in a new legal definition of the 'continental shelf' which would be at least of the same breadth.[7] The effect of these legal developments would be to confer jurisdictional and related benefits on five classes of nations, viz:

(a) coastal states;
(b) narrow margin states;
(c) very broad margin states;
(d) states in special geographical circumstances;
(e) states with a special environmental vulnerability;

but also important guarantees to another category of otherwise unbenefited states, viz.

(f) landlocked states.

Coastal States: This is, of course, the broadest grouping of intended beneficiaries under a system of such extensive national jurisdiction. As suggested in Chapter One of this book, a consensus on 200-mile limits could be regarded as the juridical confirmation of 'the rise of the coastal state' in political and economic history. Within this grouping of over 100 nations with a coastline the chief beneficiaries would be those states which border on open ocean and can therefore gain full advantage from the grant of authority without suffering curtailment, for example, through the presence of an adjacent foreign state within 400 miles or a contraction by dint of a concave coastline. The jurisdictional grant to coastal states will affect all natural resources of the seabed, subsoil and superjacent waters, both renewable and non-renewable; probably also the conduct of scientific research and the preservation of the marine environment; and possibly some other activities.[8]

Narrow Margin States: More specifically, the legitimation of 200-mile EZ limits would guarantee the 'sovereign rights' of the nearest coastal state to the resources of the seabed and subsoil within these limits, regardless of the breadth of its continental shelf. Under existing treaty law, these rights extend only to the present limits of 'exploitability',[9] so that it might be difficult to convince investors that a coastal state's claim beyond the outer edge of a narrow continental margin is legally secure. After UNCLOS III there will be no disputing the claim of such a state because of its EZ authority up to 200-mile limits.

Very Broad Margin States: In a different way, the new law of the sea might also favour states with a continental margin extending much further than 200 miles, if there emerged a treaty similar on this point to ISNT Part II. According to Article 62 of this document, the coastal state's rights in these circumstances would extend 'beyond its territorial sea throughout the natural prolongation of its land territory to the outer edge of the continental margin.' It is doubtful, however, that this provision will prevail precisely because it seems 'inequitable' to most delegations that a state should prosper so handsomely through the bounty of nature.[10]

States in Special Geographical Circumstances: It is somewhat more likely, on the other hand, that the equity of UNCLOS III may flow to the advantage of archipelagic and island states. The former are likely to be treated preferentially along the lines of Articles 117 to 131 in ISNT II, and the latter along the lines of Article 132. It is probable that an archipelagic state may be deemed to have sovereignty or sovereign rights over the seabed and subsoil, the superjacent waters, and the superjacent airspace enclosed by 'straight baselines joining the outermost points of the outermost islands and drying reefs of the archipelago provided that such baselines enclose the main islands and an area in which the ratio of the area of the water to the area of the land' falls within designated parameters.[11] Other restrictions will certainly be applied to the drawing of such baselines,[12] but if this category of states is to be treated preferentially at all the net effect is likely to be a very considerable extension of maritime jurisdiction for archipelagic states.[13]

Under the suggested 'régime of islands' island states would be authorized to determine their territorial sea, contiguous zone, economic zone and continental shelf in the same manner that is applicable to states on the land mass, with the result that they would gain geometrically as well as by virtue of geographical circumstances.[14]

States with a Special Environmental Vulnerability: It is still uncertain precisely what kind of general environmental authority will be vested in the coastal state within its economic zone.[15] It seems likely, however, that a coastal state will be recognized as entitled to exercise special preventive measures if it can show that it has a special vulnerability. Such a state might, for example, be permitted to establish 'appropriate non-discriminatory laws and regulations for the protection of the marine environment in areas within the economic zone, where particularly severe climatic conditions create obstructions or exceptional hazards to navigation, and where pollution of the marine environment, according to accepted scientific criteria, could cause major harm to or irreversible disturbance of the ecological balance.'[16] It has also been suggested that where there are no internationally agreed rules or standards for pollution control in an EZ area, or they are inadequate to meet special circumstances, the coastal state should be permitted to apply to 'the competent international organization' for the area to be recognized as a 'special area' within which the coastal state would be authorized to adopt 'special mandatory measures'.[17] These two provisions should presumably be regarded as alternative approaches: it is difficult to predict which would prevail.[18]

Landlocked States: This last category would seem to be the only one that is totally excluded from the benefits that might be derived from a uniform massive extension of coastal state jurisdiction. But the case for remedial treatment of landlocked states has been strongly argued by many delegations at UNCLOS III.[19] In their case it might be regarded as equity in a somewhat different sense, denoting an intention to remedy a defect, to correct an injustice, albeit one which is imposed by geography and not by man. The proposed remedy would take the form of a treaty confirmation that landlocked states have 'freedom of transit' through neighbouring territories 'by all means of transport' in order to exercise the 'right of access' to and from the sea.[20] In this way it is intended that landlocked states should be enabled to enjoy not only the rights generally available under the freedom of the high seas and in accordance with the principle of the 'common heritage of mankind' beyond the limits of national jurisdiction,[21] but also the right of participation in the exploitation of the living resources of the economic zone of adjoining coastal states.[22] It should be noted, then, that these equitable provisions for guaranteed access are designed to bring landlocked states closer to parity with coastal states, despite the facts of geography, rather than to confer upon them a positive advantage through reverse discrimination.

(iii) Participation in the International Seabed Authority

In the First Committee, on the other hand, the most important questions do directly raise the question of deliberate discrimination in favour of the disadvantaged as a matter of equity: questions related to control over the proposed International Seabed Authority and the sharing of expected benefits from deep ocean mining and other activities under the Authority's jurisdiction. Proposals injected into ISNT Part I suggest the following classification of states deemed to be entitled to preferential treatment, viz.:

(a) developing countries;
(b) countries in the most critical economic need;
(c) states with a particular economic vulnerability;
(d) landlocked states;
(e) other geographically disadvantaged states.

Developing Countries: Throughout ISNT there are numerous references to the 'interests and needs of the developing countries'. Indeed this kind of reference is virtually the dominant motif under the new equity in the law of the sea. Not surprisingly, it is especially conspicuous in ISNT Part I, which deals with the new régime proposed for 'the seabed and the ocean floor and the subsoil thereof beyond the limits of national jurisdiction', where very substantial mineral wealth is available for extraction and distribution among the most deserving recipients. In Articles 2 to 19 ('Principles') there are nine references to 'developing countries' in five articles (7,9,10,11 and 18); and in Articles 20 to 41 ('The International Seabed Authority') there are eight, also in five articles (23,26,26,27,28 and 30).

These references are made in different ways at different levels of specificity. For example, Article 7 provides as a general principle that activities in the area in question 'shall be carried out for the benefit of mankind as a whole ... taking into particular consideration the interests and needs of the developing countries'. Article 11, dealing with transfer of technology, is of course intended exclusively for the benefit of developing countries; and, more specifically, Article 9 provides:

> The development and use of the Area shall be undertaken in such a manner as to: ...
>
> (b) avoid or minimize any adverse effects on the revenues and economies of the developing countries, resulting from a substantial decline in their export earnings from minerals and other raw materials originating in their territory which are also derived from the Area.

Countries in the Most Critical Economic Need: No effort has been made in ISNT to distinguish carefully the various levels of economic need under the general heading of 'developing countries', but in Article 27(1) (b) it is suggested that the sub-classes of 'states with large populations' and 'least developed countries' should each be entitled to separate representation on the 36-member Council of the Authority, as well as having a less direct kind of representation among the 24 members who would be elected 'in accordance with the principle of equitable geographical representation'.

States with a Particular Economic Vulnerability: The infusion of a new hardship ethic in the UNCLOS III proposals is further evidenced by the emphasis in ISNT I on the special needs of 'land-based mineral producing countries' whose economies might be seriously damaged by a drastic fall in prices caused by deep ocean mining activities under the jurisdiction of the International Seabed Authority.[23] Article 30(2) (b) requires the Economic Planning Commission of the proposed Authority to try 'to avoid or minimize adverse effects on *developing* countries whose economies substantially depend on the revenues derived from the export of minerals and other raw materials originating in their territories which are also derived from the resources of the Area under exploitation, taking into account all sources of these minerals and raw materials' (italics added). Fears of this kind prompted the Secretary-General of the United Nations to produce a report on probable consequences, entitled *Economic Implications of Seabed Mineral Development in the International Area*,[24] which had the effect of introducing commodity-related issues into the law of the sea and complicating further the difficulties of instituting appropriate considerations of equity into the new order.[25]

Landlocked States: In ISNT Part I seven articles contain references to landlocked states (Articles 7,8,9,18,23,26 and 27). Sometimes, as in Articles 9 and 23, the purpose of the reference is simply to underline that landlocked as well as coastal developing countries are intended to be treated preferentially under the new law of the sea. But more specifically, Article 27 guarantees that at least one of the 36 members of the Council of the proposed International Seabed Authority must be a landlocked developing country, elected as such. On the other hand, the landlocked developed countries, such as Switzerland and Austria, would not be guaranteed representation on the same body. It is often assumed that in any equitable system for sharing in the benefits to be derived from seabed activities under the Authority's jurisdiction landlocked developing countries would have the highest preferential standing of all, but this is not yet expressly acknowledged. It should be noted that Article 23(3) of ISNT Part I merely suggests 'taking into particular consideration the interests and needs of the developing countries whether coastal or landlocked'; and this de-emphasis on a special priority for the latter is found also in Article 18.[26]

Other Geographically Disadvantaged States: This category receives occasional reference in the ISNT, but its entitlement to special treatment receives even less accentuation than the category of landlocked states. Unlike the latter, the phrase 'other geographically disadvantaged states' is nowhere defined in ISNT. In general debate it is supposed to refer to states which for geographical reasons would gain relatively little from a considerable extension of coastal jurisdiction: for example, because they have a narrow or concave coastline, or border on a gulf or semi-enclosed sea. By virtue of a secondary order of equity, such a state is considered by some to be entitled to some degree of preferential treatment in the law of the sea, especially of course if it is also a developing country. This tendency is reflected only in several references in ISNT Part I: namely, in Articles 18, 26(2) (xi), and 27(1) (b) (v). In the last of these provisions, 'geographically disadvantaged states' are treated on a par with landlocked states, in being accorded separate representation on the Council of the International Seabed Authority.

(iv) Equity in Other Contexts

Although most of the major 'ethical' or 'ideological' developments at UNCLOS III can be considered under one of the two headings discussed above, mention should also be made of other trends of possibly even larger significance.

Obligation to Enter into Regional Arrangements: As noted above, ISNT II proposes that landlocked states, both developed and developing, 'shall have the right to participate in the exploitation of the living resources of the exclusive economic zones of adjoining coastal States on an equitable basis, taking into account the relevant economic and geographic circumstances of all the States concerned.'[27] The benefits available under such a right are seen as based upon an obligation to enter into regional arrangements ('The terms and conditions of such participation shall be determined by the States concerned through bilateral, subregional or regional agreements'[28]); and this obligation is regarded as fair only in circumstances where the arrangements would not aggravate the existing economic disparities in the region ('*Developed* landlocked States shall, however, be entitled to exercise their rights only within the exclusive economic zones of neighbouring *developed* coastal States'[29] (italics added).)

The same idea is carried further in proposals for a 'regional economic zone' in certain geographical circumstances, or at least for a regional fishing zone. The ISNT II version of the latter proposes that 'the right to participate, on an equitable basis, in the exploitation of living resources in the exclusive economic zones of other States in a sub-region or region' should be granted to:

> (a) 'developing coastal States which are situated in a subregion or region whose geographical peculiarities make such States particularly dependent for the satisfaction of the nutritional needs of their populations upon the exploitation of the living resources in the economic zones of their neighbouring States'

and

> (b) 'developing coastal States which can claim no exclusive economic zones of their own.'[30]

Primary Interest of State of Origin: ISNT II also includes the proposal that coastal states 'in whose rivers anadromous stocks originate shall have the primary interest in and responsibility for such stocks.'[31] The state of origin would be authorized to establish total allowable catches, but only 'after consultation with other States fishing these stocks'.[32] Other provisions reflect the view that the equities in this kind of situation can only be served by an effective consultation mechanism.[33]

Development and Transfer of Technology: Of much wider significance are the draft articles in ISNT III dealing with the development and transfer of technology[34] – a matter to which most developing countries attach a very high priority as they prepare for the acquisition of the new rights and privileges likely to be conferred upon them. Although most of these provisions are couched in mandatory, not merely permissive, language, and although they refer to fairly specific activities, the obligations so created would be nothing more in effect than appeals to 'promote' and 'co-operate' addressed to those nations possessing the technology. In a law-making treaty of this kind, this may be as far as the conference can go in norm-making. The problems are essentially ethical and institutional.[35]

Dispute Settlement: There cannot, of course, be any specific prescription on the quality of justice to be administered in dispute settlements under the new law of the sea. But many delegates from developing countries have referred to the need for 'third world justice' to correct the injustices of the past.[36] The closest approximation to a textual reflection of this sentiment is perhaps the provision for a Tribunal within the International Seabed Authority. As part of its mandate, this body would have jurisdiction over disputes out of a 'contract or arrangement' and submitted to it in accordance with the Convention.[37] This refers to contracts or arrangements between the Enterprise, another organ of the Authority, and governments or commercial organizations. It is intended, of course, that the Enterprise operate primarily for the benefit of the developing countries; and it is expected that in most cases, at least initially, the governments and enterprises with which it negotiates will tend to reflect or represent the interests of the developed world. In theory, equity would seem to require that the proposed system of dispute settlement should be placed outside the structure of the Authority in order to avoid the possibility that either 'side' – in this case the developing majority – would be judge and jury in its own cause. It might be argued, however, that the same result would follow whatever forum was to be used for the settlement of such disputes, since the same majority interest is now represented in all sectors of global organization. If equity in the form of 'impartiality' is indeed possible in the settlement of such disputes, it may be as likely to appear within the structure of the Authority as outside.

3. The Relevance of Efficiency in the Law of the Sea

(i) Introduction

As suggested above, the current developments in the law of the sea should be evaluated not only by reference to contemporary 'ideological' concepts of equity, but also by reference to modern 'technological' standards of efficiency. If the ocean is to be regarded essentially as a resource, then it must surely be brought within a regulatory framework that makes it amenable to rational processes of 'management'. Indeed, within a context of economic considerations, it follows that the maximum benefits of a system of equitable distribution cannot become available except at the highest level of efficiency in 'ocean management'. Since most arguments based on equity at UNCLOS III are economically motivated, it is illogical to regard efficiency and equity as incompatible objectives.[38] But the constant intrusion of legitimate social, political and psycho-cultural factors in the claim-making process means that it is unrealistic to deny that there are different 'orders of rationality' at work.

In this section ISNT will be examined for evidence of the potential efficiency (or effectiveness) of a future UNCLOS III treaty in various functional areas of concern. The sophistication of these provisions will be discussed by reference to these six aspects of ocean management, viz.:

(a) the articulation of objectives;
(b) the scope and distribution of authority;
(c) methods of organization;
(d) maintenance of standards;
(e) conflict avoidance and dispute settlement provisions;
(f) enforcement procedures.

(ii) Ocean Management

Objectives: The major purpose of the 200-mile economic zone, as far as fisheries management is concerned, is to secure an extensive area of unimpeded control to the coastal state, enabling it to meet all reasonable developmental and nutritional needs. The rationale is that propinquity (or adjacency) gives entitlement to priority of use and exclusiveness of managerial authority. Implicit in this approach is the assumption that national fishery management in the EZ areas will operate not only more equitably, but also in the long run more effectively, than international fishery management. The coastal state alone, according to

ISNT Part II, would determine both the allowable catch of the living resources of the EZ and its own capacity to harvest these resources.[39] Its priority of use would be limited by the principle that where the coastal state does not, by its own admission, have the capacity to harvest the entire allowable catch prescribed by that state, it shall 'give other States access to the surplus of the allowable catch'.[40] The principle of 'full utilization' yields here to the objective of 'optimum utilization' and interpretation and application are matters that would lie within the discretion of the coastal state. Reference is made to the need to avoid overexploitation[41] and to obtain the 'maximum sustainable yield',[42] but the latter is to be understood as 'qualified by relevant environmental and economic factors, including the economic needs of coastal fishing communities and the special requirements of developing countries, and taking into account fishing patterns, the interdependence of stocks and any generally recommended sub-regional, regional or global minimum standards.'[43]

Almost identical language is used in ISNT Part II to describe the objectives of fishery conservation on the 'high seas': that is, beyond the EZ limits of national jurisdiction.[44]

Authority: The potential functional effectiveness of a coastal state régime within EZ limits is obviously impaired by the setting of uniform spatial limits which have no particular relevance to the various managerial activities to be carried out by a coastal state within the zone. The arbitrariness of 200-mile EZ limits, as they are likely to be defined, is especially evident in fishery management and pollution prevention.[45] In some situations these limits are clearly too wide,[46] in others too narrow,[47] to permit maximum efficiency in these areas of managerial responsibility. Moreover, the ISNT proposals are extremely vague in determining guidelines for the drawing of baselines, and also for the drawing of the outer edge of the continental margin.[48] This vagueness should be construed as another source of predicted inefficiency in ocean management, creating unnecessary risks of confusion and confrontation which are likely to jeopardize efforts to establish rationally determined lines of managerial authority.

Organization: From an organizational viewpoint, the best test of the future effectiveness of the new law of the sea is the structure proposed for the International Seabed Authority. Here again efficiency seems to have been sacrificed to other considerations. Many of the provisions contained in ISNT Part I are, admittedly, likely to be changed in the course of compromise diplomacy before the Authority is actually established, but the proposed structure itself may not be very different from that envisaged in the Negotiating Text prepared for the New York session. As it now stands, the Authority would be composed of five principal organs: an Assembly, a Council, a Tribunal, an Enterprise and a Secretariat.[49] In addition, an Economic Planning Commission[50] and a Technical Commission[51] would be set up as organs of the Council, and an Arbitration Commission[52] would supplement the services of the Tribunal in dispute settlement. The very complexity of this structure raises doubts about the potential bureaucratic efficiency of the Authority, doubts that are reinforced after an examination of the powers and functions assigned to these various bodies within the Authority. The Council, which is described as the 'executive organ',[53] would be the crucial decision-making body. Its competences would be many and varied: supervisory;[54] constitutive;[55] contractual;[56] creative;[57] legislative;[58] recommendatory;[59] and administrative.[60] The criteria for the election of members of the Council[61] are, perhaps inevitably, such as to guarantee a highly political atmosphere for decision-making in an organization that is at least semi-technical in its purpose. It also seems certain that the important work of the Economic Planning Commission will be highly charged with political implications.[62] Accordingly, one may doubt whether the Enterprise, responsible for the conduct of the Authority's activities on the seabed, will be able within this structure to operate effectively at a level of efficiency comparable to that of the corporations with which it will have to deal as a contracting party to technically complicated arrangements.[63]

Standards: One of the chief efficiency-related concerns at UNCLOS III is whether sufficiently high standards will be established in the new structures and processes of the law of the sea. In ISNT I there are a number of provisions on the qualifications expected of persons elected to various bodies. Members of the Economic Planning Commission, for example, would have 'appropriate qualifications and experience relevant to mining and the management of mineral resource activities, and international trade and finance';[64] and members of the Technical Commission would have 'appropriate qualifications and experience in the management of seabed resources, ocean and marine engineering and mining and mineral processing technology and practices, operation of related marine installations, equipment and devices, ocean and environmental sciences and maritime safety, accounting and actuarial techniques.'[65] The impression of a concern for high efficiency is strengthened by the provision that they should be 'persons of high moral character who may be relied upon to exercise independent judgment' serving 'in their individual capacity';[66] but, on the other hand, some lowering of standards might be expected to result from the requirement that the Council, in appointing such persons, should have 'due regard to not only the need for Members highly qualified and competent in the technical matters which may arise in such programs but also to special interests and the principle of equitable geographical distribution.'[67] No particular qualifications are prescribed in ISNT I for members of the Governing Board of the Enterprise, despite the presumed desirability of attracting persons of the highest competence and long experience in mining and related fields. Instead their appointment is left to the processes at work within the Assembly, upon the recommendation of the scarcely less political Council.[68]

But perhaps the clearest expression of suggested policy in ISNT on professional qualifications is Article 38(2) which deals with the staff of the Secretariat:

> The paramount consideration in the recruitment and employment of the staff and in the determination of their conditions of service shall be to secure employees of the highest standards of efficiency, competence and integrity. Subject to this consideration, due regard shall be paid to the importance of recruiting staff on as wide a geographical basis as possible.

The appearance of an official determination to maintain the highest standards in the Secretariat is somewhat marred, however, by the directive that the Authority 'shall be guided by the principle that its permanent staff shall be kept to a minimum.'[69] The concept of 'minimum' size is unlikely, perhaps, to coincide with that of optimum size.[70]

There are, of course, numerous references to 'standards' other than human qualifications in the Informal Single Negotiating Text – indeed too many to be discussed fully here. In Part II, for instance, it is provided that the coastal state is required to '[take] into account applicable international standards' in determining the breadth of the safety zones around artificial islands, installations and structures constructed in its economic zone;[71] and in the vicinity of these erections '[s]hips of all nationalities must respect these zones and shall comply with generally accepted international standards regarding navigation.'[72] The safety at sea requirements in Article 80 are set out fairly specifically, and it is further prescribed that, in taking these measures, 'each State is required to conform to generally accepted international regulations, procedures and practices ...'[73] As another reflection of efficiency-awareness, Article 106 on high seas fishery conservation prescribes that:

> 1. In determining the allowable catch and establishing other conservation measures for the living resources in the high seas, States shall:
>
> > (a) adopt measures which are designed, *on the best evidence available* to the States concerned, to maintain or restore populations of harvested species at levels which can produce the *maximum sustainable yield, as qualified by relevant environmental and economic factors*, including the special requirements of developing countries, and taking into account fishing patterns, the interdependence of stocks and *any generally recommended sub-regional, regional or global minimum standards*. (italics added)

It should be noted that this mix of criteria is similar to that suggested for fishery conservation measures taken by the coastal state within its own economic zone.[74] Surprisingly perhaps, there is little, if any, textual evidence that lower standards would be expected within the limits of national jurisdiction than outside in the high seas.

An entire section of ISNT Part III is devoted to 'Standards' for protection of the marine environment. Articles 16 to 21 deal with various kinds of marine pollution: pollution from land-based sources (Art. 16); pollution arising from activities concerning exploration and exploitation of the seabed and from installations under the jurisdiction of coastal states (Art. 17); pollution from dumping of wastes and other matter (Art. 19); pollution from vessels (Art. 20); pollution from atmospheric sources (Art. 21); and pollution from activities concerning exploration and exploitation of the international seabed area (referred in Art. 18 to Part I of the Text). The level of standards envisaged varies with the type of pollution. The greatest concern for effective standards is reflected in a provision that the requirements of anti-pollution laws and regulations enacted by *flag states* 'shall be no less effective than generally accepted international rules and standards' established by 'the competent international organization or by general diplomatic conference'.[75] In the same article it is recognized that special measures, based on more rigorous environmental standards, may be taken by coastal states in 'special circumstances':

> 4. Where internationally agreed rules and standards are not in existence or are inadequate to meet *special circumstances* and where the coastal State has reasonable grounds for believing that a particular area of the economic zone is an area where, *for recognized technical reasons* in relation to its oceanographical and ecological conditions, its utilization, and the particular character of its traffic, the adoption of *special mandatory measures* for the prevention of pollution from vessels is required, the coastal State may apply to the competent international organization for the area to be recognized as a '*special area*'. Any such application shall be supported by *scientific and technical evidence* and shall, where appropriate, include plans for establishing sufficient and suitable land-based reception facilities. (italics added)
>
> 5. Nothing in this article shall be deemed to affect the establishment by the coastal State of *appropriate non-discriminatory laws and regulations* for the protection of the marine environment *in areas within the economic zone, where particularly severe climatic conditions create obstructions or exceptional hazards to navigation*, and where pollution of the marine environment, *according to accepted scientific criteria, could cause major harm to or irreversible disturbance of the ecological balance*. (italics added)

In summary, there is abundant evidence of concern at UNCLOS III with the problem of standards for the management of the ocean, but for reasons of political distrust and economic disparity the conference is not likely to establish uniform global standards that will seem impressive in the ideal managerial perspective.

Conflict Management: By almost any concept of 'functionality' – and certainly by that of rational and effective 'ocean management' – both the actual and the prospective existence of conflict will tend to impair the efficiency of ocean uses. It is, therefore, highly pertinent to evaluate developments in the law of the sea by reference to the adequacy or inadequacy of conflict avoidance and dispute settlement procedures likely to be accepted at UNCLOS III. Generally speaking, it is likely to be easier to secure a consensus on the former than on the latter. Dispute settlement provisions were still sufficiently far from acceptance at the 1975 Geneva session that no effort was made to graft overarching provisions on the Informal Single Negotiating Text prepared by the chairmen of the three Main Committees.[76]

In ISNT Part I, however, there is provision for the establishment of a Tribunal, as one of the five principal organs of the International Seabed Authority.[77] Its jurisdiction is broadly defined, and it would be empowered to render advisory opinions on request as well as to adjudicate disputes.[78] The Tribunal would be composed of nine 'independent judges, elected regardless of their nationality from among persons of high moral character, who possess the qualifications required in their respective countries for appointment to the highest judicial offices, or are jurisconsultants [sic] of recognized competence in law of the sea matters and other areas of international law.'[79] If language such as this is retained in final treaty form, it raises the prospect of highly contentious issues coming before a tribunal composed partly of non-specialist, judicially trained (or oriented) lawyers, and partly of experts closely attuned to the special or even unique characteristics of marine resource issues. One envisages, then, a mixture of judges: some, close to the tradition of litigation, tending to put a premium on the virtue of consistency with the past decisions of other tribunals, such as the International Court of Justice; and the remainder more comfortable with the technique of arbitration, tending to resolve disputes on a more *ad hoc* basis with special sensitivity to the particular variables in the situation at hand. Whether this kind of dynamic tension could create solutions or a source of difficulty for future ocean managers is, of course, hard to predict without knowing more about the mix of individuals constituting the Tribunal.

As things stand at the time of writing the likeliest approach to dispute settlement in the law of the sea treaty is to have two kinds of mechanisms: one a tribunal of limited functional jurisdiction of the kind described, limited to the purposes of the International Seabed Authority; the other a set of settlement procedures, from which disputing states would be more or less free to choose one that is mutually acceptable for the purposes at hand. This would mean, among other things, that no special emphasis would be placed on the need for other specialized tribunals, such as that provided for in the 1958 Geneva Convention on Fishing and Conservation of the Living Resources of the High Seas.[80] Yet the same functional logic that supports the case for specialized treatment of disputes arising out of deep ocean mining would seem to justify similar treatment of disputes (say) in the field of fishery conservation or environmental protection.

The absence at the global level of a single-purpose tribunal for other activities might have the effect of inducing states to submit their disputes to *ad hoc* tribunals or regional bodies; and conceivably this could result in a trend towards diversification that does not serve the long-term global interests of rational and orderly ocean management.

More progress has been made at UNCLOS III in agreeing on procedures of conflict avoidance, as distinguished from dispute settlement. One of the battles still being fought on this front is against the so-called 'territorialist' states whose 'sovereign' conception of coastal state authority within the limits of national jurisdiction does not even tolerate the notion that coastal states might be legally required to resort to internationally agreed consultative procedures for the purposes of conflict avoidance. In deference to territorialist sentiment presumably, no such requirements are included in the ISNT II version of the economic zone. In view of the capability limitations of most coastal states, the absence of 'duty to consult' provisions might be regarded as a potential source of inefficiency, particularly in fishery management.[81] On the other hand, the coastal state's discretion in the economic zone is not likely to be left absolutely unfettered. For example, as noted above,[82] coastal states will be expected, if not strictly required, to comply with international standards in varying degrees in the exercise of pollution control authority. Outside limits of national jurisdiction, all states would be under 'the duty to adopt, or to co-operate with other States in adopting, such measures for their respective nationals as may be necessary for the conservation of the living resources of the high seas',[83] and similar duties for the protection and preservation of the marine environment.[84] Unfortunately – perhaps inevitably – the conference has missed opportunities to develop and tighten state responsibility in the law of the sea.[85] The ISNT III text has failed conspicuously to go beyond the principles of environmental responsibility and liability affirmed at the 1972 United Nations Conference on the Human Environment.[86] There are other kinds of limitations on the prerogatives of coastal states,[87] but in the main it is fair to conclude that important opportunities in conflict avoidance techniques have been neglected, increasing one's apprehension that an UNCLOS III treaty will be generative of unnecessarily frequent disputes over the exercise of coastal state discretion.

Enforcement: One of the most frequent criticisms of the 200-mile economic zone is that few, if any, coastal states have the capability to enforce their regulations over such an extensive area. Even within

12-mile territorial limits, it is argued, many coastal authorities have difficulty in policing these much more restricted areas to ensure that 'innocent passage' of foreign vessels remains 'innocent': that is, that 'it is not prejudicial to the peace, good order or security of the coastal State.'[88] It should not, however, be assumed that the policing requirements existing within a 12-mile territorial sea would automatically be expanded by the ratio of 200 to 12 with the establishment of a 200-mile economic zone. Within such a zone the enforcement problem is likely to occur mostly in the context of fishery management and to a lesser extent pollution control. In ISNT Part II the former is dealt with very simply: by virtue of the coastal state's 'sovereign rights' of fishery management, foreign nationals permitted to fish in the former's economic zone would be required to comply with the 'terms and conditions established in the regulations of the coastal State', including those regulations relating to 'enforcement procedures'.[89] The enforcement provisions for pollution control in ISNT III are, by contrast, numerous and conflicting. At present, until further negotiation clarifies matters, it can only be said that UNCLOS III is trying to find an eclectic approach to the issue of enforcement jurisdiction in this context which would accommodate diverse proposals for coastal state jurisdiction,[90] flag state jurisdiction,[91] port state jurisdiction,[92] and international jurisdiction.[93] Until the drafting is further advanced it is impossible to guess how efficient or inefficient the enforcement machinery might be.

(iii) Dissemination of Knowledge and Development of Skills

Relevance to Ocean Management: The dissemination of oceanographic knowledge and the development of maritime skills can, of course, be regarded as tasks of 'ocean management'. But for most of the developing coastal states it is more to the point to regard these value goals as *pre-conditions* to the establishment of any effective kind of ocean management within their limits of national jurisdiction. The proposed switch, for example, from international to national fishery management within 200-mile limits is likely to lead to a loss in managerial effectiveness in some regions of the world unless remedial measures are taken to raise the levels of scientific and economic knowledge and administrative skill most relevant to 'economic zone management' by coastal authorities. To envisage a substantial improvement in the short term one would have to anticipate a large-scale investment not only in the marine sciences but also in a variety of 'crash courses' in 'marine policy studies' designed to equip government officials with the training most appropriate to their particular responsibilities and the national milieu of policy-making in which they operate. To enable coastal states to participate more effectively, for example, in shipping control, and to comply with internationally agreed standards in pollution prevention and control, it will be necessary to develop technical training programmes in such areas as marine law, shipping economics, port and sea terminal management, and marine technology ranging from ship construction to management, engineering and navigation.

Accordingly, the movement towards the expansion of coastal state jurisdiction and 'economic zone management' must be evaluated in light of accompanying provisions on scientific research and transfer of technology.

Scientific Research: In the ISNT II proposal, the coastal state would have 'exclusive jurisdiction' over scientific research within its economic zone.[94]

> The consent of the coastal State shall be obtained in respect of *any research concerning the exclusive economic zone* and undertaken there. Nevertheless, the coastal State shall not normally withhold its consent if the request is submitted by a qualified institution with a view to *purely scientific research*, subject to the proviso that the coastal State shall have the right, if it so desires, to participate or to be represented in the research, and that the results shall be published after consultation with the coastal State concerned.[95] (italics added)

Whether one thinks of a consent régime such as this as antithetical to the world community interest in scientific research depends on whether one assumes that a loss of freedom of enquiry will necessarily result in a reduction of the volume and quality of scientific effort. The truth surely is that no one can make a prediction one way or the other. The questionable phrases underlined above certainly seem to give the coastal authorities an easy pretext for withholding their consent to foreign research in their zone. The phrase 'purely scientific research' is especially open to criticism that it can be given almost any meaning that suits the immediate purposes of the coastal state. With this kind of wording, its discretion is nearly absolute. The picture changes considerably, however, when one looks at the section on 'Marine Scientific Research' in ISNT III, reflecting the work of Committee III at the Conference. This section is said to be without prejudice to the rights of coastal states in the territorial sea, the economic zone and the continental shelf,[96] but the provisions represent nonetheless a different approach to scientific research, suggesting internationally agreed criteria and guidelines which would be linked with the manner in which coastal states exercise their discretion.[97] At the time of writing it remains uncertain which philosophy will prevail[98] – and how much difference it will make to the volume and quality of marine research throughout the world.

Transfer of Technology: As noted above, the ISNT III provisions in 'Development and Transfer of Technology' are weak, although they are perhaps sufficiently numerous and detailed to identify the need for marine-related training and skills. Perhaps the most significant proposal is that for 'regional marine scientific and technological centres, in co-ordination with the International Seabed Authority when appropriate as well as with international organizations and national marine scientific and technological institutions ...'[99] It is expected that a high priority will be given to marine studies within the projected United Nations University.[100] There is little evidence, however, that marine policy studies, involving the social sciences, will receive as much attention as science and technology. If this goes uncorrected, it may result in technocratic, rather than humanistic, approaches to 'economic zone management'.

4. Equity and Efficiency in Coastal Zone Management

(i) The Concept of Coastal Zone Management

The 'coastal zone' is commonly conceived as a narrow band skirting all coastlines in which the sea and land environments have an immediate impact upon each other, so as to create a set of special or unique resource problems.[101] Frequently, these problems are aggravated by unusually severe population pressures characterized as 'urbanization' and 'industrialization'.

In North America, and perhaps elsewhere, it has been found difficult to determine precisely where the spatial limits of coastal zone management should be drawn. Any solution applied to this problem of delineation is bound to be somewhat arbitrary, both on the seaward and landward sides. Generally, at least, it is agreed that the seaward limits should not be further out than the seaward limits of the territorial sea, so that the coastal zone is regarded as a concept of national, but not international, law.[102]

Given the prospect of a 200-mile economic zone soon to be established in international law, drawn from the baseline of a 12-mile territorial sea, it is entirely likely that sooner or later the concept of coastal zone management will be enlarged to swallow up the entire economic zone, at least for specific purposes, under the functional jurisdiction of the coastal state.[103] For example, one can easily envisage in the not-too-distant future the construction of artificial islands between 12-mile and 200-mile limits for the establishment of research, monitoring and data processing purposes under the administration of government agencies belonging to the coastal state. With a little imagination one can also foresee the use of such installations for the day-to-day regulation of shipping movements and fishing activities from what would be tantamount to marine branch offices of government departments.

(ii) Equity in Coastal Zone Management

In the context of coastal zone management, as distinguished from the law of the sea, the above scenario raises questions of equity from the viewpoint of the traditional land-based coastal community. Technological trend projections of this kind may be disconcerting to such a community which tends to be especially suspicious, and even resentful, of the 'intrusions' of central government. One of the intangible rewards for the traditional fisherman, like the traditional farmer, is the feeling or illusion that he is less 'regulated' than others. The possibility of new, technologically sophisticated, island stations and communities rising up eventually in his domain may be a dismaying prospect for the typical seafarer from the traditional land-based coastal community. The establishment of any such trend would probably be construed as further evidence of the central government's determination to destroy the community's way of life.[104]

Yet one would like to think that the development of sea-based marine technology is not necessarily antithetical to the interests or attitudes of the coastal community. Indeed it would seem important to consider the development of the community as concomitant with the development of the technology in question. The serious danger is that sociological considerations will be totally disregarded, and that ocean technology will be allowed to have its head regardless of the interests and inclinations of village and small-town communities in the coastal zone. There is little in the recent history of such communities to afford them comfort.

No human being or community is entitled to immunity from change.

Change is the only constant. But each should be free to participate in the processes that determine the rate and direction of change. It is suggested, then, that marine policy-making proceed on the premise that coastal communities have a special interest in participating in the development as well as the regulation of marine technology. Whether one looks to the future construction of artificial islands and related technologies, or to the immediate problems of the traditional coastal community, it is hard to deny the justice of the case for community involvement in the implementation of marine policy on the basis of extended coastal state jurisdiction in the aftermath of UNCLOS III. Traditional coastal communities are, in many ways, 'underdeveloped' within the national society in a degree that is comparable to the 'underdevelopment' of many disadvantaged nations in the international society. The case for preferential treatment of such communities in national marine policy is supported by much the same considerations of equity that sustain the privileged status claimed by the disadvantaged in the law of the sea.

(iii) Efficiency in Coastal Zone Management

The problems of efficiency in coastal zone management are much too complex to be dealt with sufficiently at the end of this final chapter. The legal and institutional issues are especially complicated in federal systems like the Canadian and the American.[105] But regardless of whether the state is unitary or federal, the potential effectiveness of a coastal zone management system will vary with the mix of functional activities brought within the scheme and with the mix of 'competences' assigned to the managers. If the activities are mostly confined to the protection of the natural environment of the coastal zone (e.g. preservation of sand dunes, wildlife areas, salt marshes and other localized areas of environmentally critical significance), the problems would appear to be manageable;[106] and few, if any, complications would arise from developments in the new law of the sea. If the scheme does not have to deal with competing priorities of use (e.g. development versus conservation), there is no reason why a relatively efficient regulatory system should not be devised, given appropriate investments of funds and personnel.

The concept of coastal zone management might, on the other hand, be accepted as a new and useful approach to the treatment of many different kinds of conflict and priority problems peculiar to coastal areas and communities. If inshore fishing activities, for example, came under such a regulatory system, the actual or potential conflict with offshore fishing would have to be taken into account, and this problem would have to be recognized as having an international as well as a national (and local) aspect. The same would be true if a coastal zone regulatory authority were established in such a way as to deal with the discharge of effluents, since this is an important source of marine pollution from the land-mass.[107]

Likewise, more complicated issues arise from the establishment of a coastal zone management authority if it is assigned regulatory powers than if only research, supervisory, co-ordinative, or other non-regulatory responsibilities are entrusted to it. It remains to be seen how much regulatory authority can usefully be undertaken by a coastal zone management entity. At present it should be noted that the concept of coastal zone management has evolved rather as an efficiency, not an equity, concept. At least in North America the prevailing rationale is that the primary purpose is to facilitate the solution of problems arising from the existence of numerous agencies, each of which has an involvement in some aspect of coastal zone management but none with a direct responsibility for such management as a whole. The lack of effective co-ordination is at the heart of the problem.[108]

Despite the origin of this concept, it remains important to ensure that coastal communities are properly represented in whatever mechanisms might be established for regulatory purposes. Since the community will often be the crucial focus in the implementation of coastal zone management measures, community participation will serve the ends of efficiency as well as equity. Accordingly, it seems possible to conclude on an optimistic note: the increasing involvement of coastal states in ocean management, within extensive limits of national jurisdiction, provides a new opportunity for coastal communities to become involved both in the making and implementation of marine policy, and more specifically in the development and regulation of modern marine technology.

Notes

1. The demands for equity and efficiency can be seen as evidence of a political phenomenon with widely significant effects on law-making. The law of the sea is in the process of transformation under the impact of developmental, welfare, and environmental concepts. To the extent that disparities in equity and efficiency may be the cause of future wars the current revision of the law of the sea might be regarded as a 'peace-keeping operation' of an unusually basic and systematic kind. For a strikingly innovative 'polemological' study of trends of this kind in the context of international development law, see Wil D. Verwey, *Economic Development, Peace, and International Law*, 1972.

2. See, for example, *Proceedings of the United Nations Conference on Trade and Development*, Third Session, Santiago de Chile, 13 April to 21 May 1972.
3. This resonant phrase, as generally used, seems intended to convey an efficiency orientation to the problems of regulating ocean uses, based on the perception of the sea as a 'system', or a set of interlocking systems, and on a quasi-scientific determination to regulate them in a 'rational' manner through the maximum availability of 'hard' data.
4. 'Formerly, international law fulfilled its functions among the self supporting, developed states. This function was especially to harmonize the freedom of one state with the freedom of others, while the economic life was left to the economic laws of the market ... In our time, the majority of the family of nations consists of poor, vulnerable states, late-comers in an industrialized world. They have different needs, and impose different demands on international law. They want to see the legal principle of freedom filled in with the legal principle of protection of the economically weak against the economically strong and with the legal principle of assistance which must be made available and promoted by the rich countries.

   This endeavour of the young, poor countries coincides and is related with the internal development in the old, rich countries, who evolved from the liberal 'Rechtsstaat' to the social welfare state: the state which concerns itself with the fate of all its members as expressed in its attempt to reach full employment and to attain a decent standard of living for all members of its community. This promoted the idea that also the international community ought to be developed into a welfare community ...

   In connection with their particular situation, the developing countries demand a particular place in such a welfare community. They ask for a new inequality – now an inequality in their own favour ... Just as in the Covenant of the League of Nations war was 'a matter of concern ... to the whole League' (Art. 11), so has world poverty become 'a matter of concern' to the UN community. But the consequences have not yet been drawn, neither in the UN Charter, nor in the UN practice. The world community has not yet recognized nor realized an international law that is attuned to this new task and which would lead to a legal arrangement in the economic field contributing to the abolishment of world poverty.' B.V.A. Roling, in *Preface* to Verwey, note 1 above, at pp. vii–viii.
5. This document (UN Doc. A/Conf. 62/WP 8), drafted by the chairmen of the three Main Committees was issued in three parts. (It will be referred to in this article as ISNT I, ISNT II, and ISNT III.) At the beginning of each part there is a cautionary note by the President of the Conference which stresses that: '... the single text should take account of all the formal and informal discussions held so far, would be informal in character and would not prejudice the position of any delegation, nor would it represent any negotiated text or accepted compromise. It should, therefore, be quite clear that the single negotiating text will serve as a procedural device and only provide a basis for negotiation. It must not in any way be regarded as affecting either the status of proposals already made by delegations or the right of delegations to submit amendments or new proposals.' When the Text emerged on the final day of the Geneva session of UNCLOS III (9 May 1975), it became evident that although in some places it provided an accurate reflection of the results of negotiations to date, in other places it represented merely the Chairman's personal views on a possible compromise between opposing proposals.
6. Articles 45–61, in ISNT II, pp. 19–26.
7. Article 62, ibid., p. 27.

8. Article 45, ibid., p. 19.
9. Convention on the Continental Shelf (1958), Article 1.
10. 'The definition of the continental shelf, however, is linked in the Text with another article imposing on the coastal state the duty of sharing with the international community the revenues it derives from exploiting the mineral resources of its continental margin beyond 200 miles. It is felt, by and large, that only such an obligation would, in a sense, counterbalance the confirmation by the conference of the coastal state's exclusive sovereign rights to its margin beyond 200 miles and so provide the *necessary element of equity* that might lead to a satisfactory resolution of the issue'. (italics added) Robert Auger, 'Prelude to a Finale provided by a Single Negotiating Text?', *International Perspectives* July/August 1975, p. 38.
11. Article 118(1) of ISNT II suggests that the ratio should be 'between one-to-one and nine-to-one.'
12. See Article 118 of ISNT II for a variety of suggested restrictions.
13. It has been calculated that if this kind of archipelagic claim were accepted in addition to a 200-mile economic zone throughout the world, the combined effect would be to bring more than one-third of the total surface of the world's ocean under national jurisdiction régimes of one kind or another. More pertinent, from the point of view of global equity, is the estimate that 46 per cent of the newly enclosed ocean area would go to high-income countries which make up less than a quarter of the world's population. *A New Regime for the Oceans,* Report of Oceans Task Force of The Trilateral Commission, 1976, pp. 5–6.
14. In the case of islands, the only suggested restriction is that '[r]ocks which cannot sustain human habitation or economic life of their own shall have no exclusive economic zone or continental shelf.' Article 132(3) of ISNT II. It is far from certain, however, that this proposal will finally be accepted. See Auger, note 10 above, p. 38.
15. On this question the 'philosophy' of ISNT II is totally different from that of ISNT III. According to the former (Article 45), the coastal state in its EZ would have 'jurisdiction with regard to the preservation of the marine environment including pollution control and abatement.' ISNT III, on the other hand, sets out suggested provisions for an 'umbrella' chapter, which 'disregards the import of the 200-mile economic zone and the concomitant jurisdiction of the coastal state to preserve the marine environment therein ... To all intents and purposes coastal states [in ISNT III] are denied any enforcement rights.' Auger, note 10 above, p. 39.
16. Article 20(5), ISNT III, p. 8.
17. Article 20(4), ibid.
18. It is expected that some role will be given to IMCO as the 'competent international organization' in matters of marine pollution by vessels, but it seems unlikely that IMCO or any other organization will be given a veto over the coastal state's exercise of environmental jurisdiction in its own EZ.
19. This case is stronger, of course, when the landlocked state is economically as well as geographically disadvantaged, but the poorer landlocked states have found that it lies in their interest in conference negotiations to make common cause with the wealthier landlocked states. See Edward Miles, 'The Dynamics of Global Ocean Politics', pp. 167–9 above.
20. Article 109(1) ISNT II, p. 40.
21. Ibid.
22. Article 116, ibid., p. 41; and Article 57, ibid., p. 24.
23. 'The extent to which deep seabed mining would have an adverse economic effect on mineral-exporting countries is hard to assess due to the technical and

economic uncertainties involved. Some United Nations studies indicate that nodule mining will increase total supplies only minimally over the next ten years in terms of copper supply (1–2 per cent in 1985), somewhat more with respect to manganese (8–16 per cent) and nickel (14–29 per cent), and substantially in the case of cobalt (33–66 per cent).' *A New Regime for the Oceans*, op. cit., p. [35].

24. This document (UN Doc. A/Conf. 62/25) was published on 22 May 1974, just before the Caracas session of UNCLOS III.
25. 'In 1972 the developing countries accounted for only 13 per cent of the world's total nickel production, but the share has been growing. Only one developing country (Gabon) is dependent on manganese exports. The cobalt producers include developing countries like Zaire, Zambia, Cuba and Morocco. It has been estimated that the developing countries' export earnings from the four minerals in question – which are roughly $2 billion per annum at present and which will probably double over the next decade – could be $300–$400 million lower in 1985 than would be the case in the absence of seabed mining.' *A New Regime for the Oceans,* op. cit., p. 21. On the political implications within UNCLOS III, see Miles, op. cit., pp. 151–8.
26. 'Participation in the activities in the Area of developing countries, including the landlocked and other geographically disadvantaged States among them, shall be promoted, having due regard to their special needs and interests.' Article 18, ISNT I, p. 7.
27. Article 57(1), ISNT II, p. 24.
28. Ibid.
29. Ibid.
30. Article 58(1), ibid.
31. Article 54(1), ISNT II, p. 23.
32. Article 54(2), ibid.
33. The rest of Article 54 identifies situations where the state-of-origin and other states fishing these stocks would be required to co-operate with one another. A similar approach is suggested in the case of catadromous species. See Article 55, ISNT II, p. 24.
34. Articles 1–11, ISNT III, pp. 22–5. The 'technology' referred to here is the combination of 'marine sciences and marine technology' (Article 1(1), *ibid.*, p. 22). In a note circulated by the Conference Secretariat in July 1974, at the Caracas session of UNCLOS, the following definition was suggested: 'For all practical purposes, "Marine technology" may be understood as the body of knowledge and hardware needed for the uses of the ocean space and for surveying and developing marine resources. In its general sense, it includes such components as: technical information, designs, know-how, engineering, hardware, processing technology and management. It encompasses the equipment and technical know-how employed in the traditional marine industries such as naval architecture and shipbuilding, fishing or coastal development, as well as in the newer activities of exploration and exploitation of deep seabed minerals and hydrocarbons.' (UN Doc. A/Conf. 62/C.3/L.3 at p. 6.) In this paper, transfer of marine technology is viewed as '(i) a process of making available to the countries needing it the relevant technology for the better use of marine resources and environment, and (ii) as a process of implanting such technology in the recipient country ... The aim of marine technology transfer is therefore to get a specific ocean industry working in the recipient country, and concurrently to enable the country to achieve a certain amount of technological autonomy in terms of skill, know-how and trained personnel so that it can make its own technological decisions with full awareness of what is available'. (Ibid., p. 9.)

35. On the moral and legal aspects of technology transfer generally, see Charles C. Okolie, *Legal Aspects of the International Transfer of Technology to Developing Countries*, 1975. For a comparison of general and regional approaches to technology transfer, see Report of the Secretary-General prepared for the Geneva session of UNCLOS III ('Description of Some Types of Marine Technology and Possible Methods for their Transfer', Doc. A/Conf. 62/C.3/L.22, pp. 3–8).
36. The literature on this trend is quite new. See, for example, Charles C. Okolie, *International Law Perspectives of the Developing Countries* (1973). Many Third World writers trace the trend to the writings of Frantz Fanon, especially his famous work *The Wretched of the Earth*, 1964.
37. Article 32(1), ISNT I, p. 17.
38. In other words, the two objectives run counter to each other only when the equity demands are fuelled by the desire for historic revenge, tolerating the prospect of economic losses in order to enjoy the non-economic satisfaction of inflicting political damage to putatively exploitative powers.
39. See Articles 50(1) and 51(2), ISNT II, p. 21.
40. Article 51(2), ibid.
41. Article 50(2), ibid.
42. Article 50(3), ibid.
43. Ibid.
44. Article 106(1), ibid., p. 38.
45. Some 80 per cent of the world's fishing catch is taken within 200 miles from the coast but in some regions a 200-mile limit cuts across the major fisheries: for example the Grand Banks in the North-West Atlantic. For the purposes of environmental management a uniform jurisdictional limit is even more difficult to justify, in managerial terms, except as a conflict avoidance device.
46. A 200-mile zone may be considered larger than the optimal size for the prevention of pollution by vessels in light of the costs of effective enforcement that would arise for such an extensive area. It is also too wide for the management of traditional inshore stocks which are still the chief focus of fishery conservation in many parts of the world.
47. In certain major fisheries, such as the Grand Banks mentioned in footnote 45, the area of fishery management authority should be even larger, co-extensive with the range of distribution of the species. This rationale cannot, of course, be applied to the most highly mobile species, like tuna, which are too widely dispersed throughout the oceans to be brought under a single management system on an area basis.
48. See, for example, the provisions in Article 61, (ISNT II, p. 25) on the delimitation of the economic zone between adjacent or opposite states and in Article 70 (ibid., p. 28) on the delimitation of the continental shelf between adjacent or opposite states. The text provides no guidelines at all for determining the outer edge of the continental margin.
49. Article 24, ISNT I, p. 10.
50. Article 30, ibid., p. 16.
51. Article 31, ibid., p. 17.
52. Articles 32–34, ibid., pp. 17–19.
53. Article 28, ibid., p. 13.
54. Article 28(i), (ix) and (x), ibid., pp. 13–14.
55. Article 28(iii), ibid., p. 14.
56. Article 28(v), ibid.
57. Article 28(xi), ibid.
58. Article 28(iv) and (xii), ibid., pp. 14–15.
59. Article 28(ii), (xiv), (xv) and (xvi), ibid.

60. Article 28(vi), (vii), (viii) and (xiii), ibid.
61. Article 27(1), ibid., pp. 12–13.
62. This Commission is charged, for example, with the politically sensitive task of recommending to the Council '[a] ppropriate programmes or measures, including integrated commodity arrangements and buffer stock arrangements, to avoid or minimize adverse effects on developing countries whose economies substantially depend on the revenues derived from the export of minerals and other raw materials originating in their territories which are also derived from the resources of the Area under exploitation, taking into account all sources of these minerals and raw materials.' Article 30(2), ibid., p. 16.
63. A political orientation in the Enterprise seems inescapable if the members of the Governing Board of that organ are to be appointed by the Assembly, as proposed in Article 26(2) (ii), ibid., p. 11.
64. Article 30(1), ibid., p. 16.
65. Article 31(1), ibid., p. 17.
66. Article 29(5), ISNT I, p. 15.
67. Article 29(1), ibid.
68. See footnote 63 above.
69. Article 38(1), ibid., p. 20.
70. Efficiency is not, of course, a function of size. A large staff and a small staff, operating under the same terms of reference, may be equally inefficient. But the causes of inefficiency may be related to size: a large staff, inflated by political pressures for 'equitable geographical representation', may owe its inefficiency to low standards of personal competence and to wasteful duplication of effort, whereas a small staff, reduced by false conceptions of economy, may be condemned to different kinds of inefficiency arising from overtaxed personnel, inadequate equipment, and superficial analysis of problems. The Text seems, on the face of things, to be flirting with the latter danger; but the history of international organizations – and of bureaucracies generally – suggests that the former danger is more probable.
71. Article 48(5), ISNT II, p. 20.
72. Article 48(6), ibid.
73. Article 80(5), ibid., p. 32.
74. Article 50(3), ibid., p. 21.
75. Article 20, ISNT III, p. 7.
76. At the end of the Geneva session of UNCLOS III, in the spring of 1975, the general questions of dispute settlement were still in the hands of an informal group. Since the ISNT was drafted by the chairmen of the three Main Committees, the work of informal groups such as this is not always reflected in the Text. It is assumed, however, that an effort will be made within the official committee system to graft the work of the dispute settlement group on to the negotiating text, perhaps during the New York session in the spring of 1976.
77. Articles 32–4, ISNT I, pp. 17–19.
78. Article 33, ibid., p. 18.
79. Article 32(3), ibid.
80. Convention on Fishing and Conservation of the Living Resources of the High Seas (1958), Articles 9–12.
81. Within the economic zone, the coastal state, according to Article 45(1) of ISNT II, would have 'sovereign rights' over fishery management. Article 45(2) provides, however, that in exercising these rights '... the coastal State shall have some regard to the right and duties of other States.' More specifically, Article 52 would create a limited 'duty to consult' in two situations:

1. Where the same stock or stocks of associated species occur within the exclusive economic zones of two or more coastal States these States shall seek either directly or through appropriate sub-regional or regional organizations to agree upon the measures necessary to co-ordinate and ensure the conservation and development of such stocks without prejudice to the other provisions of this Part.

2. Where the same stock or stocks of associated species occur both within the exclusive economic zone and in an area beyond and adjacent to the zone, the coastal State and the States fishing for such stocks in the adjacent area shall seek either directly or through appropriate sub-regional or regional organizations to agree upon the measures necessary for the conservation of these stocks in the adjacent area.

On this matter, see *A New Regime for the Oceans,* op. cit., pp. 46–7.

82. Ibid., pp. [27–32].
83. Article 104, ISNT II, p. 38.
84. The first 44 articles in ISNT III deal with the general principles of protection and preservation of the marine environment, culled mostly from existing treaties that apply to the high seas, but in many cases it is not made clear whether these principles apply equally to the economic zone and to areas outside.
85. The relative neglect of the need to develop state responsibility at UNCLOS III is apparently the result of overemphasis upon assertions of new, or newly enlarged, rights – mostly rights of an acquisitive nature. Paradoxically, then, the neglect of state responsibility can be traced to the ethical claims of the coastal states. A return to international co-operative obligation may eventually be made after a period of trial by error in national ocean management. *The Future of the Oceans*, op. cit.
86. On the emergence of the Stockholm principles on marine pollution, see Douglas M. Johnston, 'International Environmental Law: Recent Developments and Canadian Contributions,' in Macdonald, Morris and Johnston (eds.), *Canadian Perspectives on International Law and Organization*, 1974, pp. 555–611.
87. See, for example, the restraints on the coastal state's enforcement powers in Article 60, ISNT II, p. 25.
88. Article 16(1), ibid., p. 8.
89. Article 51(4), ibid., p. 22.
90. Articles 28–32, ISNT III, pp. 10–12.
91. Article 26, ibid., p. 9.
92. Article 27, ibid., p. 10.
93. Article 24, ibid., p. 9.
94. Article 45(1) (c), ISNT II, p. 19.
95. Article 49, ibid., p. 21.
96. A general provision to this effect is included in Article 5, ISNT III, p. 15 ('Marine scientific research shall be conducted subject to the rights of coastal States as provided for in this Convention'.) But this text makes a clear distinction between the territorial sea, where an unqualified consent régime would continue to operate (Article 13, ibid., p. 17) and the economic zone and continental shelf where non-coastal states and 'appropriate international organizations' would apparently have a carefully qualified right to engage in the conduct and promotion of marine scientific research. (Articles 14 to 24, ibid., pp. 17–19.)
97. The central feature of the qualified consent régime proposed in ISNT III for the economic zone and continental shelf areas is the suggested distinction

between research projects 'of a fundamental nature' and projects 'related to the resources of the economic zone or continental shelf'. Projects belonging to the latter category would be conducted only with the explicit consent of the coastal state. Conflict avoidance and dispute settlement procedures are proposed for situations where there is a difference of opinion on the nature of a project, and research of both kinds is made subject to a variety of conditions. Articles 18 to 22, ibid., pp. 18–19.

98. The language in ISNT III is based on a working paper co-sponsored by Colombia, El Salvador, Mexico and Nigeria – states which can be regarded as moderates among the Third World supporters of the economic zone. As it stands, the text is a compromise between the extreme *laissez faire* positions of some oceanographic powers (Japan, the Soviet Union, the United Kingdom and the United States) and the extreme sovereignty positions of the territorialists who demand an absolutely unqualified consent régime governing all research in the economic zone.

99. Article 10, ISNT III, p. 24.

100. As early as 1971 it was proposed that studies undertaken within a UN-sponsored university should deal in large part with developmental problems and the impact of technology on the environment. 'Question of the Establishment of an International University', Report of the Secretary-General (Doc. A/8510, 11 November 1971), Annex 1 (Report and Comments of the Director-General of UNESCO), p. 13.

101. See Bostwick H. Ketchum (ed.), *The Water's Edge: Critical Problems of the Coastal Zone,* 1972.

102. This is the seaward limit of the zone recognized in US federal legislation. Coastal Zone Management Act of 1972, s. 304(a).

103. Douglas M. Johnston, A. Paul Pross and Ian McDougall, *Coastal Zone: Framework for Management in Atlantic Canada,* 1975, pp. 15–18.

104. cf. Geoffrey Stiles, 'The Small Maritime Community and its Resource Management Problems: A Newfoundland Example,' pp. 233–52 above.

105. On the statutory complications within the Canadian system, see Johnston, Pross and McDougall, note 103 above, pp. 29–53.

106. Ibid., pp. 151–3.

107. It might be more realistic to anticipate the development of coastal zone management concurrently at several different levels of organization. Ibid., pp. 149–63.

108. Ibid., pp. 91–112.

Further Readings

1. J.R. Stevenson and B.H. Oxman, 'The Third United Nations Conference on the Law of the Sea: The 1975 Geneva Session', *American Journal of International Law,* 69, 1975, pp. 763–97.

INDEX